The Calendar and Qua
General George
Fort Jefferson, Kent

Compiled and edited by Kenneth C. Carstens

HB

HERITAGE BOOKS, INC.

Another Heritage Book by the author:
The Personnel of George Rogers Clark's Fort Jefferson and the Civilian Community of Clarksville [Kentucky] 1780-1781
Based on the Lost Vouchers of George Rogers Clark

Published 2000 by

HERITAGE BOOKS, INC.
1540E Pointer Ridge Place, Bowie, Maryland 20716
1-800-398-7709
www.heritagebooks.com

ISBN 0-7884-1525-5

Table of Contents

Acknowledgements

Many individuals assisted with the archival portion of the Fort Jefferson project and have effected to varying degrees my perception, interpretation, and presentation of the information within the Calendar and Quartermaster sections of this book.

Individuals at other institutions and archives who assisted me include Jane H. Pairo, Conley L. Edwards, III, and Paul I. Chestnut, Virginia State Library, Archives Division, Richmond; James J. Holmberg, The Filson Club, Louisville, Kentucky; Samuel W. Thomas, historical consultant, Louisville; Robert B. Kinnaird and his staff at the Kentucky Historical Society, Frankfort; Kandie Adkinson, Land Office, Secretary of State's Office, Frankfort, Kentucky; Richard K. Boyd and Sandra S. Jones, Public Relations Managers, Westvaco, Wickliffe, Kentucky; William S. Coker, University of West Florida; Light T. Cummins, Austin College, Texas; Linda R. Baumgarten, Colonial Williamsburg Foundation; Josephine L. Harper, formerly of the State Historical Society of Wisconsin, Madison; Dennis J. Latta, and Pamela A. Nolan, George Rogers Clark National Historical Park, Vincennes, Indiana, and Robert J. Holden formerly of the GRC National Historical Park; Wilma L. Dulin, Program Archivist, Indiana Historical Society, Indianapolis; Janice C. Fox, Archivist, Missouri Historical Society, St. Louis; William E. Lind, Military Reference Branch, National Archives, Washington, D.C.; and David Hamilton, William Potter, and Gregory F. Holm, Board of Director Members, Northwest Territory Alliance, Decatur and Palos Hills, Illinois and Cleveland, Ohio, respectively.

Financial support for many different aspects of the project came from various administrative offices at Murray State University, but especially the Office of the Provost; Office of the Dean, College of Humanistic Studies (Ken Wolf), and from the Department of Sociology, Anthropology and Social Work (Frank W. Elwell, Chairman). The MSU Committee on Institutional Studies and Research (C.I.S.R.), chaired by Peter W. Whaley, consistently provided monetary support between 1986-1992 for the Fort Jefferson project. J. William Young and the late George P.

Art work for the two figures in this book was accomplished by Richard J. Mjos, Murray, and Richard Day of Vincennes, Indiana.

Throughout this project, many Murray State University students logged thousands of hours helping me transcribe, translate, and triplicate the Fort Jefferson records. Chief among these students was Cathy Biby. Without her assistance, this book would not have been possible.

A special thank you is extended to the late Robert R. Rea, Hollifield Professor of Southern History at Auburn University, for writing the Foreword, editing a final draft of the manuscript, and for his earlier research assistance with the Fort Jefferson project. It was from Professor Ray that I learned the identity of Lt. William Whitehead, a member of the British Southern Indian Department from Mobile, who had led the August 1780 Chickasaw attack against Fort Jefferson. I sincerely appreciate Dr. Rea's encouragement with the Fort Jefferson study, a rather large "history" project for which this archaeologist, trained in prehistory and anthropology, was little prepared.

I would be remiss if I did not thank the wonderful staff at Heritage Books, Inc., Bowie, Maryland, especially Roxanne Carlson and Karen Ackermann, with whom I have worked and who have helped make my Fort Jefferson books a reality.

Last, but not least, I wish to thank my family (Jason, Emily, Jameson, Ashley, and Harry) for allowing me the time to pursue my Fort Jefferson research. This book, is dedicated to my lovely wife, Nancy June, whose family genealogy in Kentucky greatly precedes mine, and whose wisdom and appreciation for history has been a true inspiration.

FOREWORD

by

Robert R. Rea

(1922-1997)

Hollifield Professor of Southern History

Auburn University

The American West, in the eighteenth century, was bounded by the Appalachian Mountains and the Mississippi River --and there was little but wilderness between them. Until 1763, the region was formally claimed by France, save for Spain's toe-hold on the eastern rim of the Gulf of Mexico, but it was populated by Indian tribes whose contact with the European powers was largely restricted to their dealings with voyageurs who traversed the rivers between New Orleans and Quebec. Into that untamed wilderness came the British, pushing westward from the Atlantic coast, involving the American West in European rivalries and wars. As a result of actions far-distant from the valleys of the Ohio and Mississippi rivers, France and Spain were forced to cede their old North American empires to Great Britain in the Treaty of Paris, 1763. New Orleans and Louisiana west of the Mississippi were transferred by France to Spain.

The Seven Years' War (or French and Indian War) had scarcely touched the American heartland, but British seizure of Fort Duquesne, renamed Fort Pitt, opened the west to future expansion down the Ohio River from Pennsylvania and Virginia. The acquisition of Canada was followed by the raising of the Union Jack over the little wooden stockades that dotted the fur-trading routes and the Great Lakes. From Fort Pitt at the head of the Ohio valley, and from Mobile on the Gulf Coast by way of the Mississippi, British military expeditions soon made their arduous river journey to Fort Chartres on the Mississippi, formerly the French stronghold in the Illinois country. Anglo-American traders led and followed the redcoats westward, and land-hungry settlers were not far behind.

When the seaboard colonies raised the standard of rebellion against Great Britain, it was the Commonwealth of Virginia that most clearly recognized the advantages of establishing an American presence on the Mississippi. The

Virginian west --Kentucky-- became a "dark and bloody ground." The British army had been withdrawn to the coastal cities long before the spirit of American independence exploded at Boston, but the Indian tribes of the Old Northwest had no love for Americans. The few Frenchmen who remained in villages such as Kaskaskia, Cahokia, and Vincennes had little use for Spanish authority across the Mississippi, but they had virtually been abandoned by British representatives from the settled parts of Canada. The Old West was ripe for the plucking, and the new Americans were keen to gather its harvest. The broad highway of the Ohio and Mississippi rivers linked the Illinois country and Kentucky with New Orleans; a common enmity toward Britain, shared with Bourbon France and Spain, encouraged Americans to look to them for aid. By 1778, France was an ally of the United States and Spain an active friend. Governor Patrick Henry of Virginia had already opened communications with the Spanish governors of New Orleans, and the financial arrangements of Oliver Pollock enabled patriot merchants to open and utilize the rivers for American commerce. An American post on the Ohio-Mississippi route was clearly desirable. Toward that end, in 1779, the adventurer James Willing headed south to raid the British settlements of Natchez and Manchac on the lower Mississippi, and Virginia's George Rogers Clark struck at the villages near the confluence of the Ohio and the Mississippi. Willing's raid caused a great stir in British West Florida but came to nought. Clark's expedition became one of the most heroic episodes in the Revolutionary history of the Old Northwest.

With less than two hundred hardy Kentuckians, Clark succeeded in making his way from the Falls of the Ohio, modern Louisville, to Kaskaskia, where in July 1779, the formerly French inhabitants peacefully accepted American military occupation. Cahokia and Vincennes were easily secured, there being no British force in the whole Illinois country. That changed shortly with the arrival at Vincennes of Colonel Henry Hamilton ("the hair-buyer") from Detroit, but Hamilton's inertia allowed Clark to take the initiative and recover Vincennes in February 1779.

George Rogers Clark had, in November 1779, drawn plans for a new post at the mouth of the Ohio River, one designed to link New Orleans and Fort Pitt and to establish by occupation Virginia's claim to lands on the Mississippi. Authorized by Governor Thomas Jefferson in January 1780, the military establishment would be named Fort Jefferson; the town beyond its walls would honor its founder and become Clarksville. After recovering Vincennes from its British occupants, Clark and his men moved south to the site selected for Fort Jefferson. The work of building the fort began on April 19, 1780. There was ground to clear, lines of fortifications to lay out, and town lots to mark, for American settlers were moving down the Ohio in significant numbers. There was also the constant threat of Indian attack, for the British had not abandoned the Illinois country. In May, Clark was called upon to lead most of his men to St. Louis, where he joined forces with Spanish and French inhabitants to frustrate a British attack. By June, Fort Jefferson was nearing completion, and Clark departed for the Falls of the Ohio, leaving the new post in the hands of Captain Robert George. At that time Fort Jefferson contained a garrison of about one hundred and fifty men, and the settlement boasted forty families on whose labor and productivity the post might hope to depend.

Success on the eighteenth-century frontier was unpredictable, survival uncertain. Crops might be planted, but harvests were not assured; lacking sufficient quantities of livestock, game must be hunted, and over-burdened settlers had need to keep a sharp eye on the surrounding woods, for Indian attacks came without warning. The first Chickasaw raid struck Fort Jefferson on June 7, when the defenses were scarcely complete. Repeated assaults followed in July, August, and early October. From August 27 to August 30, Fort Jefferson was under siege by a British-led Indian war party. The Indians' impact on the agricultural and hunting economy of Fort Jefferson was severe, and though the loss of life was not great, the threat of tomahawk and captivity was momentarily paralyzing to the little settlement on the western-most edge of the United States. Fields that had been burned did not produce, and hunting parties became overly-cautious and less successful. Failing to find an easy prosperity on the

Mississippi, soldiers deserted and settlers turned back toward the older Kentucky settlements; many sickened and died as want and disease took their toll.

Fort Jefferson had been established with an eye to its commercial potential, and the river trade kept its people alive during the winter of 1780-1781. From November to January, only the arrival of boats from New Orleans and from posts farther up the Ohio enabled the post to survive. The frontier soldier was not the sort to thrive on the boredom of winter garrison duty, and while the ready availability of liquor provided a certain relief, it inevitably produced a loss of discipline and caused dangerous disorders among men and officers.

Kentucky's defense required the destruction of hostile British influence over the Indians north of the Ohio, and toward that end George Rogers Clark and other American leaders sought to concentrate Kentucky's manpower above the Falls of the Ohio in the spring of 1781. Withdrawals and desertions reduced the defenders of Fort Jefferson to a mere fifty-eight men by May. With military evacuation in prospect, few would choose to remain behind at Clarksville. On June 8, 1781, the last contingent of the garrison headed up the Ohio, and Fort Jefferson became a footnote in history. The future would be American, but the centers of Kentucky and the Illinois country would arise elsewhere.

Brief though the history of Fort Jefferson was, its records provide fascinating and heretofore unplumbed insights to the life of a frontier outpost. Kenneth C. Carstens has brought these materials together for the first time, and to sources long known in printed and manuscript form he has added the great collection of documentary material in the archives of Virginia. Largely unknown or overlooked, these records provide the building materials with which a new history of Fort Jefferson can be constructed. The "Calendar" locates and identifies the documentation of the day-by-day life of the post, the sinews of its narrative history. The actors on the scene --548 by name-- are isolated and their activities are specified. It is a broad vein of gold for the prosopographer, the genealogist, and the historian of Kentucky's earliest settlers. It gives flesh and blood to the narrative and fills the scene with living men and women. The other part of Carstens's work, "the Quartermaster

Books" of John Dodge and Martin Carney, sets forth the material basis of Fort Jefferson's history. Here, in precise detail, is the physical existence of a frontier post, its economy, and a window to its sociology as well. The archaeologist may search in vain for the artifacts of George Rogers Clark's Fort Jefferson, but its historical record has been recovered in such detail that the modern investigator may truly find that he can know more of its life and history than any man who stared up at its wooden palisade from the muddy banks of the Mississippi in 1780-1781. This is a unique record of the old American West, formerly frozen in time and now released.

Part I

Fort Jefferson, 1780-1781:
A Calendar of Events

Kenneth C. Carstens

Introduction

Several "histories" have been written about Fort Jefferson since the end of the 19th century, but their authors relied on very few original documents from which to tell their story. Now, however, many of the original Fort Jefferson papers are available for study. The history of how those documents came to rest in the Virginia Archives is still somewhat unclear, but it appears that they were first discovered during the turn of this century by E.G. Swem, the Virginia State Librarian (Swem 1927). Few researchers made use of these terrifically rich vouchers and letters, even after they were brought to the public's attention in Indianapolis by Mary Jane Meeker (Meeker 1976) in preparation for this country's bicentennial. Several of the documents were used by Seineke in her wonderful compilations of Clark's Illinois Country papers (Seineke 1981). Still, this phenomenally rich collection of more than 20,000 individual documents, which are now microfilmed and saved, has rarely been studied from beginning to end (Carstens 1999).

This examination of Fort Jefferson took six years to create (1984-1990), but is only now coming to publication. Finding time to work on the project between full-time teaching, running the anthropology and archaeology programs at Murray State University, and remodeling an older home has not been an easy chore. Added to that the waxing and waning of several other publishers and it becomes understandable that it has taken longer to publish the enclosed pages (nine years!), than it did to prepare the original copy. Yet, funded by grants from Murray State University's Committee on Institutional Studies and Research (CISR), I was able to travel to Richmond, Virginia, twice to examine every document within the unpublished George Rogers Clark Papers. Within the Clark collection of approximately 20,000 papers were about 4,000 items dealing with the activities at Clark's Fort Jefferson. Permission was secured from the Virginia State Library to have each record reproduced and shipped to Murray State University where from

1984-1990, each handwritten paper was deciphered (some handwriting was better than others), and entered into three separate filing systems. As a result, three book length manuscripts began to take shape, one of which was published by Heritage Press in 1999 (Carstens 1999).

The Fort Jefferson "Calendar" (Part I of this book) focuses chiefly on the contents of the unpublished Virginia documents, although previously published and unpublished primary records from other archives (Filson Club in Kentucky, Kentucky Historical Society, and Missouri Historical Society) have been used also to detail the day to day experience at George Rogers Clark's Fort Jefferson. A tremendous wealth of additional information remains untapped within the unpublished Clark collection, especially for the sites of Kaskaskia, Cahokia, Vincennes, the Falls of the Ohio (Louisville), and several of the more centrally-located interior forts and stations of Kentucky. The "Quartermaster" section (the second portion of this book) reproduces the individual tabulations maintained by John Dodge and Martin Carney, two of Fort Jefferson's quartermasters. These quartermaster records, unlike the paraphrased and edited commentary in the "Calendar" section of the book, is a faithful reproduction of Dodge and Carney's line by line entries of each page of their accounting records. Much is to be learned from these 18th century accounting records even though these records are incomplete.

A list references cited in the "Calendar" appears at the end of this section and also the section dealing the Historical Background and Context. Several abbreviations for some of the references were used within the body of the "Calendar." MHS, represents the William Clark Collection at the Missouri Historical Society (followed by "B" for Box, and "F" for Folder number); GRC I or GRC II reference the James Alton James' edited version of the George Rogers Clark Papers (1972, AMS reprinted version); and last but not least, VSA symbolizes the abbreviation for the unpublished George Rogers Clark papers in the Archives Division of the Virginia State Library. The number following the abbreviation depicts the box in which the document was found within the collection. When I visited the collection in 1984 and 1986, the Clark papers were organized somewhat by date, sometimes by subject, and were all filed in 50 separate acid-free Princeton folder boxes. This collection is now available on microfilm from the Virginia State Library and is posted on the internet.

A referenced glossary of 18th century terms is provided at the end of the "Calendar" section of the book, and will be useful, too, for the ensuing "Quartermaster" division of the text. The definitions of terms were pulled from both historic, period, dictionaries as well as specialized books. Many of the terms relate to fabrics in use during the 18th century as they were dispersed by the quartermaster corps at Fort Jefferson. From reading the list, one gains respect for the knowledge these quartermasters must have retained and the records that they were required to keep. It is hoped that this section of the book will be particularly useful to historical re-enactors who strive for authenticity in their historic costume designs. Here, in great detail, is a description of what fabrics were actually dispersed and used on the 18th century American frontier.

References Cited

Carstens, Kenneth C., editor and compiler
1999 The Personnel of George Rogers Clark's Fort Jefferson and the Civilian Community of Clarksville [Kentucky], 1780-1781. Heritage Books, Inc. Bowie, Maryland.

Draper, Lyman C.
n.d. The Draper Manuscripts. Wisconsin Historical Society, Madison.

James, James Alton, editor
1972 George Rogers Clark Papers, 1771-1784, Vols. I and II. Reprinted AMS Press, New York.

Meeker, Mary Jane
1976 Original Vouchers in the George Rogers Clark Bicentennial Exhibition. Indiana History Bulletin, June, 53(6), Indianapolis.

Missouri Historical Society
n.d. The William Clark Papers. The Missouri Historical Society, Forest Park, St. Louis.

Seineke, Katherine Wagner
1981 The George Rogers Clark Adventure in the Illinois and Selected Documents of the American Revolution at the Frontier Posts. Polyanthos Press, New Orleans.

Swem, E. G.
1927 The Lost Vouchers of George Rogers Clarke (sic). Virginia Journal of Education, Vol. XXII (June).

Virginia State Library
n.d. The Unpublished Papers of George Rogers Clark. Virginia State Library, Archives Division, Boxes 1-50. Richmond.

Historical Background and Context

The origin of George Rogers Clark's Fort Jefferson dates from the summer of 1777, when Clark first developed his plans to capture British posts in the Illinois Country (Kaskaskia and Vincennes) (Henry 1777). By the fall of that year, Clark had received word from his spies that the Illinois Country could be taken easily (James, ed. 1972). Clark formulated plans that included constructing a fort near the mouth of the Ohio River to facilitate trade with the Spanish and French settlements (Figure 1). A fort located at the mouth of the Ohio also would support through possession, Virginia's revised (1763) "paper claim" to her western boundary (Carstens 1994). By January, 1778, Clark received permission from Virginia Governor Patrick Henry to proceed with his secret plans (James, ed. 1972).

Clark captured Kaskaskia, a French community under British control on July 4, 1779, without firing a shot. Even more remarkable was his success in approaching that community completely undetected. Clark and his small force of about 150 of the Illinois Battalion had traversed the entirety of the Ohio River from Fort Pitt to the mouth of the Tennessee River and traveled overland from the Tennessee River to Kaskaskia without being observed (James, ed. 1972).

To counter Clark's ambitious move westward, British Governor Henry Hamilton brought his combined forces of British regulars and Native Americans south from Detroit to take control of the garrison at Fort Sackville (Vincennes) on the Wabash (James, ed. 1972). Arriving at Fort Sackville late in the year, Hamilton decided to wait out the winter in Vincennes before attacking Clark at Kaskaskia. Clark, however, seized the initiative.

Leaving Kaskaskia in the dead of an Illinois winter, Clark and his followers (accompanied by newly allied Frenchmen), left Kaskaskia in February and headed northeast toward Vincennes. This move by Clark was planned both to surprise the British garrison at Vincennes by bringing the fight to the them and to catch the British off guard and without their usual compliment of Indian allies who had been released for winter hunting activities (James, ed. 1972).

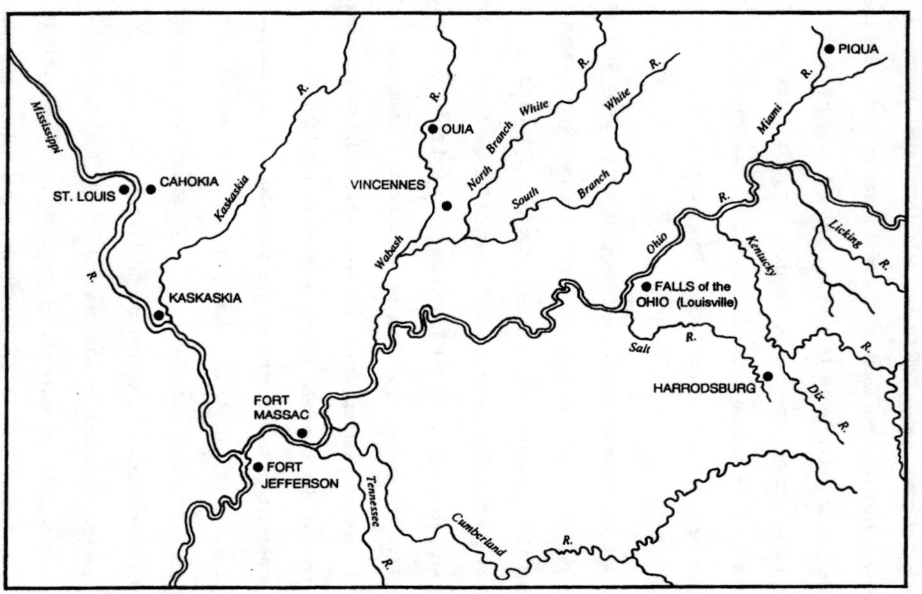

Figure 1: Location of sites mentioned in text.

Fort Jefferson Calendar

Clark's strategy worked. Hamilton and his forces surrendered Fort Sackville after a few days of half-hearted defense on February 25, 1779. The Americans, jubilant over their two victories, renamed the Vincennes fort, Fort Patrick Henry, to pay homage to the Virginia governor who initially backed the enterprise (James, ed. 1972).

Everybody loves a winner and George Rogers Clark was a winner. Between March and November, 1779, Clark's Illinois Battalion grew steadily as word of his undertaking reached the frontier settlements. Recruitment for the Illinois Battalion improved as a result of Clark's battlefield successes.

In November, 1779, Clark called a Council of War meeting with his junior officers to discuss the final part of his enterprising campaign: the building of a fort and a civilian community near the mouth of the Ohio River (Carstens 1994, James, ed. 1972) (Figure 2).

In January, 1780, the new governor of Virginia, Thomas Jefferson, wrote letters to Joseph Martin, Daniel Smith and Thomas Walker, and George Rogers Clark (James, ed. 1972). Jefferson directed Martin to contact the "Cherokee" Indians and purchase land for the new fort from the Indians. Jefferson did not know at that time that the Chickasaw Indians --allies of the British-- claimed the area on which the fort would be constructed, not the Cherokees.

Jefferson further instructed Daniel Smith and Thomas Walker to meet Clark at the site and determine precisely the exact location (latitude) of Clark's new fort, making sure it fell within Virginia and not North Carolina (Sioussat 1915).

In his communication to Clark, Jefferson gave permission to build the fort and an adjacent civilian community (Carstens, In press-b, 1993). The latter, Jefferson wrote, could be used to support the fort by growing the supplies Virginia could not afford to send. A civilian community would also attract young men and families from whom Clark could actively recruit (James, ed. 1972).

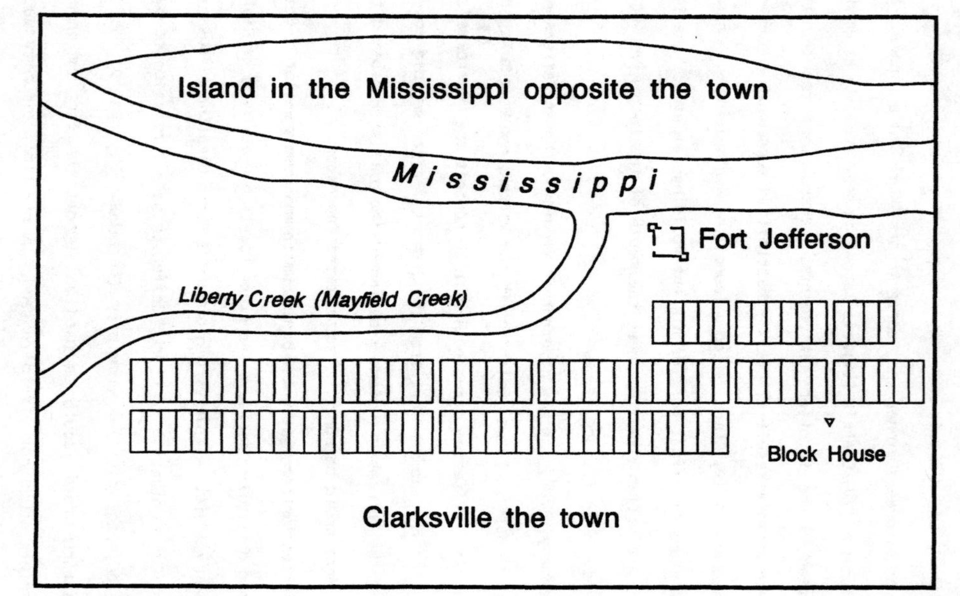

Figure 2: The William Clark map of Fort Jefferson and the community of Clarksville (Draper Manuscripts, 1M11, Courtesy of the Wisconsin Historical Society, Madison).

Clark and Robert Todd discussed the feasibility of reducing the garrisons in the Illinois country and concentrating their populations at and around the new fort. Some resettlement did occur, but Kentucky County (the western most county of Virginia in 1780), was about to see its single largest influx of settlers, more than 10,000 in a single year. By mid-year, reshuffling the Illinois population no longer seemed necessary.

To obtain settlers for the community and additional soldiers for his army, Virginia authorized Clark to grant 300 land warrants, each worth 560 acres, to every new soldier (James, ed. 1972). By April, 1780, only a few additional supplies were needed before Clark could leave the Falls of the Ohio (Louisville) for the new post. So promising were the prospects of the new settlement and garrison, that William Shannon, Clark's Commissary at the Falls, requested provisions for 1,000 men for six months (James, ed. 1972).

By April 19, 1780, Clark, 175 soldiers, and an untold number of civilians arrived at the spot selected for the new settlement (Carstens 1994). In honor of the current Virginia governor, Clark called the new post Fort Jefferson. The civilian community became known as Clarksville (also Clark's Town or Iron Banks). The fort and community were on a slightly elevated floodplain between Mayfield Creek (also then called Liberty Creek), and a series of eroded bluffs located to the north (Carstens 1993). The main stream of the Mississippi River was then about one-half mile west of the fort (Figure 2). Clark's men and the settlers set to the task at hand, clearing the woods and constructing the outpost and town. Clark, however, would have little time to further invest in the fort or settlement.

Jefferson, writing from Williamsburg, suggested Clark lead a force into the Shawnee country to counter their attacks on the central Kentucky settlements. Jefferson did not realize that a more pressing issue was developing nearer Clark's new post.

Word arrived Fort Jefferson that Indians and British soldiers were expected to attack Pancore (St. Louis) and Cahokia (McDermott 1980). Taking all but 18 regulars from Fort Jefferson, and leaving Captain Robert George in charge of the new post, Clark proceeded north to Cahokia, arriving May 24th, the day before the battle of St. Louis (Virginia State Library, n.d.). Clark and the united French, Spanish, and American forces, promptly defeated Charles Langlade's British and Indian raiders (McDermott 1980).

Meanwhile, word reached Fort Jefferson from O'Post (Fort Patrick Henry in Vincennes), that British attacks on the central Kentucky settlements were expected any day. News also was received that the Spanish planned to attack the British strongholds at Mobile and Pensacola, which would help free trade on the Mississippi.

By June first, Clark's triumphant Illinois Battalion began to relocate at Fort Jefferson. On June 4, 1780, Captain Robert George, Fort Jefferson commandant, advised Clark that the construction of the new post was nearing completion (Carstens In press-b). Captain George hoped to have the garrison enclosed with pickets by the end of that week, and the settlers, George wrote, were nearly finished with their planting.

The fort was enclosed none too soon. By June 7, marauding Chickasaw Indians killed members of the Clarksville militia who were surprised on the outskirts of the town (Carstens 1991, 1997). Although not a full-scale attack, the Indians' presence was a considerable menace to the fort and settlement.

By June 10, Clark returned to Fort Jefferson with his soldiers and the Indian problem faded into the background. A more demanding obstacle redirected Clark's attention.

A messenger from the Falls of the Ohio (Louisville) brought word of an increased number of hostile Shawnee Indian attacks in the central Kentucky regioin. Colonel Daniel Brodhead at Fort Pitt wrote to Clark that he preferred not to deal with the Shawnee problem, recommending instead that Clark attack the Shawnee "from his quarter."

On June 10, 1780, Clark left Fort Jefferson with two others for the Falls of the Ohio. Between June 10 and 14, considerable issues of goods and clothing were made at Fort Jefferson to outfit Clark's army for the Shawnee campaign (Carstens 1990). By mid-June, half of the Fort Jefferson troops left their post to meet Clark at the mouth of the Licking River (across from Cincinnati) to launch the expedition against the Shawnee (Carstens 1997). Simultaneously, Clark began recruiting for the operation as soon as he reached the Falls.

The civilian community (Carstens 1996) at Fort Jefferson continued to grow and prosper. On June 13th, several Clarksville magistrates (Piggott, Johnson, Smith, Hunter, and Iles) wrote the Virginia government to have Clarksville and its surrounding area recognized as a new county, which, if recognized, would give them a vote in the Virginia legislature and financial support for their town. Their petition was sent along with Clark's troops who left Fort Jefferson to go on the Shawnee expedition on June 14, 1780 (James, ed. 1972).

For the next two weeks, all went well at the post on the Mississippi -- variously known as Fort Jefferson, Iron Banks, Camp at the Mouth of the Ohio, Camp Jefferson, and Camp on the Mississippi. Numerous issues for dry goods to be made into soldiers' clothing were made for officers and enlistees alike. The fort's bartering system was well established, as witnessed by the type and kind of payments received by the tailors and seamstresses who made clothing for the soldiers (Carstens 1990, 1996). A company of Virginia Light Dragoons (cavalry) commanded by Captain John Rogers, a maternal cousin of George Rogers Clark, was newly-outfitted and provisioned at Fort Jefferson --with everything but horses! On July 14, 1780, Rogers' Company departed for Cahokia, and Lieutenant Colonel John Montgomery left for Fort Clark at Kaskaskia.

At day break, three days later, the Chickasaw Indians attacked the Clarksville community, killing two of the militia and wounding several others (Carstens 1997, 1999). The fight, however, was brief and led to relatively little destruction. The shooting was more of a test by the Chickasaw to determine the military strength of fort and community; after obtaining the information they needed, the Indians withdrew (Carstens 1997).

Fort Jefferson Calendar

By July 20, 1780, messengers (Laurence Keenan and Joshua Archer), were sent to Lt. Col. Montgomery at Fort Clark in Kaskaskia for assistance. On July 31, 1780, 65 Kaskaskia Indians and 10 members of Captain Richard McCarty's Company of French soldiers arrived from Fort Clark to assist Fort Jefferson (Virginia State Archives, n.d.). The Indian allies were employed primarily by Captain George to hunt for the garrison (Carstens In press-a). Also arriving from Fort Clark was Captain John Bailey and William Clark (paternal cousin to George Rogers Clark, son of Benjamin Clark, not George's younger brother). Bailey and William Clark brought with them 1,400 pounds of flour, 50 bushels of corn, and 28 men from Bailey's Company of Infantry.

The fort and community entered August pleased that they had successfully thwarted two attacks by the Chickasaws, and they were undoubtedly proud that they had helped defeat the combined Anglo-Indian assault on St. Louis and Cahokia the preceding May. Recent arrivals at Fort Jefferson (Captain Richard McCarty and his company and Major Timothe B. Monbreun) added to the feeling of security at the post. But, it was now understood that an attack by the Chickasaw might occur at any time and come from any quarter (Carstens 1997). Therefore, a higher status of alert was ordered, and arms and munitions were issued to the troops to maintain a "prepared" normalcy.

On the morning of August 27, 1780, the civilians and the soldiers of Fort Jefferson were once again tested by the Chickasaw (Carstens 1997, Seineke 1981). This time, however, a greater band of Chickasaws attacked the community and its garrison. Estimates of their number vary; the most conservative figure comes from Captain George, who suggested 150 Chickasaw attacked the post. In this encounter, the Chickasaw were led by Lieutenant William Whitehead, a member of the British Southern Indian Department, and by James Colbert, a Chickasaw half-breed "Big Man."

Part way through the battle, Colbert appeared with a flag of truce and demanded the surrender of the post to prevent additional civilian bloodshed...an age old ploy. Captain Helm, Captain George's second in command, told Colbert the

Americans would not surrender. Wheeling to walk away from the parley, Colbert was shot in the back by a Kaskaskia Indian from a nearby blockhouse. Fighting recommenced later that evening. At the end of the fourth day of battle, August 30th, the Chickasaw retreated, but not before they had destroyed much of the corn crop and had killed many of the settlers' cattle and sheep (Carstens 1997). In addition to these losses, several Negro slaves had been shot by the Chickasaw, and a number of the militia were either severely wounded or lost their lives during the battle. Most notable during the battle was the heroic act of Nancy Ann Hunter, who recovered lost livestock during the flag of truce which insured the survival of the fort's inhabitants (Carstens 1997). Meanwhile, Captain John Bailey's Company had been ambushed by the Chickasaws while on a hunting party. Four members of his troop were killed and a fifth (Private Jarrell) had been taken prisoner (Virginia State Archives, n.d.). Nevertheless, the state of preparedness in early August probably saved many more lives at the post.

September was a very depressing month for the inhabitants and soldiers of Fort Jefferson. With much of the corn crop destroyed, and Chickasaw Indians stalking the nearby country side looking for stragglers and hunters, there was little, if any, hope for food for the following months (Carstens In press-a). The few bushels of corn garnered from the devastated fields would barely feed the garrison, let alone the men, women, and children of the town. Fearful of spending a winter with little or no food, 24 of the town's 40 families moved between September 12th and 14th, either going down the Mississippi to New Orleans or up the Mississippi and Ohio Rivers to Kaskaskia or the Falls area (Carstens 1997, James, ed. 1972, Jameson, n.d.). To make matters worse, there were many desertions from Clark's Illinois Battalion. Although there were now fewer mouths to feed at Fort Jefferson, there were also fewer inhabitants and soldiers to defend the post or assist with the continued construction of the new town (Virginia State Archives, n.d.).

September marked the beginning of the "sickly" season, as Captain George called it, the season when ague and malaria were worse (James, ed. 1972) An examination of the vouchers for September vividly illustrates that many persons, soldiers and civilians alike, became sick with the ague (flu) or began suffering from the effects of malaria (Virginia State Archives, n.d.). Few persons, save the officers, had access to Jesuit bark, a tree bark containing quinine used to stay the affects of malaria. As a result, the garrison and town had fewer people than before, and those who remained were generally too ill to move or desert their posts.

Not all was gloomy, however. On September 6th, a load of supplies arrived by boat from New Orleans from Oliver Pollack, the American agent in New Orleans supporting Clark's western theater of operations; part of the cargo included 1,200 pounds of gunpowder (Carstens 1990, 1991). On September 10th, a party of Kaskaskia Indian allies were granted permission by Captain George to seek revenge against the Chickasaw for the recent hostilities (Missouri Historical Society, n.d.). George must not have thought his position to be too precarious thereby risking another retaliatory raid by the Chickasaws.

October was not much of an improvement over September. Between the 4th and 5th, four more persons were killed near the fort (Draper n.d., Harding 1981). Although additional ammunition was issued to the post and town, the Indians never showed themselves fully, keeping just outside the community where they could harass the settlers and soldiers. Sickness continued to prevail as did further desertions (Harding 1981).

Physical problems were now accompanied by political intrigue (James, ed. 1972). Lt. Col. John Montgomery arrived with Captain John Williams from Kaskaskia on October 22, 1780. Col. Montgomery wanted Captain George to relinquish his command to Captain Williams. George refused, subsequently writing to Col. Clark to explain that he would not forego his command unless ordered to do so by Clark. Williams, obviously caught in an awkward situation, also wrote to Clark stating that he would not take command until he received orders from Clark. Although Lt. Col. Montgomery and Captain George did not get along, Montgomery did assist Captain George in his efforts to save the post. By October

28th, Montgomery left Fort Jefferson to go to New Orleans to procure additional supplies for the garrison and community. Writing later that day, Captain George observed that Fort Jefferson had been severely reduced by famine, desertion and death (James, ed. 1972, Seineke 1981). Now, during near drought conditions, low water in the Mississippi hampered efforts to get supplies to the fort.

Montgomery's assistance in New Orleans paid off when a shipment of new supplies arrived in November (Carstens 1990, James 1970). Even so, soldiers and civilians spent most of their time, when not too ill, making nets in order to seine for fish in the shallows of the Mississippi River (Virginia State Archives, n.d.). December, 1780, was, relatively speaking, a better month for the American frontiersmen. In his letter to George Rogers Clark during the first few days of December, John Donne, Deputy Commissary at the fort, reported that Major (of Militia) Silas Harlan and other hunters had been successful in bringing more than 8,000 pounds of buffalo, bear, and dear meat into the fort (Carstens In press-a, James, ed. 1972). Unfortunately, there were still more than 150 persons in garrison, 20 civilian families that had to be fed, and the expectation that several new military companies might arrive any day (Virginia State Archives, n.d.). Food, although now available, was still in short supply (Carstens In press-a).

On the 12th of December, and again on the 15th, cargo supplies arrived from Pollack in New Orleans and from the Falls of the Ohio (Carstens 1990, James 1970). Both shipments included primarily munitions and dry goods, and while the shipment of new shoes was welcomed, the newly-arrived dry goods would have to be used in Kaskaskia and other Illinois towns to barter for food. In spite of a bleak outlook, Christmas was saluted by Captain George's Company of Artillery by expending 60 pounds of gunpowder in salutes fired from Fort Jefferson's five swivels and two cannon (Carstens 1991).

Within a few days another shipment from New Orleans was delivered by Captain Philip Barbour on behalf of Oliver Pollock, American agent in New Orleans (Carstens 1990). Barbour, seeing the depressed condition of the fort and civilian community, negotiated the sale of his $25,000 cargo to $237,320 hard specie (Carstens 1990, 1994, James, ed. 1972). A true capitalist!

Not wanting to lose the needed supplies, Captain George conferred with his fellow officers and agreed to pay Captain Barbour's outrageous demand and explained his actions in a letter to Oliver Pollack. The cargo, consisting primarily of dry goods and tafia (watered-down rum), was immediately put to use.

In high spirits, the community and soldiers raised their cups to what appeared to be a bright and shiny New Year (Virginia State Archives, n.d.). Supplies were unloaded, repacked, and sent to Kaskaskia and the Falls to procure foodstuffs for the garrison and civilian community (Carstens 1990).

Another part of the shipment included munitions. Just about every member of the garrison, including militia and Indians, received a sword, and Clark's Illinois Battalion officers received their new clothing allotments for the year (Carstens 1991). In addition, the Kaskaskia Indians were granted permission once again to attack the Chickasaw (Virginia State Archives, n.d.).

The month of January revealed the growing dislike shared by the fort's officers and civilians for Captain John Dodge, Indian Agent and Quartermaster for the Illinois Department. Although Dodge would have but a few months left at Fort Jefferson (he spent the first part of the Spring at Kaskaskia, then took leave to settle his books at Richmond), the majority of the inhabitants felt cheated by his dealings, and he proved to be a constant source of friction with the officers (Draper Manuscripts, n.d., James, ed. 1972).

On January 23rd, another boat load of supplies was received at Fort Jefferson. A tafia ration (one gill each) for January 30th showed that 110 men remained in garrison, Captain John Bailey and his Company of Infantry having departed for O'Post (Vincennes) earlier that month (Harding 1981).

February and March of the new year witnessed several activities that would dominate post functions for the next several months. Fort Jefferson became the hub for the distribution of arms, munitions, dry goods, and liquor. Military companies arrived from other Illinois outposts and soldiers from Fort Jefferson delivered supplies to them (Carstens 1990). Fort Jefferson was finally becoming the economic hub and military stronghold that Clark had intended, a point not unnoticed by the distant central Kentucky settlements who wanted Clark's army to be protecting them and not the Mississippi region.

The prosperity of Fort Jefferson began to erode as quickly as it had been achieved. Although the post now had more dry goods, munitions, and rum (and whiskey) than it could possibly use, its larder was still quite empty in spite of daily hunting by parties of soldiers and Indians from the post (Carstens In press-a). No matter how much tafia was consumed (and incredible amounts were!), daily meals consisted of little solid food. Grumbling and discontent with the post's conditions were no longer restricted to whispers among friends. Serious charges were made which only could be settled through courts of inquiry (Draper Manuscripts, n.d.).

In March, court activities convened to examine the conduct and character of two of the fort's newly arrived officers: Captains Edward Worthington and Captain Richard McCarty (Draper Manuscripts, n.d.). Worthington, who had postponed his trip from the Falls to Fort Jefferson for months was accused of retailing liquor, gambling with the soldiery, and frequent disobedience of orders. McCarty, on the other hand, was charged with threatening to leave the service (and Virginia) and insulting a fellow officer. The outcome of Worthington's court of inquiry is unknown. McCarty was found guilty, and a general court martial was recommended. His chief accuser was John Dodge. McCarty would never suffer the embarrassment of a court martial, however. He was killed by Indians two months later while en route to the Falls (Harding, 1981).

Near the end of March, a third court of inquiry was held in the public store at Fort Jefferson to examine the conduct of Captain John Rogers, who had been in command at Fort Clark in Kaskaskia (Draper Manuscripts, n.d.). The charges had been brought by Dodge again, but this time the court found them to be without substance and acquitted Rogers.

Fort Jefferson Calendar

March was a "happy" month for the majority of the American-Irish officers and soldiers. Their consumption of large quantities of tafia and whiskey was truly amazing, as were their excuses for imbibing the libations (Carstens, In press-a, Virginia State Archives, n.d.). Whether drinking to Saint Patrick's health, death, or Saint Patrick's wife Shealy, the Fort Jefferson community properly celebrated their ethnic customs (Virginia State Archives, n.d.).

On the other side of the coin, however, there was discontent and boredom. Lieutenant John Girault, for example, pleaded in a letter to George Rogers Clark that he might be sent on an expedition or otherwise employed somewhere usefully, implying that nothing of consequence was occurring at Fort Jefferson (Seineke 1981). As tensions relaxed, so did discipline. James Taylor and David Allen were court-martialed on charges of speaking disrespectfully to an officer, beating an officer's servants, and robbing an officer's kitchen. Taylor was acquitted, but Allen was found guilty and received 50 lashes on his bare back (Draper Manuscripts, n.d.).

April brought heavy rains, which in turn raised water levels dangerously high in nearby Mayfield Creek and the Mississippi River. As a result, by April 25th, many items in the public store had to be moved to higher ground by the fort's soldiers (Carstens 1994, Virginia State Archives, n.d.).

Several letters were received in April from General George Rogers Clark. The content of those letters is unknown, but as Clark had received permission to plan an assault against Fort Detroit, it is possible that these letters focused on Detroit and that Clark suggested to his officers' that they begin planning the evacuation of Fort Jefferson (James, ed. 1972).

By the 10th of May, Lt. Col. John Montgomery returned to Fort Jefferson. Shortly after his arrival, increased unhappiness at the post led a militia man to break into the fort's public store, forcing Captain George to call for an inspection of the town (Virginia State Archives, n.d.). The culprit was not found.

Evidence of decline was all too apparent. By the first of May, the number of men remaining in the garrison was down to 58 (Virginia State Archives, n.d.). It is evident that the decision to evacuate Fort Jefferson was made prior to June 5th. On that date Captain Abraham Keller's Company left the fort for the Falls area. The remaining soldiers and civilians departed June 8th, the official date of evacuation (James, ed. 1972). Numerous goods, far too cumbersome to remove, were left at the old fort, as were the earthly remains of at least 38 men, women, and children who were buried in the post's cemetery (Virginia State Archives, n.d.).

The fort, occupied for only 416 days, had served its function. Its presence on Virginia's western boundary even though short-lived provided the physical evidence Virginia needed to justify her claim to her chartered western boundary (as did the Virginian military occupation of Kaskaskia and Vincennes). It also provided fodder for the American negotiators of peace, then meeting in France, to shore up an American claim to the Mississippi as a western boundary. This simple American occupation also hampered British and Spanish control of the mid-Mississippi valley for the time being --a point that would be challenged severely in less than two decades by the inhabitants of Kentucky-- and provided a civilian stronghold on the western edge of what would become the fifteenth state in the Union.

On July 12, 1781, tired and exhausted, the Fort Jefferson survivors arrived at General Clark's new stronghold at the Falls of the Ohio, Fort Nelson, and the saga of George Rogers Clark's Fort Jefferson came to an end.

References Cited

Carstens, Kenneth C.

In Press-a Subsistence Practices at George Rogers Clark's Fort Jefferson, 1780-1781. Current Archaeology, edited by Charles Hockensmith and Kenneth Carstens, Kentucky Heritage Council, Frankfort.

In Press-b The Structural Composition of George Rogers Clark's Fort Jefferson, 1780-1781. Filson Club History Quarterly, Louisville, Kentucky.

1990 Issues at Fort Jefferson, 1780-1781: The Quartermaster Books of John Dodge and Martin Carney. Selected Papers from the 1987 and 1988 George Rogers Clark Trans-Appalachian Frontier History Conferences, edited by Robert J. Holden, Vincennes, Indiana.

1991 Praise the Lord and Pass the Ammunition: Munition Supplies at George Rogers Clark's Fort Jefferson, 1780-1781. Selected Papers from the 1989 and 1990 George Rogers Clark Trans-Appalachian Frontier History Conferences, edited by Robert J. Holden, Vincennes, Indiana.

1993 The William Clark Maps of Fort Jefferson: An Exercise in 18th Century Scaling. Filson Club History Quarterly, 67:23-43).

1994 Fort Jefferson, 1780-1781: A Summary of Its History. Selected Papers from the 1991 and 1992 George Rogers Clark Trans-Appalachian Frontier History Conferences, edited by Robert J. Holden, Vincennes, Indiana.

1996 The Role of Women in Kentucky's Western Frontier, 1780-1781. Historical Archaeology in Kentucky, edited by Stephen and Kim McBride and David Pollack, Kentucky Heritage Council, Frankfort.

1997 George Rogers Clark's Fort Jefferson, 1780-1781. The Filson Club History Quarterly, 71(3):259-284.

1999 The Personnel of George Rogers Clark's Fort Jefferson and the Civilian Community of Clarksville [Kentucky], 1780-1781. Heritage Books, Inc., Bowie, Maryland.

Draper, Lyman C.

n.d. The Draper Manuscripts. Wisconsin Historical Society, Madison.

Harding, Margery Heberling

1981 George Rogers Clark and His Men: Military Records, 1778-1784. The Kentucky Historical Society, Frankfort.

Henry, Patrick

1777 Letter to Governor Galvez. Archivo General de Indias Seville, Estante 87, Cajon´1, legajo 6, Spain.

James, James Alton

1970 Oliver Pollock: The Life and Times of an Unknown Patriot. Books for Libraries Press, New York.

James, James Alton, editor

1972 George Rogers Clark Papers, 1771-1784, Vols. I and II. Reprinted AMS Press, New York.

Jameson, Ann McMeans

n.d. The Personal Narrative of Ann McMeans Jameson. Unpublished manuscript, The Filson Club, Louisville.

McDermott, John Francis
1980 The Battle of St. Louis 26 May 1780. Bulletin of the Missouri Historical Society, St. Louis.

Missouri Historical Society
n.d. The William Clark Papers. The Missouri Historical Society, Forest Park, St. Louis.

Seineke, Katherine Wagner
1981 The George Rogers Clark Adventure in the Illinois and Selected Documents of the American Revolution at the Frontier Posts. Polyanthos Press, New Orleans.

Sioussat, St. George L.
1915 The Journal of General Daniel Smith, one of the Commissioners to Extend the Boundary Line between the Commonwealths of Virginia and North Carolina, August, 1779, to July, 1780. The Tennessee Historical Magazine, 1(1): 40-65, Nashville.

Virginia State Library
n.d. The Unpublished Papers of George Rogers Clark. Virginia State Library, Archives Division, Boxes 1-50, Richmond.

Summer 1777
Clark prepares his plans to seize the British posts of Kaskaskia, Cahokia, and Vincennes. Clark sends Benjamin Linn and Samuel Moore into the Illinois Country as scouts. He also receives information from Thomas Bentley and Daniel Murray (Seineke 1981: xx-xxi).

Fall 1777
Clark suggests to Governor Patrick Henry that the British posts in the Illinois Country can be taken by the Virginians and will alleviate the Indian problem (GRC, I: 30-32).

January 2, 1778/Friday
Governor Patrick Henry proposes to the Virginia Privy Council that Clark be allowed to begin his campaign against Kaskaskia (GRC, I: 33).

Governor Patrick Henry issues his secret instructions to Clark, including the proposal to build "a post near the Mouth of the Ohio" (GRC, I: 35).

July 4, 1778
Clark and his forces take Kaskaskia without firing a shot (GRC,I: 1xiii; Seineke 1981: xxiv-xxv).

January 14, 1778/Wednesday
Governor Patrick Henry proposes, in a letter to Spanish Governor Galvez at New Orleans, that a Virginian fort be built at the mouth of the Ohio River in order to secure communications with New Orleans (Draper Manuscripts 58J105).

September-November, 1778
Letter from Bernardo De Galvez to Governor Patrick Henry. Galvez states that an establishment at the Mouth of the Ohio would be very valuable to "facilitate navigation of the Mississippi" (Seineke 1981: 301-303).

August-November, 1779
British Lt. Governor Hamilton proposes to capture Clark and his Virginian forces by first taking Vincennes and Kaskaskia, then building a fort at the Mouth of the Ohio River (GRC, I: 1xix-1xxi).

February 25, 1779
Before Hamilton sets out for Clark, George Rogers Clark and his combined French and American forces travel to Vincennes. Lt. Governor Hamilton surrenders to George Rogers Clark at Fort Sackville, which was renamed Fort Patrick Henry (GRC, I: 1xxiv-1xxxv; 162-163).

March 10, 1779/Monday
Francis Villier enlists on this date as a sergeant in Captain Richard McCarty's Company (Harding 1981: 27).

May 24, 1779/Monday
Edward Murray enlists as a private in Captain John Bailey's Company (Harding 1981: 46).

May 29, 1779/Saturday
James Rubedo enlists on this date in Captain John Williams' Company (Harding 1981: 26).

May 30, 1779/Sunday
Jesse Piner enlists as a private in Captain Richard McCarty's Company (Harding 1981: 27).

May 31, 1779/Monday
Ebenezer Suverns is discharged. Suverns was formerly of Captain John Williams' Company at Kaskaskia (Harding 1981: 2).

Daniel Tolley is discharged from Captain John Williams' Company (Harding 1981: 2).

June 4, 1779/Friday
Henry Haul enlists as sergeant in Captain Robert George's Company (Harding 1981: 30).

Joseph Anderson enlists as a sergeant in Captain Robert George's Company (Harding 1981: 29-30).

George Armstrong enlists as a Matross in Captain Robert George's Company (Harding 1981: 29-30).

John Ash enlists as a Matross in Captain Robert George's Company (Harding 1981: 29-30).

Valentine Balsinger enlists as a sergeant in Captain Robert George's Company (Harding 1981: 29-30).

September 20, 1779/Monday
Mathias Prock enlists as a private in Captain John Bailey's Company (Harding 1981: 45-46).

September 23, 1779/Thursday
Letter from George Rogers Clark to Thomas Jefferson. Clark states he is happy Jefferson agrees to the need for a fortification at or near the Mouth of the Ohio. Clark mentions several possible locations for the post. Clark feels the fort would be an advantage to trade in the western country and for the Indian Department. Clark recommends a garrison of 200 men for the fort and 100 families for a settlement (Seineke 1981: 400-401).

September 24, 1779/Friday
Letter from George Rogers Clark at the Falls of Ohio to Col. Daniel Broadhead at Fort Pitt. Clark mentions he will station a small floating battery at the Mouth of the Ohio (Seineke 1981: 401-402).

September 25, 1779/Saturday
Richard Turpin enlists as a Matross in Captain George's Co. (Harding 1981: 32).

September 30, 1779/Thursday
Letter from George Rogers Clark to Silas Harlan. Clark states that a fort will be built near the Mouth of Ohio "immediately." Clark orders Harlan to raise settlers to live at the post. The settlers will be paid as militia for as long as necessary. Clark tells Harlan to be at the post by December 1, 1779 (GRC, I: 368-369; VSA, September 1779).

November 4, 1779/Thursday
Letter from Silas Harlan at Harrodsburg to George Rogers Clark at Falls of Ohio. Their setting off to the Iron Banks (Mouth of Ohio), was approved by the commissioners, and he believes it will also be approved by the Virginia Assembly. Harlan is going on an expedition to procure cattle and horses (MHS: B1, F11).

November 8, 1779/Monday
Letter from Jefferson to Governor Galvez. Jefferson seeks Galvez's approval of Virginia to build a post on the Mississippi River near the Mouth of Ohio for promoting trade between Virginia and Spain (Seineke 1981: 407-408).

November 15, 1779/Monday
Jacob Decker enlists as a private in Captain Kellar's Company (Harding 1981: 24).

November 16, 1779/Tuesday
Clark calls a Council of War and discusses with his junior officers the size of the post and garrison for the Mouth of the Ohio (GRC, I: 375-377).

November 17, 1779/Wednesday
Beverly Trent enlists as a sergeant in Captain John Bailey's Company of the Illinois Regiment in the Virginia State Service (Harding 1981: 45-46).

November 18, 1779/Thursday
Jeremiah Horn [also Hern] enlists for three years by Lt. Valentine T. Dalton into Captain Robert George's Company of Artillery (MHS: B1, F23).

November 29, 1779/Monday
Thomas Laney [also Delany, Leney] enlists for three years by Lt. Valentine T. Dalton into Captain Robert George's Company of Artillery (MHS: B1, F23).

Patrick Marr, Samuel Coffy, and John Anderson enlist for three years by Lt. Valentine T. Dalton into Captain Robert George's Company of Artillery (MHS: B1, F23).

December 1, 1779/Wednesday
James Ballanger enlists as a member of Captain Mark Thomas' Company of Infantry commanded by Col. George Slaughter (Harding 1987: 37).

December 8, 1779/Wednesday
James Thompson enlists as a private in Captain Kellar's Company (Harding 1981: 24).

December 11, 1779/Saturday
Benjamin Lewis enlists for three years by Lt. Valentine T. Dalton into Captain Robert George's Company of Artillery (MHS: B1, F23).

January 1, 1780/Saturday
Thomas Bolton enlists for three years into Captain Robert George's Company of Artillery by Lt. Valentine T. Dalton (MHS: B1, F23).

Letter from Governor Jefferson to George Rogers Clark. Clark is directed to complete his battalion. He should station 100 men at the Falls of Ohio under Major Slaughter in preparation for Detroit (Seineke 1981: 418).

January 5, 1780/Wednesday
Henry Hutton, by order of George Rogers Clark, issued 200 yards of flannel, 225 yards of cloth, 320 skeins of thread, and 277 dozen buttons to Thomas Wilson at the Falls of the Ohio for making soldiers clothing (MHS: B1, F14).

January 6, 1780/Thursday
George Smith enlists as a Matross in Captain George's Company (Harding 1981: 32)

January 10, 1780/Monday
Paul Quibea [Quibeo] enlists for three years in Captain Robert George's Company of Artillery by Lt. Valentine T. Dalton (MHS B1, F23).

January 24, 1780/Monday
Jefferson's writes letter to Joseph Martin, Indian Agent. States desire of having a fort at the Mouth of Ohio. Mentions that this fort, together with other posts, are meant to establish a chain of defense for the Western frontier and the protection of trade with New Orleans. Jefferson requests Martin to seek the permission of the Cherokee and/or purchase the land at the Mouth of the Ohio from them (GRC, I: 385-386).

January 29, 1780/Saturday
Letter from Jefferson to George Rogers Clark. Encloses letters with his to Joseph Martin and Daniel Smith and Thomas Walker which discuss the new location of a fort at the Mouth of Ohio. Jefferson describes his agreement with building a fort near the Mouth of Ohio. Jefferson also discusses land warrants and other means to induce enlistment and settlement near the proposed fort (GRC, I: 386-391; Seineke 1981: 481-419).

Jefferson's letter to Thomas Walker and Daniel Smith. Jefferson mentions proposing to fortify a post near the Mouth of Ohio and needs to know the exact latitude of the post. Jefferson requests that either Walker or Smith go to the Falls of Ohio where George Rogers Clark will furnish escorts and other necessities and then travel to the Mouth of Ohio. Jefferson requests the return of a map of their work to him and one to Col. Clark (GRC, I: 392-392; Seineke 1981: 420).

January 31, 1780/Monday
James McDonell [McDonald] enlists for three years by Lt. Valentine T. Dalton into Captain Robert George's Company of Artillery (MHS: B1, F23).

February 3, 1780/Thursday
Daniel Baber enlists as Matross in Captain Robert George's Company (Harding 1981: 29-31).

February 4, 1780/Friday
Peter Angley enlists as a private in Captain John Bailey's Company (Harding 1981: 45-46).

February 22, 1780/Tuesday
George Rogers Clark writes to Governor Jefferson describing the location he has selected for building Fort Jefferson (GRC, I: 414)

March, 1780/Miscellaneous
Letter from George Rogers Clark at Louisville to Col. John Todd. Clark suggests that in order to maintain authority in Illinois, it may be necessary to evacuate the Illinois posts and let their forces center at the Mouth of the Ohio. If militia families would settle there, Clark feels they would be followed by two or three times their number of young men (GRC, I: 404-406; Seineke 1981: 429).

March 1, 1780/Wednesday
Account of arms received by Martin Carney at the Falls of Ohio, the property of the Commonwealth of Virginia, from John Donne, Commissary, two rifles and three muskets (VSA-16,50).

March 10, 1780/Friday
Patrick McAuley enlists for three years by Lt. Valentine T. Dalton into Captain Robert George's Company of Artillery. He was not included on the payroll because Dalton neglected to give account of what has become of him or when and how his time expired (Harding 1981: 30; MHS: B1, F23).

Page Certain enlists as a private in Captain Worthington's Company (Harding 1981: 47).

March 13, 1780/Monday
Jacob Ditterin enlists as a Matross in Captain George's Company (Harding 1981: 32).

March 20, 1780/Monday
Andrew Conor enlists as a private for three years by Lt. Valentine T. Dalton into Captain Robert George's Company of Artillery (MHS: B1, F23).

March 24, 1780/Friday
Larken Ballenger enlists on this date as a member of Captain John Bailey's Company (Harding 1981: 45-46).

March, 26, 1780/Sunday
Peter Blain enlists as a private in Captain John Bailey's Company of Illinois Regiment in the Virginia State Service (Harding 1981: 45-46).

William Carr enlists as a private in Captain John Bailey's Company of the Illinois Regiment in the Virginia State Service (Harding 1981: 45-46).

James Hays enlists as private in Captain John Bailey's Company of Illinois Regiment in the Virginia State Service (Harding 1981: 45-46).

March 28, 1780/Tuesday
John Hazzard enlists for three years by Lt. Valentine T. Dalton into Captain Robert George's Company of Artillery (MHS: B1, F23).

April 4, 1780/Tuesday
Letter from George Rogers Clark in Louisville to Col. William Fleming at Harrodsburg. Clark says he is very sorry for the great loss of blood and property by the Kentuckians. They have sent Clark several petitions wanting an expedition against the Shawnee (Piqua). Clark does not want to interfere with an expedition already planned by Jefferson. The success of that expedition depends on the Kentuckians and will give them immediate and permanent peace from the Indians. Clark also states that he has workman engaged building 100 boats in order to transport himself into the heart of Indian country (GRC, I: 407-408).

April 5, 1780/Wednesday
Martin Carney at the Falls purchased one wagon and gears and four gallons of tar, equal to 1,148 pounds; five flat-bottomed boats for sake of the plank to build a garrison and barracks at or near the Mouth of Ohio River by order of Col. Clark (VSA-50: 2).

Joshua Pruitt enlists on this date as a Matross in Captain Robert George's Company (Harding 1981: 31).

April 6, 1780/Thursday
Articles purchased by Martin Carney for the State of Virginia by order of Col. Clark: one bateau for 275 pounds to be paid to Eliasha Freeman (VSA-50: 2).

April 7, 1788/Friday
Daniel Smith and Thomas Walker, about 160 miles east of the Cumberland River, received the January 29, 1780, letter from Thomas Jefferson from Col. Henderson (Souissant 1915).

Articles purchased by Martin Carney for the State of Virginia by order of Col. Clark: purchased from William Pope, two muskets and a rifle for 330 pounds (VSA-50: 2).

April 8, 1780/Saturday
Daniel Smith and Thomas Walker recruit guard to accompany them to the Falls of the Ohio [thinking they would meet with Col. Clark there to carry out Governor Jefferson's January 29, 1780, orders to them] (Souissant 1915: 62).

Articles purchased by Martin Carney for the State of Virginia by order of Col. Clark: had appraised one rifle gun the property of Nathanal Randal valued to 180 pounds (VSA-50: 2).

Account of arms received by Martin Carney at the Falls the property of the Commonwealth of Virginia: received of Col. Clark at the Falls of Ohio, three rifles and 27 muskets (VSA-50: 16).

Sundry disbursements made by John Donne in behalf of the Commonwealth of Virginia: to cash paid James Young in part for a boat for Fort Jefferson, 31 2/6 dollars (VSA-10).

April 10, 1780/Monday
Articles purchased by Martin Carney for the State of Virginia by order of Col. Clark: one large bateau to be paid to John A. Johns per receipt, 1,000 pounds (VSA-50: 2).

William Purcell enlists as a Matross in Captain Robert George's Company (Harding 1981: 31-33).

April 11, 1780/Tuesday
William Shannon received six land warrants containing 560 acres each from George Rogers Clark. Shannon promises to deliver one able bodied soldier per warrant. Signed by John Thruston, James Sullivan, and William Shannon (GRC, I: 412).

Citizens of Cahokia write to George Rogers Clark of fear if Indians attack their village, hoping Clark will render assistance (GRC, I: 410-412).

April 12, 1780/Wednesday
Abraham Kellar and William Shannon sign they received of Col. George Rogers Clark, four land warrants containing 560 acres each, for recruiting four soldiers during the war to serve in Col. Clark's regiment (GRC, I: 413).

Edward Worthington and William Shannon sign they received of Col. George Rogers Clark, 20 land warrants containing 560 acres each, for recruiting 20 soldiers during the war to serve in Col. Clark's regiment (GRC, I: 413).

Letter from William Shannon at Falls of Ohio to Evan Baker, Commissary of Washington County, Virginia. Shannon states that he is directed to draw on Baker for six months provision for 1000 men to be at the Mouth of Ohio by June 1, 1780 (GRC, I: 413-414).

William Shannon's deposition of August 25, 1781 states on this date he received 39 land warrants containing 360 acres each from George Rogers Clark to furnish provisions for use of troops under Clark's command in the Illinois Department to the amount of 8,771 pounds, 2 shillings, Virginia Currency (GRC, I: 593).

Francis Puccan enlists for three years by Lt. Valentine T. Dalton into Captain Robert George's Company of Artillery. Puccan was not on the payroll because Dalton neglected to give an account of what has become of him or when or how his time expired (MHS: B1, F23).

Account of arms delivered by Martin Carney to Captain George's Company of Artillery of the Illinois Virginia Regiment: delivered to Sergeant Walker, two rifle guns (VSA-50: 3).

Account of arms delivered to Captain John Bailey's Company: delivered to Sergeant Trent by Col. Clark's verbal orders, two rifles (VSA-50: 4).

William Robeson enlists as a private in Captain Worthington's Company (Harding 1981: 47, 53).

April 14,1780/Friday
William Pursley enlists as a Matross in Captain Robert George's Company of Artillery (Harding, 1981: 140, 156, 203).

April 15, 1780/Saturday
James Brown enlists as a private in Captain Worthington's Co. (Harding 1981: 47).

April 19, 1780/Wednesday
George Rogers Clark and Illinois Regiment arrive at the Mouth of the Ohio (GRC, I: 417-418).

Thomas Jefferson at Richmond writes to George Rogers Clark answering Clark's letter of February 22, 1780, regarding location of fort at Mouth of Ohio. Jefferson discusses several options within letter concerning a site for a new fort (GRC, I: 414-416).

Thomas Jefferson at Richmond writes George Rogers Clark at Falls regarding murders by the Indians between Fort Pitt and Kentucky. Jefferson believes Clark is at the Mouth of Ohio, and suggests Clark should carry out an expedition against the Indians immediately (GRC, I: 416-417).

Valentine T. Dalton at Fort Patrick Henry (Vincennes) writes George Rogers Clark at Mouth of Ohio informing him of opposition to building a fort at the Ohio by the English (MHS: B1, F16).

Privates Peter Angley, Ephraim Dragoon, and Mathias Prock desert from Captain John Bailey's Co. (Harding 1981: 46).

April 20, 1780/Thursday
George Rogers Clark, at Mouth of Ohio, writes to John Dodge stating he arrived at Mouth of Ohio yesterday [4-19-80]. Dodge should send Clark's furniture, seeds for garden, and "beans the French plant to make shades." Clark states Captain Bentley will give Dodge the news (GRC, I: 417-418).

Captain John Ozala signs he received of Zephaniah Blackford, 230 lbs of Indian meal for a command of 30 men from Fort Patrick Henry to the Mouth of the Ohio (VSA-10).

John Bouden enlists for three years by Lt. Valentine T. Dalton into Captain Robert George's Company of Artillery. Bouden was not on the payroll because Dalton failed to give account of what has become of him or when and how his time expired (MHS: B1, F23).

Jacob Ditterin enlists for three years by Lt. Valentine T. Dalton into Captain George's Company of Artillery (MHS: B1, F23).

April 21, 1780/Friday
William Bartholomew, John Breeding, William Bohman, John Cowan, John Deck, George King, Bob Logan and Daniel Tyger are stationed at Fort Clark; some are later at Fort Jefferson (VSA-10).

April 22, 1780/Saturday
Articles purchased by Martin Carney for the State of Virginia by order of Col. Clark include two horses the property of Captain Worthington, valued at 1,800 pounds (VSA-50: 2).

April 25, 1780/Tuesday
Thomas Walker and Daniel Smith are within 12 miles of the Falls when they are informed by Captain Kellar that Col. Clark had left for the Iron Banks on April 14, 1780. Captain Kellar offers to take Walker and Smith with him as he was just leaving to go there. "Agreed to go with him" (Souissant 1915: 63).

Letter from Captain Richard McCarty [possibly at Cahokia] to George Rogers Clark. McCarty congratulates Clark on his arrival at the Mouth of Ohio. Speaks of expected Indian attack at McCarty's location by a much superior force. "Health good but pockets low." Wishes George Rogers Clark was at McCarty's location (MHS B1, F16).

Col. John Montgomery at Fort Clark [Kaskaskia] writes George Rogers Clark at Mouth of Ohio. Montgomery is pleased Clark has arrived. Lt. Richard Brashears delivers letter and awaits at Fort Jefferson for Clark's response. Montgomery states condition at Fort Clark not good, but he will do all he can in bringing Clark goods (MHS B1, F16).

April 26, 1780/Wednesday

Daniel Smith, Thomas Walker, and Captain Kellar embark for Iron Banks from Falls of Ohio. Smith writes: "If Paper was plenty I would attempt a description of our uncomfortable situation --with a Xantippe of a Landlady, something like a petruchio of Shakespeare of Nabal for a landlord, their Dirty children, leaky boat, Drunkenness &c., but I am by no means equal to the task" (Souissant 1915: 63).

Account of arms delivered by Martin Carney to Captain George's Company of Artillery of the Illinois Virginia Regiment: delivered to Captain George, one rifle gun (VSA-50: 3).

Account of arms delivered to Captain John Bailey's Company: delivered to Ensign Slaughter, one rifle; delivered to Captain John Bailey, one rifle (VSA-50: 4)

John Bailey signs he received of Martin Carney, one rifle gun for the use of Bailey's Company (VSA-10).

James Dean enlists as a private in Captain Worthington's Company (Harding 1981: 47).

The Commonwealth of Virginia in account with Abraham Kellar: to cash paid Edward Matthews as per receipt, 180 pounds (VSA-19).

April 27, 1780/Thursday

Captain John Rogers and George Rogers Clark sign request at "Camp on Mississippi," for 20 yards of cloth with facings and trimmings for making clothing for part of Rogers' Company of Virginia Light Dragoons (MHS: B1, F16).

John Rogers and George Rogers Clark sign request at "Camp on Mississippi," to deliver 30 yards flannel with thread to make the same in shirts for part of Rogers' company of Virginia Light Dragoons (MHS: B1, F16).

Laurence Slaughter signs he received of George Rogers Clark five land warrants containing 560 acres each, promising to return five soldiers to serve in Clark's battalion (MHS: B1, F16).

April 28, 1780/Friday

Richard Brashears and George Rogers Clark sign request to let Shadrack Bond, one of the artificers, have one suit of clothes and flannel for one shirt (MHS: B1, F16).

George Rogers Clark requests that Mr. Brashears be issued 20 suits of soldiers clothes. Also issued Brashears flannel for ten shirts (MHS: B1, F16). Lt. Richard Brashears signs he received the items from William Clark (MHS: B1, F16).

Account of arms received by Martin Carney in this department the property of the Commonwealth of Virginia: received of Captain John Rogers, entered before in another place [April 1, 1780], two rifles; purchased of William Pope, one rifle and two muskets; appraised and taken into service belonging to N. Randolph, one rifle (VSA-50: 16).

John Rogers and George Rogers Clark sign request for 40 yards of cloth with trimmings and facing for making for Rogers' Company (MHS: B1, F16).

John Rogers and George Rogers Clark sign request for three hundred yards of flannel for shirting, overalls and over jackets. The troops will wear these when cleaning their horses (MHS: B1, F16). John Rogers signed he received the within contents from William Clark (MHS: B1, F16).

April 29, 1780/Saturday
Letter from Batisst, Chief of the Kaskaskia Indians, at Fort Clark to George Rogers Clark, stating he has heard of Clark's arrival at the Mouth of the Ohio and Batisst plans to visit Clark along with Col. John Montgomery (GRC, I: 418).

Letter from Richard McCarty at Fort Clark [Kaskaskia] to George Rogers Clark. McCarty is sending something with Mr. Gratiot to Clark; Clark's presence is wanted at Fort Clark (MHS: B1, F16).

April, 1780/Miscellaneous
Anne McMeans "Sailed to Fort Jefferson with husband and 7 children" (Personal Narrative, A. McMeans Jameson Filson Club).

Micajah Mayfield "finds" Mayfield Creek (Draper Manuscripts 8J64-65).

May 1, 1780/Monday
Richard Harrison and George Rogers Clark sign request to William Clark to deliver the bearer 48 yards flannel for the use of the troops under Harrison's command (MHS: B1, F17).

John Aldar enlists as private in Captain George Owens' Company of Militia of the District of Clarksville in the State of Virginia (GRC, I: 464; Harding 1981: 48-49).

Private Peter Blain deserts from Captain John Bailey's Company of Militia (Harding 1981: 46).

John Hutsil enlists as a private in Captain George Owens' Company (Harding 1981: 49).

Conrad Ker enlists as a private in Captain George Owens' Company of Militia (GRC, I: 464; Harding 1981: 48-49).

Henry Ker enlists as a private in Captain George Owens' Company of Militia (GRC, I: 464; Harding 1981: 48-49).

Jonas Ker enlists as a private in Captain George Owens' Company of Militia (GRC, I: 464; Harding 1981: 48-49).

Mark Ker enlists as 1st Lieutenant in Captain George Owens' Company of Militia (GRC, I: 464; Harding 1981: 48-49).

Buckner Pittman enlists as a sergeant in Captain George's Company of artillery (Harding 1981: 31-33).

Edward Wilson enlists as an Ensign in Captain Owens' Co. of Militia (GRC, I: 464; Harding 1981: 48).

Joshua Archer enlists as a private in Captain George Owens' Company (GRC, I: 465; Harding 1981: 48-49).

James Barnett enlists as a private in Captain George Owens' Company of Militia (Harding 1981: 48-49).

May 2, 1780/Tuesday
Lt. Richard Harrison signs he received four muskets and three carabin's from Martin Carney at Clarksborough [Clarksville] for the use of Harrison's Company (VSA-11; 50: 3).

May 3, 1780/Wednesday
Daniel Smith and Thomas Walker write: "This morning at break of day opposite old Fort Massac. This afternoon at five o'clock got to the Mouth of the Ohio; then own the Mississippi about five miles to Col. Clark's encampment, who we saw this evening and had some conversation with respecting our business." Captain Kellar and untold number of individuals in party also arrives (Souissant 1915: 64).

May 4, 1780/Thursday
Daniel Smith and Thomas Walker "staid [sic] at the Intended Town" [Fort Jefferson] (Souissant 1915: 64).

Letter from Oliver Pollack to George Rogers Clark regarding bills of Clark's and Montgomery's which are for $60,000 and are unpaid (Draper Manuscripts 40J35).

May 5, 1780/Friday
Smith and Walker write: "staid [sic] at the Intended Town." Note: journal entry combines May 4 and 5 as one entry (Souissant 1915: 64).

May 6, 1780/Saturday
Smith and Walker write: "Went down to the Iron Bank, encamp'd on the Spanish Shore a little below---rather hazy" (Souissant 1915: 64).

In a letter to George Rogers Clark from Charles Gratiot in Kaskaskia, reference is made to Col. Montgomery taking the opinions of the officers, military, and militia to determine whether they wish to proceed with the expedition [Gratiot had previously mentioned this expedition to George Rogers Clark]. The vote was to proceed in order to scatter the enemy and strike terror in the Indians. About 30 men will stay at Kaskaskia for its defense. Gratiot apologizes for not being able to send tafia to Clark. It is scarce at Kaskaskia. He promises to send some from Cahokia. Gratiot hopes there is some tafia left from what he had reserved for his own use and will divide it with Clark. Gratiot asks that his respects be given to all the gentlemen and for Clark to tell them that all the garden seeds were sent down by Mr. Lindsay and there are no more in Kaskaskia (MHS: B1, F17).

May 7, 1780/Sunday
Smith and Walker write: "Cloudy. Rain last night" (Souissant 1915: 64).

Letter from Col. Montgomery at Cahokia to George Rogers Clark at Fort Jefferson. Trip planned will not take place because inhabitants won't furnish Col. Montgomery with the needed supply of flour and corn to feed his troops for two months. Mentions a Mr. Gillespe, who is to make a voyage with a party of men. Mr. Gillespe will deliver to George Rogers Clark part of the artillery, some salt, 2000 lbs of lead. The balance of the provisions will be brought by Col. Montgomery (MHS: B1, F17; Seineke 1981: 431-432).

May 8, 1780/Monday
Smith and Walker write: "Clear in morning but cloudy at noon. Ran some lines to determine the width of the river" (Souissant 1915: 64).

Laurence Slaughter signs he received from Martin Carney one rifle gun for Slaughter's own use (VSA-11) (VSA-50: 4).

John Bailey signs request to the quartermaster to issue one gun to one man of Bailey's company (VSA-11a). Bailey signs he received the gun from Martin Carney (VSA-11).

Joseph Thornton enlists on this date as a private in Captain Worthington's Company (Harding 1981: 47 & 53).

May 9, 1780/Tuesday
Smith and Walker write: "Cloudy, but being convinced we were north of the line [North Carolina-Virginia] moved to the South end of the Island about five miles" (Souissant 1915: 64).

Letter from John Rogers at Kaskaskia to George Rogers Clark at Fort Jefferson. Rogers will be leaving May 10 for Cahokia with his company. Mr. Dodge has purchased horses for Rogers. Rogers is asking for instructions to receive saddles, bear skins, and reams of clothing for his soldiers (MHS: B1, F18).

May 10, 1780/Wednesday
Smith and Walker write: "Observed" (Souissant 1915: 64).

Matross's John Fitzhugh, Christopher Lowerback, and Adam Payne desert from Captain George's Company (Harding 1981: 30-31).

May 11, 1780/Thursday
Smith and Walker write: "Agreed with yesterday's observation. We were 3'19" in Virginia. From this point of the Island we ran east to the main land where I marked a buck eye elm and sugar tree. Then we surveyed south three miles, 265 poles; thence west 106 poles to the river [96 poles of which we mark'd]. New land is forming here; nothing to mark but cotton [wood?] trees. Moved up the river until we were about one mile below west clift. A creek about 1-4 m. above west cliff; lay in the wet without fire" (Souissant 1915: 64).

Letter from George Rogers Clark at Camp Jefferson to Oliver Pollock, Esq., New Orleans. Clark arrived at Fort Jefferson to execute orders for establishing a post for the convenience of trade and other purposes. Clark hopes Pollack will assist in obtaining the clothes and other possessions stolen by the deserters (GRC, I: 418-419; Seineke 1981: 432-433).

Col. John Montgomery signs request to John Dodge to accept and pay the within contents. Gasper Butcher signs he received the goods from John Dodge [what contents are requested is not mentioned] (VSA-11).

Richard Clark and John Montgomery write on May 6, 1780 that Gasper Butcher was employed as artificer in repairing the fort at Kaskaskia [Fort Clark], for three days in the month of March at the rate of 3/pr day payable in goods as they were sold in 1772 (VSA-11).

May 12, 1780/Friday
Smith and Walker write: "Got up to Col. Clarke" (Souissant 1915: 64).

John Bailey signs he received from Martin Carney, three fusees for Captain Worthington's Company (VSA-11).

May 13, 1780/Saturday
"Embark'd again for Kaskaskios [sic]" wrote Daniel Smith upon leaving Fort Jefferson (Souissant 1915: 64).

George Rogers Clark probably leaves Fort Jefferson sometime between May 13, 1780 and May 18, 1780 to go to St. Louis and Cahokia by way of Kaskaskia. Note, Captain Robert George is signing vouchers by May 18, 1780 (VSA-11).

May 14, 1780/Sunday
Account of ammunition received by Martin Carney at Fort Jefferson: received from the French boats [Kaskaskia], by order of Col. Clark, ten kegs gunpowder 100 weight each which equals 1,000 lbs; received from Captain George by Col. Clark's verbal order, three kegs gunpowder, none of them full. [Document states that the

kegs were said to contain 100 weight each, but it had been crossed out], equals 200 lbs gunpowder; received from Captain John Dodge, 21 piggs of lead, said to be 1,600 lbs (VSA-50: 5).

May 15, 1780/Monday
Letter from Captain John Rogers at Fort Clark to George Rogers Clark at Fort Jefferson. Rogers speaks of the dirty condition and need for repair of the fort at Cahokia and his efforts to clean it. Rogers also speaks of Col. Montgomery [on the Spanish side], who is supposed to make an expedition with 100 men. Clark told John Rogers to remain at Cahokia (MHS: B1, F17; Seineke 1981: 434).

Letter from Col. Montgomery at Fort Bowman [Cahokia] to George Rogers Clark at Fort Jefferson. Montgomery has a handful of troops and he wants to join with Spanish troops because of the approach of the enemy. They will try to prevent the enemy from attacking the villages [of Cahokia]. The Spanish will furnish 100 men with artillery and ammunition. Montgomery believes he will depart in a few days with 250 men, but will retreat down stream if the enemy is too hard. If the enemy are not more than two to one, nothing but death will prove a surrender (MHS: B1, F17).

May 16, 1780/Tuesday
Letter from Captain Valentine T. Dalton at Fort Clark to George Rogers Clark. Dalton had gone to O'Post [Vincennes] from Fort Clark [Kaskaskia] to pick up salt. Letter mentions Lt. Timothy Montbreuen and his latest actions at Ouiatenon (Seineke 1981: 435).

May 17, 1780/Wednesday
Letter from Major de Peyster at Detroit to Gen. Haldimand tells of several Indian tribes. De Peyster also informs Haldimend that Clark has gone to the Iron Mines on the Mississippi, below the Ohio to establish a fort (Seineke 1981: 435-436).

May 18, 1780/Thursday
Captain Richard Brashears signs request to the quartermaster to issue one case bottle of tafia for Brashears' own use (VSA-11).

Valentine T. Dalton signs request at Fort Clark, to issue pork for the use of Captain George's company at Fort Jefferson (VSA-11).

Captain Robert George at Fort Jefferson writes to George Rogers Clark at Cahokia informing him of Captain Shannon and Doctor Smith's arrival at Fort Jefferson a few days ago; additionally only 18 men including non-commissioned officers are present, but George is not worried as he expects no action. The doctor is short of medicines. Captain George is keeping the doctor at Fort Jefferson, but is sending a letter with Shannon to Cahokia. George refers to the sickly season approaching (MHS: B1, F17).

Col. George Rogers Clark amends several entries of land deeds to include 73,962 acres of "drowned lands from Mouth of Tennessee River down Ohio to Mississippi River" (Draper Manuscripts 5K3) (MHS, B1: F17).

May 19, 1780/Friday
Laurence Slaughter signs request to the armourer to please repair Slaughter's rifle gun as quickly as possible (VSA-11).

Account of ammunition received by Martin Carney at this post Clarksville: received from Kaskaskia, five piggs lead said to be 480 lbs (VSA-50: 5).

Account of ammunition delivered by Martin Carney by order of Col. Clark: to Captain Richard Harrison at Kaskaskia, 23 1/2 lbs gunpowder; to Silas Harlan, Major of Militia, three lbs gunpowder and six lbs lead; to John Bailey, Captain of Regulars at Kaskaskia, 9 1/2 lbs gunpowder and 19 lbs lead; to Mr. Perault,

Lt. of Regulars at Kaskaskia, 1/2 lb gunpowder; to Doctor [Conard?] and Lt. Girault, of Regulars at Kaskaskia, one lb gunpowder and two lbs lead (VSA-50: 8).

May 20, 1780/Saturday
Col. Daniel Broadhead at Fort Pitt writes to George Rogers Clark regarding primary forces. Broadhead wishes that Clark with his forces would make an attack on the Shawnee. Broadhead feels an attack by himself would be impractical for want of resources. Major Slaughter and his 100 men will be joining Clark. Letter to be delivered to George Rogers Clark by Slaughter (GRC, I: 419-420).

Captain Edward Worthington at Falls of Ohio writes to George Rogers Clark at Mouth of Ohio explaining why he did not accompany Col. Legras and Mr. DeJean from Williamsburg to Fort Jefferson. There are several dissatisfied people at the Falls of Ohio. Worthington speaks of supplies that are being prepared by the Commissary in Clark's department that will be sent to Clark (MHS: B1, F17).

May 22, 1780/Monday
Letter from Lt. James Robertson at New Orleans to George Rogers Clark. Robertson has just arrived in New Orleans and informs Clark of his plans in that location to join Clark. He also tells of the Spainards getting ready to attack Mobile and Pensacola (Seineke 1981: 437).

Daniel Williams enlists as a private in Captain Worthington's Company (Harding 1981: 47, 53).

May 24, 1780/Wednesday
Lieutenant Thomas Wilson writes from Vincennes informing Clark of rumored British and Indian attacks in Kentucky (Seineke 1981: 437-438)

May 25, 1780/Thursday
Letter from Captain William Shannon at Kaskaskia to George Rogers Clark at Cahokia. Shannon arrived at Kaskaskia after an eight day trip from Clarksville. He plans on seeing Clark in two days if his horse can hold out. Indians are daily being hostile with the inhabitants at the Falls and Clark's return is much hoped for (MHS: B1, F17; Seineke 1981: 439).

May 26, 1780/Friday
Account of ammunition delivered by Martin Carney by order of Col. Clark: to Richard Brashears, Captain of Regulars at Cahokia, 4 3/4 lbs gunpowder and 9 1/2 lbs lead; to Richard Brashears, Captain of Regulars at Cahokia, five lbs gunpowder and 11 lbs lead; to Captain John Rogers of Regulars at Cahokia, six lbs gunpowder; to Captain Richard Harrison of Regulars at Cahokia, 136 lbs gunpowder; to John Bailey at Cahokia, 4 1/2 lbs gunpowder and nine lbs lead; to Mr. Brady for Indians at Cahokia, three lbs gunpowder and four lbs lead; to John Duff, Spy at Cahokia, 1/4 lb gunpowder and 1/2 lb lead; to John Bailey at Cahokia, 9 1/2 lbs gunpowder and 19 lbs lead; to Captain McCarty at Cahokia, 4 3/4 lbs gunpowder and 9 1/2 lbs lead; to Jarret Williams, Ensign at Cahokia, 3 1/2 lbs gunpowder and seven lbs lead; to Captain Richard Harrison at Cahokia, 21 lbs gunpowder (VSA-50: 8).

The Battle of St. Louis (and Cahokia) occurs (McDermott 1980: 131-151). Clark and his forces from Fort Jefferson, Kaskasia, Cahokia, and St. Louis foil the British-led attack and are victorious. Clark sent Col. John Montgomery after the retreating Indians (GRC, I: cxxxv; McDermott 1980: 141-142).

May 29, 1780/Monday
Account of ammunition received by Martin Carney at Clarksville: received from Kaskaskia, one keg gunpowder, said to be 40 lbs gunpowder (VSA-50: 5).

Matross Mark Foley, Thomas Snellock, and David Wallace are discharged on this date from Captain Robert George's Company (Harding 1981: 30).

May 30, 1780/Tuesday
Samuel Allen enlists as a sergeant in Captain Brashears' Company (Harding 1981: 51).

The following men enlist as privates in Captain Brashears' Company (Harding 1981: 51-52).

1. Jon Allin
2. William Bartholomew
3. John Blair
4. Mark Foley
5. Richard Harrison
6. James Morris
7. Francis Rubedo

James Dawson enlists for three years in Isaac Taylor's Co. (Harding 1981: 141).

May 31, 1780/Wednesday
Account of arms delivered to Captain John Bailey, one carabin (VSA-50: 4).

Account of ammunition delivered by Martin Carney by order of Col. Clark: to Captain of Militia at Cahokia, 34 lbs gunpowder, 56 lbs lead; to Daniel Flanery at Cahokia, five lbs gunpowder (VSA-50: 8).

June 1780/Miscellaneous
Lt. Richard Clark receives from Mr. William Clark three yards flannel and three skeins of thread for his own personal use (MHS: B1, F19).

Fred Guion receives one lb lead to kill meat for garrison at Fort Jefferson per Captain George's orders (VSA-11).

Thomas Kirk is discharged from Captain Todd's Co. at Fort Clark. He later came to Fort Jefferson with Col. Montgomery (VSA-13).

Josiah Phelps is sent from Louisville to see George Rogers Clark, at Fort Jefferson (Draper Manuscripts 26J4).

June 1, 1780/Thursday
William Shannon is listed as a Captain. He is to supply Fort Jefferson from Louisville (GRC, I: 413-414).

Lewis Pines time of enlistment expires. He was a member of Captain Robert Todd's Co. (Harding 1981: 12).

June 2, 1780/Friday
Col. John Todd, Jr. [Louisville] writes to Thomas Jefferson [at Richmond] regarding consolidating all Illinois troops to Fort Jefferson. Todd granted "a number of families 400 acres each" [sent list to Jefferson] (GRC, I: 422-423; Seineke 1981: 439-440; VSA-11).

Joseph Lindsay writes about his and Israel Dodge's trip to Illinois describing the losses they encountered as a result of a hurricane. Lindsay asks that the public make amends for Israel Dodge's clothing loss, because he was not paid for his trouble or time. Lindsay and I. Dodge bring with them a quantity of goods from the Falls. Also included were forms for "justice of peace" and "judges of the court" signed at Fort Jefferson by William Shannon and Henry Smith (VSA-11).

Captain A. Kellar lists 17 men who had served in his unit at one time or another during the war (MHS: B1, F19). [Those known to go to Fort Jefferson are in boldface]:

1. Christopher McGinnis
2. Martin Faggin
3. John Williams
4. **John Chappel**
5. **James Thompson**
6. Leaving Dossey
7. **Geo. Hoit**
8. Petter Boofry

9. Petter Balfau
10. **Baptist Raper**
11. James Macintos
12. **John Shank**
13. **Jacob Decker**
14. **Anthony Montroy**
15. Wm Montgomery
16. Franway Larose
17. **Joseph Panther**

According to Harding (1981: 23-24), the above 8 men, who were at Fort Jefferson, have the following dates of enlistment and discharge dates: private John Chappel (also Chappell), May 9, 1779; Discharged July 29, 1779: private Baptist Raper (also Rapkin) May 9, 1779; Deserted September 5, 1780 (Harding 1981: 23-24). Private John Shank, November 15, 1779; Discharged September 16, 1781: private Jacob Decker; November 15, 1779; Died October 7, 1780: private James Thompson, December 8, 1779; Died October 20, 1780: private Geo. Hoit (also Hoyt), May 9, 1779; Deserted October 15, 1780: private Anthony Montroy, May 9, 1779; On command at St. Vincents: private Joseph Panther (also Panter), November 15, 1779; Discharged July 8, 1781.

June 3 1780/Saturday

Conductor Thomas Wilson requests Edward Taylor, who is employed by Wilson, to be paid for his service to Wilson by going express from Fort Patrick Henry [Vincennes] to Fort Jefferson [Iron Banks] to Fort Clark [Kaskaskia] and back to Fort Patrick Henry [Vincennes] and taking 19 days to do so (VSA-11). This request was granted and Taylor was paid one dollar/day and supplies. Signed by George Rogers Clark (VSA-11).

In a letter written by Col. John Montgomery at Cahokia, Captain Brashears received by Col. Clark's order, 24 men belonging to the Illinois Regiment (MHS: B1, F19).

Account of ammunition received by Martin Carney at Clarksville from Kaskaskia, 10 1/2 piggs, said to be 1,000 lbs lead (VSA-50: 5).

Account of ammunition delivered by Martin Carney by order of Col. Clark to Captain John Rogers, at Cahokia, 80 lbs gunpowder (VSA-50: 8).

Matross John March dies. He was a member of Captain George's Company of Artillery (Harding 1981: 32).

June 4, 1780/Sunday

Captain Robert George writes from Fort Jefferson to George Rogers Clark. Letter will be delivered by Col. LeGras who is accompanied by Mr. Dejean from Williamsburg. The trenches for Fort Jefferson are ready for the pickets which the inhabitants are bringing. The inhabitants are not yet finished planting. Hope to have the fort enclosed within the week. Provisions are being spared; issuing single rations of corn. Mr. Donne has tried to procure meat without success. Present stock of corn is a little more than 100 bushels (MHS B1, F19; Seineke 1981, 441).

June 5, 1780/Monday

According to the journal entry of Daniel Smith, "Not well the night of 5th June. Left this place [Kaskaskia] to go homeward. Arrived at Camp Jefferson" (Souissant 1915: 64).

George Rogers Clark at Kaskaskia signs request to William Shannon (also at Kaskaskia), five gallons of tafia to take to Fort Jefferson (VSA-11).

Patrick Kennedy writes to certify that Col. Thomas Walker and son lived at Mr. Charlesvilles for 20 days at the rate of $2 per person per day [17 May-5 June, 1780] (VSA-11).

Account of ammunition delivered by Martin Carney by order of Col. Clark to Captain John Rogers, Captain at Cahokia, 40 lbs gunpowder; to Richard Winston at Kaskaskia, 50 lbs gunpowder (VSA-50: 8).

George Rogers Clark "with a few men" left Kaskaskia by boat to go to Fort Jefferson. Clark later left Fort Jefferson with Major Josiah Harlan and Captain Herman Consola for Harrodsburg on Saturday, June 10, 1780 (GRC, I: cxxxviii; VSA-11).

June 6, 1780/Tuesday
Letter from Captain John Rogers at Kaskaskia to George Rogers Clark at Fort Jefferson. Rogers wants to go on dangerous expedition to learn more about the service and to better serve his country (MHS: B1, F19; Seineke 1981: 442).

June 7, 1780/Wednesday
According to the journal of Daniel Smith, "A few minutes after the Indians had murdered three men (the Ker brothers) near the town [Clarksville], two others were missing and were supposed to be made prisoners; it appears that the Indians had killed another last Monday from the bloody clothes found in the Indian canoes. People at Fort Jefferson are much distressed for want of provisions and in confusion" (Souissant 1915: 64).

Pay Abstract of a company of Milita commanded by Captain George Owens of the district of Clarksville in the State of Virginia. The following members were killed on June 7, 1781: 1st Lt. Mark Ker, Pvt. Henry Ker, and Pvt. Conrad Ker. Private Samuel Cooper advanced on June 7, 1781 (GRC, I: 464-465).

Martin Carney draws up records of "ammunition received" and "ammunition issued" finding a mistake in the "issued" records. Carney is charged with 3,235 weight gunpowder and 4,145 weight lead. The issues exceed that amount by 46 1/2 weight in gunpowder, and 149 1/2 weight in lead (VSA-11).

George Rogers Clark arrives Fort Jefferson (Draper manuscripts, 26J1)

June 8, 1780/Thursday
Captain George Owens signs he received 13 lbs gun gunpowder and 26 lbs lead for his Company of Militia at Clarksborough. Silas Harlan is at Clarksville and signs issue of ammunition for Captain Owens' Company of Militia (VSA-11; 50: 8).

Issued to Major Harlan for expresses per order of Col. Clark, 2 1/4 yards blue cloth and three scalping knives (VSA-48: 77).

Martin Carney, quartermaster, signs he has received four quire of writing paper and has sent six quire of paper to the Falls of Ohio per Col. Clark's order (VSA-48: 77).

June 9, 1780/Friday
George Rogers Clark requests Silas Harlan receive two pairs leggings and two knives for going express to the Falls of Ohio from Fort Jefferson (VSA-11).

George Rogers Clark requests John Dodge for the Commissary Department at Fort Jefferson, two quire of paper (VSA-11; 48: 77).

George Rogers Clark signs request for John Dodge to issue two quire of paper to Captain Robert George. George signs that he received the paper (VSA-11; 48: 77).

George Rogers Clark signs request to John Dodge at Fort Jefferson to issue six quire paper to troops and staff at Falls of Ohio. William Shannon received the six quire from John Dodge (VSA-11).

Martin Carney at Clarksville acknowledges he received five pairs of hand millstones for the use of George Rogers Clark's troops from Archibold Lockard.

They cost $200/pair [$100, or 300 pounds, Virginia currency] (VSA-11; 50: 2). Arch. Lockard at Fort Jefferson received a receipt from Martin Carney for the five pairs of millstones to be paid by the State of Virginia (VSA-11).

Valentine T. Dalton writes from Fort Patrick Henry that Monsr. Ambress sold a pirogue for 200 livres peltry. Dalton notes that the pirogue measures 45'x 3' and can carry 5,000 lbs. The pirogue is now employed to carry artillery stores to headquarters at Clarksville (VSA-11).

Col. George Rogers Clark at Fort Jefferson signs request to Captain George to allow Quartermaster Carney the same clothing privileges as an officer of the regiment (VSA-11).

Col. George Rogers Clark signs request of John Dodge to issue Col. Walker and Maj. Smith four pairs cotton overalls, two pairs linen drawers, six linen shirts, one osnaburg shirt, and one pair scissors for them on their public service at Fort Jefferson (VSA-11).

Account of ammunition delivered by Martin Carney by order of Col. Clark to Harman [Herman] Consola at Camp Jefferson, 1/2 lb gunpowder (VSA-50: 8).

Captain Robert George is appointed Commander of Fort Jefferson [Day before Clark leaves for Louisville] (VSA-June 1782).

William Poston at Fort Jefferson is issued two shirts by order of Captain George (VSA-11).

__June 10, 1780/Saturday__
According to the journal of Daniel Smith,"Col. Clark with two men leave by land for the Falls of the Ohio" (Souissant 1915: 64).

Lt. Richard Harrison requests and receives from Martin Carney, 40 flints and 1 1/2 lbs lead for use of his troops going up the Ohio from Fort Jefferson (VSA-11; 50: 9).

Captain Robert George writes to John Dodge that George Rogers Clark ordered the issuance of clothing to Captain Lieut. Harrison (VSA-11).

Captain Robert George signs request to Martin Carney to deliver 1 1/2 lbs lead to Captain Harrison for his use on his expedition to the Falls of the Ohio (VSA-11).

Issued for use of Expresses to the Falls of Ohio by order of Col. Clark: 1 3/4 yards blue bath coating, 1 1/2 yds. scarlet cloth, one yd blue cloth, 12 yards ribbon, two skeins silk, one clasp knife, one pair scissors, one pair ravelled gartering, one weight vermilion, and three ruffled shirts 3 1/4 yards each (VSA-48: 77).

Issued to George Rogers Clark the following list of items by verbal orders, for use of slaves when setting off on expedition: one check linen handkerchief, seven yards osnaburg for two shirts for Negro man, five yards damaged linen for Wench, seven yards osnaburg for Wench & boy, 2 1/2 yards dark ground calico for Wench, three yards spotted flannel for Wench, one Indian handkerchief for Wench, one check linen handkerchief for Wench, four skeins thread, one scalping knife for Negro man, and 5 1/2 yards osnaburg for two pr trousers (VSA 48:1).

Issued to George Rogers Clark the following items when going to the Falls of Ohio to make an expedition against the Indian towns: three ruffled shirts 3 1/4 yards each, 1 3/4 yards blue bath coating, 1 1/2 yards scarlet cloth, one yd blue cloth, 12 yards ribbon, two skeins silk, one clasp knife, one pr scissors, one pr ravelled gartering, one lb vermilion (VSA 48: 1).

Issued to George Rogers Clark the following items paid to Mr. Eyler for a mortar: four lbs white sugar and one lb coffee (VSA 48: 1).

Issued to George Rogers Clark, 18 check handkerchiefs paid to Lafont for 18 Plates (VSA 48: 1).

Issued to George Rogers Clark, one snaffle bridle paid for two saltcellars for Do. [18 check handkerchiefs paid for 18 plates and two saltcellars which were listed but crossed out] (VSA 48: 1).

Issued for George Rogers Clark, six gallons tafia sent to Fort Jefferson by Captain Brashears (VSA 48: 1).

Issued for George Rogers Clark, 60 lbs peltry paid to Gratiot for one dozen China plates (VSA-48: 1).

Captain Robert George's sundry merchandise drawn out of the public store more than his quota for which in part no returns or receipts have been issued or passed: 26 yards blue stroud, 32 ruffled shirts, 20 plain shirts, 26 butcher knives, one ink holder, one bridle, and 26 skeins thread per order, issued to Captain Harrison, no receipt (VSA-48: 90).

Issued to Captain Lt. Richard Harrison: six yards superfine broadcloth; 2 1/2 yards shalloon; issued for six vests and six pair breeches: eight yards casimir, ten yards thickset, 7 1/2 yards corduroy, one yd spotted persian, 2 1/2 yards linen; 19 1/2 yards linen for six shirts; 2 3/4 yards cambric for ruffling six shirts and making six stocks; one silk handkerchief; one romal handkerchief; two cotton handkerchiefs; two linen handkerchiefs; three pair thread hose; 5 1/4 dozen metal buttons; two sticks silk twist; six skeins silk; 12 skeins thread; and one fine hat. John Donne certifies that the list is a true inventory of articles issued to Captain Lt. Richard Harrison agreeable to his receipt taken in Receipt Book A (VSA-48: 67).

Lt. James Merriwether belongs to Captain John Rogers' Light Dragoons (VSA-12).

Samuel Smyth is present at Fort Jefferson. He signed an invoice from New Orleans for Mr. Lindsay (VSA-11).

An inventory of goods delivered to Captain John Dodge being a cargo purchased at New Orleans in behalf of the State of Virginia (VSA 11): 10 1/5 ells brown cloth; 5 1/3 ells brown cloth; 14 ells brown cloth; 11 1/2 ells pampadown; 5 3/4 ells grey cloth; 22 1/2 grey cloth; 14 1/2 ells scarlet cloth; 12 1/2 ells brown cloth; 3 7/8 ells bath coating; 50 Pair blankets 2 1/2 points; 10 pieces blue stroad; 20 Ells bath coating; 18 pieces chintz; 55 pieces white linen some damaged; 8 pieces white linen 482 1/2 ells; 1 piece corded demitee some damaged; 33 dozen and 11 linen handkerchiefs; 28 English blankets; 92 lbs brown twine; 22 1/2 lb brown thread some damaged; 3 3/4 lb white thread; 2 pieces Ossnaburgs 226 1/2 ells including 12 ells damaged; 3 dozen and 9 pair thread hose some damaged; 3 pieces fine linen 57 ells some damaged; 4 pieces calendry; 3 pieces seyseys; 7 1/2 pieces indian handkerchiefs; 2 pieces damascus; 1 piece flowered muslin 8 ells; 2 pieces muslin 6 ells deducted; 8 red handkerchiefs; 7 pieces and remnants deep ground callicoe 67 1/4 ells; 2 dozen hats; 3 dozen and 11 silk handkerchief; 21 dozen and nine combs sundry kinds; 8 dozen butcher knives; 1 dozen and 5 clasp knives; 23 ells white flannel; 2 pieces cambrick 11 ells; 2 pieces lawn 11 ells; 26 1/4 ells thick set; 44 1/4 ells spotted and cotton velvet; 5 pieces salune; 2 pieces camblet 56 1/3 ells; 3 callimancoe 95 ells; 13 1/2 ells spotted icana; 7 3/4 ells fustain; 41 buttons metal; 2 dozen hair buttons; 1 ream writing paper; 2 dozen and 10 ink pots different kinds; 6 cases horse flems; 11 razors; 2 dozen and 10 pair scissors; 21 1/2 pieces raveled gartering; 2 boxes wafers; 21 1/2 pieces of remnants of ribbon; 1 dozen and 11 bridles; 19 pair knee garters; 35 1/2 ells holland some damaged; 1 bordered apron; 1 large chest; 1 large trunk; 3 pieces gingums 82 1/2 ells; 9 blue hankerchiefs; 1 3/4 ell brittannia; 4 pieces cottonade 61 ells; 2 pieces persian 23 1/3 ells; 90 ells ribbon; 240 skeins silk; 167 lbs. coffe damaged; 11 dozen and 9 butcher knives; 38 skeins hair twist; 400 needles; 6 pieces ferreting; 5 1/2 packs pins; 30 1/2 ells cotton de 16 a schachque; 9 sticks blackbase; 5 pieces toille greys; 1 2/5 ell fine grey cloth; and 8 pieces calico.

Col. George Rogers Clark leaves Fort Jefferson with Josiah Harlan and Herman Consola for Harrodsburg (GRC, I: cxxxviii; Souissant 191564).

June 11, 1780/Sunday
Lt. Richard Harrison receives from Martin Carney 24 yards osnaburg made into bags to carry corn for the troops on their trip to Falls of Ohio from Camp Jefferson (VSA-11).

Captain Robert George signs request to John Dodge to give Martin Carney clothing as directed by Col. Clark [Fort Jefferson]. Martin Carney received clothing (VSA-11).

June 12, 1780/Monday
Captain Robert George signs request to John Dodge to furnish Richard Harrison with the following: for 26 men of George's Co. going to the Falls by order of Col. Clark: 26 yards of stroud for making leggings and breech cloths for 26 men, 52 shirts, 26 knives, one ink pot, one bridle, and thread to make leggings (VSA-11).

1. John Walker
2. L. Keinan
3. John Taylor
4. M. Hacketon
5. M. Tinklee
6. I. Floyd
7. P. Marr
8. Wm. Freeman
9. John Wheat
10. William Moore
11. P. Hup
12. William White
13. D. Kennedy
14. V. Balsinger
15. E. Fair
16. P. McCalley
17. G. Smith
18. John Bush
19. L. Ryan
20. P. Long
21. B. Damewood
22. D. Baber
23. John Oakly
24. John Megarr
25. A. Miller
26. D. Bush

Captain Robert George signs request to John Dodge to furnish Sam Smyth with one knife, two combs [one horn, one ivory], 1 1/4 yard white half-thicks for leggings, bath coating for a breech cloth, four yd. gartering, one ink stand, one pair blankets, and one bridle for the use of the expedition to the Falls by Col. Clark's orders. Sam Smyth signed he received the goods (VSA-11).

Issued to William Clark, secretary to Col. Clark, three vests and three pair breeches to be made from: 5 1/4 yards fustian, five yards spotted velvet, and 2 1/2 yards sycee; 9 3/4 yards linen for three shirts, 3/8 yard cambric for ruffling shirts, one yard muslin for three stocks; two pair thread hose, one silk handkerchief; one check linen handkerchief, 13 skeins thread; four skeins silk; one stick silk twist, 2 1/2 yards linen for lining for vests and breeches, and five yards toile gris for two pair trousers (VSA-48: 69).

John Donne signs that the above is a true inventory of the articles issued to Secretary Clark as taken from Receipt Book A, agreeable to William Clark's receipt therein (VSA-48: 69).

Captain Robert George signs request to John Dodge to furnish William Shannon with the following by Col. Clark's orders: chintz for two pair trousers, cloth or other stuff for two waistcoats, two pair breeches, one breech cloth, one bridle, one blanket, one ink stand, one knife, one course and one fine comb (VSA-11).

William Shannon received from John Dodge, five yards check linen, 2 3/4 yards thickset, 1 1/2 yards course white linen, 1/2 yard. blue bath coating, one stick mohair, one blanket, one snaffle bridle, one large knife, one ink stand, one course and one fine comb (VSA-11).

Captain Robert George signs request to John Dodge by Col. Clark's orders to furnish Sergeant Walker with, two pair stockings, as much cottonade to make two trousers, and 12 yards red tape (VSA-11).

Sergeant John Walker received, 5 1/4 yards cottonade, two pair thread hose, and 12 yards ferret (VSA-11).

Captain Robert George signs request to John Dodge by Clark's orders to furnish Captain Lieut Harrison with the following for the expedition to the Falls, three knives, three horn and one ivory combs, 1 1/2 yards white half-thicks for leggings, bath coating for breech cloth, four yards gartering, one pair blankets (VSA-11). Captain Lt. Harrison received the goods (VSA-11).

Captain Robert George signs request to John Dodge by Clark's orders to furnish Lt. William Clark with the following: linen for three shirts with ruffling, stuff for four summer vests, two pair of breeches, two pair of trousers with proper trimming, two pair thread stockings, and two handkerchiefs (VSA-11). Lt. William Clark received the items (VSA-11).

Captain Robert George certifies that Martin Carney did everything in his power to preserve the boat, that was delivered to him by Col. Clark, which sunk unavoidably and became lost enroute to Fort Jefferson (VSA-11).

Letter from Captain Valentine T. Dalton at Fort Patrick Henry writes to George Rogers Clark about activities at Fort Patrick Henry (Seineke 1981: 442-443).

Isaac Allen is issued clothing at Fort Jefferson as a member of Ensign Williams' Company (VSA-12).

Capt. John Bailey is going on the expedition with Capt. Lt. Harrison to the Falls of the Ohio (VSA-11).

Captain Robert George's sundry merchandise drawn out of the public store more than his quota for which no returns or receipts have been issued or passed: twenty-four yards osnaburg and 15 skeins thread. Receipt signed by Martin Carney (VSA-48: 91).

Captain Robert George's sundry merchandise drawn out of the public store for which no returns or receipts have been issued or passed: three clasp knives, two horn combs, one ivory comb, 1 1/2 yards white half-thicks, 1/2 yard blue bath coating, four yards gartering, two 2 1/2 point blankets, and one leather ink pot, delivered to Captain Harrison per receipt (VSA-48: 90).

Captain Robert George's merchandise drawn out of the public store for which no returns or receipts have been issued or passed: two pair thread hose, 5 1/4 yards cottonade, and 12 yards ferret. Per order, delivered to Sergeant Walker per receipt (VSA-48: 90).

Captain Robert George's merchandise drawn out of the public store more than his quota for which no returns or receipts have been issued or passed: three, 2 1/2 point blankets, 26 horn combs, 13 ivory combs, and 2 1/2 yards blue bath coating. Issued to Captain Harrison per his receipt (VSA-48: 91).

Issued to Samuel Smyth, Surgeon Illinois Department: 1 3/4 yards blue bath coating for issued for three vests and three pair breeches: 7 1/2 yards spotted cotton velvet, one yard spotted persion, 2 1/2 yards gingham or check, and 7 1/2 yards linen for lining; 7 1/2 yards linen for three pair trousers; 9 3/4 yards for three shirts; one silk handkerchief; one romal handkerchief; one check linen handkerchief; 1 3/8 yards cambric for three stocks and ruffling three shirts; two sticks silk twist; 15 skeins thread; four skeins silk; one pair knee garters; and six yards ferretting (VSA-48: 71).

John Donne certifies that the above is a true inventory of the articles issued to Samuel Smyth, Surgeon, agreeable to Smyth's receipt taken in receipt Book A (VSA-48: 71).

Issued to Captain William Shannon, Conductor General by orders of Captain Robert George, Commandant per Captain Shannon's receipts on said orders: five yards check linen for two pair trousers, 2 3/4 yards thickset for one pair breeches, 1 1/2 yards linen for lining, 1/2 yard blue bath coating for breech cloth, one, 2 1/2 point blanket; one snaffle bridle; one clasp knife; one ink holder, one stick silk twist; one ivory comb, and one horn comb (VSA-48: 75).

June 13, 1780/Tuesday

James Pigot, Ezekiel Johnson, Henry Smith, Joseph Hunter, and Mark Iles write a petition as trustees of Fort Jefferson making a request that the new Clarksville settlement be granted its own county status (GRC, I: 425-426).

Daniel Smith and Thomas Walker write that they each received from the public stores: five pairs of cottonade overalls, one pair of brown linen drawers, six linen shirts [three ruffled, three plain], one pair blue leggings, one blue coating breech cloth, one scalping knife, 4 1/2 yards of binding, one pair leg garters, one ivory comb, one linen shirt, and one osnaburg shirt (VSA-11).

John Dodge signs an invoice of goods he received for the use of the Illinois troops and other purposes (VSA-11). Joseph Lindsay signs it is a true invoice with errors corrected (VSA-11).

Captain Robert George signs request of John Dodge to issue black calamanco to make a short gown for Mistress Flor. (VSA-11). Mistress Flor signs she received the four yards requested (VSA-11).

Captain Robert George signs request to Martin Carney to deliver to Richard Harrison 500 lbs gun gunpowder, 1,000 lbs lead for the expedition to the Falls (VSA-50: 9). Richard Harrison signed he received the items for the expedition (VSA-11).

Captain Robert George orders Martin Carney to purchase tobacco from Mr. Lindsay for the use of the troops at Fort Jefferson (VSA-11).

Joseph Lindsay receives of Martin Carney a receipt for 161 lbs. tobacco equal to 240.50 livres in peltry (VSA-11).

Martin Carney purchases for the State of Virginia by order of Col. Clark 161 lbs tobacco for the use of the troops at this post at 241 livres in peltry, equals 30 pounds and 8 shillings (VSA-50: 2).

Captain Robert George signs request at Fort Jefferson to John Dodge by Clark's orders to deliver the following for the use part of George's Co. going to the Falls three blankets, 26 horn combs, 13 ivory combs, 2 1/2 yards blue bath coating, and thread (VSA-11). Richard Harrison signed he received the listed items (VSA-11).

Richard Harrison writes that he received from Martin Carney by Col. Clark's orders: one large barge, one small canoe, 28 oars, 13 fathom cable, and one grapling [hook] (VSA-11).

Richard Harrison and Robert George sign request to the quartermaster 1/2 lb lead for use on expedition to Falls (VSA-11) (VSA-50: 9).

Captain Robert George signs request to Martin Carney to issue 1/2 lb of gunpowder and one lb lead each, to Josiah Phelps and John Montgomery (VSA-11) (VSA-50: 9).

Captain Robert George signs request to John Dodge to furnish 24 yards of osnaburg and thread to make bags for the trip to the Falls (VSA-11). Martin Carney signed he received the above from John Dodge (VSA-11).

Captain Robert George signs request to Martin Carney to deliver six carots of tobacco for his company's use on the trip to the Falls (VSA-11). John Walker signed he received tabacco (VSA-11).

Captain Robert George signs request to John Dodge by Clark's orders to furnish Captain Shannon with 1/2 yard linen, 1/4 yard check [linen], one Indian handkerchief, one pair small scissors, one silk handkerchief, one linen handkerchief, and six skeins brown thread (VSA-11). William Shannon signed that he received the items (VSA-11).

Issued to Captain William Shannon Conductor General, by orders of Captain Robert George, Commandant, per Captain Shannon's receipts: 1/2 yard white linen, 1/4 yard check linen, one Indian handkerchief, one silk handkerchief, one linen handkerchief, one pair scissors, and six skeins thread (VSA-48: 75).

Jacob Ditteren [Dittering] enlists for three years by Lt. Valentine T. Dalton into Captain Robert George's Company of Artillery (MHS: B1, F23).

Account of ammunition delivered by Martin Carney by Captain Robert George's order at Camp Jefferson: to Captain George for the use of the troops, 3/4 lb gunpowder and 1 1/2 lbs lead (VSA-50: 9).

Account of tobacco delivered by Martin Carney by order of Captain Robert George at this place: to Captain Lt. Harrison going up the Ohio, six carots equal to 18 pounds (VSA-50: 12).

Captain Robert George's merchandise drawn out of the public store for which no returns or receipts have been issued or passed: four yards black calamanco per order and receipt of Mark Eyler (VSA-48: 91).

Captain Robert George's merchandise drawn out of the public store for which no returns or receipts have been issued or passed: four, 2 1/2 point blankets per order and receipt of William Moore (VSA-48: 91).

Issued for Doctor Walker and his party by order of Col. Clark: 12 1/2 yards cottonade made into five pair overalls, 2 1/2 yards toile gris made into one pair drawers, 22 3/4 yards linen made into seven shirts, 3/8 yard muslin made into ruffling for three shirts, one yard blue cloth made into one pair leggings, 1/2 yard blue coating made into one breech cloth, one scalping knife, 4 1/2 yards worsted binding, one pair garters, one ivory comb and 3 1/4 yards osnaburgs made into one shirt (VSA-48: 77).

Captain Robert George signs request to John Dodge by Col. Clark's orders to issue four blankets for the use of his company on the trip to the Falls (VSA-11). William More "marked" that he received the blankets (VSA-11).

__June 14, 1780/Wednesday__
According to Daniel Smith's journal "Embarked to go to the Falls of Ohio with no more provisions than one quart of unsound corn per day for ten days" (Souissant 1915: 64).

Captain Robert George signs request to John Dodge to issue William Shannon three yards of the best ribbon by order of Col. Clark. William Shannon signed that he received the ribbon (VSA-11) (VSA-48: 75).

Captain Robert George requests that 3 1/4 lb. gunpowder and 1 1/2 lb lead be delivered for the use of the Fort Jefferson garrison by order of Col. Clark (VSA-11).

Richard Harrison writes a return to William Shannon for 27 gallons tafia for the use of his escort party [for Col. Walker] to the Falls from Fort Jefferson. John Donne signs that the above was delivered (VSA-11).

Captain Robert George signs request to John Dodge to deliver to the bearer, two shirts, one blanket, and one hat for his use on the expedition to the Falls of the Ohio (VSA-11). John Walker signs he received the above (VSA-11).

John Dodge was issued one small fusse of Isreal Ruland's of Vincennes by orders of George Rogers Clark (VSA-11).

Gov. Jefferson in Council to the Speaker of the House: mentions Fort Jefferson and the building of the civilian community adjacent to the fort. The lands on which the fort is built belong to the Chickasaw Indians who have entered into war with the U.S. (GRC, I: 427-428; Seineke 1981: 443).

Account of ammunition delivered by Martin Carney by Captain Robert George's order at Camp Jefferson: to Captain George's men going to the Falls of Ohio, two lbs gunpowder (VSA-50: 9).

Issued to Martin Carney Deputy Quartermaster: three yards brown broadcloth 7/4 wide and three yards shalloon, issued for six vests and six pair breeches, five yards spotted cotton velvet, six yards casimir, 2 1/2 yards thickset, 4 1/2 yards cottonade and five yards sycee; 2 1/4 yards linen for lining the vests and breeches; 19 1/2 yards linen for six shirts; two yards muslin for six stocks; 3/4 yard fine holland for ruffling six shirts, one silk handkerchief, one India handkerchief, one red cotton handkerchief, one blue cotton handkerchief, two check linen handkerchiefs, two sticks silk twist, two skeins silk, 12 skeins thread, one pair knee garters, five dozen metal buttons, and one fine hat (VSA-48: 73).

John Donne signs that the above is a true inventory of the articles issued to Martin Carney, Deputy Quartermaster agreeable to Carney's receipt taken from receipt Book A (VSA-48: 73).

Issued to Samuel Smyth, Surgeon Illinois Department: one clasp knife, one ivory comb, one horn comb, 1 1/4 yards white half-thicks for leggings, 1/2 yard bath coating for a breech cloth, four yards gartering for binding, one brass ink stand, one pair blankets, 2 1/2 point, and one bridle (VSA-48: 71).

John Donne signs the above was also issued [additional list dated June 12] to Surgeon Smyth by order of Captain Robert George Commandant agreeable to Col. Clark's orders as per inventory and receipt taken from receipt Book A (VSA-48: 71).

Captain Robert George's merchandise drawn out of the public store for which no returns or receipts have been issued or passed: one ruffled shirt; one plain shirt; one hat; and one, 2 1/2 point blanket per receipt of John Walker (VSA-48: 91).

June 15, 1780/Thursday

Captain John Dodge writes he received several goods from Lt. William Clark belonging to the State of Virginia, most of which was cloth with some brass buttons (VSA-11).

For sundry articles Robert George has taken out of the public store for which no return or receipt has been passed: 2 1/8 yards superfine gray cloth 7/4 wide, and four yards brown cloth 7/4 wide, 1/4 yard overdrawn (VSA-48: 89).

Robert George's merchandise drawn out of the public store for which no returns or receipts have been issued or passed: 1/4 yard superfine broad cloth 7/4 wide; 1 1/8 yards chintz; 2 1/2 yards shalloon; 1 3/4 yards linen; one pair scissors;

six skeins fine white thread; six skeins coarse white thread; one snaffle bridle; one ruffled shirts; 3 1/2 yards osnaburgs; one skein thread; and two metal dozen buttons (VSA-48: 90).

One silk handkerchief and one Indian handkerchief were paid Nancy Hunter per receipt for making six ruffled shirts (VSA-48: 79).

June 16, 1780/Friday
Lt. William Clark writes to the State of Virginia wanting payment in the amount of 27 Spanish milled dollars in merchandise for the delivery of goods he brought to John Dodge by order of John Todd at the Falls (VSA-11).

Paid to William Clark by order of Col. John Todd in lieu of 20 Spanish milled dollars for Clark's services in bringing to this place a quantity of cloth saved from Col. Rogers' defeat: one pair 2 1/2 point blankets = 15 1/2 dollars; one check linen handkerchief = one dollar; one brass ink pot = one dollar; one large clasp knife = 1/2 dollar; four yards ribbon = 2 dollars. Total order = 20 dollars (VSA-48: 79).

Captain Robert George signs a request to John Dodge to deliver to Martin Carney, one brass ink stand, one clasp knife, one small and one large tooth comb, and six yards ferretting. Martin Carney signs he received the items (VSA-11).

Captain Robert George signs a request to John Dodge to deliver the following for the use of the artillery, 2 1/2 yards flannel, twine, 2 1/2 yard. osnaburg, one pair scissors, and two needles. Daniel Bolton "marks" he received the items (VSA-11).

Issued per order of Captain George, Commandant, and receipt of Daniel Bolton to make cartridges for the cannon: 2 1/2 yards white flannel, 2 1/2 yards osnaburgs, one pair scissors, eight skeins twine, and two needles (VSA-48: 77).

Three yards calico are paid Margaret Bolting [Bolten] for making six plain shirts (VSA-48: 79).

Daniel Bolton delivers munition supplies to Lawrence Keinan [Keenan] in Captain George's Co. (VSA-11).

Francis Bredin is paid 1 1/2 yards chintz, one linen handkerchief, one horn comb, and one pair scissors for making seven plain shirts (VSA-48: 80).

Mary Brien is paid 9 1/2 yards calico for making 19 plain shirts (VSA-48: 79).

Elizabeth Burk is paid five yards calico for making six ruffled and six plain shirts per receipt (VSA-48: 80).

Mary Damewood is paid 4 1/2 yards calico for making three ruffled shirts and three plain shirts (VSA-48: 79).

N. Doliride is paid 4 1/2 yards ribbon for making three ruffled shirts (VSA-48: 79).

Mary Groots is paid five yards calico for making six ruffled and six plain shirts per receipt (VSA-48: 80).

Ann Johnson is paid 11 1/4 yards calico for making 12 ruffled and 24 plain shirts (VSA-48: 80).

B. King is paid five yards calico for making six ruffled and six plain shirts per receipt (VSA-48: 80).

Chastity King is paid 1 1/2 yards calico and two linen handkerchiefs for making six ruffled shirts (VSA-48: 80).

Mary Lundsford is paid one India handkerchief and two linen check handkerchiefs for making five plain shirts (VSA-48: 80).

Elizabeth Phelps is paid five yards calico for making six ruffled and six plain shirts (VSA-48: 80).

Mary Shilling is paid 1 1/2 yards calico, one ivory comb, and 3/8 yard muslin for making three ruffled and three plain shirts per receipt (VSA-48: 80).

Rachel Yates is paid one silk handkerchief for making three ruffled shirts per receipt (VSA-48: 80).

Sarah Burk is paid two yards calico and two linen handkerchiefs for making six ruffled and one plain shirt (VSA-48: 80).

June 17, 1780/Saturday

Issued to William Clark (cousin of George R. Clark), Secretary to Col. Clark, one hat (VSA-48: 69).

E. Johnson is paid five yards calico for making six ruffled shirts and 12 plain shirts (VSA-48: 80).

E. (Mrs. John) McCormick is paid 1 1/4 yards calico, one ivory comb, and one horn comb for making five ruffled shirts per receipt (VSA-48: 80).

Sarah Smith is paid 5 1/4 yards calico for making 19 plain shirts (VSA-48: 80).

E. (Mrs. Michael) Wolf is paid five yards calico and one paper pins for making three ruffled shirts and 15 plain shirts (VSA-48: 80).

Margery (Mrs. James) Young is paid 2 3/4 yards calico and one linen handkerchief for making nine plain shirts (VSA-48: 80).

June 18, 1780/Sunday

Anthony Montroy enlists for three years into Captain Robert George's Company of Artillery by Lt. Valentine T. Dalton (MHS: B1, F23).

John Dodge is issued for his own use: six yards brown broadcloth 7/4 wide; 2 1/2 yards shalloon; 5 5/12 dozen metal buttons; two sticks silk twist; six skeins silk; one pair knee garters; issued for six vests and six pair breeches: six yards white casimir, 2 1/2 yards corduroy, four yards chintz, 2 1/2 yards corduroy, 2 1/2 yards thickset, 1 1/4 yards spotted persian, and 4 1/2 yards cottonade; 21 yards linen for six shirts; 3/4 yard fine holland for ruffling; issued for six stocks: one yard fine holland and one yard cambric; three pair thread hose; two silk handkerchiefs; one cotton red handkerchief; one India handkerchief; two check linen handkerchiefs; one hat; two pair shoes; and two pair silk hose (VSA-48: 57).

June 19, 1780/Monday

Captain Robert George signs request to John Dodge to issue two shirts each for 23 men of his Artillery Co. by orders of Col. Clark (VSA-11):

1. Joseph Anderson
2. Matthew Jones
3. John Ash
4. George Venshiner
5. Richard Turpin
6. Peter Wagoner
7. Francis Little
8. John Dorrely
10. John Smothers
11. James McDaniel
12. Isaac Pruit
13. Thomas Win
14. Matthew Murray
15. Andrew Clark
16. John Bryan
17. William Posten
18. Richard Hopkins
19. Charles Bush
20. Cesar
21. John Hacker
22. Lazarus Kening
23. Daniel Balton
24. William Fever

Captain Robert George's merchandise drawn out of the public store for which no returns or receipts have been issued or passed: twenty-three ruffled shirts and 23 plain shirts. Per order to Captain George, no receipt (VSA-48: 91).

M. Bolton is paid two yards white linen for washing stains out of damaged linen (VSA-48: 81).

Captain Robert George's merchandise drawn out of the public store more than his quota for which no returns or receipts have been issued or passed: one brass ink pot, one large clasp knife, one ivory comb, one horn comb, and six yards ferret. Per order and receipt of Martin Carney (VSA-48: 91).

R. Ford is paid two India handkerchiefs for making six shirts plain (VSA-48: 80).

Charlotte Owens (Owings) is paid five linen handkerchiefs for making ten plain shirts (VSA-48: 81).

Esther Ford is paid one India handkerchief, one linen handkerchief, and one coarse handkerchief for making six plain shirts (VSA-48: 81).

June 20, 1780/Tuesday
Captain Robert George signs a request to John Dodge to issue two shirts each to Joseph Thornton, John Sword, and Zachariah Williams of Captain Worthington's Co. Reuben Kemp signed he received the shirts (VSA-11).

Captain Robert George writes to John Dodge to ask him to deliver to Mr. Blackford 187 hard dollars worth of bread and such goods for the use of Kaskaskia and its neighborhood. Zephaniah Blackford signed he received the goods (VSA-11).

Issued to Zephaniah Blackford by order Captain George to purchase and disposed of agreeable to the return made John Dodge for 187 hard dollars: provisionsMr. John Girault was paid 1 1/2 yards shalloon, one ink pot, one one pair damask - 5 1/8 yards; one pair flowered lawn - 13 yards; five ribbon; one dozen check linen handkerchiefs; one piece chintz no. 12; piece chintz no. 6; and one piece chintz no. 10; (VSA-48: 79).

Captain Robert George signs a request to John Dodge to deliver to Mr. John Donne, one leather ink pot and one fine and one course comb for the use of the Commissary Dept. John Donne signed he received the items (VSA-11).

Captain Robert George signs a request to John Dodge to issue Mr. Blackford [Commissary], linen for three shirts, stuff for three summer jackets and trousers, two pocket handkerchiefs with thread to make them, one ink pot, and stuff for three stocks. Zephaniah Blackford signed he received the items (VSA-11).

Captain Robert George requests John Dodge to issue Zephaniah Blackford with trimmings for three jackets. Z. Blackford signed he received 3 3/4 yards linen (VSA-11).

Captain Robert George signs a request to John Dodge to pay Mrs. Mary Smith, 12 shillings and six pence, for making a suit of soldiers clothes for Jacob Wheat (VSA-11).

Mary Smith writes that she received from John Dodge two yards of white flannel [which was in full of her demand] (VSA-11).

Captain Robert George signs a request to John Dodge to pay John Bryan 15 pounds four shillings, and six pence in goods for making clothing for Captain George's Co. (VSA-11). John Bryan "marked" he received the following goods in full of his demand, one piece chintz, 6 3/4 yards linen, one paperfold of pins, two silk handkerchiefs, 1 1/2 yard. ribbon (VSA-11).

Captain Robert George signs a request to Martin Carney to issue two guns for the use of Fort Jefferson (VSA-11).

Account of arms delivered by Martin Carney to Captain George's Company of Artillery of the Illinois Virginia Regiment: delivered to Captain George at Camp Jefferson, one rifle gun and one musket (VSA-50: 3).

Account of tobacco delivered by Martin Carney by order of Captain Robert George at this place: to Mr. Donne, Commissary, one carot equal to three pounds (VSA-50: 12).

Issued to Mr. Blackford, Deputy Commissary of Issues: 3 3/4 yards sycee for three vests; issued for three pair trousers: 5 1/4 yards cottonade and 2 1/2 yards toile gris; 9 3/4 yards white linen for three shirts; 1 1/2 yards muslin for three stocks and ruffling; two linen handkerchiefs; nine skeins white thread; one brass ink pot; and 3 3/4 yards linen for lining for jackets (VSA-48: 65). Mr. Z. Blackford signed he received the items (VSA-48: 65).

Mary Smith is paid four yards flannel per order of Captain George for making one suit of soldiers clothes (VSA-48: 78).

Mr. John Girault is paid 1 1/2 yards shalloon , one ink pot, one ivory comb, one horn comb, three yards ribbon in lieu of his charge for assisting in Translating in Public Business (VSA-48: 79).

John Nash is a soldier in Captain Shelby's Co. He received a suit of clothing made by J. Bryan, tailor at Fort Jefferson (VSA-11).

The interpretor exchanges 2 1/2 yards osnaburgs and one yard linen for a set of buttons (VSA-48: 79).

John Dodge notes that six yards osnaburgs were issued to make into bags for public use and two India handkerchiefs paid for writing paper (VSA-48: 79).

Issued in the Indian Department, to a party of friendly Kaskaskia Indians sent to hunt and scout for the garrison while it was weak, and delivered by orders Col. Montgomery: 13 3/4 yards blue stroud for blankets and breech cloths, 6 1/4 yards white half thicks for leggings, 12 yards white linen for shirts, two yards dark green calicoe for shirts, three scalping knives, two horn combs, eight skeins thread, one bolt ravelled gartering, three linen handkerchiefs, 5 1/2 yards ribbon, one piece ribbon, one pair blue stroud leggings, one plain shirt, and two scalping knives (VSA-48: 46).

Reuben Kemp is issued three ruffled and three plain shirts per order Captain George (VSA-48: 43).

Captain Robert George's sundry merchandise drawn out of the public store more than his quota for which in part no returns or receipts have been issued or passed: one ink pot, one ivory comb, and one horn comb. Per order and receipt of John Donne (VSA-48: 91).

<u>**June 21, 1780/Wednesday**</u>

Captain Robert George signs a request to Martin Carney to issue Mr. Donne one carot tobacco and charge him the customary price of others in public service (VSA-11). John Donne signs he received the tobacco (VSA-11).

Account of ammunition delivered by Martin Carney by Captain Robert George's order at Camp Jefferson: to Mr. Donne, Commissary, one lb gunpowder and two lbs lead; to Lt. Thomas Wilson, two lbs gunpowder and four lbs lead; to Captain George for the troops at Camp Jefferson, 2 1/4 lbs gunpowder and 4 1/2 lbs lead; to the Indians going to Kaskaskia, one lb gunpowder, two lbs lead and six flints (VSA-50: 9).

Issued per order of Captain George and receipt of John Bryan for making soldiers clothing: one pair chintz no. 23; 6 3/4 yards white linen; one paper pins; two silk handkerchiefs; and 1 1/2 yards ribbon (VSA-48: 78).

Sarah Burk is paid two silk handkerchiefs and one India handkerchief for making 11 shirts plain (VSA-48: 81).

Mary Shilling is paid two Indian handkerchiefs for making six plain shirts (VSA-48: 81).

S. (Mrs. Thomas) Winn is paid one silk handkerchief for making three ruffled shirts (VSA-48: 81).

June 22, 1780/Thursday
Captain Robert George signs a request to John Dodge to issue Andrew Clark truck [credit] for two pairs of trousers, check handkerchief, and a small-tooth and large-tooth comb. Andrew Clark signs he received the items (VSA-11).

M. McMeans is paid 1 1/2 yards calico, two Indian handkerchiefs, and one linen handkerchief for making 12 plain shirts (VSA-48: 81).

S. (Mrs. Thomas) Winn is paid 2 3/4 yards calico and 1 1/4 yards ribbon for making six shirts and five pair trousers (VSA-48: 81).

J. (The Widow) Witzel is paid two Indian handkerchiefs and two linen handkerchiefs for making ten plain shirts (VSA-48: 81).

Captain Robert George's merchandise drawn out of the public store for which no returns or receipts have been issued or passed: five yards toile gris, one check linen handkerchief, one ivory comb, one horn comb, and two skeins thread. Per receipt of Andrew Clark (VSA-48: 91).

Captain Robert George's merchandise drawn out of the public store for which no returns or receipts have been issued or passed: one brass ink stand receipt of Joseph Anderson (VSA-48: 91).

June 23, 1780/Friday
Captain Robert George signs a request to John Dodge to issue 16 shirts to Reuben Kemp, Daniel Williams, Richard Bradin, Charles Evans, Andrew Johnston, Isaac Yeates, Archibold Lockard and William Nelson who are members of Worthington's Co. Reuben Kemp signs he received 15 plain and one ruffled shirt (VSA-11; 48: 43).

Captain Robert George signs a request to John Dodge to issue a brass ink stand to Sergeant Anderson (VSA-11). Joseph Anderson signs he received the inkstand (VSA-11).

Account of ammunition delivered by Martin Carney by Captain Robert George's order at Camp Jefferson: to Captain George for the troops at this place, 3/4 lb gunpowder and 1 1/2 lbs lead; to Sergeant Anderson, 1/2 lb lead and one flint (VSA-50: 9).

Issued to Israel Dodge, Deputy Agent: two yards brown cloth 7/4 wide; 3 1/2 yards blue bath coating 7/4 wide; 2 1/2 yards shalloon, 4 1/4 dozen metal buttons; two sticks silk twist; six skeins silk; one pair knee garters; issued for six vests and six pair breeches: five yards cottonade, three yards chintz, two yards toile gris, 2 1/2 yards spotted velvet, 2 1/2 yards thickset, 4 1/4 yards casimir, and 2 1/2 yards chintz; four yards linen damaged for lining; 21 yards linen for six shirts; 3/4 yard fine holland for ruffling; two yards brittanca's for six stocks; one silk handkerchief; one Indian handkerchief; three linen check handkerchiefs; three pair thread hose; and one hat (VSA-48: 59).

Rachel Kennedy is paid one silk handkerchief for making four plain shirts (VSA-48: 81).

Charolette Kimly is paid 1 1/4 yards calico and one Indian handkerchief for making three ruffled and three plain shirts (VSA-48: 81).

William Robeson is issued two shirts at Fort Jefferson from John Dodge per Captain George's orders; member of Worthington's Co. (VSA-11).

S. Winn is paid one Indian handkerchief for making three plain shirts (VSA-48: 81).

Captain Robert George's merchandise drawn out of the public store for which no returns or receipts have been issued or passed: four ruffled shirts per order for soldiers going for provisions (VSA-48: 90).

Captain Robert George requests four shirts to be issued to the men going to Illinois for provisions (VSA-11).

James Ballanger is issued a shirt at Fort Jefferson to go to the Illinois for provisions; formerly a member of Captain Robert Todd's Co. of Foot under Col. John Montgomery; discharged at Fort Jefferson (VSA-11).

Jacob Huffman is issued a shirt at Fort Jefferson to go to the Illinois for provisions; was formerly a member of Captain Jesse Evans' Company of Infantry under Col. John Montgomery (VSA-11).

Richard Senet is issued one shirt at Fort Jefferson to go to the Illinois for provisions. Formerly member of Isaac Taylor's Co. of volunteers under Col. Montgomery (VSA-11).

June 24, 1780/Saturday
Jane Archer is paid one blue cotton handkerchief, one linen handkerchief, three yards ribbon, one paper pins, and one pair scissors for making six ruffled shirts (VSA-48: 81).

Elenor (Mrs. James) Piggott is paid one Indian handkerchief, two linen handkerchiefs, one paper pins, and one ivory comb for making three ruffled and four plain shirts (VSA-48: 81).

June 25, 1780/Sunday
Letter from Captain Valentine T. Dalton at Fort Patrick Henry [Vincennes] to George Rogers Clark telling they recently fought a battle with the enemy and won. Dalton feels prepared and confident to win another battle if one should occur (MHS: B1, F19; Seineke 1981: 443-444).

June 26, 1780/Monday
Andrew McMeans is paid 1/2 paper pins, one pair scissors, 3 1/2 yards narrow ribbon, four linen handkerchiefs, and one paper pins for making two ruffled and nine plain shirts per receipt (VSA-48: 82).

June 27, 1780/Tuesday
Mary Groots is paid one ivory comb, one pair scissors, and one paper pins for making three plain shirts (VSA-48: 82).

M. (Mrs. Archibald) Lockart is paid one Indian handkerchief for making three plain shirts (VSA-48: 82).

June 28, 1780/Wednesday
Ann Helms is paid one paper pins for making one plain shirt (VSA-48: 82).

Luvana (Lorana) Meredith is paid one Indian handkerchief and one ivory comb for making four plain shirts (VSA-48: 82).

Elizabeth Phelps is paid four linen handkerchiefs, one pair scissors, and one ivory comb for making ten plain shirts (VSA-48: 82).

Captain Robert George's merchandise drawn out of the public store for which no returns or receipts have been issued or passed: eight plain shirts per order and receipt of John Johnston (VSA-48: 91).

June 29, 1780/Thursday
Captain Robert George signs a request to John Dodge to issue eight shirts to James Thompson, Joseph Panther, John Shank, and Jacob Decker of Captain Kellar's Co. (VSA-11).

Account of ammunition delivered by Martin Carney by Captain Robert George's order at Camp Jefferson: to Daniel Bolton, gunner, 15 lbs gunpowder (VSA-50: 9).

Charlotte King is paid one India handkerchief and one yard ribbon for making four plain shirts (VSA-48: 82).

June 30, 1780/Friday
Account of ammunition delivered by Martin Carney by Captain Robert George's order at Camp Jefferson: to Lt. Wilson for a party of men going hunting, 2 1/4 lbs gunpowder and 4 1/2 lbs lead; to Michael Hacketon a soldier in Captain George's Company, one lb lead; to Sergeant Anderson for the use of the garrison, 4 1/2 lbs gunpowder, nine lbs lead, and eight flints (VSA-50: 9).

Jane Thompson signs a receipt for eight plain shirts per order of Captain George (VSA-48: 42).

Robert George's merchandise drawn out of the public store for which no returns or receipts have been issued or passed: five yards cottonade per self (VSA-48: 90).

June 1780/Miscellaneous
Lt. Richard Clark receives from Mr. William Clark three yards flannel and three skeins of thread for his own personal use (MHS: B1, F19).

Fred Guion receives one lb lead to kill meat for garrison at Fort Jefferson per Captain George's orders (VSA-11).

Thomas Kirk is discharged from Captain Todd's Co. at Fort Clark. He later came to Fort Jefferson with Col. Montgomery (VSA-13).

Josiah Phelps is being sent from Louisville to see George Rogers Clark, at Fort Jefferson (Draper Manuscripts 26J4).

July 2, 1780/Sunday
Zephaniah Blackford requests at Fort Clark [Valentine T. Dalton signs] an issuance of rations for 10 men for six days [July 2 - July 7] going from Fort Jefferson to get provisions for the fort (VSA-13).

July 3, 1780/Monday
Captain Robert George signs a request to Captain John Dodge to issue two pairs of leggings of half-thicks to Sergeant Anderson and Michael Hacketon of his company going on command by Col. Clark's orders (VSA-12).

Captain George Owens requests of the Quartermaster to issue ammunition for seven men of his militia company: 1 3/4 lb gunpowder, 3 1/2 lb lead, two guns and 45 gun flints (VSA-12).

Captain Robert George's merchandise drawn out of the public store for which no returns or receipts have been issued or passed: 2 1/2 yards half-thicks. Per order and receipt of Joseph Anderson (VSA-48: 91).

Account of ammunition delivered by Martin Carney by Captain Robert George's order at Camp Jefferson to Mr. Kennedy, Conductor, one lb gunpowder and two lbs lead (VSA-50: 9).

Patrick Kennedy signs that he sent Joseph Duncan, Samuel Watkins, and John Cox to Camp Jefferson with provisions and they were to be paid in linen for two shirts each. Captain Robert George requests an issuance of linen and thread enough to make each man two shirts (VSA-12).

Joseph Duncan, Samuel Watkins, and John Cox received: 16 1/4 yards white linen and 3 1/4 yards check linen (VSA-48: 78).

Captain Robert George signs a request to Martin Carney to issue Patrick Kennedy, Joseph Duncan, Samuel Watkins and John Cox, one lb gunpowder and two lb ball [lead] for their return to the Illinois (VSA-12).

Joseph Duncan signs, John Cox and S. Watkins sign their "mark" that they received the linen (VSA-12b).

Captain Robert George's merchandise drawn out of the public store for which no returns or receipts have been issued or passed: one pair garters per order and receipt of John Donne (VSA-48: 91).

Issued to Patrick Kennedy Assistant Conductor of Stores: 9 3/4 yards linen for three shirts; 1 5/8 yards fine holland for three stocks and ruffling three shirts; 3 3/4 yards calender for three vests; 4 5/8 yards check linen for three pair trousers; issued for three pair breeches: 3 1/4 yards toile gris and 2 1/2 yards corded dimity; 4 1/4 yards linen for lining; one ink pot; one ivory comb; one horn comb; one pair garters; and 15 skeins thread issued by order of Captain Robert George per Patrick Kennedy's receipt on said orders; and six check handkerchiefs per order Captain Rogers (VSA-48: 63).

James Piggott is mentioned as being a participant at Court of Inquiry at Fort Jefferson (DMS 56J22-24).

<u>July 4, 1780</u>/<u>Tuesday</u>
According to the journal of Daniel Smith "arrived at the falls" trip took 21 days from Fort Jefferson to Falls (Souissant 1915: 64).

John Crawley's enlistment voucher, witnessed by Harmen Eagle, for enlisting three years with Captain Abraham Kellar's Company [probably at Fort Jefferson, but not stated] (MHS B1, F20).

Richard Underwood's receipt for one land warrant, dated 4 July 1780 at Cohos [Cahokia] for enlisting for three yrs. Company not specified, but attested by Captain Richard Brashears (MHS B1, F20).

<u>July 5, 1780</u>/<u>Wednesday</u>
Zephaniah Blackford requests John Montgomery to issue two days allowance of beef for 10 men on command from Fort Jefferson (VSA-12).

An invoice written for rations is issued to Francois Tratie (VSA-13).

Account of ammunition delivered by Martin Carney by Captain Robert George's order at Camp Jefferson: to the militia at this place, 1 3/4 lb gunpowder, 3 1/2 lbs lead, and 46 flints (VSA-50: 9).

M. Brien is paid two Indian handkerchiefs and two coarse check handkerchiefs for making eight plain shirts (VSA-48: 82).

Robert George's articles taken out of the public store for which no return or receipt has been passed: 1/8 yd scarlet cloth 7/4 wide; for six vests and six breeches: four yards white casimir fine, 3 3/4 yards sycee, and 8 3/4 yards chintz; 21 yards fine white linen for six shirts; 3/4 yd fine holland for ruffling shirts; two yards holland for six stocks; three silk handkerchiefs; three red silk and cotton handkerchiefs; 2 1/2 yards white linen for lining; 2 1/2 yards shalloon for lining; 5 7/12 dozen metal buttons, 2/12 dozen overdrawn; five skeins silk; two skeins silk twist; 12 skeins fine white thread; and 12 skeins coarse thread a skein of each overdrawn (VSA-48: 89).

Francis McMeans is paid one fine linen handkerchief and four coarse linen handkerchiefs for making six plain shirts (VSA-48: 82).

Judy King is paid three yards white flannel for making six plain shirts (VSA-48: 82).

Sidy Smith is paid 2 1/4 yards calico and 2 1/2 yards ribbon for making six ruffled shirts (VSA-48: 82).

July 6, 1780/Thursday

Francis Brenid [Bredin] was paid five linen handkerchiefs and one yd ribbon for making ten plain shirts and one pair leggings (VSA-48: 82).

Rachel Kennedy is paid one Indian handkerchief and one linen handkerchief for making five plain shirts to (VSA-48: 82).

E. (Mrs. John) McCormick is paid six yards white flannel and one razor for making 14 plain shirts (VSA-48: 82).

Luvana (Lovana) Meredith is paid one coarse linen handkerchief for making one plain shirt (VSA-48: 83).

July 7, 1780/Friday

Samuel Cooper, a private in Captain George Owens' Co. of Militia, is advanced in rank on this date to Lieutenant (Harding 1981: 48).

July 8, 1780/Saturday

Captain Robert George at Fort Jefferson signs a request to Martin Carney to issue 1 1/4 lbs gunpowder for Lt. Wilson's scouting party (VSA-12).

Account of ammunition delivered by Martin Carney by Captain Robert George's order at Camp Jefferson: to Lt. Wilson going on command, 1 1/4 lbs gunpowder and 2 1/2 lbs lead (VSA-50: 9).

July 9, 1780/Sunday

Baptist Daquoin [Le Quang] at Kaskaskia writes ["marks"] to Captain Dodge that he needs help. He says he is naked and he has no gunpowder. He says he would like to see Dodge, that he can not convince the enemy he is an American, and that he realizes that these are trying times for all men (VSA-12).

Ensign Jarret Williams requests provisions for three men [one officer and two privates] for four days [July 9 - July 12] going to Fort Jefferson (VSA-12).

John Williams at Kaskaskia requests 30 lbs flour for the detachment going to Camp Jefferson (VSA-12).

John Williams requests 250 rations for his voyage to Camp Jefferson (VSA-12).

John Williams requests provisions for one soldier for 10 days going [July 9 - July 18] to Fort Jefferson (VSA-12).

July 10, 1780/Monday
Captain John Rogers lists men of his company of Lt. Dragoon who are entitled to clothing and who have more than one year to serve (VSA-12):

1. William Merriwether
2. Thomas Key
3. Rice Curtiss
4. David Pagan
5. Domenick Welch
6. Nathaniel Mershon
7. David McDonald
8. Casper Cailer
9. Joseph Irwin
10. Frederich Dohaty
11. George Key
12. George Snow
13. Henry Blankinship
14. William Campbell
15. William Goodwin
16. James Spillman
17. Francis Spillman
18. William Booton
19. Travis Booton
20. William Gruin
21. William Leer
23. Charles Martin
24. Mikel O'Harrah
25. John Jones
26. Barney Wigins
27. John Murphey
28. William Kendall
29. James Hammit
30. William Frogget
31. Robert Barnit
32. Mikiel Glass

Captain Rogers requests from John Dodge 62 shirts and black stuff for as many stocks and thread or silk to make up the stocks for 31 men (VSA-12).

Rogers signs he was actually issued: 17 ruffled shirts, 45 plain shirts, 11 yards of black persian, and 15 yards fine linen-damaged (VSA-12).

Captain George signs request John Dodge issue Captain Abraham Kellar his quota of clothing allowed by law [passed in 1779] (VSA-12).

Captain Robert George requests John Dodge issue Captain John Rogers and his two officers their full quota of clothing which they are entitled to by law passed in June, 1779 (VSA-12).

Captain Robert George requests John Dodge issue Mr. Montbreuen his full quota of clothing as an officer (VSA-12).

Captain Robert George requests John Dodge issue Captain John Bailey and Ensign Slaughter their full quota of clothing which they are entitled to by law (VSA-12).

Captain John Rogers and Valentine T. Dalton sign they received of John Dodge two yards blue persian and one piece binding (VSA-12).

Antoine Gamelin, Indian Agent [probably Vincennes] signs he received of Sergeant John Moore of Captain Worthington's Co., two soldiers of the same company: Louis Brown and David Allen. They are to be delivered to the commanding officer. [Not known if Allen arrives at Fort Jefferson; no other record of Brown at Fort Jefferson occurs] (MHS: B1, F20).

James Mulboy and Joseph Lonion are enlisted by Lt. Valentine T. Dalton into Captain Robert George's Company of Artillery. They are not on the payroll because Dalton failed to give account of what had become of them or when or how their time expired (MHS: B1, F23).

Issued to Captain John Rogers for his company, 17 ruffled shirts; 45 plain shirts; issued for 62 stocks, 11 yards black persian and 15 1/2 yards fine linen damaged and two yards blue persian, and one piece silk ferret (VSA-48: 44).

July 11, 1780/Tuesday
Lt. Col. John Montgomery at Fort Jefferson writes that Ann Elms attended the sick in the hospital at Fort Clark from 10 February until 5 June, and that she is entitled to receive the same pay as anyone else employed for the same purpose. She is to be paid out of the country store at Fort Jefferson. Lt. Col. John

Montgomery, signing as Fort Jefferson Commandant, writes to Captain John Dodge, Agent, stating that Captain Dodge should, at his leisure, pay Mrs. Ann Elms and her daughter a petticoat each (VSA-12).

Captain Robert George signs a request to John Dodge to issue Lt. Girault the clothing he is entitled to by law. Lt. Girault received part of the contents as appears by the receipt he signed (VSA-12).

Captain George signs request to John Dodge that Captain Richard Brashears be issued his full quota of clothing which he is entitled to by law (VSA-12).

Captain George signs request to John Dodge that Major McCarty be issued the clothing he is entitled to by law (VSA-12).

Captain George signs request to John Dodge that Col. John Montgomery be issued the clothing which he is entitled to by law (VSA-12).

Col. Montgomery signs request to John Dodge that Doctor Ray be issued his full compliment of clothing as is allowed to officers by Act of Assembly. Reverse states that Dr. Ray received part of the within contents as per the receipt (VSA-12).

Captain Abraham Kellar issued one comb, one inkstand, and one scalping knife at Camp Jefferson from Captain John Dodge per Captain George's orders (VSA-12).

Mr. Frederick Guion was issued one ink holder for use of the Commissary Dept. at Fort Jefferson from Captain John Dodge, Agent by order of Col. Rogers per Captain George's order (VSA-12; 48: 93).

Thomas Wilson signs he received 99 5/8 yards blue cloth, 125 3/8 yards white cloth and 200 yards flannel. John Donne attested. John Wilson signed that he had measured the cloth and that the above quantities were what he had measured. This also attested by John Donne. Thomas Wilson once again signed that he received from George Rogers Clark by the hand of Henry Hutton, 277 dozen buttons and 320 skeins of thread in addition to the 225 yards cloth and 200 yards flannel. Wilson also certifies that three men who were sent to the Falls for clothing, received a suit of clothes each (MHS: B1, F14).

Lt. Richard Clark is issued his quota of clothing at Fort Jefferson. Member of Captain Worthington's Co. (VSA-12).

Lt. Perrault is issued full quota of clothing per order of Captain George (VSA-12).

July 12, 1780/Wednesday

Captain Robert George signs request to John Dodge that twenty-three men of Captain Abraham Kellar's Company be issued full clothing. The first six enlisted the others have over one year to serve.

1. John Chappel
2. George Hoit
3. Baptist Raper
4. Francis Laycore
5. Anthony Montrey
6. James Thompson
7. James Pritchet
8. Harman Eagle
9. Thomas Hays
10. George Smith
11. John Crawley
12. Joseph Cooper
13. Barny Cooper
14. John Kella
15. David Russill
16. David Humble
17. James Davis
18. John Kearnes
19. Philip Duly
20. Haymore Duly
21. John Shank
22. Joseph Panther
23. Jacob Decker

Four of the above mentioned men (James Thompson, John Shank, Joseph Panther, and Jacob Deckart), have received two shirts each in part of their clothing. Abraham Kellar signs to certify that the first six of the above mentioned men are enlisted, and all the rest have more than one year to serve (VSA-12).

Abraham Kellar signs he received at Fort Jefferson from Captain John Dodge, 80 1/2 yards blue cloth, 69 yards white flannel, thread and buttons to make up the same, three ruffled shirts, and 35 plain shirts for the use of Captain Abraham Kellar's company of the Illinois Regiment agreeable to the within order (VSA-12b).

John Williams signs that one man of Captain Brashears' Company has been issued provisions at Fort Jefferson (VSA-12).

Captain Robert George signs request to John Dodge by order of Col. Clark that Joseph Momeral, Louis Lepaint, James Brown, and Jacke Rubedo, four soldiers of Captain Williams Company, be issued cloth and trimmings for a complete suit of clothes each, also two shirts each, they being entitled to the same by law having more than one year to serve (VSA-12). John Williams certifies he received the items (VSA-12).

Captain Robert George signs request to John Dodge, that full clothing be issued for three men enlisted who have never received any part thereof. Also for one man enlisted for one year. The above men were recruited by Lt. Col. Montgomery; their names are William Buchanan, Robert Whitehead, William Whitehead, and John Roberts. John Roberts enlisted for one year; the other three enlisted during the war. John Montgomery signs that he received 14 yards blue cloth, 12 yards flannel, thread and buttons, and eight shirts (VSA-12).

Captain Robert George signs request to John Dodge, that Deputy Conductor John Donne be issued the same allowance of clothing as the officers of the line (VSA-12).

Jarrett Williams certifies that James Curry, William Elms, James Morris, William Barthalomew, James Dawson, James Elms, and John Elms are enlisted (VSA-12). Robert George signs request to John Dodge, by order of Col. Clark, that full clothing be issued for their seven men of Captain Brashears' company which the law allows (VSA-12).

Jarrett Williams signs that 14 shirts, 21 yards flannel, and 24 1/4 yards of blue cloth with thread and buttons were issued to Brashear's seven men to make up the shirts. John Donne attests (VSA-12).

Col. Montgomery requests he be issued ten lbs of pork for the use of his mess at Fort Jefferson (VSA-12).

Captain Robert George signs a request to John Dodge that Ensign Slaughter be given 44 shirts for 22 men of Captain John Bailey's Co. which are enlisted during the present war. Slaughter signs that he received of Captain John Dodge the full contents agreeable to the above order (VSA-12). List of the 22 men:

1. John Vaughan
2. William Brauly
3. Graves Morris
4. James Jerril
5. George Shepard
6. Peter Shepard
7. Robert Whit
8. Frances Harden
9. James Hays
10. Levi Theel
11. John Conner
12. Larken Ballenger
13. David Shaffer
14. Randel White
15. Henery Phillips
16. Willian Carr
17. Nicholas Tuttle
18. Edward Murray
19. William Thompson
20. Hugh Young
21. William Bush
22. Edward Parker

Robert George signs request to John Dodge that Frederick Guion, a sergeant enlisted during the war in George's Company of Artillery, be issued full clothing and scarlet cloth sufficient to face his coat, at Fort Jefferson (VSA-12).

Frederick Guion signs that he received 3 1/2 yards of blue cloth, three yards of white flannel, two ruffled shirts, thread and buttons (VSA-12).

John Montgomery signs a request to to John Dodge that Quartermaster James Finn be issued the same portion of clothing as other state officers in the service. This is the 2nd order of the same date, at Fort Jefferson (VSA-12).

Captain Robert George requests that four enlisted men be issued full clothing by Lt. Girault. The four men are: Francis Villier, Charles Martin Laughlan, John LaRichardy, and Francis Bennoit. Lt. Girault certifies that the above mentioned men are all enlisted to serve during the war (VSA-12).

Lt. Girault signs he received the within 14 yards blue cloth, 12 yards flannel thread and buttons, eight shirts VSA-12).

John Rogers and Robert George sign a request to Martin Carney to let four men of Captain Rogers' Company be issued one lb gunpowder and one lb lead, at Fort Jefferson (VSA-12).

Captain Robert George signs request to John Dodge that Ensign Jarret Williams be issued his full quota of clothing which he is entitled to by law (VSA-12). Captain Robert George signs a request to Martin Carney that Captain Kellar be issued one lb of gunpowder and one lb of lead at Fort Jefferson for his own use (VSA-12).

Captain Robert George requests of Captain Dodge that William Clark be issued one hat (VSA-12). William Clark signs he received the hat from Captain Dodge (VSA-12).

Captain John Williams requests he be issued ten lbs pork at Fort Jefferson from the quartermaster for his mess (VSA-12).

Ensign Jarret Williams certifies that the following men were enlisted during the war. Robert George requests of John Dodge that 36 shirts be issued for 18 of the men who are entitled by law. The others (marked with an x) have previously received clothes (VSA-12).

The men are enlisted as follows:

1. James Curry x
2. John Joins
3. John Mackever
4. Charles Morgan
5. John Boils
6. John McMichael
7. Daniel Tyger
8. John Blair
9. James Dawson x
10. Isaac Allen
11. James Harry
12. John Cowen
13. David Wallis
14. Francis Rubedo
15. William Elms x
16. James Morris x
17. Wm. Bartholemew x
18. Cagy Mayfield
19. Joseph Ross
20. James Elms x
21. John Elms x
22. Peter Howell
23. Samuel Allen
24. Charles Ouncler
25. Patrick Curry

Ensign Jarret Williams signs he acknowledged the receipt of the requested number of shirts agreeable to the order (VSA-12).

List of sundry articles issued Major John Williams: two yards fine holland for six stocks; 3/4 yd fine cambric for ruffling six shirts; issued for nine vests and breeches four yards cottonade, 2 1/2 yards sycee, 2 1/4 calender, 2 1/2 corded dimity, 2 1/2 yards thickset, and 2 1/2 yards spotted cotton velvet; three yards brown broadcloth 7/4 wide; three pair thread hose; six yards of cotton sycee for three vests and breeches; two dozen and nine metal buttons; 21 yards of white linen for six shirts; two sticks silk twist; six skeins of silk; one pair knee garters; ten skeins white thread; two silk handkerchiefs; two Indian handkerchiefs; two linen handkerchiefs; 2 1/2 yards of shalloon; one fine hat; four yards coarse linen for lining; and three yards broadcloth 7/4 wide (VSA-48: 3).

Major John Williams, Illinois Battalion signed he received from Captain John Dodge, Agent, the within mentioned goods in part of the clothing allowed Williams by law. John Donne attested (VSA-48: 4).

Sundry articles overdrawn by Major John Williams above the clothing allowed him by law: one 2 1/2 point blanket and one snaffle bridle issued by order of Montgomery; 5 1/2 weight soap and two weight coffee (VSA-48: 4).

List of sundry articles issued Major Richard McCarty: 1 1/2 yards brown broadcloth 7 1/4 wide; 1 1/2 yards scarlet broadcloth 7 1/4 wide; issued for two pair breeches 2 1/2 yards thickset and 2 1/2 yards corded dimity; issued 2 1/2 yards shalloon; issued for four pair breeches and six vests 2 1/4 calender, four yards camlet, six yards calamanco, four yards toile gris, and three yards chintz; issued two dozen metal buttons; 21 yards white linen for six shirts; 3/4 yd fine holland for ruffling; two yards muslin for six stocks; two pair thread hose; one silk handkerchief; one Indian handkerchief; four linen handkerchiefs; two skeins of silk; 12 skeins white thread; three yards coarse linen for lining; three yards broadcloth 7/4 wide (VSA-48: 5).

Major John Williams signs in behalf of Major Richard McCarty that he received from Captain John Dodge, Agent the goods listed above in part of the clothing allowed McCarty by law. John Donne attested (VSA-48: 6).

Sundries issued Captain John Rogers: 1 3/4 yards broadcloth 7/2 wide; 1 1/2 yards blue bath coating 7/2 wide; for five vests and breeches, 2 1/2 yards of corded dimity, 1 1/4 yards of sycee, 1 1/4 yards of calender, four yards toile gris; 14 yards white linen for four shirts; two yards fine holland for six stocks; 1/2 yd cambric for ruffling; two linen handkerchiefs; two silk handkerchiefs; 1 1/4 yards blue persion [did state for one vest but had been crossed out]; 12 skeins silk; one stick silk twist; 2 1/4 yards of thickset for one pair breeches; two pair thread hose; 2 1/2 yards of shalloon; three yards spotted flannel for two vests and breeches; three yards of gray cloth for three vests and breeches; seven yards of white linen for two shirts; 1/4 yd of fine holland for ruffling; 2 1/2 yards coarse linen for lining; two linen handkerchiefs; 2 3/4 yards broadcloth 7/4 wide (VSA-48: 7).

Captain John Rogers, Virginia Light Dragoons signs he received from Captain John Dodge the within mentioned sundry goods, in part of the clothing allowed Rogers by law. John Donne attested (VSA-48: 8).

Sundry articles overdrawn by Captain John Rogers: one English blanket, 3 3/4 ells ribbon per receipt, four skeins silk, one comb, and six lbs coffee (VSA-48: 8).

Sundries issued Captain Kellar: 1 1/2 yards brown broadcloth 7/4 wide; 1 1/2 yards scarlet broadcloth 7/4 wide; 2 1/2 yards shalloon; one stick silk twist; 1 1/4 yards sycee for one vest and breeches; six skeins silk; 2 1/2 yards calender for one vest and breeches; two yards toile gris for two vests or breeches; 2 1/2 yards thickset for one pair breeches; 2 1/2 yards corded dimity for one pair breeches; 3 1/2 yards chintz for three vests; 14 yards white linen for four shirts; two yards muslin for six stocks; 1/2 yd fine holland for ruffling; seven skeins white thread; one silk handkerchief; one Indian handkerchief; four linen handkerchiefs; two pair thread hose; one fine hat -- returned; 3 1/2 yards coarse linen for lining; one pair knee garters; three yards broadcloth 7/4 wide; 5 1/2 yards white linen for two shirts (VSA-48: 9).

Captain Abraham Kellar, Illinois Battalion, signs he received from Captain John Dodge, Agent, the within sundry goods in part of the clothing allowed Kellar by law. Attested by John Donne (VSA-48: 10).

Sundries issued Captain John Bailey: 1 1/2 yards brown broadcloth 7/4 wide; 1 1/2 yards scarlet broadcloth 7/4 wide; one stick silk twist; eight skeins silk;

2 1/4 yards thickset for one vest or breeches; two yards toile gris for one vest or breeches; 2 1/2 yards shalloon; two yards toile gris for one vest or breeches; 4 1/2 yards check linen for two vests or breeches; 3 1/8 yards calender for three vests or breeches; 5/8 yd sycee; two yards chintz for two vests or breeches; 19 1/2 yards white linen for six shirts; two yards muslin for six stocks; 3/4 yd fine holland for ruffling; nine skeins white thread; one silk handkerchief; one Indian handkerchief; four linen handkerchiefs; two pairs thread hose; one hat fine -- returned; 3 1/2 yards coarse linen for lining; three yards broadcloth 7/4 wide; 2 3/4 yards calamanco for one vest or breeches; 3/4 yard spotted flannel for one vest or breeches (VSA-48: 11).

Ensign Laurence Slaughter, Illinois Battalion, signs in behalf of Captain John Bailey, that he received from Captain John Dodge, Agent, the within sundry goods in part of the clothing allowed Bailey by law. Attested by John Donne (VSA-48: 12).

Overdrawn by Captain John Bailey: four yards osnaburg and 5/8 yd stroud for leggings (VSA-48: 12).

Issued Captain Richard Brashears: 1 1/2 yards scarlet cloth 7/4 wide, 1 1/2 yards broadcloth 7/4 wide, 2 1/2 yards shalloon, two yards calender for two small garments, four yards toile gris for two small garments, eight yards toile gris for four small garments, three yards gray cloth 7/8 wide for two small garments, 19 1/2 yards white linen for six shirts, 3/4 yd fine holland for ruffling, two yards muslin for six stocks, ten skeins thread, 2 1/2 check for one small garment, 2 1/2 yards coarse linen for lining, one pair thread hose, one silk handkerchief, one Indian handkerchief, four linen handkerchiefs, four skeins silk, one hat, 2 3/4 calamanco for one small garment, three yards blue cloth 7/4 wide (VSA-48: 13).

Ensign Jarret Williams, Illinois Regiment, signs in behalf of Brashears that he received from Captain John Dodge, Agent, the within mentioned goods in part of the clothing allowed Brashears by law. Attested by John Donne (VSA-48: 14).

Issued to Lt. John Girault, 1 1/2 yards brown broadcloth 7/4 wide; 2 1/2 yards brown broadcloth damaged; three yards gray cloth 7/8 wide; 2 1/2 yards shalloon; four skeins silk; one stick silk twist; for 11 vests and breeches: two yards calender, four yards camlet, 2 1/2 yards dimity, two yards chintz, four yards toile gris, six yards calamanco 1/2 yd wide; 1 1/2 yards shalloon -- error; 3 1/2 yards coarse linen for lining; one silk handkerchief; one Indian handkerchief; four check linen handkerchiefs; two yards muslin for six stocks; 19 1/2 yards white linen for six shirts; 3/4 yard fine holland for ruffling; 12 skeins white thread; two pairs thread hose; one pair knee garters and 1 1/2 yards blue cloth; one hat; and 2 1/4 yards calamanco 1/2 yd wide for one vest or breeches (VSA-48: 15).

Lt. Girault receives from Captain John Dodge, Agent, the within mentioned quantity of goods, in part of the clothing allowed Girault by law. John Donne attested (VSA-48: 16).

Issued to Lt. Michael Perrault: three yards brown broadcloth 7/4 wide; 2 1/2 yards shalloon; one stick silk twist; three skeins silk; 19 1/2 yards white linen for six shirts; 3/4 yd of white holland for ruffling; two yards muslin for six stocks; issued for 12 vests or breeches: two yards casimir, 2 1/2 yards chintz, 2 1/2 yards spotted flannel, three yards camlet, two yards shalloon, four yards toile gris, and 2 1/4 yards check linen; one silk handkerchief; one Indian handkerchief; four linen handkerchiefs; eight skeins thread; two pairs thread hose; one hat; four yards damaged linen for lining; and three yards broadcloth 7/4 wide (VSA-48: 17).

Andrew Rey, Surgeon, signs in behalf of Lt. Michael Perrault, that he received from Captain John Dodge, Agent, the within quantity of goods, in part of the clothing allowed Perrault by law. Attested by John Donne (VSA-48: 18).

Issued to Lt. Richard Clark: 1 1/2 yards scarlet cloth 7/4 wide, 1 1/2 yards brown cloth 7/4 wide, 2 1/2 yards shalloon, two yards calender, four yards toile gris, three yards spotted flannel, three yards gray cloth 7/8 wide, 19 1/2 yards white linen, 3/4 yards fine holland, two yards muslin, one pair thread hose, six yards check linen, four skeins silk, one silk handkerchief, one Indian handkerchief, four linen handkerchiefs, 12 skeins thread, and 2 1/2 dozen buttons. [The entire list had been x'd out] (VSA-48: 19).

Captain John Rogers, Virginia Light Dragoons, signs in behalf of Lt. Richard Clark, that he received from Captain John Dodge the within quantity of goods in part of the clothing allowed Clark by law. Attested by John Donne (VSA-48: 20).

Issued to Lt. Merriwether: 1 1/2 yards scarlet cloth 7/4 wide; 1 5/8 yd brown broad cloth; 2 1/2 yards shalloon; issued for four vests and four breeches: two yards callender, four yards toile gris, three yards spotted flannel, and three yards gray cloth 7/8 wide; 19 1/2 yards white linen for six shirts; 3/4 fine holland for ruffling; two yards muslin for six stocks; six yards check linen for two vests and two breeches; four skeins silk; 12 skeins thread; one silk handkerchief; one Indian handkerchief; four linen handkerchiefs; and three yards white cloth 7/4 wide (VSA-48: 21).

Captain John Rogers, Virginia Light Dragoons, signs in behalf of Lt. James Merriwether, that he received from Captain John Dodge, Agent the above quantity of goods in part of the clothing allowed Merriwether by law. John Donne attested (VSA-48: 21).

Overdrawn by Lt. Merriwether: one English blanket per Captain Rogers and 1/8 yd brown broadcloth (VSA-48: 22).

Issued to Ensign Jarret Williams: 1 1/2 yards scarlet cloth 7/4 wide; 1 1/2 yards broadcloth; 2 1/2 yards shalloon; issued for five vests and five pair breeches: two yards calender, four yards toile gris, eight yards toile gris, three yards gray cloth 7/8 wide; 19 1/2 yards white linen for six shirts; two yards muslin for six stocks; 3/4 yd fine holland for ruffling; ten skeins thread; 2 1/2 yards check for one pair breeches; 2 1/2 yards coarse linen for lining; one silk handkerchief; one Indian handkerchief; four linen handkerchiefs; four skeins silk; one hat; 2 3/4 yards black calamanco for breeches; and three yards blue cloth 7/4 wide (VSA-48: 23).

Ensign Jarret Williams signs he received from Captain John Dodge, Agent, the within mentioned quantity of goods in part of the clothing allowed him by law. Attested by John Donne (VSA-48: 24).

Issued to Ensign Slaughter: 1 1/2 yards broadcloth 7/4 wide; 1 1/2 yards scarlet cloth 7/4 wide; one stick silk twist; four skeins silk; issued for one vest and one pair breeches: 2 1/4 yards thickset and two yards toile gris; 2 1/2 yards shalloon; issued for three vests or breeches: two yards toile gris and 4 1/2 yards check linen; 3 1/8 yards calender for three vests for breeches; issued for two vests or breeches: 5/8 yd sycee and two yards chintz; 19 1/2 yards linen for six shirts; two yards muslin for six stocks; 3/4 yd fine holland for ruffling; nine skeins thread; one silk handkerchief; one Indian handkerchief; four linen handkerchiefs; two pair thread hose; one hat; 3 1/2 yards coarse linen for lining; three yards blue cloth 7/4 wide; 2 3/4 yards calamanco for one vest; and 3/4 yd spotted flannel for one vest (VSA-48: 25).

Ensign Laurence Slaughter, Illinois Regiment, signs he received from Captain John Dodge, Agent, the within mentioned quantity of goods in part of the clothing allowed him by law. John Donne attested (VSA-48: 26).

Issued to Cornet Thruston: 1 1/2 yards scarlet cloth 7/4 wide; 1 5/8 yards brown cloth; 2 1/2 yards shalloon; issued for four vests and four breeches: two yards calender, four yards toile gris, three yards spotted flannel, and three yards gray cloth 7/8 wide; 19 1/2 yards white linen for six shirts; 3/4 yd fine holland for ruffling; two yards muslin for six stocks; six yards check linen for two vests and two breeches; four skeins silk; one silk handkerchief; one Indian handkerchief; four linen handkerchiefs; 12 skeins thread; three yards white cloth; one hat -- returned (VSA-48: 27).

Captain John Rogers, Virginia Lights Dragoons, signs in behalf of Cornet Thruston, that he received from Captain John Dodge, Agent, the above mentioned quantity of goods in part of the clothing allowed Cornet Thruston by law. Attested by John Donne (VSA-48: 27).

Overdrawn by Cornet Thruston: one English blanket per Captain Rogers and 1/8 yd brown cloth (VSA-48: 28).

Issued to Doctor Rey [Ray]: 1 1/2 yards scarlet cloth 7/4 wide; 1 1/2 yards brown cloth; 2 1/2 yards shalloon; one stick silk twist; three skeins silk; 19 1/2 yards white linen for six shirts; 3/4 yd fine holland for ruffling; two yards muslin for six stocks; issued for six vests and six pair breeches: two yards casimir, 2 1/2 yards chintz, 2 1/2 yards spotted flannel, three yards camlet, three yards shalloon, four yards toile gris, and 2 1/4 yards check linen; one silk handkerchief; one Indian handkerchief; four linen handkerchiefs; eight skeins thread; one skein thread; two pair thread hose; one hat; four yards damaged linen for lining; and three yards broadcloth 7/4 wide (VSA-48: 29).

Andrew Rey [Ray], Surgeon, signs he received from Captain John Dodge, Agent, the within mentioned quantity of goods in part of the clothing allowed Rey by law. Attested by John Donne (VSA-48: 30).

Issued to Lt. Montbreuen: three yards broadcloth 7/4 wide; 2 1/2 yards shalloon; issued for six breeches and three vests: two yards calender, four yards camlet, two yards corded dimity, 1/2 yd camlet, two yards chintz, four yards toile gris; 3 1/2 yards coarse linen for lining; one silk handkerchief; one Indian handkerchief; four linen handkerchiefs; two yards muslin for six stocks; 19 1/2 yards white linen for lining; 3/4 yd fine holland for ruffling; 12 skeins white thread; two pair thread hose; one pair knee garters; 5 1/2 yards spotted flannel for three vests; three yards blue cloth 7/4 wide; and one hat (VSA-48: 31).

Lt. Timothe Montbreuen signs he received from Captain John Dodge, Agent, the above mentioned goods in part of the clothing allowed him by law. Attested by John Donne (VSA-48: 31).

Issued to Mr. James Finn, Quartermaster: 9 3/4 yards white linen for three shirts; six yards toile gris for three breeches; issued for three trousers: four yards check linen and 2 1/4 yards toile gris; one yd fine holland for three stocks; three yards chintz for three vests; three yards damaged linen for lining; ten skeins thread; one silk handkerchief; one linen handkerchief; one ink holder; 4 1/4 yards camlet for a coat; one hat; issued for trimmings to his coat: 2 1/2 yards toile gris, one skein silk and two skeins thread (VSA-48: 33).

Issued to Mr. John Donne, Deputy Conductor: 1 3/4 yards blue bath coating 7/4 wide; three yards gray cloth 7/8 wide in lieu of 1 1/2 yards 7/4 wide; three yards coarse linen for lining; 5 1/4 yards coarse linen for lining in lieu of 2 1/2 yards shalloon; 21 yards linen for six shirts; two yards cambric for six stocks; 3/4 yards cambric for ruffling six shirts; issued for six pair breeches: five yards spotted velvet, 2 1/2 yards thickset, 2 1/2 yards check linen, and five yards white linen; issued for six vests: 1 1/2 yards blue persian, 3 3/4 yards sycee and five yards linen; one silk handkerchief; one romal handkerchief; four check linen handkerchiefs; 26 skeins thread; four skeins silk; two sticks twist; two pair knee garters; 6 1/2 yards ferretting; one hat; and 2 3/4 yards white cloth (VSA-48: 35).

Issued to Lt. Richard Clark: 1 1/2 yards scarlet cloth 7/4 wide; 1 1/2 yards brown cloth 7/4 wide; 2 3/4 yards shalloon for lining; issued for six vests: two yards calender, 1 3/4 yards spotted flannel, three yards gray cloth 7/8 wide, and 1 3/4 yards white casimir; issued for six breeches: 4 1/2 yards fustian and six yards check linen; 21 yards fine linen for six shirts; 3/4 yards fine holland for ruffling shirts; two yards muslin for six stocks; four yards coarse linen for lining - damaged; two pair thread hose; one silk handkerchief; one Indian handkerchief; four check linen handkerchiefs; 17 skeins thread; four skeins silk; one stick silk twist; one hat; two dozen large metal buttons; 1/2 dozen small metal buttons; and three yards blue cloth 7/4 wide (VSA-48: 39).

Lt. Richard Clark, Illinois Regiment, signs he received from Captain John Dodge, Agent, the above quantity of merchandise in part of an order drawn on Dodge in Richard Clark's favor by order of Col. George Rogers Clark, dated the 11th inst. Attested by John Donne (VSA-48: 39).

Issued to Major John Williams for his company, two ruffled shirts, six plain shirts, 14 yards blue cloth, 12 yards white flannel, skeins thread, and a dozen buttons (VSA-48: 41).

Issued to Col. Montgomery for clothing for four men of Captain Quirk's Company, 14 yards blue cloth, 12 yards white cloth say flannel, four shirts, 13 yards linen for four shirts (VSA-48: 41).

Issued to Lt. John Girault for four men of Majr. Richard McCarty's Company, 14 yards blue cloth, 12 yards white flannel, four shirts, and 13 yards linen for four shirts (VSA-48: 41).

Account of ammunition delivered by Martin Carney by Captain Robert George's order at Camp Jefferson: to Captain Abraham Kellar going to Cahokia, 1/2 lb gunpowder and one lb lead (VSA-50: 9).

July 13, 1780/Thursday

Sergeant Matthews is issued a flat bottomed boat and a swivel at the Falls of the Ohio for the use of carrying corn and other provisions to the troops stationed at Fort Jefferson from William Shannon per Col. Clark's order (VSA-12).

Sergeant Matthews signs his mark that he received of William Shannon, one large flat bottomed boat and one swivel (VSA-12).

Lt. Col. John Montgomery at Fort Jefferson, requests the quartermaster issue Mr. Finn, 20 lbs gunpowder and 40 lbs lead, in a small keg for the use of the troops at Coho [Cahokia]. Mr. Finn, Quartermaster, signs he received the above mentioned ammunition (VSA-12; 50: 14).

Captain Robert George, Commandant, requests Captain John Dodge to issue Major John Williams his full quota of clothing, which he is entitled to by law (VSA-12).

Lt. Col. John Montgomery, signs as Commandant, requests of Captain John Dodge, Agent, to issue Maj. John Williams for the use of Batist Le Quang [Da Quoin], two shrouds, two blankets, two pair leggings, and four shirts as he is entitled to them for his good service to the State on an expedition with Montgomery (VSA-12).

John Williams signs he received the items plus an additional five ells of ribbon to bind the leggings (VSA-12).

Lt. Col. John Montgomery, who signs as Commandant, requests Captain John Dodge, Agent, to issue Montgomery 5 3/4 yards of muslin, one snaffle bridle, one black ball, and 3 1/4 yards of ribbon (VSA-12).

Montgomery signs that he received the within contents (VSA-12).

Captain John Rogers, Virginia Light Dragoons, requests Captain John Dodge at Fort Jefferson the following for the use of his company of Dragoons: 18 yards of osnaburg for the purpose of padding saddles, one lb thread, and 1 1/2 dozen course needles (VSA-12).

Issued to Captain John Rogers for his company, 18 yards osnaburgs for saddle pads, one lb thread, and 1 1/2 dozen needles (VSA-48: 44).

Lt. Col. John Montgomery, signing as Commandant, requests Captain John Dodge to deliver to Major John Williams, one stroud [it being 2 1/2 yards], and one shirt which he borrowed to bury an Indian which was killed by mistake by one of the Light Horse men; also one stroud and a shirt which Montgomery borrowed for a chief of the Sauk nation in Dodge's absence at Coho [Cahokia]. John Williams signed that he received the within account (VSA-12).

John Montgomery at Fort Jefferson requests flour be issued to one man for three days "going up the river" (VSA-12).

Lt. Col. John Montgomery, signs as Commandant at Fort Jefferson, requests Captain John Dodge issue Shadrack Bond, two shirts and as much course linen that will make a pair of trousers in part of an account Bond has against the State, for which he is to be paid from the country store. Bond signed he received the within contents (VSA-12).

Unsigned document titled Camp Jefferson: Sir Deliver half pound gunpowder and one pound lead [writing appears to be John Montgomery's] (VSA-12).

Lt. Col. John Montgomery, signs as Commandant, requests Captain Dodge to issue James Brown, a sergeant in Captain Brashears' company, one ink pot. James Brown signs he received the within contents (VSA-12).

Court of Inquiry held at Fort Jeffferson regarding Captain John Dodge's disrespectful language against Captain George. The court of inquiry was held at the public store. President of the inquiry was Captain John Williams; Captain John Rogers and John Girault sat on the board. Other members and participants of the inquiry were (DMS 56J22-24):

1. Robert George
2. John Dodge
3. Dr. Andrew Ray
4. Laurence Slaughter
5. James Piggott
6. Captain Smith
7. James Sherlock
8. Mrs. Mary Smith
9. John Montgomery
10. Martin Carney
11. E. Johnson
12. Joseph Hunter

Captain Dodge was acquitted.

The daughter of Mary Smith, no name given, had been badly paid by Israel and John Dodge for making shirts for them according to Mary Smith's testimony at Fort Jefferson Court of Inquiry (DMS 56J22).

John Montgomery, signing as Lt. Col. Commandant, at Fort Jefferson writes to Mr. William Clark to issue one box of Jesuit Bark to Doctor Ray. Doctor Ray receives box of Jesuit Bark at Fort Jefferson (MHS B1, F20).

Account of arms received by Martin Carney in this department, the property of the Commonwealth of Virginia: received of Lt. Wilson at Fort Jefferson, five muskets (VSA-50: 16).

Issued to Captain John Bailey for his company: 43 plain shirts and one ruffled shirt per Ensign Slaughter (VSA-48: 42).

Issued per order of Col. Montgomery and receipt of Shadrack Bond, per account for public services: 6 1/2 yards linen, 2 3/4 yards osnaburg, and four skeins thread (VSA-48: 78).

Issued to Ensign Jarrett Williams for 25 men of Captain Brashears' Company: one ruffled shirt, 49 plain shirts, 21 yards flannel, 24 1/4 yards blue cloth, thread and buttons and one ink pot to Sergeant Brown by Col. Montgomery's order (VSA-48: 43).

The following individuals were discharged at Fort Jefferson from Captain Jesse Evan's Company:

1. Richard Chapmen	4. Jacob Huffman	7. James Potter
2. Sgt. Andrew Clark	5. John Lastly	8. Leonard Shoemaker
3. Joshua Hollis	6. John McGuire	9. Joseph Smith

Captain Robert George's sundry merchandise drawn out of the public store more than his quota for which in part no returns or receipts have been issued or passed: one horn comb, one scalping knife, and one ink stand per order and receipt of Captain Abraham Kellar (VSA-48: 92).

Issued in the Indian Department, 7 1/2 yards blue stroud, six plain shirts, 2 1/2 yards half-thicks, five yards ribbon - five ells, two, 2 1/2 point blankets all delivered Captain Williams by Col. Montgomery's orders (VSA-48: 46).

Captain Robert George's sundry merchandise drawn out of the public store for which no returns or receipts have been issued or passed: 3 1/2 yards blue cloth, three yards white flannel, two ruffled shirts, and thread and buttons for clothes. Per order and receipt of Fred Guion (VSA-48: 92).

July 14, 1780/Friday

John Montgomery requests Captain Dodge issue Major Williams, one English blanket for Montgomery's use, and also one 2 1/2 point blanket and one snaffle bridle for Williams' use at Fort Jefferson. Williams received the within articles from Captain Dodge same day (VSA-12b).

Captain John Rogers requests of John Dodge that his Company of Light Dragoons be issued 11 coarse combs, 11 fine combs, three ink stands, two rolls black ball and 24 skeins fine thread to make the officers' shirts, two horse fleams, and 1/2 lb of coarse thread, at Fort Jefferson. Rogers signs he received the items (VSA-12;48-92).

John Montgomery requests of Martin Carney issue Ensign Slaughter 1/4 lb of gunpowder and 1/2 lb lead at Fort Jefferson; Slaughter is going to Oka[illeg.] (VSA-12; 50: 14).

Captain Robert George requests John Dodge to issue Frederick Guion, one coarse and one fine comb (VSA-12).

John Montgomery requests Captain John Dodge issue the following men one shirt each (VSA-12):

1. John Wilson	9. Jacob Huffman	17. Richard Linnett
2. Edward Taylor	10. Ebenezer Suverns	18. John Lastly
3. Henry Hutton	11. James Ballenger	19. John McQuire
4. Andrew Clark	12. James Potter	20. Daniel Tolley
5. Lou Brown	13. Joseph Smith	21. James Kincade
6. Leonard Shoemaker	14. Samuel Johnston	22. Joshua Hollis
7. William Hall	15. Richard Chapman	23. Abner Etheridge
8. Lewis Pines	16. Peter Freeman	24. William Carmack

John Wilson signs he received from Captain John Dodge, 24 shirts for self and party within mentioned. John Donne attested (VSA-12).

John Rogers requests John Dodge issue thirty-one men of Captain Rogers' company of Light Dragoons, 77 1/2 yards blue cloth and thread to make cloaks which they are entitled to by law, having more than one year to serve (VSA-12).

John Rogers signs he received the within cloth with the allowance of one yd for damage and [unclear] amount of thread (VSA-12).

Daniel Tolley is discharged from Captain Williams' Company at Fort Jefferson (VSA-12).

John Montgomery requests John Dodge issue to James Finn material [no quantity stated] to make coat and trimmings and one hat at Fort Jefferson (VSA-12).

Finn signs he received the within mentioned articles (VSA-12).

Jarrett Williams and John Montgomery sign request for one man of Captain Brashears' company to be issued five days provisions from July 14 - July 18 at Fort Jefferson (VSA-12).

John Montgomery requests of quartermaster issue Lt. Girault 1/4 lb gunpowder and 1/2 lb lead or balls at Fort Jefferson (VSA-12; 50: 14).

John Dodge, Agent, certifies Lt. Girault is due three pair silk hose, one pair thread hose, two pair shoes, and buttons for one suit of clothes. This was to complete an order drawn on Dodge in Girault's favor by George Rogers Clark for the clothing allowed by law. Lt. Girault signs request to let Lt. Clark have the within or part thereof (VSA-12).

John Montgomery requests John Dodge issue Lt. Thomas Wilson as much linen as will make two shirts and two pair trousers which will be part of his clothing if acquitted, if not Lt. Col. Montgomery will see them paid for, as it is impossible to keep a prisoner naked. Lt. Wilson signs he received the within contents (VSA-12).

Captain John Rogers requests he and two officers be issued one cover lid each; Rogers signs he received the lid (VSA-12).

Captain Dodge to John Williams: for four gallons of tafia delivered to Williams for the Indian Dept. at 30 weight peltry per gal, 120 lbs peltry; John Williams signs he received at Fort Jefferson the full contents (VSA-12).
Captain Robert George requests John Dodge issue Richard Sennet, Peter Freeman, James Ballenger, and Jacob Huffman one shirt each or linen to make the same with thread in payment for services performed when going to Kaskaskia for provisions for the troops. Charge the State of Virginia for this. Richard Sennet signs his mark that he received the within contents; attested to by John Donne (VSA-12).

Account of ammunition delivered by Martin Carney by Captain Robert George's order at Camp Jefferson: to Captain John Rogers going to Cahokia, one lb gunpowder and one lb lead (VSA-50: 9).

Account of ammunition delivered by Martin Carney by Col. Montgomery's orders: to James Brown, Sergeant Majr. of Illinois Regiment, 3 1/2 lbs gunpowder and seven lbs lead; to Sergeant Wilson of Illinois Regiment, 5 1/2 lbs gunpowder and 11 lbs lead (VSA-50: 14).

Lt. Col. John Montgomery at Fort Jefferson writes a return for ammunition for 14 men going to Kaskaskia stating 1/8 lb gunpowder and 1/4 lb lead be issued to each of the 14 men. James Brown signs he received the items (VSA-12).

Issued per order of Col. Clark in favor of John White for public services paid to John Williams per his receipt - L 26:10 V.C.: eight yards white linen at 2 1/2 dollars = 20 dollars; one embroidered apron = 20 dollars; two paper pins = two dollars; one English blanket = 16 dollars; 9 1/2 yards white linen at 2 1/2 dollars = 23 3/4 dollars; 2 1/2 yards calamanco at 2 1/2 dollars = 6 1/4 dollars; and thread = 4/3 dollars. Total order 88 1/3 dollars (VSA-48: 78).

James Finn, quartermaster, signed he received from Captain John Dodge, Agent, the above mentioned goods [July 12 list] by order of Lt. Col. John Montgomery. Attested by John Donne (VSA-48: 33).

Abner Etheridge [Abram Estridge?] was discharged at Fort Jefferson (VSA-12).

John Donne, Deputy Conductor Western Department, signed he received from Captain John Dodge, Agent, the within mentioned quantity of goods [July 12 list], in part of an order drawn on Dodge in Donne's favor by order of Col. George Rogers Clark of the 12th Inst. Attested by Leonard Helm (VSA-48: 36).
Issued in the Indian Department, three yards blue persian at four dollars = 12 dollars, 1/2 yd fine cambric at 12 dollars = six dollars, 7 1/2 yards ribbon at one dollar = 7 1/2 dollars, thread = one dollar, one ivory comb, two horn combs, 7 1/2 yards calamanco at 2 1/2 dollars = 18 3/4 dollars. Total order equals 47 1/4 dollars. Paid Major John Williams for liquor furnished for the savages in lieu of 120 lbs peltry per receipt (VSA-48: 46).
James Kincade was discharged at Fort Jefferson, but do not know from who's company (VSA-12).

Captain Robert George's sundry merchandise drawn out of the public store more than his quota for which in part no returns or receipts have been issued or passed: four plain shirts per order and receipt of Richard Linnett (VSA-48: 92).

Elizabeth Phelps is paid one pair scissors and two paper pins for making three plain shirts (VSA-48: 83).

Ebenezer Suverns is discharged at Fort Jefferson. He may have re-enlisted with Captain Williams at Kaskaskia before being discharged (Harding 1981: 2; VSA-12).

John Williams is paid twenty yards osnaburgs, 12 linen handkerchiefs, 3 3/4 yards ribbon and one paper pins for making 40 plain shirts (VSA-48: 83).

Sergeant John Wilson of Isaac Taylor's Co. is discharged at Fort Jefferson (Harding 1981: 13).

John Montgomery signs return for ammunition to Martin Carney for 22 men discharged: 1/4 lb gunpowder and 1/2 lb lead for each man. John Wilson signs that he received the items (VSA-12).

John Williams signs he received from John Dodge the contents of an account from November 7th, 1779, for John White. The account had been a request that White be paid for 53 days of blacksmith work at Kaskaskia -- six pounds, ten shillings (VSA-12).

Captain Robert George's merchandise drawn out of the public store for which no returns or receipts have been issued or passed: one ivory comb and one horn comb. Per order and receipt of Fred Guion (VSA-48: 92).

Martin Carney issues to Captain John Rogers, one lb gunpowder and one lb lead at Fort Jefferson (VSA-22).

July 15,1780/Saturday
John Montgomery requests John Dodge pay Mrs. Ann Elms and her daughter as much of something as will make each of them a petticoat (VSA-12). This action was first requested on July 11, 1780.

Ann Elms signs her mark she received seven yards of calico in compliance with Lt. Colonel John Montgomery's order. Leonard Helm attests (VSA-12; VSA-48: 78).

Zephaniah Blackford, Deputy Commissary and Lt. Valentine T. Dalton, Lt. of Artillery, at Fort Clark, sign a provision return for two men from 15 July 1780 - 24 July 1780 on command from Fort Jefferson there obtaining provisions for Fort Jefferson. Reverse states that 25 pounds flour and 25 pounds pork were issued (VSA-12).

Account of arms delivered by Martin Carney to Captain George's Company of Artillery of the Illinois Virginia Regiment: to Sergeant Anderson, five muskets and five carabins (VSA-50: 3).

Account of ammunition delivered by Martin Carney by Captain Robert George's order at Camp Jefferson: to Martin Carney, quartermaster, given in lieu of meat, one pound gunpowder (VSA-50: 9).

Nancy Ann Hunter is paid seven yards calico for making ten plain and three ruffled shirts (VSA-48: 83).

M. Murry [Murray] is paid one pair scissors and one linen handkerchief [had stated one paper pins but was crossed out] for making three plain shirts (VSA-48: 83). A list of Captain Edward Worthington's Company of Regulars:

1. Andrew Johnston
2. John Yeates
3. John Bowdery
4. John Moore
5. Reuben Kemp
6. Edward Johnson
7. William Crump
8. John Tulfor
9. James Bryant
10. Issaac Yeates
11. George Leviston
12. Charles Evans
13. Page Certain
14. Lawerence Sutherland
15. Moses Nelson
16. William Brading
17. John Anderson
18. Abraham Lockard
19. John Hargis
20. John White
21. Henry Dewit
22. John Nelson
23. Enoch Nelson
24. John Robinson
25. John Jewel
26. Modiack McKensey
27. Daniel Williams
28. Jonathon Sworden
29. James Kerkely
30. Christopher Hatten
31. Thomas Cox
32. George Gilmore
33. James Eastis
34. Joseph Thornton
35. Zachariah William
36. John Wilson
37. Jacob Willis
38. Francis Harris
39. David Allen
40. Moses Lunsford

The above are enlisted for three years or during the war, except John Wilson and John Yeats (MHS: B1, F20; VSA-12).

<u>**July 16, 1780/Sunday**</u>

At the Falls, George Rogers Clark signs, and Sergeant Edward Matthews signs his mark, that he received of George Wilson, an eight gallon pot for the use of the party going to Fort Jefferson. The State of Virginia is indebted for $600 (VSA-12).

Major Harlan signs for one batteau, one swivel, one canoe, and three pounds gunpowder and three pounds lead for Doctor [illeg.]'s party (VSA-12).

Captain Robert George, Commandant, requests Captain John Dodge, Agent, to furnish James Sherlock, Indian and French interpreter for the State of Virginia in the Illinois Dept, one broadcloth coat, one capot of bath coating, one summer coat, three summer vests, two pair of breeches, two pair of trousers, four ruffled shirts, four cambrick stocks, four handkerchiefs, two pair of shoes, two pair stockings, and one hat (VSA-12).

Issued to James Sherlock Indian and French Interpreter by order of Captain Robert George, Commandant: for one coat: 1 1/2 brown broadcloth 7/4 wide, 1 1/2 yards shalloon, 1/8 yard scarlet cloth, 2 1/2 dozen buttons, three skeins silk, one stick silk twist, skeins thread, and two yards course linen - damaged; issued for one capeau: 3 1/2 yards gray cloth 7/8 wide, six yards silk ferret for binding, four skeins silk, four skeins thread; for one summer coat: 2 1/2 yards chintz, 2 1/2 yards linen for lining, and four skeins thread; for three vests and two pair breeches: 4 3/4 yards corded dimity, 3 1/2 yards linen for lining, 2 1/2 yards gray cloth 7/8 wide, 1 1/4 yards cotton 16 de sachque, six skeins silk, and ten skeins thread; five yards cottonade for two pair trousers; four skeins thread; four ruffled shirts; four cambric stocks; one silk handkerchief; one romall handkerchief; two check linen handkerchiefs; two pair thread hose and one stock say hat (VSA-48: 62).

George Rogers Clark at the Falls writes to William Shannon, Conductor Secretary, to furnish Sergeant Mathas [Matthews?] with one barrel of whiskey for the use of the troops stationed at Clarksville on the Mississippi River (VSA-12).

Edward Matthews, sergeant, signs his mark he received from William Shannon, 29 gallons and three quarts of good whiskey, which Matthews promises to deliver to Mr. John Donne, Deputy Commissary at Fort Jefferson, the danger of the enemy and weather accept. Document attested by Benj. Hawson (VSA-12).

Captain Robert George at Fort Jefferson requests Captain John Dodge, Agent, to furnish Captain Leonard Helm, Superintendent of Indian Affairs, with such necessary clothing as he shall think proper to take, not exceeding quantity allowed by law to an officer of the line (VSA-12).

Issued to Captain Leonard Helm, Superintendent of Indian Affairs: two yards brown cloth 7/4 wide; 2 1/2 yards shalloon; 1 3/4 yards blue bath coating 7/4 wide; 2 1/4 yards white cloth 7/4 wide; issued for six vests: 3 1/2 yards brown camlet, 2 1/4 yards chintz, 2 1/2 yards cottonade, and one yard chintz [two yards toil gris had been listed but was crossed out]; issued for six pair breeches: 8 1/4 yards toile gris, 2 3/4 yards thickset, and one yard chintz; 3 1/2 yards damaged linen for lining; 20 3/4 yards linen for six shirts; 3/4 yard fine holland for ruffling; two yards cambric for six stocks; one silk handkerchief; one Indian handkerchief; four linen handkerchiefs; two pair thread hose; 16 skeins thread; one stick silk twist; four skeins silk; one hat; and one pr knee garters (VSA-48: 37).

Leonard Helm, Superintendent of Indian Affairs signs he received from Captain John Dodge, Agent, the goods drawn on Dodge in Helm's favor. Attested by John Donne (VSA-48: 38).

July 17, 1780/Monday

In letter from John Dodge to Thomas Jefferson, dated August 1, 1780, Dodge tells of an Indian attack on Fort Jefferson's village at daybreak on July 17, 1780 the troops defeated them (GRC, I: 435-438)

Captain George writes to George Rogers Clark telling of a gun being fired a little before daybreak. It was fired by an Indian with the intention of drawing the troops into an ambush. One man was killed and another was tomahawked. At the upper end of town, the militia sentinel was fired on by three Indians and wounded [later died]. The firing continued for 2 1/2 hours. Another soldier was wounded. The swivel was of great service (Seineke 1981: 448-449).

Private John Aldar, a member of Owens' militia, is killed on this date (Draper Manuscript 26J28; GRC, I: 465; Harding 1981: 49).

Pvt. Daniel Meredith, a member of Owens' militia, is killed on this date. John Montgomery stated Meredith was killed by the Indians. Meredith was married (GRC, I: 465; Harding 1981:49; VSA-13).

Issued for use of wounded men: 5 1/2 yards linen damaged, one yard ribbon, and one piece gartering (VSA-48: 78).

Account of ammunition delivered by Martin Carney by Captain Robert George's order at Camp Jefferson: to Sergeant Anderson for the defense of this place, 22 pounds gunpowder and 104 pounds lead (VSA-50: 9).

George Rogers Clark, at the Falls, requests William Shannon to send seven pounds gunpowder and two pounds lead for use of the boat crew, embarking for Clarksville (Fort Jefferson). Edward Matthews signs his mark he received the items (VSA-12).

Issued to John Dodge for his own use: 8 1/2 yards coarse linen for sheets, 6 3/4 ells at six pair (VSA-48: 58).

Issued to Archibald Lockart, for honing and setting public razors which were damaged, one check linen handkerchief (VSA-48: 78).

M. McMeans is paid one linen handkerchief, three yards ribbon, one pair scissors, one ivory comb, and one horn comb for making three ruffled and three plain shirts (VSA-48: 83).

Lt. Thomas Wilson's house at Clarksville was attacked by the Indians said Captain John Rogers in his letter to Col. Clark (MHS B1, F21).

<u>July 20, 1780/Thursday</u>
John Montgomery signs a provision return written by Fred Guion for one new recruit and one washerwoman for three days in Captain George's Company of Artillery (VSA-12).

Captain Robert George at Fort Jefferson requests Captain John Dodge, Agent, to issue Lawrence Keinan [Keenan], of Captain George's Artillery unit, one pair leggings, one breech cloth, one handkerchief, and to Joshua Archer [a resident of Clarksville] one pair leggings, one breech cloth; they being employed as expresses carrying dispatches to Colonel Montgomery. John Archer signs as having received within contents from John Dodge (VSA-12).

Daniel Bolton is paid three yards white linen by order of Colonel Montgomery in lieu of 15 days public work per his receipt (VSA-48: 78).

<u>July 21, 1780/Friday</u>
Captain Robert George at Fort Jefferson requests the quartermaster to furnish Lawrence Keinan (Keenan), a soldier in George's company, and Thorington, a soldier in Captain Worthington's Company, with half a carot of tobacco each (VSA-12).

Account of tobacco delivered by Martin Carney by order of Captain Robert George at this place: to Laurence Keinan [Keenan], by Captain George's orders, 2/3 carot equal to two pounds (VSA-50: 12).

Captain Robert George's merchandise drawn out of the public store for which no returns or receipts have been issued or passed: 2 1/2 yards half-thicks, one yard blue stroud, and one linen handkerchief per order and receipt of Joshua Archer (VSA-48: 92).

<u>July 22, 1780/Saturday</u>
Letter of Captain John Rogers at Kaskaskia to George Rogers Clark. Rogers is on his way from Camp Jefferson. Speaks of the people being very disturbed and Colonel Montgomery not sending troops to them. The Indians are continually attempting to cut off communication. They have killed several persons on the river and have chased several boats in canoes (MHS, B1: F20; Seineke 1981: 445-446).

Zephaniah Blackford, Deputy Commissary on command at Fort Clark, signs provision return for four men on command from Fort Jefferson for three days, commencing the 22nd and ending the 24th July 1780 (VSA-12).

Patrick Kennedy at Kaskaskia signs he has received the articles mentioned for immediate use of the troops at Fort Jefferson agreeable to letters sent by the commanding officer at that post (VSA-12).

July 24, 1780/Monday
Private James Dean deserted from Captain Worthington's Company (Harding 1981: 47).

James Piggott is paid seven yards damaged linen for making seven plain shirts (VSA-48: 83).

July 25, 1780/Tuesday
Account of tobacco delivered by Martin Carney by order of Captain Robert George at this place: to Thorntons, a soldier in Captain Worthington's Company by Captain George's order 1/3 carot equal to one pound (VSA-50: 12).

July 26, 1780/Wednesday

Captain Robert George requests the Fort Jefferson quartermaster furnish Joseph Anderson, John Ash, Matthew Jones, James McDannel, Peter Waggoner, and Richard Hopkins of George's Company, with three carots of tobacco [1/2 carot each]. Joseph Anderson, sergeant, signs he received the tobacco (VSA-12).

William Poston is issued three carots of tobacco for six men (VSA-12).

July 27, 1780/Thursday
Captain Robert George at Fort Jefferson writes an order to furnish William Elms and Micajah Mayfield, belonging to Captain Brashears' Company, with one carot of tobacco. William Elms signs he received the tobacco (VSA-12).

Captain Robert George signs a return to the quartermaster to issue 1/2 carot of tobacco for the following men in Captain Worthington's company: Daniel Williams, Jonathon Swordin, Archibold Lockard, William Ralesone[?]. Patrick Mains, sergeant, signs he received the tobacco (VSA-12).

July 28, 1780/Friday
Captain Robert George requests Martin Carney, quartermaster at Fort Jefferson, to furnish Lt. William Clark with one carot tobacco and charge him with the same [equals three pounds] (VSA-12; 50: 12).

Captain Robert George requests the quartermaster at Camp Jefferson to furnish Andrew Clark, artificer, with half of a carot of tobacco. This amount is equal to 1 1/2 pounds (VSA-12; 50: 12).

Captain Robert George, commandant at Fort Jefferson, requests the quartermaster furnish Frank Settle with 1/2 pound gunpowder and 1 pound lead. Settle is a soldier in George's company; Settle signs he received the lead (VSA-12).

Captain George writes to Colonel Montgomery - letter missing. See reference to this letter in George to Montgomery, 2nd Sept., 1780 (Seineke 1981: 457-459).

Account of tobacco delivered by Martin Carney by order of Captain Robert George at this place: to Sergeant Anderson in Captain George's Company, three carots equal to nine pounds; to Sergeant Mains in Captain Worthington's Company, two carots equal to six pounds (VSA-50: 12). Tobacco was orginally requested on July 27, 1780.

July 29, 1780/Saturday
Captain Robert George, Commandant at Fort Jefferson requests Captain John Dodge, Agent, to let Mr. Donne have six pounds coffee to assist his family during these times of great scarcity. John Donne, Deputy Conductor, Western Dept., signs he received the within contents (VSA-12).

Captain Robert George requests the quartermaster at Fort Jefferson furnish the "bearer" [one of the militia soldiers] with 1/2 pound gunpowder and one pound of lead (VSA-12; 50: 9).

Captain Robert George at Fort Jefferson requests Captain John Dodge, Agent, issue one hat to Peter Wagoner of George's Company as he is entitled to by law. Peter Wagoner signs his mark, and James Sherlock attests that the within contents were received (VSA-12).

Captain Robert George's merchandise drawn out of the public store for which no returns or receipts have been issued or passed: one hat per order and receipt of Peter Wagoner (VSA-48: 92).

Benjamin Roberts, Captain conductor, request the quartermaster issue three pounds flour to a sick soldier by the name of William Abbett (VSA-12).

Francis Little is issued 1/2 pound gunpowder and one pound lead by order of Captain George (VSA-12).

July 30, 1780/Sunday
Issued in the Indian Department, 31 linen handkerchiefs to wear as tokens, 23 yards blue cloth damaged, 13 3/4 yards white half-thicks, 45 yards blue stroud, 15 1/2 yards blue stroud, 29 plain shirts, two prs ravelled gartering, one pound vermilion, 1 1/2 units thread, 32 scalping knives, 1 3/4 yards blue cloth, three ruffled shirts, 15 plain shirts, one small shirt -- 1 3/4 yards, 12 piece ribbon, nine, 2 1/2 point blankets, six yards ribbon, one silk handkerchief, one ruffled shirt, one plain shirt, one pr leggings of half-thicks, three yards ribbon, one linen check handkerchief, one pair blue stroud leggings, one coarse hat bought for 20 dollars paper cury, four yards white flannel, two linen check handkerchiefs, two pair garters, four scalping knives, two yards ribbon, and eight yards white flannel for hunting shirts (VSA-48: 47).

July 31, 1780/Monday
Captain Robert George, Commandant at Fort Jefferson requests the quartermaster furnish Mr. Sherlock, two carots tobacco for the use of the Kaskaskia Indians now stationed at this place (VSA-12).

Letter of Captain George to George Rogers Clark tells of Indian attack on July 17. Also tells of Colonel Montgomery's promise to supply provisions which must be paid out of the store. Colonel Montgomery also sent Kaskaskia Indians to hunt. He promises to send a company of men for defense. Letter added telling of Lt. Clark and Captain Bailey's arriving from Kaskaskia with 1400 pounds flour, 50 bushels of corn, and 28 men (MHS, B1: F20; Seineke 1981: 448-449).

August 1, 1780/Tuesday
John Dodge at Fort Jefferson writes to Thomas Jefferson: tells of poor conditions at Fort Jefferson, Indian attack of July 17, 1780 on village and of Kaskaskia Indians he has hunting for them (GRC, I: 435-438; Seineke 1981: 449-450).

Robert George requests the quartermaster furnish Mr. Jacob Pyatt with 1/2 pound gunpowder and one pound lead for his journey to the Falls (VSA-12) (VSA-50: 10).

Robert George requests the quartermaster furnish 28 men of Captain John Bailey's Company with seven pounds gunpowder and fourteen pounds lead for the defense of Fort Jefferson. Sergeant John Vaughan signed he received the ammunition (VSA-12; 50: 10).

Col. George Rogers Clark's Shawnee Campaign officially begins with his 1,000 troops [many from Fort Jefferson], crossing the Ohio at the Licking River (GRC, I: 451).

Account of ammunition delivered by Martin Carney by Captain Robert George's order at Camp Jefferson: to Francis Little, a soldier at this place, 1/2 pound gunpowder, one pound lead (VSA-50: 9).

Robert George requests the quartermaster furnish David Allen, a soldier in Worthington's Company, with a gun. Joseph Anderson signs he received the gun which was a rifle, Martin Carney (VSA-12).

Robert George requests the quartermaster furnish James Sherlock with ten pounds gunpowder and 20 pounds lead for a party of the Kaskaskia Indians now stationed at this place to hunt for the garrison (VSA-12; 50: 10).

August 2, 1780/Wednesday

Robert George requests John Dodge issue six pounds coffee each to Mr. Clark, Mr. Carney, and himself, stating this was the second written order for the same. William Clark signs he received the 18 pounds of coffee (VSA-12).

Lt. Richard Clark requests John Dodge issue 14 shirts to the following men of Captain Worthington's Company who are enlisted for three years, and which to they are entitled by law (VSA-12):

1. George Leverston
2. Edward Johnson
3. Moses Lunsford
4. William Crump
5. Moses Nelson
6. John Pulford
7. James Bryant

Lt. Richard Clark signed he received the 14 shirts from John Dodge (VSA-12).

Issued to Captain Worthington's Company: 14 plain shirts by order of Captain George issued to Lt. Clark (VSA-48: 43).

Captain John Rogers at Cohos [Cahokia] writes to Col. George Rogers Clark at Louisville and includes a discussion of the Indian attack at Fort Jefferson on 17 July 1780 (MHS B1, F21).

August 3, 1780/Thursday

Robert George requests the quartermaster issue Sergeant Anderson one pound gunpowder and two pounds lead for the use of George's troops (VSA-12; 50: 10). Sergeant Joseph Anderson signed he received the within amount (VSA-12).

Account of tobacco delivered by Martin Carney by order of Captain Robert George: to Sergeant Anderson, 1 1/2 carots equal to 4 1/2 pounds; to Mr. Sherlock, Interpreter to the Indians, two carots equal to six pounds; to Sergeant Elms for Captain Brashears' Company, one carot equal to three pounds; to Mr. Sherlock, Interpreter to the Kaskaskia Indians, one carot equal to three pounds (VSA-50: 12).

Captain Robert George's merchandise drawn out of the public store for which no returns or receipts have been issued or passed: 18 weight coffee per order and receipt of William Clark and six weight coffee per order and receipt of John Donne (VSA-48: 92).

August 4, 1780/Friday

Robert George requests the quartermaster issue Matthew Murray of Kellar's Company, 1/2 carot of tobacco out of public store. Matthew Murray signed that he received the tobacco (VSA-12: 50-12).

John Bailey requests the quartermaster issue Sergeant Vaughan 10 pounds tobacco for the use of Bailey's Company. John Vaughan signed he received the tobacco (VSA-12).

Lt. Richard Clark signs a return for articles for his own use: one English blanket, two linen handkerchiefs, two yards silk ferretting, one leather ink pot, one fine and one coarse comb, seven skeins of thread, five yards blue ferretting, and four skeins silk. Richard Clark signs he received the articles from John Dodge (VSA-12).

Matross Daniel Baber deserted from Captain George's Company (Harding 1981: 29-30).

August 5, 1780/Saturday
Account of tobacco delivered by Martin Carney by order of Captain Robert George: to Sergeant Vaughan of Captain Bailey's Company, 3 1/3 carots equal to ten pounds; to Francis Little for taking care of the State boats, one carot equal to three pounds (VSA-50: 12).

Lt. Timothe Montbreuen comes to the relief of Fort Jefferson with Captain McCarty (Draper Manuscript 26J23).

Incomplete document: civil case held in the Borough of Clarksville between Israel Dodge and Mary South and Sarah (Burke).

August 7, 1780/Monday
Inventory of sundry articles lost by Israel Dodge on his passage from the Falls of Ohio to post St. Vincent on public business: one broadcloth coat superfine; one waistcoat superfine; two pair fine cloth breeches; one nankeen waistcoat; two shirts; five stocks [one cambric, four linen]; one black persian stock; one pair silk stockings; one pair worsted stockings; two pieces thread stockings; one piece yarn stockings; one, four point blanket and one blanket coat; one butcher knife; and one tomahawk (VSA-48: 136).

John Donne signs that Israel Dodge personally appeared before Donne and swore that about the 25th of February, lost the above mentioned articles by unavoidable accident on his passage from the Falls of Ohio to post St. Vincennes in company with Mr. Lindsay while in public service. The goods have not yet been found and are not expected to be found (VSA-48: 136).

August 8, 1780/Tuesday
Leonard Helm and Robert George sign a request to the quartermaster to issue Helm one carot of tobacco. Leonard Helm signs that he received the tobacco (VSA-12; 50: 12).

Zephaniah Blackford signs he received from Martin Carney one pine barge and nine oars [property of State of Virginia] to carry provisions from Illinois to Fort Jefferson (VSA-12).

Ezekial Johnston signs his mark he received from Martin Carney an order on the Treasury of Virginia for $225, for 4 1/2 days work with two horses and a slide, hauling timber for Fort Jefferson (VSA-12).

John Bailey requests John Dodge to issue Bailey four yards osnaburg and blue stroud for one pair of leggings. John Bailey signs that he received the material (VSA-12).

John Bailey and Robert George sign a request of John Dodge to issue Bailey and Lt. Clark seven pounds of coffee each. Richard Clark signs that he received the coffee (VSA-12).

Robert George requests John Dodge issue Martin Carney, one English blanket, one snaffle bridle and one stick blackball. Martin Carney signs he received the items (VSA-12).

Vetale Baruais signs he received a list of articles for the use of the troops of the State of Virginia and paid 482 1/3 dollars for them. John Montgomery signs that the above exchange took place (VSA-12).

Account of tobacco delivered by Martin Carney by order of Captain Robert George to Martin Carney, quartermaster, for his own use, one carot equal to three pounds (VSA-50: 12).

Richard McCarty is present at Fort Jefferson with ten soldiers from Fort Clark, and 65 Kaskaskia Indians. Lt. Timothe Montbreuen is also present (Draper Manuscript 26J23).

Captain Robert George's merchandise drawn out of the public store for which no returns or receipts have been issued or passed: one English blanket, one snaffled bridle, and one stick black ball per order and receipt of Martin Carney (VSA-48: 92).

August 9, 1780/Wednesday
Robert George requests 11 2/4 pound gunpowder and 46 pounds lead for the use by 46 men of Captain Owen's Company. Jacob Girod signs he received the above ammunition from Martin Carney (VSA-12; 50: 10).

Robert George requests John Dodge issue Sergeant Keinan [Keenan] three yards flannel for the purpose of making cannon cartridges; Keinan signs his mark that he received the within contents (VSA-12; 48: 78).

August 10, 1780/Thursday
Robert George requests John Dodge issue Richard Hopkins, a soldier in George's Company, a knife. Richard Hopkins signs his mark he received the knife (VSA-12).

Captain Robert George's merchandise drawn out of the public store for which no returns or receipts have been issued or passed: one scalping knife per order and receipt of Richard Hopkins (VSA-48: 92).

Patrick Kennedy signs he received 50 pounds flour and 50 pounds meal from William Charleville for the use of Captain Bailey's Company for their trip to Camp Jefferson (VSA-12).

Private John Allen enlists on this date in Captain Kellar's Company (Harding 1981: 24).

August 12, 1780/Saturday
Thomas Bentley writes to General Haldimand regarding spying. Removal of troops to Fort Jefferson vacating all Illinois (Seineke 1981: 452-453).

Robert George requests John Dodge issue Paul Quibea and Jeremiah Horn, four shirts which they are entitled to by law, being enlisted during the present war. Robert George signs he received the shirts (VSA-12).

Captain Robert George's merchandise drawn out of the public store for which no returns or receipts have been issued or passed: four plain shirts per order and receipt of Captain George (VSA-48: 92).

Richard Clark and Robert George sign a request to John Dodge to issue David Allen of Worthington's Company, two shirts which he is entitled to by law being engaged as a soldier for three years or during the war. Richard Clark signs he received the shirts. Two plain shirts were issued for David Allen per Lt. Clark's receipt and Captain George's orders (VSA-12; 48: 43).

Private John Blair dies. He was a member of Captain Brashears' Company (Harding 1981: 51, 52).

John Grimshaw enlists on this date in Captain George's Company (Harding 1981: 31-33).

August 13, 1780/Sunday
John Bailey and Robert George sign a request to John Dodge to issue Nicholas Burk of Bailey's Company two shirts. John Bailey signs he received the shirts (VSA-12; 48-42).

August 14, 1780/Monday
Robert George requests Paul Quibea be issued 1/2 carot of tobacco. Paul Quibea signs his mark he received the tobacco (VSA-12).

Robert George requests Sergeant Anderson be issued 1/2 pound gunpowder and one pound lead for the use of the troops. Joseph Anderson signs he received the above ammunition (VSA-12).

Account of ammunition delivered by Martin Carney by Captain George's order: to Sergeant Anderson for a hunter at this place, 13 1/2 pounds gunpowder (VSA-50: 10).

Robert George requests the quartermaster furnish Lawrence Keinan [Keenan], gunner, with 13 1/2 lbs gunpowder to use in a swivel at Joseph Ford's house for the defense of this place. Lawrence Keinan signs his mark that he received the ammunition; also receives 2 1/2 yards flannel (VSA-12; 50: 10).

John Dodge and Robert George sign a request to Martin Carney to issue three small axes or tomahawks to the Indians for the use of killing meat for the troops. James Sherlock, Indian Interpreter, signed he received the within from Martin Carney (VSA-12; 50: 40).

Captain Robert George's merchandise drawn out of the public store for which no returns or receipts have been issued or passed: 2 1/2 yards toile gris per order and receipt of D. Bolton (VSA-48: 92).

August 15, 1780/Tuesday
Captain John Rogers and Captain Abraham Kellar sign a court martial order for John Carnes [parts missing, document torn] (VSA-17).

Robert George requests John Dodge issue Daniel Bolton, gunner at the blockhouse, with as much toile gris or other linen as needed to make a pair of trousers. Daniel Bolton signs his mark he received the linen (VSA-12).

Robert George requests John Dodge issue Richard Hopkins, a soldier in George's Company, a blanket out of the Public Store. Hopkins has been eight months in service doing duty without a blanket and is enlisted for the present contest. Hopkins marked he received the blanket (VSA-12).

Captain Robert George's merchandise drawn out of the public store for which no returns or receipts have been issued or passed: one English blanket per order and receipt of Richard Hopkins (VSA-48: 92).

August 16, 1780/Wednesday
Robert George requests Martin Carney issue Richard Clark 1/2 pound gunpowder and one pound lead; also receives one flint (VSA-12; 50: 10). Richard Clark signs he received the within contents of Martin Carney (VSA-12).

Charolette Kimly is paid one linen handkerchief for making two hunting shirts paid (VSA-48: 83).

E. Springer is paid one, 1/2 yard blue stroud for plowing and harrowing a turnip patch for public use (VSA-48: 83).

August 17, 1780/Thursday
Richard Clark and Robert George sign a request to Martin Carney to issue David Allen of Worthington's Company, 1/4 pound gunpowder and 1/2 pound lead. Richard Clark signs he received the ammunition from Martin Carney (VSA-12; 50-10).

Account of arms delivered by Martin Carney to Captain George's Company of Artillery of the Illinois Virginia Regiment: delivered to Sergeant Anderson for "Sailor" Worthington, one rifle gun (VSA-50: 3).

August 18, 1780/Friday
Robert George requests John Dodge issue John Ash, of George's Company, one fine and one course comb, and one butcher knife. John Ash signs his mark he received the items (VSA-12).

Francis Bredin is paid one linen handkerchief for making two hunting shirts (VSA-48: 83).

John Bryan is paid 3/4 yard black persian, 1/2 yard thickset, six yards binding, and two linen handkerchiefs for making a suit of clothes for the interpreter (VSA-48: 83).

Francis Little is paid one pair blue stroud leggings for opening and drying public cloths (VSA-48: 83).

L. Meredith is paid two linen handkerchiefs for making four hunting shirts (VSA-48: 83).

August 19, 1780/Saturday
Robert George requests John Dodge issue Thomas Delany, Charles Morgan, James McMullan, John Grimshaw and Charles Morgan, all of George's Company, one suit clothes and one blanket. Also issue one suit clothes each for Daniel Bolton and James McDaniel also of George's Company. Robert George signs he received from Dodge, 21 yards B Cloth, 18 yards white flannel, thread, and buttons for making the suits (VSA-12).

Robert George requests the quartermaster issue a rifle from public store to Captain Leonard Helm. Leonard Helm, Superintendent of Indian Affairs, signed he received the rifle from Martin Carney (VSA-12).

Robert George requests the quartermaster issue Lieut. Richard Clark a rifle out of the public store. Richard Clark signed he received the above from Carney (VSA-12).

Captain Robert George's merchandise drawn out of the public store for which no returns or receipts have been issued or passed: one ivory comb, one horn comb and one scalping knife per order and receipt of John Ash. Twenty-one yards blue cloth, 18 yards white flannel, and thread and buttons per order and receipt of Robert George. Fourteen weight of coffee per order and receipt of Richard Clark (VSA-48: 92).

Zephaniah Blackford is paid twenty-nine ells blue cloth and 85 ells white flannel to Madam Valle for 52 bushels of corn, 1417 weight flour, and six empty barrels. Paid by order Lt. Colonel Montgomery (VSA-48: 85).

August 20, 1780/Sunday
Robert George requests Martin Carney issue Captain Leonard Helm 1/2 pound gunpowder and one pound lead or ball. Leonard Helm signed he received the ammunition from Martin Carney (VSA-12).

John Harry signs he received $600 from Colonel Montgomery on behalf of the country for one large pirogue used to transport provisions to the relief of Fort Jefferson (VSA-12).

Zephaniah Blackford is paid forty ells white linen in lieu of 100 dollars worth of goods to purchase provisions for Fort Jefferson (VSA-48: 85).

August 21, 1780/Monday
Robert George requests the quartermaster issue Paul Quibea, a soldier in George's Company, 1/4 pound of gunpowder (VSA-12).

Account of ammunition delivered by Martin Carney by Captain George's order: to Captain Leonard Helm for his own use, 1/2 pound gunpowder and one pound lead; to a French man in Captain George's Company, 1/4 pound gunpowder (VSA-50: 10).

Account of arms delivered by Martin Carney by order of Captain Robert George, to individuals: to Captain Leonard Helms for his use, one rifle; to Lt. Richard Clark for his use, one rifle (VSA-50: 17).

August 22, 1780/Tuesday
Col. George Rogers Clark writes to Thomas Jefferson regarding his successful Shawnee expedition (Seineke 1981: 455-457).

Anne Elms is paid two linen handkerchiefs and one coarse comb for making one hunting shirt and three plain shirts (VSA-48: 84).

L. Meredith is paid one paper for making one plain shirt (VSA-48: 84).

August 24, 1780/Thursday
Richard Clark and Robert George sign a request to the quartermaster to issue Joseph Thornton of Worthington's Company, one carot of tobacco. Reuben Kemp signed he received the tobacco (VSA-12; 50: 12).

Robert George requests the quartermaster issue Michael Hacketon 1/4 pound gunpowder and 1/2 pound lead (VSA-12).

Robert George requests Martin Carney issue one carot tobacco out of the public store to Richard Clark. Richard Clark signed he received the tobacco from Martin Carney (VSA-12; 50: 12).

Richard Clark and Robert George sign a request to John Dodge to issue one knife out of the public store to Reuben Camp [Kemp] of Captain Worthington's Company. Reuben Kemp signs he received the knife (VSA-12).

Captain Robert George's merchandise drawn out of the public store for which no returns or receipts have been issued or passed: one scalping knife per order and receipt of R. Kemp (VSA-48: 93).

Account of ammunition delivered by Martin Carney by Captain George's order: to a man of Captain Bailey's Company, 1/4 pound gunpowder and 1/2 pound lead; to a soldier of Captain George's Company, 1/4 pound gunpowder and 1/2 pound lead (VSA-50: 10).

August 25, 1780/Friday
Robert George requests John Dodge to issue eight shirts to Thomas Leney, John Grimshaw, James McMullen and Charles Morgan of George's Company, who are enlisted for three years or during the war. Thomas Leney, gunner, signed he received the shirts (VSA-12).

Captain Robert George's merchandise drawn out of the public store for which no returns or receipts have been issued or passed: eight plain shirts per order and receipt of Thomas Leney (VSA-48: 93).

August 26, 1780/Saturday
Robert George requests the quartermaster issue Joseph Anderson 1/2 carot of tobacco. Joseph Anderson signed he received the tobacco from Martin Carney; 1/2 carot equals 1 1/2 pounds (VSA-12; 50: 12).

Account of ammunition delivered by Martin Carney by Captain George's order: to Thomas Laney, gunner at the blockhouse, one pound gunpowder and two pounds lead (VSA-50: 10).

E. Wolf is paid three yards white flannel for making five plain shirts (VSA-48: 84).

E. Wolf is paid one yard flannel and two yards ribbon for doubling and twisting six pounds twine for making a net for public use (VSA-48: 84).

August 27, 1780/Sunday
In Captian Robert George's September 2, 1780 letter to Lt. Col. John Montgomery, Captain George states "Indians fire on Fort Jefferson at sunrise at a party of Captain Smith's negros. At dark parley between "houses in lower end of the town" and an Indian spokesman named Jas. or William Whitehead from Pensacola; Whitehead expressed determination of Indians to drive Fort Jefferson personnel out (Seineke 1981: 457).

Indians attack and destroy cornfields, kill livestock and horses (MHS: B1, F23).

Pay Abstract of a Company of Militia commanded by Captain George Owens of the district of Clarksville in the State of Virginia: Pvt John Hutsill, a member of Owens' militia is killed on August 27, 1780 (GRC, I: 465).

Thomas Laney and Robert George sign request to the quartermaster to issue one pound of gunpowder and two pounds lead for four men in George's Company. Thomas Laney signed he received the ammunition (VSA-12).

Robert George requests the quartermaster issue 25 pounds gunpowder and 50 pounds lead to the artillery (VSA-12; 50: 10).

Robert George requests the quartermaster issue 22 pounds gunpowder and 44 pounds lead to the soldiery for the protection of this place (VSA-12; 50: 10).

Matthew Jones and Archibold Lockard sign their marks and James Sherlock signs that Jones, Lockard and Ensign Gage will dig a well in the fort for 20 yards white linen (VSA-12).

Robert George requests John Dodge issue the quartermaster a piece of flannel and thread out of the public store for the use of the artillery at the post (VSA-12).

Captain Robert George's merchandise drawn out of the public store for which no returns or receipts have been issued or passed: 1 1/4 yards blue stroud and three pair mocasins to John Ash, who will leave the fort as an express (VSA-48: 94).

Captain John Bailey's hunting party encounters hostile Indians; four men are killed and one is captured (Seineke 1981: 458).

Private James Jarrell is taken prisoner; he is a member of Captain Bailey's Company (Harding 1981: 46).

Unspecified amount in yards of flannel and thread per order delivered for use of the artillery per receipt of Martin Carney (VSA-48: 84).

Lt. Richard Clark commands one of the blockhouses (Seineke 1981: 459).

August 28, 1780/Monday
John Donne receives from Thomas Phelps, 88 pounds of tame beef for the use of the troops during an attack on the fort (VSA-20).

Robert George requests John Dodge to issue John Ash, a soldier in George's Company, with cloth for a breech cloth and leggings and three pairs of moccasins for his trip to Illinois. John Ash signed he received the material. Leonard Helm signs as witness (VSA-12).

John Dodge and Robert George sign request to Martin Carney, deputy quartermaster, to issue one carot tobacco for the use of the friendly Indians (VSA-12).

According to Captain Robert George's September 2, 1780 letter to Col. Montgomerty, Captain Helm met with Colbert, an Indian spokesman; Colbert was shot by Fort Jefferson Indians at conclusion of talk. At dark, Indians attacked "Fords and Donne's Houses at the Lower End of the town, and also the Garrison" (Seineke 1981: 457).

Account of tobacco delivered by Martin Carney by order of Captain Robert George at this place: to Mr. Sherlock, Interpreter for the Indians, one carot equal to three pounds (VSA-50: 12).

Issues in the Indian Department, paid Duplasse [Duplasy] his account for bread and tobacco, 24..0..0; paid Joneast his account of bread and pork, 145 (VSA-48: 48).

Martin Carney issues Captain John Rogers 20 lbs gunpowder at Fort Jefferson (VSA-22).

August 29, 1780/Tuesday
According to Captain George's September 2, 1780 letter, in the evening, the Indians attacked the "Upper end of the town and the blockhouse" (Seineke 1981: 457).

Issues in the Indian Department, paid Nicholas Canada for his account of smith work per receipt, 40 pounds (VSA-48: 48).

August 30, 1780/Wednesday
Robert George requests the quartermaster to issue 1/2 carot of tobacco out of the public store to Jesse Kerns of George's Company (VSA-12).

According to Captain George's September 2, 1780 letter, the Indians "decamped," killed remaining sheep and cows, and destroyed almost all of the corn crop. Bailey's hunting party returns in evening; Bailey reports four men dead and one "taken" (Seineke 1981: 458).

August 31, 1780/Thursday
Robert George requests of Captain George Owens that all inhabitants of the fort bring in all the corn and other substances left from the ravages of the enemy. Captain Helm and Mr. William Clark were chosen to estimate the value of the corn and other subsistence before the enemy's appearance (VSA-12).

September, 1780/Miscellaneous
Richard Clark and John Montgomery request the quartermaster issue David Allen, a soldier in Worthington's Company, one quart [crossed out] and one pound sugar (VSA-13).

Sugar issued at Fort Jefferson by waste book by order of Col. Montgomery, 247 1/2 lbs (VSA-19).

September 1, 1780/Friday
Robert George requests the quartermaster issue John Grimshaw 1/2 carot of tobacco; 1/2 carot equals 1 1/2 pounds (VSA-13; 50: 12).

William Clark and Leonard Helm after making their assessment of the crops the Indians destoyed gave the following credit (1M8): Joshua Archer farmed with Joseph Hunter, had 1 3/4 acres [45 bushels] destroyed by Indians. John Burk farmed one acre [potential of 20 bushels] which was burned by Indians. Joseph Ford farmed four acres; would have produced 100 bushels had Indians not burned it. Robert Ford farmed 3 1/2 acres an estimated 87 1/2 bushels. Daniel Graffen farmed 16 acres with seven others from Clarksville, totaling 320 bushels had Indians not burned crop (others include: Jacob Groats, Charles King, James King, Daniel Merrideth, Daniel Miller, Jacob Shillings, James Young, and Mrs. Rion).

John Hutsil farmed two acres that would have yielded 50 bushels total had Indians not burned it. John Johnston farmed 1 1/2 acres that would have produced 37 1/2 bushels had Indians not burned it. John McCormack farmed one acre at Clarksville that would have produced 30 bushels had Indians not burned it. Thomas Phelps farmed six acres at Clarksville that would have produced 200 bushels had Indians not burned it. Henry Smith farmed five acres at Clarksville that would have yielded 125 bushels had Indians not burned it. Edward Wilson farmed two acres at Clarksville, would have yielded 60 bushels had Indians not destroyed it. Michael Wolf farmed two acres at Clarksville that would have yielded 50 bushels had it not been burned by Indians (Draper Manuscripts 1M8).

September 2, 1780/Saturday
Letter from Captain Robert George to Col. John Montgomery. George details attack at Fort Jefferson of Aug 27, 1780. He writes about the fort and the distressed situation there, the destruction of corn crop, and fear that men might evacuate the fort; mentions that Captain Smith owned a few slaves, one being female and was killed by the Indians (MHS: B1, F21; Seineke 1981: 457-459).

John Montgomery, at Kaskaskia, requests Martin Carney issue the widow of Daniel Meredith, who was killed by the savages on the 17th of July at Fort Jefferson, two lbs sugar (VSA-13).

Robert George requests John Dodge issue Mr. Joshua Archer goods, in payment for going express to Kaskaskia on public business in time of great danger, and charge it to the State of Virginia. John Archer signed he received 5 1/2 yards white linen (VSA-13).

Joshua Archer is paid 5 1/2 yards linen per order for going express to Kaskaskia in time of an attack (VSA-48: 84).

Robert George requests the quartermaster issue Richard Hopkins, a soldier in George's Company, two carots of tobacco for corking and paying public boats, two carots equals to six pounds. Richard Hopkins signs his mark he received the tobacco from Martin Carney (VSA-13; 50: 12).

Robert George requests John Dodge pay six men for 12 days work bringing provisions to the fort (VSA-13).

Martin Carney signs he received ten yards white linen and two linen handkerchiefs from Robert George for transporting provisions (VSA-13; 48-84).
Abraham Kellar receives pay voucher for bounty of men (VSA-13).

September 3, 1780/Sunday
A payment voucher for bounty of men directed to Abraham Kellar (VSA-13).

Col. John Montgomery, at Kaskaskia, compliments Sharlow Veele and begs him to send him some bread for his trip to Fort Jefferson (VSA-13).

Robert George requests the quartermaster furnish Sergeant Anderson with 16 lbs tobacco for the use of George's Company. Joseph Anderson signs he received the tobacco from Martin Carney; 16 lbs equals to 5 1/2 carots (VSA-13; 50: 13).

Invoice and receipt of $1,000 worth of goods delivered by Israel Dodge at Fort Jefferson and received by Patrick Kennedy at Kaskaskia (VSA-13).

John Bailey and Robert George sign a request of the quartermaster to issue 16 lbs of tobacco for the use of Bailey's Company. Sergeant John Vaughan signed he received the tobacco from Martin Carney (VSA-13; 50: 12).

Patrick Kennedy signs he received 307 lbs of fresh beef from Mons. Charleville for the use of Montgomery's troops on their way to the relief of Fort Jefferson (VSA-13).

Ten ells blue stroud, ten ells blue cloth, 20 ells osnaburgs, eight 2 1/2 point blankets, 4 3/8 ells fine linen, 24 ells 2d linen, eight ells flowered muslin, six ells spotted flannel, 12 ells calico, 9 7/8 ells linen and seven check handkerchiefs delivered to Patrick Kennedy Esquire, Deputy Conductor per his receipt and Lt. Col. Montgomery's orders, to purchase provisions for the relief of Fort Jefferson (VSA-48: 85).

Issued to Patrick Kennedy, ten ells of blue stroud, ten ells of blue cloth, 20 ells of osnaburgs, eight, 2 1/2 point blankets, 4 3/8 ells of calico, 9 7/8 ells of linen, and seven checked handkerchiefs to pay for $1,000 of supplies to be sent from Fort Clark to Fort Jefferson (VSA-13).

September 4, 1780/Monday

Richard Clark writes that the following men are enlisted for three years in Captain Worthington's Company (VSA 13):

1. Joseph Thornton
2. Zachariah Williams
3. Daniel Williams
4. William Robison
5. David Allen
6. Archibold Lockard

Robert George requests John Dodge issue cloth with trimmings for five coats and waistcoats and five pair of overalls for the above soldiers. Richard Clark signs he received the items from John Dodge (VSA-13).

Note to the quartermaster for 10 oars for the troops under command of Richard McCarty going to Fort Jefferson (VSA-12).

Matross Edmund Fair dies. He was a member of Captain George's Company (Harding 1981: 31, 32).

Issues in the Indian Department: two ruffled shirts; four plain shirts; nine yards blue cloth damaged; 3 3/4 yards blue stroud; three yards blue cloth; one English blanket; one, 2 1/2 point blanket; 1 1/2 yards blue cloth for a stroud; 5/8 yd blue cloth for leggings; two yards flannel; one ruffled shirt; six plain shirts; four pairs containing 200 yards linen; 145 yards white flannel; 50 scalping knives; one, 2 1/2 point blanket; one stroud 1 3/4 yards; 1 1/4 yards stroud; two linen shirts; four calico shirts; two pieces ribbon; eight gallons tafia; 5/8 yd stroud for leggings; 1/2 yd stroud for breech cloth; 15 weight flour; one, 2 1/2 point blanket; three gallons tafia; 17 scalping knives; 5/8 yd stroud for leggings; two yards ribbon; four gallons tafia; six check handkerchiefs; 1 1/4 yd blue stroud for two pair leggings; three calico shirts; 3 1/4 yards blue stroud; six yards white linen for two shirts; two white blankets, 2 1/2 points; 16 weight tobacco; one English blanket; 15 bushels corn; one hundred weight flour; six yards ribbon; six linen shirts; three calico shirts; 24 bushels corn; one hundred weight flour; six weight sugar paid for ferriage to Missouri; five ells linen paid Pierre Gamlin for tafia; six gallons tafia; four bushels corn; ten weight brown sugar; 50 weight flour; 20 weight tobacco; 15 combs; 16 scalping knives; two pair ravelled gartering; six weight coffee; five weight brown sugar; one hat; three gallons tafia; two shirts plain; ten bushels corn; 60 weight flour; three bags six ells each; ten weight tobacco; five bushels corn; 15 weight flour; 33 weight bread; five gallons tafia; 12 weight soap; six weight brown sugar; three bushels corn; six check handkerchiefs; two pieces ribbon; two dozen fine combs; one dozen coarse combs; 100 weight flour; four gallons tafia; 17 weight lead; 20 weight lead; one bushel salt; 1/2 bushel salt; ten weight lead; 1/2 bushel salt; 15 weight tobacco; 1/2 bushel salt; four bushels corn; four looking glasses; four yards gitt lace; two quarts tafia; two weight vermilion; peltry paid for tafia and tobacco to Isaac Levy, 35 livres and ten dollars; paid I. Camp for medicine for the interpreter, 16 livres peltry; paid I. Camp for a keg for the savages, 12 livres peltry; paid for 20 1/2 gallons tafia and cask to Isaac Levy per receipt, 193 livres peltry; paid Captain Joneast for sundries for Indians at different times 675; ten in cash per receipt; paid Lafortaine for interpreting ten days, ten dollars cash per receipt; paid Canada for repairing Indian Arms and 200 flour per receipt, 120 livres peltry; paid Gratiot for tafia, 45 livres peltry; paid Gratiot for 2 1/2 weight tobacco, ten shillings, seven livres peltry; paid Gratiot for five weight vermilion 100 livres peltry; paid Gratiot for three ells ticken given for tobacco for Indians, 45 peltry; four ells cotton of 16 Sachaque given Major Bosson for assisting Dodge in the Indian Department at O'Post; three check handkerchiefs to Chapeau for carrying a speech to the Savages; issued for a coat and jacket for a friendly Indian Chief: eight yards red calamanco, 1/2 yd casimir, three yards linen (VSA-48: 48-52).

September 5, 1780/Tuesday
John Donne signs he received from John Dodge, 11 bags to transport provisions to the garrison, which were destroyed by the soldiers (VSA-13).

Robert George requests Carney and Dodge to issue 20 lb of ball to Mr. Perault (VSA-13).

Richard Clark and John Montgomery request the quartermaster issue James Keney 3/4 lb gunpowder in payment of the same quantity of his own that was used during the attack (VSA-13).

John Martin[?] writes on the reverse of the above voucher, "a man of understanding will be governed by reason" (VSA-13).

September 6, 1780/Wednesday
John Dodge and Robert George sign a request to Martin Carney to issue the friendly Indians five lbs gunpowder and ten lbs lead for their killing meat for the troops (VSA-13; 50: 10).

John Dodge and Robert George sign a request to issue Mr. Perault, 20 lbs ball to be paid to John Dodge at Kaskaskia (VSA-13).

Account of ammunitions received by Martin Carney at this post Clarksville: received from a French bateau, arrived from N. Orleans, 12 kegs of gunpowder sent by Mr. Pollock, said to be 1,200 lbs gunpowder (VSA-50: 5).

Account of ammunition delivered by Martin Carney by Captain George's order: to John Dodge, Agent, for a French boat going to Pancore [St. Louis], 20 lbs lead (VSA-50: 10).

September 7, 1780/Thursday
Daniel Graffen[?] signs he received one rifle gun with mold and wipers and seven yards white linen for a milk cow [six yrs old, branded with figure 4 on each rump]. Attested by Girault (VSA-13). John Dodge signs that the gun and wiper were the property of James Sherlock to which the State is indebted to him (VSA-13).

John Montgomery requests the quartermaster issue Mr. Oiles, one quart tafia for his sick family (VSA-13).

John Montgomery requests the quartermaster issue Archibold Lockard, one quart tafia for his sick family (VSA-13).

John Montgomery requests the quartermaster issue John McCormick one quart of tafia for his wife and charge him with the same (VSA-13).

James Young signs he received from Martin Carney a certificate for five days [sawing?] at public work [$250] (VSA-13).

John Dodge requests Martin Carney issue six gallons tafia to the friendly Indians (VSA-13).

September 8, 1780/Friday

Silas Harlan signs he received from William Shannon, 58 lbs beef for the use of the party going to Fort Jefferson (VSA-13).

Robert George requests the quartermaster let the bearer have one bottle tafia and three lbs of sugar (VSA-13).

Mr. Perrault and John Montgomery sign a request to the quartermaster for issue one bottle tafia to Perrault (VSA-13).

Leonard Helm and John Montgomery sign a request to Martin Carney for Leonard Helm one quart tafia for Helm's use (VSA-13).

John Montgomery writes a return for two wounded men of Captain Owens' Company, for one lb sugar, and one lb coffee (VSA-13).

John Montgomery requests Martin Carney issue Mr. Joshua Archer one quart tafia for behaving well when sent as an express on an extraordinary occasion (VSA-13).

Richard Clark and John Montgomery sign a request to the quartermaster to issue Joseph Thornton, Pat Morre's wife, and one child, one pint tafia and two lb sugar. They are members of Captain Worthington's Company (VSA-13).

John Montgomery requests the quartermaster issue the troops at this garrison, one box soap and one box sugar (VSA-13).

John Montgomery writes a return for one pint tafia, one lb coffee, and two lbs sugar (VSA-13).

John Montgomery requests the quartermaster issue Nathan Allen two lbs sugar and one pint tafia (VSA-13).

John Montgomery requests the quartermaster issue Mr. Andrew McMean's family, three lbs sugar (VSA-13; 50: 20).

John Montgomery requests the quartermaster issue John Bryan[t], one quart tafia for his sick family (VSA-13).

John Montgomery requests the quartermaster issue Jacob Shilling, one quart tafia and two lbs sugar for his sick family (VSA-13).

John Montgomery requests the quartermaster issue Francis Gamlin, 2 1/2 lbs sugar and one quart tafia (VSA-13).

John Montgomery writes a return for five lbs sugar, one quart tafia and 10 lbs coffee for eight sick persons at Clarksville (VSA-13).

John Montgomery requests the quartermaster issue Joseph Hunter's family three lbs sugar (VSA-13).

Robert George and John Montgomery sign a request to the quartermaster to issue two sick soldiers, Charles Morgan and James McDaniel, four lbs sugar (VSA-13).

John Montgomery requests the quartermaster issue Matthew Murray and family two lb sugar (VSA-13; 50: 20).

John Montgomery requests one quart tafia to be issued James Young for a grubbing hoe for public use (VSA-13).

John Bailey and John Montgomery sign a request to the quartermaster for Edward Parker, Francis Hardin and John Clark [of Bailey's Company], three pints tafia and three lb sugar (VSA-13).

John Montgomery requests the quartermaster issue Thomas Kirk one lb sugar (VSA-13).

John Montgomery requests the quartermaster issue Madam Hutsel, three lbs sugar for her sick children (VSA-13).

John Montgomery requests the quartermaster issue Mr. Ouler's [Oiler] sick family, four lb sugar (VSA-13).

John Montgomery requests Martin Carney issue the troops and Indians one hogshead tafia (VSA-13).

John Dodge requests Martin Carney issue the Indians, who came with Major McCarty, one gallon tafia (VSA-13).

John Montgomery writes a return for a woman and two sick children of Captain Worthington's Company, for two lbs sugar and one pint tafia (VSA-13).

John Montgomery requests the quartermaster issue Zephaniah Blackford, one quart tafia for his use (VSA-13).

John Montgomery requests the quartermaster issue Frederick Guion, one bottle tafia and charge it to his account (VSA-13).

Thomas Jefferson writes to George Rogers Clark that the "situation" on the Mississippi is left to Col. Clark's decision (Draper Manuscripts 50J56; GRC, I: 455-456).

Joseph Thornton received two lbs sugar and one pint tafia for his use, along with Patrick Mains, wife and child (VSA-13).

Account of tobacco delivered by Martin Carney by order of Captain George at Fort Jefferson: to Captain John Dodge for the Indians by Col. Montgomery, two carots equal to six pounds (VSA-50: 13).

Account of ammunition delivered by Martin Carney by Col. Montgomery's orders: to James King, 3/4 lb gunpowder (VSA-50: 14).

Account of sugar delivered by Martin Carney by order of Col. Montgomery at Fort Jefferson: to two soldiers in Captain Worthington's Company, two lbs; to three men of Captain Bailey's Company, three lbs; to two soldiers of Captain Worthington's Company, three lbs; to one woman and children of Captain Worthington's Company, two lbs; to two men in Captain George's Company, four lbs (VSA-50: 20).

Tafia issued at Fort Jefferson to the officers, troops, and Indians by order of Captain Robert George, one hogshead tafia (VSA-19).

Tafia received at Fort Jefferson from John Dodge, one hogshead tafia (VSA-19).

Sugar received at Fort Jefferson from John Dodge, one case (VSA-19).

September 9, 1780/Saturday
Overdrawn by Captain Richard Brashears: one English blanket per receipt and order of Lt. Col. Montgomery (VSA-48: 14).

Overdrawn by Lt. Girault: one English blanket per order of Lt. Col. Montgomery (VSA-48: 16).

Overdrawn by Lt. Perrault: one English blanket per order of Lt. Col. Montgomery (VSA-48: 18).

Richard Clark and John Montgomery sign a request to issue Archibold Lockard, two lbs sugar for his sick family (VSA-13).

An agreement made with Frederick Guion for goods: one rifle gun $1,000, $250 for a side saddle and collar; $80 for four sickels; $20 for collar; $200 for saddle; 55 weight iron at five dollars per pound; $600 for two spinning wheels; $1,000 for one wagon and one rifled gun; $200 two ells of blue cloth; and ten pounds of tobacco; borrowed from Ryly for different times 500, 200, 50 dollars (VSA-13).

John Montgomery requests John Dodge issue an English blanket out of the public store to Lt. Perrault. Perrault signed he received the blanket from John Dodge (VSA-13).

John Montgomery requests the quartermaster issue Nelly Lewis, two lbs sugar, as she is sick (VSA-13; 50: 20).

Richard Clark and John Montgomery sign a request to issue William Crump and Dan Williams, both of Worthington's Company, who are sick, three lbs sugar and one bottle of tafia (VSA-13).

John Bailey and John Montgomery sign a request to the quartermaster to issue to Anthony Lunsford's sick family, two lbs sugar (VSA-13; 50: 20).

John Montgomery writes a return to the quartermaster for four lbs sugar to be given to Lt. James Merriwether (VSA-13; 50: 20).

John Montgomery requests an issuance of two lbs sugar to Macajah Mayfield's sick family (VSA-13; 50: 20).

Robert George and John Montgomery sign a request to the quartermaster to issue Frederick Guion, 1/2 lb gunpowder and one lb lead (VSA-13; 50: 14).

John Montgomery requests one blanket be issued Lt. Girault (VSA-13).

John Bailey and John Montgomery sign a request to the quartermaster that says, "Good for one bottle tafia" (VSA-13).

John Dodge requests two gallons tafia for the Indian allies (VSA-13).

John Montgomery requests the quartermaster issue Lt. Williams one lb soap out of the public store (VSA-13).

Robert George requests Martin Carney issue Mr. Donne, four lbs of soap (VSA-13).

John Montgomery requests Martin Carney to issue Captain George Owens, two lbs sugar for his sick family (VSA-13; 50: 22).

John Bailey and John Montgomery sign a request to issue one lb sugar and one pint tafia for John Johnston and William Brauley, of Bailey's Company, who are sick (VSA-13).

John Montgomery signs a return for one lb sugar and one pint tafia for Henry Stuart, of Captain Owens' Company, who is sick (VSA-13).

Slaughter and Montgomery sign a return to the quartermaster for 2 1/2 lbs sugar for five sick men of Bailey's Company (VSA-13; 50: 21).

John Bailey and John Montgomery sign a request to issue two lbs sugar and one quart tafia for Levi Theel, William Thompson, Robert Witt, and Peter Shepard, who are sick. They are members of Bailey's Company (VSA-13).

John Montgomery requests the quartermaster to issue Matthew Jones, a soldier of George's Company, two lbs sugar and one pint tafia for a sick member of his family (VSA-13).

Richard Clark and John Montgomery sign a request to John Dodge to issue full clothing to Richard Underwood of Captain Worthington's Company, enlisted for three years (VSA-13). Richard Clark signed he received 3 1/2 yards blue cloth, eight yards white flannel, and buttons and thread along with two shirts (VSA-13).

Issued by order of Lt. Col. Montgomery for Richard Underwood and per receipt of Richard Clark: 3 1/2 yards blue cloth; three yards white flannel; two plain shirts; buttons and thread for cloth (VSA-48: 43).

John Montgomery requests Martin Carney to issue Mary Demore [washerwoman for George's Company], two lbs sugar (VSA-13; 50: 21).

An account of sugar and tafia delivered to Fort Jefferson by Col. Montgomery's orders: Mrs. Ezekiel Johnston, four lbs sugar, one qt. tafia, cost of one pound, six shillings, zero pence; to Widow Witzel paid by Mr. Carney, three lbs sugar, cost zero pounds, 15 shillings, zero pence; two wounded men of the militia paid by Henry Steward, two lbs sugar, one pint tafia, cost zero pounds, two shillings, zero pence; Widow Meredith paid two lbs sugar, cost zero pounds, ten shillings, zero pence; to eight sick people of the inhabitants, four lbs sugar, one quart tafia, cost one pound, six shillings, six pence; to Robert Ford, seven lbs sugar, one pint tafia, cost zero pounds, 13 shillings, zero pence; to Mr. Oiles, four lbs sugar, cost one pound, zero shillings, zero pence; to Nathan Allen, two lbs sugar, one pint tafia, cost zero pounds, 13 shillings, zero pence, Allen is referred to as an "inhabitant of this place; to Mr. Joseph Hunter, paid, three lbs sugar, cost zero pounds, 15 shillings, zero pence, Hunter is referred to as an "inhabitant of this place"; to Mrs. Andrew McMeans, five lbs sugar, one pint tafia, cost zero pounds, 18 shillings, zero pence; Mr. Jacob Shilling, two lbs sugar, cost zero pounds, 16 shillings, zero pence; to Captain Owens paid, two lbs sugar, cost zero pounds, ten shillings, zero pence; to Mr. James Young, three lbs sugar, cost zero pounds, 15 shillings, zero pence; to Francis Gamlin, 2 1/2 lbs sugar, one quart tafia, cost zero pounds, 18 shillings, six pence, Gamlin is referred to as an "inhabitant of this place; to John McCorrmich paid by a Phelps, one quart tafia, cost zero pounds, six shillings, zero pence; to Mr. Oiler, one quart tafia, cost zero pounds, six shillings, zero pence (VSA-13).

Account of sugar delivered by Martin Carney by order of Col. Montgomery at Fort Jefferson: to the widow Meredith, two lbs; to two wounded militia men, two lbs; to Jacob Shilling a militia man, two lbs; to Joseph Hunter a militia man, three lbs; to Francis Gamlin a militia man, 2 1/2 lbs (VSA-50: 22).

Account of sugar delivered by Martin Carney by order of Col. Montgomery at Fort Jefferson, to Nathan Allen of militia, two lbs (VSA-50: 21).

John Montgomery requests the quartermaster issue one pint tafia to Baptist, the Kaskaskia chief (VSA-13).

John Bailey and John Montgomery sign a request to John Dodge to issue John Clark of Bailey's Company, two shirts, which he is entitled to by law for enlisting during the war. Laurence Slaughter signed he received the shirts from John Dodge (VSA-13).

John Montgomery and John Dodge sign a request to Martin Carney to issue the friendly Indian allies "who came to our relief when besieged by the enemy," one hundred lbs of gunpowder and two hundred lbs of lead. James Sherlock signed he received the ammunition from Martin Carney (VSA-13).

Robert George requests the quartermaster issue seven lbs sugar to Robert Ford for 57 lbs beef for use of the officers mess (VSA-13).

John Montgomery requests one blanket for Captain Richard Brashears, for Brashears' own use (VSA-13). Brashears signed he received the blanket from Dodge (VSA-13).

Account of sugar delivered by Martin Carney by order of Col. Montgomery at Fort Jefferson, to David Allen, a soldier in Worthington's Company, one lb (VSA-50: 20).

Account of ammunition received by Martin Carney at this post Clarksville: received of Lt. Dalton, guns, 23 lbs gunpowder, and 15 lbs lead (VSA-50: 5).

Account of ammunition delivered by Martin Carney by Col. Montgomery's orders to John Dodge, Agent for the Indians, 100 lbs gunpowder and 200 lbs lead (VSA-50: 14).

Account of sugar delivered by Martin Carney by order of Col. Montgomery at Fort Jefferson: to Thomas Kirk, one lb; to Col. Montgomery's order, three lbs; to Groves Morris, a man in Captain Bailey's Company, two lbs; to a man and his sick children, one lb; to Thomas Kirk, two lbs; to eight sick people of the Inhabitants, four lbs; to a sick woman and children of Captain Brashears' Company, two lbs; to two men of Captain Bailey's company, two lbs; to Matthew Jones, a soldier in Captain George's company, two lbs; to Mr. Donne, Commissary, four lbs; to two men of Captain Bailey's Company, one lb; to Col. Montgomery's order, one lb; to John Bryan of Captain George's Company, three lbs; to Joshua Archer, three lbs; to George Lunsford of Captain Bailey's Company, 1/2 lb; to Henry Steward, a militia man, one lb; to Mrs. Witzel a widow of militia, three lbs; to Mr. Oiler's sick family, four lbs; to Captain Kellar for his own use, four lbs; to Jacob Ditterin, one lb (VSA-50: 20-21).

Account of sugar delivered by Martin Carney by order of Col. Montgomery at Fort Jefferson, to Charles Evans, a soldier in Captain Worthington's Company, one lb; to the Widow Hughes of militia, three lbs; to Captain Brashears and Doctor Ray, three lbs (VSA-50: 22).

Account of soap delivered by Martin Carney by order of Col. Montgomery and Captain George at Fort Jefferson, to Fredrick Guion, two lbs (VSA-50: 50).

Received of Captain John Dodge one pair steelyards [balanced weights], for use of the Commissary Dept. by John Donne (VSA-13).

Issued to John Dodge for his own use: paid Moses Henry, four ells black calamanco house expense; six yards ferretting; three skeins silk; one ivory comb; 1 1/2 weight sugar; one snaffle bridle; ten skeins silk; three ells ticken bought of Gratiot, 45 livres peltry; 13 ells linen; and ten weight soap [house expense] (VSA-48: 58).

Account of sugar delivered by Martin Carney by order of Col. Montgomery at Fort Jefferson, to Ezekial Johnston, a militia man, four lbs (VSA-50: 22).

Mrs. Ezecal Johnston is referred to as an inhabitant (VSA-13).

Sugar and tafia provided to inhabitants [25+] of Fort Jefferson via the quartermaster stores (VSA-13).

Fragment of a letter from Williams to someone, gives reference to "my wife Nancy" and as postscript "pray send me a line" (VSA-13).

Account of sugar delivered by Martin Carney by order of Col. Montgomery at Fort Jefferson: to Archibold Lockard in Worthington's Company, two lbs (VSA-50: 20).

<u>September 10, 1780</u>/<u>Sunday</u>

John Montgomery requests the quartermaster issue one boat and 23 oars for his trip to Kaskaskia (VSA-13).

Robert George requests John Dodge issue the following to the quartermaster; barrack of tafia, one large cross cut saw, one case sugar, one case soap, one fish sein, 166 lb of ball, and what other articles are needed for the use of the troops (VSA-13).

John Montgomery requests John Dodge issue Lt. Valentine T. Dalton the clothing he is entitled to by law (VSA-13).

John Donne signs he received one pair steelyards for the use of the Commissary Dept. from John Dodge (VSA-13).

Richard McCarty signs he received from Col. Montgomery a set of bills for $1,000 for recruiting services in favor of Lawrence Slaughter (VSA-13).

John Montgomery requests Martin Carney issue Joshua Archer three lb sugar for good behavior when sent as an express on an extraordinary occasion (VSA-13).

John Montgomery requests the quartermaster issue Jacob Ditterin, who is in George's Company of Artillery and, who is sick, one lb sugar (VSA-13).

Reverse of sugar issue to ditterin is a portion of another document with a list: three sergeants, one drummer, 17 rank and file, one junior officer, one boman[?] (VSA-13).

Abraham Kellar and John Montgomery sign a request to Martin Carney to give the bearer four lbs sugar and four lbs coffee for Kellar's use (VSA-13).

John Montgomery requests the quartermaster issue Widow Hughes, three lbs sugar for her sick family (VSA-13).

Slaughter and Montgomery sign a return for 1/2 lb sugar for George Lunsford of Bailey's Company, who is sick (VSA-13).

Laurence Slaughter and John Montgomery sign a request for two lbs sugar for Graves Morris of Slaughter's Company, who is sick (VSA-13).

Col.[?] Merriwether and John Montgomery sign a request to the quartermaster for Merriwether, one lb gunpowder and two lbs lead (VSA-13; 50: 14).

Lt. Col. John Montgomery signs a request to John Dodge to issue Captain McCarty full clothing for his men as they are entitled to by law (VSA-13).

Richard McCarty signs he received 63 yards blue cloth, 55 yards white flannel, and thread to make the clothing. He also wants one hat and a pair of shoes for each man (VSA-13; 48: 41).

List of Captain Richard McCarty's Company of Regulars raised by order of Col. George Rogers Clark in 1779, who have received no clothing and are enlisted during the war (VSA 13):

1. Jean Andree'
2. Jess Piner
3. Grolais Pere
4. Grolais Fils
5. Laform P. Blanihar
6. Jean Pepin
7. Jas Metivce
8. Wil Mulby
9. James Harrison
10. Pursley F. L'Enfant
11. Jacque Gagnier
12. Richard Lovin
13. Louis G. Lamarine
14. John M. Pepin

Captain Abraham Kellar and John Montgomery sign a return to Martin Carney for 1/2 lb gunpowder and 1 lb lead for each of eight men in Kellar's company (VSA-13).

John Montgomery signs a return for 1/2 lb gunpowder and one lb lead for three volunteers who went with Montgomery on an expedition (VSA-13; 50: 14).

John Dodge and John Montgomery sign a request to Martin Carney to issue 10 lbs gunpowder, 20 lbs lead, and two carots of tobacco to a party of warriors going to get revenge on the injury of their father, Big Knife (VSA-13).

John Montgomery signs a request to John Dodge to issue 20 of the Kaskaskia Indians one barge and swivel to war against the Chickasaw Indians (VSA-13).

John Montgomery requests the quartermaster issue the bearer one lb gunpowder (VSA-13).

John Montgomery requests the quartermaster issue Thomas Kirk, a volunteer, two lbs sugar (VSA-13).

John Montgomery writes a return for two lbs sugar for one sick man and two children (VSA-13).

John Montgomery requests the quartermaster issue one cask gunpowder and 200 lbs lead for the troops now at Kohos [Cahokia]. Capt Richard Brashears signed he received the ammunition from Martin Carney (VSA-13).

John Montgomery requests John Dodge deliver John Ash one blanket and one shirt for his going express to Kaskaskia. John Ash signs his mark he received the contents from John Dodge (VSA-13).

Charles Gratiot writes in French to John Montgomery and requests John Dodge pay him for taking a pirogue to McCarty at Fort Jefferson for relief. Gratiot signed he received 15 ells linen from Dodge (VSA-13).

John Montgomery requests John Dodge issue Thomas Kirk, Gasper Butcher, and Stephen Stephensen one shirt each, for coming to the relief of the post and for their service of 20 months. Gasper Butcher signed he received the shirts from John Dodge (VSA-13; 48-41).

John Bailey and John Montgomery sign a request to John Dodge to issue John Bailey and Ensign Slaughter one blanket each. Laurence Slaughter signed he received the blankets from John Dodge (VSA-13).

John Montgomery requests Dodge to issue one blanket to Lt. Montbreuen. Montbreuen signed he received the blanket from Dodge (VSA-13).

John Montgomery requests four lbs coffee and one blanket for Lt. Dalton. Valentine T. Dalton signed he received the coffee and blanket from John Dodge (VSA-13).

Account of ammunition delivered by Martin Carney by Col. Montgomery's orders: to John Dodge, Agent, ten lbs gunpowder and 20 lbs lead; to Captain McCarty's Company, 4 1/2 lbs gunpowder and nine lbs lead; to Captain Brashears' Company, five lbs gunpowder and ten lbs lead; to Captain Brashears for the troops at Cahokia, 100 lbs gunpowder and 200 lbs lead (VSA-50: 14).

Overdrawn by Captain John Bailey: one blanket per receipt of E. Slaughter and order of Lt. Col. Montgomery, five yards white flannel, and 40 continental dollars to enlist a recruit (VSA-48: 13).

Account of ammunition delivered by Martin Carney by Col. Montgomery's orders: to Col. Montgomery, one lb gunpowder; to Captain Kellar's Company, four lbs gunpowder, eight lbs lead (VSA-50: 14).

Matross Fred Guion is discharged. He was a member of Captain Robert George's Company of Artillery (Harding 1981: 30).

Overdrawn by Ensign Slaughter: one blanket per receipt and order of Lt. Col. Montgomery, 1 1/4 yd thickset, and five skeins silk (VSA-48: 26).

Overdrawn by Lt. Valentine Thomas Dalton, per receipt and order of Lt. Col. John Montgomery: four weight coffee and one English blanket (VSA-48: 56).

John Williams is issued one lb gunpowder, and two lbs lead for his own use (VSA-13).

Overdrawn by Lt. Montbreuen: one English blanket per receipt and order of Lt. Col. Montgomery (VSA-48: 32).

Issued to Lt. John Girault for four men of Major Richard McCarty's Company: 14 yards blue cloth, 12 yards white flannel, four shirts, and 13 yards linen for four shirts (VSA-48: 41).

<u>September 11, 1780/Monday</u>

Jarret Williams and John Montgomery sign a return to the quartermaster for one lb gunpowder and two lbs lead for Williams' use (VSA-13; 50: 14).

John Montgomery requests the quartermaster issue Dr. Rey [Ray], 1/2 lb gunpowder and one lb lead (VSA-13; 50: 14).

Richard Brashears and John Montgomery sign a return to the quartermaster for one lb gunpowder and two lbs lead for Brashears use (VSA-13).

John Montgomery requests the quartermaster issue Zephaniah Blackford, two lbs sugar and one lb soap (VSA-13).

Richard Clark and John Montgomery sign a request to the quartermaster to issue Charles Evans of Worthington's Company, one lb sugar for sickness (VSA-13).

No signature on a request to the quartermaster to issue John Bryan three lbs sugar (VSA-13).

Robert George requests John Dodge to issue eleven blankets to men of George's Co., who are enlisted for three years (VSA-13):

1. John Hazard
2. Charles Morgan
3. John Grimshaw
4. Matthew Jones
5. Richard Turpin
6. William Pursley
7. John Smothers
8. Paul Quibea
9. James McMullen
10. Jacob Diteren
11. George Armstrong

Lawrence Slaughter and John Montgomery sign a request to the quartermaster to issue 1/2 lb sugar to a sick man of Bailey's Company (VSA-13).

Captain Brashears and John Montgomery sign a return to the quartermaster for two men of Brashears' Company, one lb gunpowder and two lbs lead (VSA-13; 50: 14).

John Montgomery requests Martin Carney issue Lt. Girault, one lb gunpowder and two lbs lead (VSA-13; 50: 14).

Lt. Valentine T. Dalton and John Montgomery sign a request to John Dodge to issue John Hazzard, John Riley, Andrew Kenore, Jacob Diteren [Ditterin], and George Armstrong, two shirts each (VSA-13).

Richard Brashears, Robert George, and John Montgomery sign a request to the Agent of Public Stores, to issue John Allen, Mark Foley, and Thomas Snellock of Brashears' Company, suits of clothing [one coat jacket, breeches and two shirts]. Richard Brashears signs he received the items (VSA-13).

John Montgomery requests John Dodge issue John Donne, one blanket being destitute of bed clothes for the approaching season. John Donne signs he received the blanket (VSA-13).

Patrick Kennedy certifies that Gasper Butcher worked as an artificer for six days at the rate of one dollar/day which he is to be paid in goods from the public store. John Montgomery requests John Dodge pay Butcher the within contents. Butcher signs he received the pay from John Dodge (VSA-13).

Robert George requests the quartermaster issue three lbs sugar to John Breare [Bryan] (VSA-13).

Reverse of John Breare [Bryan] entry above, is a ledger which reads, Jarret Willias [Williams?] to Frederick Sovereign, April 21, 1780 to 57 dollars answered[?] for Mr[?] Phandue[?], July 11 to one cow hide ten pounds of peltry, July 12 to one pair of moccasins, 40 dollars [illegible line entry] August [?] to one comb 40 [Ensign Williams at Fort Jefferson 07/12/80] (VSA-13).

John Montgomery requests John Dodge issue Doctor Rey [Ray] one blanket. Dr. Rey [Ray] signed he received the blanket (VSA-13).

Overdrawn by Doctor Ray: one blanket per receipt and order of Lt. Col. Montgomery (VSA-48: 30).

Abraham Kellar and John Montgomery sign a request to John Dodge to issue Kellar one blanket for his own use. Abraham Kellar signed he received the blanket from John Dodge (VSA-13).

Account of ammunition delivered by Martin Carney by Col. Montgomery's orders: to Col. Montgomery for his own use, one lb gunpowder and two lbs lead; to Mr. Montbreuen for his own use, one lb gunpowder and two lbs lead; to one man of Captain George's Company, 1/2 lb gunpowder and one lb lead; to Captain Brashears for his own use, one lb gunpowder and two lbs lead (VSA-50: 14).

Account of sugar delivered by Martin Carney by order of Col. Montgomery at Fort Jefferson: to Lt. Girault for his own use, one lb (VSA-50: 22).

One, 2 1/2 point blanket and one shirt per order of Lt. Col. Montgomery paid John Ash for going express (VSA-48: 84).

Account of soap delivered by Martin Carney by order of Col. Montgomery and Captain George at Fort Jefferson: Zephaniah Blackford, one lb; to Ensign Slaughter, two lbs (VSA-50: 50).

Seven yards linen per order Col. Montgomery and receipt of Richard Clark for 14 days service as engineer at Kaskaskia (VSA-48: 84).

Overdrawn by Captain Abraham Kellar: one blanket per receipt and order of Col. Montgomery (VSA-48: 10).

Overdrawn by Lt. Perrault: 2 1/2 yards toile grise (VSA-48: 18).

Overdrawn by Deputy Conductor John Donne: one English blanket per receipt and order of Lt. Col. Montgomery (VSA-48: 36).

Issued in the Indian Department, paid Fleure d'Epec for repairs on Indian arms, 40 (VSA-48: 48).

Issued to Lt. Dalton in part of the clothing allowed him by law: five yards cotton sachaque, four yards spotted flannel, 2 1/2 yards corded dimity, eight yards camlet, 13 skeins thread, 2 3/4 yards of cambric, and 21 yards white linen (VSA-48: 56).

Sundry merchandise overdrawn by Lt. Clark: one English blanket, two check linen handkerchiefs, two yards silk ferrit, one leather ink pot, one fine comb, one coarse comb, seven skeins thread, five yards blue ferriting, and four skeins silk (VSA-48: 40).

September 12, 1780/Tuesday

Pay Abstract of a Company of Militia commanded by Captain George Owens of the district of Clarksville in the State of Virginia. The following people are listed as having moved on this date (GRC, I: 464-465; Harding, 1981: 48-49):

1. Private Joseph Ford
2. Private John Ford
3. Private James McMeans
4. Private James Young
5. Private Michael Wolf
6. Private Nicholas Nedinger
7. Private Henry Steward
8. Private Francis Cimblet
9. Private Robert Ford
10. Private Andrew McMeans
11. Private Jonas Ker
12. Private John Young
13. Private John Phister
14. Private Moses McCan
15. Private James Barnet
16. Private Daniel Graffen
17. Private William Hutsil
18. Private Charles King
19. Lt. Samuel Cooper
20. Private James King

Memorandum of articles received from Jacob Groats for the Commonwealth of Virginia in Col. Clark's Dep't. (VSA-13).

John Montgomery requests Martin Carney to let John Dodge have the old barge by the landing to go to Kaskaskia on public business (VSA-13).

John Dodge requests Martin Carney to issue the bearer 1 1/2 lb sugar already paid for (VSA-13.

John Dodge requests Martin Carney to issue Mr. Gilen, four lbs sugar to pay for a mortar for Col. Clark (VSA-13).

Richard Clark and John Montgomery sign a request to the quartermaster for one man in Worthington's Company, 1/2 lb gunpowder and one lb lead (VSA-13).

Abraham Kellar and John Montgomery sign a request to the quartermaster to let two men of Captain Kellar's Company who are sick, have one lb of sugar (VSA-13; 50: 22).

Lt. John Girault and Col. John Montgomery sign a request that Lt. Girault be issued one lb sugar for his own use. Girault signs in French that he received one lb sugar for his own use (VSA-13).

Richard Brashears and John Montgomery sign a request to the quartermaster for three lbs sugar and one lb soap for the Doctor and Brashears (VSA-13).

Robert George and John Montgomery sign a request to the quartermaster to issue John Smother of artillery, who is sick, one lb sugar (VSA-13; 50: 22).

John Montgomery requests John Dodge issue 10 lbs coffee for use of Montgomery's mess. John Montgomery signs he received the coffee (VSA-13).

John Ash is paid four yards flannel for going express (VSA-48: 87).

Account of sugar delivered by Martin Carney by order of Col. Montgomery at Fort Jefferson: to a man of Captain Bailey's Company, 1/2 lb (VSA-50: 22).

Account of ammunition delivered by Martin Carney by Col. Montgomery's orders: to one man of Captain Worthington's Company, 1/2 lb gunpowder and one lb lead (VSA-50: 14).

Frank Coleman is paid 2 1/2 ells spotted flannel for ten flour casks by order of Col. Montgomery (VSA-48: 87).

Patrick Mains is discharged from Captain Worthington's Company (Harding 1981: 46-47; VSA-13).

List of sundry articles overdrawn by Col. Montgomery, beyond his quota of clothing; ten lbs coffee per order and receipt and one yd osnaburg per order and receipt "for your sadlers" (VSA-48: 2).

Francis Rubedo dies. He was a member of Captain Brashears' Company (Harding 1981: 51).

Twenty yards white flannel are issued for one cannon at Fort Jefferson (VSA-48: 87).

September 13, 1780/Wednesday

Sergeant Enoch Springer's pay ends this date; member of Owens' Militia (GRC, I: 464-465; Harding, 1981: 48).

Pay Abstract of a Company of Militia commanded by Captain George Owens of the District of Clarksville in the State of Virginia. The following men moved on September 13: private James Wiley, private Edmund Smith, private Jacob Groats, and private Jacob Shilling (GRC, I: 464-465).

John Bailey signs a return to the quartermaster for 12 lbs soap for 24 men belonging to his company (VSA-13).

John Dodge requests leave to go on business up the Mississippi (VSA-13).

William Clark and Leo Helm sign as subscribers appointed to estimate the amount of corn that could have been raised by the inhabitants of Clarksville had their crops not been burned by the Indians. Thomas Phelps had a prospect of making 190 bushels. John Montgomery certifies the estimate to be true and just and that the corn was taken by the troops at Clarksville (VSA-13).

Robert George writes a return to the quartermaster for 1 1/2 lbs sugar for a sick man in Captain McCarty's Company (VSA-13).

John Montgomery requests Martin Carney let Leonard Helm have four lbs sugar for his own use (VSA-13; 50: 22).

Richard Clark and Robert George sign a request to the quartermaster to issue a sick Zachariah Williams, of Worthington's Company, one lb sugar (VSA-13).

Valentine T. Dalton and John Montgomery sign a return for 1/2 lb gunpowder and one lb lead for two men who served at Camp Jefferson with Mr. Dalton (VSA-13).

Richard Clark and John Montgomery sign a request to the quartermaster for issue two lbs sugar to Reuben Kemp of Worthington's Company (VSA-13).

Valentine T. Dalton and Robert George sign a request to Captain Dodge to issue two shirts to Jacob Ditterin, Andrew Conors, John Hazard, George Armstrong, and John Riley who enlisted for three years. Valentine T. Dalton signed he received the shirts (VSA-13).

John Montgomery writes a return for 12 lbs soap for 24 men of Captain Bailey's Company (VSA-13; 50: 50).

John Donne writes he received a 278lb: beef cow from Martin Carney which Carney received from John Dodge for the use of the troops (VSA-13).

Reverse of John Donne's receipt of for a beef cow is a table drawn with the following information: Ensign-one, Serg.-two, volunteers-one, rank and file-ten, total 16 [14?] signed by John[?] Shelby (VSA-13).

John Montgomery requests the quartermaster issue two lbs soap to Ensign Slaughter for his use (VSA-13).

Richard Brashears and Robert George sign a return to the quartermaster for soap for 11 men of Brashears' Company (VSA-13).

Robert George requests the quartermaster issue 1/2 lb soap to 32 men of George's Company (VSA-13; 50: 50).

John Montgomery requests the quartermaster issue John Donne, three lbs soap being in need of the same (VSA-13; 50: 50).

John Montgomery signs a request for 12 blankets to Captain George's Company, eight to Captain Worthington's Company, three to McCarty's Company, four to Brashears' Company for 25 men of his company, 11 to Bailey's Company, and two to Kellar's Company (VSA-13).

Kellar signs he received two blankets from John Dodge, Valentine T. Dalton signed he received 12 of Dodge for George's Company, Richard Clark signed he received 8 for Worthington's Company, Brashears signed he received four, Slaughter signed he received 11 for Bailey, and McCarty received three for his company (VSA-13).

Richard Clark and John Montgomery sign a request to the quartermaster for 1/2 lb soap/man for 19 men of Worthington's Company (VSA-13; 50: 50).

John Montgomery requests the quartermaster issue two lbs sugar (VSA-13).

Richard McCarty and John Montgomery sign a request for 15 lbs soap for 10 men of McCarty's Company (VSA-13; 50: 50).

Abraham Kellar and John Montgomery sign a request to Martin Carney for 1 1/2 lbs gunpowder and three lbs lead for three men of Kellar's Company with himself included (VSA-13; 50: 14).

Abraham Kellar and John Montgomery sign a request to John Dodge for four lbs coffee for Kellar's use. David Rupel signed his mark he received of Captain John Dodge, four lbs coffee. Leonard Helm signed as a witness. (VSA-13).

John Montgomery requests John Dodge issue Major McCarty a blanket. Richard McCarty signed he received the blanket from Dodge (VSA-13).

Leonard Helm requests John Dodge issue him five lbs coffee for his own use. Leonard Helm signed he received the coffee from John Dodge (VSA-13).

Zephaniah Blackford signs he received 2 1/2 bushels Indian corn from Jacob Shilling for the use of the troops at Fort Jefferson. John Donne requests John Dodge to please replace the within mentioned corn (VSA-13).

Robert George requests one blanket for his use. George signs he received the blanket from John Dodge (VSA-13).

John Montgomery requests the quartermaster issue 60 lbs sugar to 10 officers of the Illinois Virginia Regiment (VSA-13).

A list of the officers of the mess:

1. Col. Montgomery
2. Major McCarty
3. Captain George
4. Captain Brashears
5. Captain Bailey
6. Lt. Clark [Richard]
7. Lt. Merriwether
8. Ensign Williams
9. Doctor Rey [Ray]
10. Mr. Clark, Secretary

Account of sugar delivered by Martin Carney by order of Col. Montgomery at Fort Jefferson: to Captain Dodge, Agent for his use, four lbs; to Lt. Dalton for his own use, 20 lbs; to Col. Montgomery for his own use, three lbs; to Reuben Kemp, a Sergeant of Worthington's Company, one lb; to Frank Little of Captain George's Company, two lbs; to Robert Ford, a militia man for 57 lbs beef for public use, seven lbs; to James Young, a militia man, three lbs; to ten officers of Col. Montgomery's mess, 60 lbs; to Captain Dodge's order by Frank Little, 5 1/2 lbs; to Carney's own use, four lbs; to Mr. Graffen for a handmill for public use, six lbs; to the Widow Witzel for a flat bottomed boat for public use, seven lbs; to James King and company for a flat bottomed boat, seven lbs (VSA-50: 22).

Account of sugar delivered by Martin Carney by order of Captain George at Fort Jefferson: three lbs [document had said to Widow Huges but was crossed out]; to Sergeant Anderson of Captain George's Company, two lbs; to Phelps of militia, six lbs (VSA-50: 24).

Account of soap delivered by Martin Carney by order of Col. Montgomery and Captain George at Fort Jefferson: to Captain Brashears' Company, 8 1/2 lbs; to Captain Brashears and Doctor Ray, one lb (VSA-50: 50).

James Brown is issued a share of two lbs sugar along with Sam Allen for being sick (VSA-13).

Account of sugar delivered by Martin Carney by order of Col. Montgomery at Fort Jefferson: to a man of Captain McCarty's Company, 1 1/2 lbs; to Col. Montgomery's order, two lbs (VSA-50: 22).

Eight blankets per receipt of Richard Clark and order of Lt. Col. Montgomery; 18 3/4 yards blue cloth per receipt of Richard Clark; 15 1/2 yards white flannel per receipt of Richard Clark; and thread and buttons for the above per receipt of Richard Clark (VSA-48: 43).

Account of ammunition delivered by Martin Carney by Col. Montgomery's orders: to Lt. Dalton for two of his men, one lb gunpowder and two lbs lead (VSA-50: 14).

Account of soap delivered by Martin Carney by order of Col. Montgomery and Captain George at Fort Jefferson, to Lt. Williams for his use, one lb (VSA-50: 50).

Captain Robert George's sundry merchandise drawn out of the public store more than his quota for which in part no returns or receipts have been issued or passed: one, 2 1/2 point blanket per order and receipt; 12, 2 1/2 point blankets per order of Lt. Col. Montgomery and receipt of Lt. Dalton for use of Captain George's Company; ten shirts for Captain George's Company per order; for making cartridges: ten yards white flannel per receipt of Martin Carney and 15 skeins thread per receipt of Martin Carney; to dress a wounded man: 1/2 yd white linen and one piece of ravelled gartering; ten plain shirts per order; and 11, 2 1/2 point blankets per order (VSA-48: 93).

James Hays deserts. He was a member of Captain John Bailey's Company (Harding 1981: 46).

Overdrawn by Captain Helm, Superintendent: five weight coffee per order and receipt, one English blanket, and 1 1/2 yards ribbon (VSA-48: 38).

Overdrawn by Major McCarty: one blanket per receipt and order of Lt. Col. Montgomery (VSA-48: 6).

Three blankets per receipt and order of Lt. Col. Montgomery and 14 shirts (VSA-48: 41).

Anne McMeans left Fort Jefferson for Natchez. Thirteen families in her boat, 19 people total; only two were men (Personal Narrative, Filson Club).

Graves Morris deserts. He was a member of Captain John Bailey's Company (Harding 1981: 45-46).

Two blankets per receipt and order of Lt. Col. Montgomery (VSA-48: 42).

Four blankets per receipt and order of Lt. Col. Montgomery (VSA-48: 43).

September 14, 1780/Thursday
Robert George requests Martin Carney issue two lbs sugar for James Brown and Sam Allen of Captain Brashears' Co., who are sick (VSA-13).

Abraham Kellar and Robert George sign a request to the quartermaster to issue James Thomson of Kellar's Company, one lb [Document torn; probably sugar] as he is sick (VSA-13; 50: 24).

Abraham Kellar and Robert George sign a request for two lbs sugar for two sick men of Kellar's Company (VSA-13; 50: 24).

Robert George requests two lbs sugar for Francis Little, who is sick (VSA-13).

Robert George requests the quartermaster issue two lbs sugar from the public store to Mr. Birks [Burks] (VSA-13).

Captain George Owens and Robert George sign a request to the quartermaster for six lbs sugar for Thomas Phelps and his sick family (VSA-13).

Account of sugar delivered by Martin Carney by order of Col. Montgomery at Fort Jefferson, to Mr. Phelps [document did list one lb of sugar but had been crossed out] (VSA-50: 23).

Account of sugar delivered by Martin Carney by order of Captain George at Fort Jefferson: to two sick soldiers of Captain Brashears' Company, two lbs; to Joseph Hunter of militia, three lbs (VSA-50: 24).

September 15, 1780/Friday
Robert George requests Martin Carney issue Joseph Hunter three lbs sugar at Fort Jefferson (VSA-13).

No signature for a request to the quartermaster for one lb of lead, 1/2 lb gunpowder, and two flints for John Hazzard (VSA-13).

Robert George requests the quartermaster issue Jacob Ditterin one lb sugar, as he is sick (VSA-13; 50: 24).

Robert George requests the quartermaster issue John Hazard 1/2 lb lead, 1/4 lb gunpowder, and two flints (VSA-13).

Captain John Bailey certifies Mrs. Bredin made four shirts, one coat, and one waistcoat for Bailey's Company. Robert George requests John Dodge pay her for the work out of the public store. Francis Bredin signs her mark that she received four yards flannel in payment for the coat and waistcoat (VSA-13).

Robert George requests the quartermaster issue one lb sugar to John Hazzard (VSA-13; 50: 24).

Robert George requests the quartermaster issue one lb sugar to Billy McCarty, a militia man who is sick (VSA-13).

Robert George requests the quartermaster issue two lbs sugar to Edward Murray and John Clark of Captain Bailey's Company (VSA-13).

George Owens and Robert George sign a request for one lb sugar to William Creton (VSA-13; 50: 24).

John Bailey and Robert George sign an ammunition return to the quartermaster for five lbs gunpowder and 32 lbs lead, for the use of 10 men of Bailey's Comapny (VSA-13).

John Bailey and Robert George sign a request to the quartermaster for 5 1/2 lbs gunpowder and 11 lbs lead for the use of Bailey's Company (VSA-13; 50: 10).

Robert George requests the quartermaster issue one lb sugar each to John Johnston, John Reid, and Paul Quibea as they are sick (VSA-13; 50: 24).

Unsigned return for 12 leven of gunpowder [assuming it is meant to be 12 lbs gunpowder], and 11 lbs lead (VSA-13).

Account of ammunition delivered by Martin Carney by Captain George's order: to John Hazard of artillery, 1/4 lb gunpowder and 1/2 lb lead; to two men of Captain McCarty's Company, one lb gunpowder and two lbs lead; to the artillery at this place, 16 lbs gunpowder, 32 lbs lead, and six yards flannel (VSA-50: 10).

Account of sugar delivered by Martin Carney by order of Captain George at Fort Jefferson: to William McCauley of militia, one lb; to Zachariah Williams, a soldier in Worthington's Company, one lb; to John Grimshaw and Mr. Mullens of George's Company, two lbs; to Edward Murray a soldier in Captain Bailey's Company, two lbs (VSA-50: 24).

Captain Robert George's merchandise drawn out of the public store for which no returns or receipts have been issued or passed: eight yards white flannel (VSA-48: 93).

September 16, 1780/Saturday

Abraham Kellar and Robert George sign a request to the quartermaster for six lbs soap for 12 men of Kellar's Company (VSA-13; 50: 50).

Robert George requests Martin Carney issue one lb soap to William Clark out of the public store (VSA-13; 50: 50).

Jarret Williams requests Martin Carney issue one quart tafia for William's use (VSA-13).

John Bailey and Robert George sign a request to the quartermaster for two lbs sugar to four sick men of Bailey's Company (VSA-13; 50: 24).

Abraham Kellar and Robert George sign a request to Martin Carney for one lb sugar to Joseph Panther of Kellar's Company, as he is sick (VSA-13; 50: 24).

George Owens signs his mark and Robert George signs a request to Martin Carney to issue Peter Hellebrant, of Owens' Company, two lbs sugar (VSA-13; 50: 24).

Robert George requests the quartermaster issue 16 lbs gunpowder, 32 lbs lead, and six yards flannel to the artillery to make cartridges for the protection of this place (VSA-13).

Robert George requests the quartermaster issue two lbs sugar to Andrew Clark, artificer of public works (VSA-13) (VSA-50: 24).

Account of soap delivered by Martin Carney by order of Col. Montgomery and Captain George at Fort Jefferson, to Lt. Richard Clark, two lbs (VSA-50: 50).

September 17, 1780/Sunday
Lt. Richard Clark and Robert George sign a request to the quartermaster to issue Richard Clark two lbs soap (VSA-13).

September 18, 1780/Monday
Robert George requests Martin Carney issue five lbs sugar to Isaac Allen, John Cowen, Joseph Ross, Thomas Snarlock [Snellock], and William Bartholomew, all sick men of Captain Brashears' Company (VSA-13).

Account of sugar delivered Martin Carney by order of Captain George at Fort Jefferson: five men of Captain Brashears' Company, five lbs (VSA-50: 24).

Lt. Richard Clark and Robert George sign a request for one lb sugar to Andrew Johnson of Worthington's Company, who is sick (VSA-13; 50: 24).

Eleven blankets per receipt of Lawrence Slaughter and order of Lt. Col. Montgomery (VSA-48: 42).

Issued to Captain Abraham Kellar for his company per his receipt: 80 1/2 yards cloth; 69 yards white flannel; thread and buttons; three ruffled shirts; 24 plain shirts [35 3/4 yards linen for 11 shirts had been listed but was crossed out], and 11 shirts (VSA-48: 42).

September 19, 1780/Tuesday
John Montgomery signs instructions to John Dodge: purchase $10,000 worth of provisions for troops at Fort Jefferson. Mainly purchase flour, corn, salt and other necessities. Montgomery also wants furniture for Col. Clark, "he can't do well without them." Also purchase a quantity of blankets and shoes sufficient for the troops (VSA-13).

Robert George requests the quartermaster issue two lbs sugar to Mrs. Elms and her sick children (VSA-13).

Robert George requests the quartermaster issue two lbs sugar to John Daughterty and his two sick children (VSA-13; 50: 24).

Robert George requests the quartermaster issue three carots tobacco out of the public store, for George's use; three carots equals to nine pounds (VSA-13; 50: 13).

Robert George requests the quartermaster issue Edward Johnson of Worthington's Company, two lbs sugar (VSA-13).

Account of sugar delivered by Martin Carney by order of Captain George at Fort Jefferson, to Edward Johnston, one lb sugar (VSA-50: 25).

Robert George requests the quartermaster issue Matthew Jones' sick family, one lb sugar (VSA-13; 50: 24).

Reverse of order for sugar for Jones shows a partial list of: one captain, one Lt., zero ensign, two sergeants, two bowmen, one artificer, one sick in hospital, 83 rank and file, zero w. women, 92 in total (VSA-13).

Robert George requests the quartermaster issue William Crump of Worthington's Company, two lbs sugar, out of the public store (VSA-13; 50: 25).

Robert George requests the quartermaster issue Bredin and family, who have been sick, two lbs sugar out of the public store. Bredin is a member of Captain Worthington's Company (VSA-13; 50: 24).

Robert George requests John Dodge issue Sergeant Vaughan of Bailey's Company, 1/4 yd white cloth to face a coat. John Vaughan signed he received the material (VSA-13).

According to Richard Winston's letter to Robert Todd, Col. Montgomery left Kaskaskia to go to Fort Jefferson with Brooks and family, and Captain Brashears; Montgomery left with large quantities of provisions (boats deeply loaded), and five black slaves. Also, Captain Brashears has left the service, and married Brook's daughter (Seineke 1981: 463-465).

Account of tobacco delivered by Martin Carney by order of Captain George at Fort Jefferson: rotten and dried away, 14 pounds (VSA-50: 13).

Account of sugar delivered by Martin Carney by order of Captain George at Fort Jefferson, to Mr. Donne, Commissary, for his family, four lbs; to James Thomson, a soldier in Captain Kellar's Company, one lb; to Helms, a soldier, two lbs (VSA-50: 24-25).

Captain Robert George's merchandise drawn out of the public store for which no returns or receipts have been issued or passed: 1/4 yd white cloth per order (VSA-48: 93).

September 20, 1780/Wednesday

John Montgomery at Kaskaskia requests Mr. Kanadey [Kennedy], Conductor, to issue 50 lbs flour to five men going express to Fort Jefferson (VSA-13).

John Montgomery requests Mr. Kanaday [Kennedy] to issue 50 lbs flour and 50 lbs beef for the use of Col. Clark's negroes and other people just arriving from Fort Jefferson. Patrick Kennedy signed that the above was received (VSA-13).

Michael Hacketon deserts. He was a member of Captain George's Company (Harding 1981: 31).

Issued in the Indian Department, four shirts to Major Williams, Commandant at Cahokia per his order for the Potawatomi chiefs, 13 yards linen; issued to the friendly savages: three clasp knives and six pair scissors; paid Tourangean for pork and tafia, 35 livres peltry; paid the sheriff for corn and two corn fields for the use of the friendly savages who came to our assistance in time of danger, 554 dollars continental; 11 yards cloth say blue cloth; nine yards white flannel; 3 1/2 yards linen; one yd toile gris; 30 skeins thread; four carots of tobacco; 1 3/4 yards cloth; and one check handkerchief (VSA-48: 52; 116).

September 21, 1780/Thursday

Major Silas Harlan was rejected pay by the Commissioners for the period of March 27-September 21, saying he was not necessary and should not have been appointed because they already had Captain Owens. It is calculated that ferriage for two horses was eight quarts of corn per day. Major Harlan, had he been paid, would have received credit for 43 1/2 bushels for two horses over his term of service (VSA-13).

September 22, 1780/Friday
Montgomery writes George Rogers Clark regarding the attack on Fort Jefferson and poor conditions; settlers waiting to evacuate. Relief of Fort Jefferson from Kaskaskia with 10 white men and 65 Indians (GRC, I: cxlii; GRC, I 456-457).

Robert George requests John Dodge issue Silas Harlan seven yards linen and two skeins of thread. Silas Harlan signed he received the items (VSA-13).

Captain Robert George's merchandise drawn out of the public store for which no returns or receipts have been issued or passed: seven yards linen and two skeins thread per order (VSA-48: 93).

Lt. Col. John Montgomery plans to return to Fort Jeff with all his men except Captain Rogers (GRC, I: 456-7).

September 23, 1780/Saturday
Robert George requests the quartermaster issue one lb sugar to Francis Little, who is sick (VSA-13; 50: 25).

September 24, 1780/Sunday
Robert George requests John Dodge issue Major Harlan 5/8 yd of blue cloth for leggings. Silas Harlan signed he received the cloth (VSA-13).

Captain Robert George's merchandise drawn out of the public store for which no returns or receipts have been issued or passed: 5/8 yd blue cloth per order (VSA-48: 93).

Two men of Captain Rogers' Company have been sick, one has since died (VSA-13).

September 25, 1780/Monday
Richard Clark and Robert George sign a request to John Dodge to issue Lt. Clark five skeins thread for the use of Captain Worthington's Company. Richard Clark signed he received the within contents (VSA-13).

Overdrawn by Lt. Montbreuen: ten weight sugar and ten weight soap per order Lt. Col. Montgomery, six yards ferretting, one dressed deer skin, four sugar and two weight coffee (VSA-48: 32).

The interpreter is paid two yards blue cloth, five yards linen, and 4 1/4 yards camlet per receipt (VSA-48: 87).

The interpreter is paid 6 1/2 yards toile gris, one yd blue stroud, one yd white flannel, one scalping knife, two pair garters, two ivory combs, and four linen handkerchiefs for making a fish net for public use (VSA-48: 88).

The interpreter is paid six ells check, six lbs brown sugar, and six lbs peltry paid for transporting goods (VSA-48: 87).

Francis Bredin is paid 2 1/2 yards linen and four yards flannel for making six shirts (VSA-48: 88).

Mary Hunter is paid four yards flannel and one pair garters for doubling and twisting twine for a net for the garrison (VSA-48: 88).

M. Guire is paid 1 1/2 weight soap for thrashing corn (VSA-48: 88).

Richard Brashears is paid three yards white linen for making six shirts (VSA-48: 88).

Sixteen check handkerchiefs are issued for hay (VSA-48: 88).

One linen handkerchief is paid Joseph Thornton for two pair moccasins per his receipt (VSA-48: 88).

Two yards cottonade are paid Andrew Johnson for two dressed skins for moccasins for an express in time of danger (VSA-48: 88).

Martha Hughes is paid one paper pins for making a shirt (VSA-48: 88).

Martha Hughes is paid 1/2 yd linen and one linen handkerchief for dressing a wounded man (VSA-48: 88).

Twenty-one yards osnaburgs are issued to make bags (VSA-48: 88).

Ann Johnson is paid one linen handkerchief for a dressed deer skin for use of an express in time of an attack (VSA-48: 88).

Twenty yards linen paid for sinking a well in time of attack at Fort Jefferson (VSA-48: 88).

One rifle gun and wipers and seven yards linen are paid Daniel Graffen for a milk cow. These are included in another where the cattle are charged (VSA-48: 88).

One blanket and one shirt are issued John Ash, express, per order of Lt. Col. Montgomery (VSA-48: 107).

One pair blue stroud leggings and one breech cloth are paid Joseph Hunter for a sheep, per certificate of John Donne, Deputy Conductor (VSA-48: 107).

Gasper Butcher is paid 3 1/2 yards white flannel and five yards white linen per order of Col. Montgomery (VSA-48: 107).

Four pieces stroud are issued at 400 dollars (VSA-48: 107).

E. Johnson are paid five weight sugar paid for a funnel (VSA-48: 107).

Two bags to John Goyles to transport flour to Fort Jefferson per order of Captain Rogers. Sixteen bags, five files and 15 weight steel to John Goyles per order of Captain Rogers and sent to Fort Jefferson (VSA-48: 108).

Five bags, 15 brass kettles = 68 weight, seven large dressed deer skins, one cask sugar, and one case soap per receipt of Lt. Clark for use of the troops at Fort Jefferson (VSA-48: 108).

Eleven bags, 2 1/4 quarts delivered to the Commissary Department for the use of transporting provisions, and lost by the troops per receipt of John Donne (VSA-48: 108).

Paid William Taylor for making soldiers clothes, 2 1/2 yards linen (VSA-48: 108).

Paid William Taylor for making soldiers clothes, two yards linen and three skeins thread (VSA-48: 108).

One hundred nails paid for repairing a public boat per order Captain Brashears (VSA-48: 108).

2,820 weight flour and 327 12/40 bushels corn by Dodge issued on the orders of Sundry Commanding Officers and sent per receipt for the relief of Fort Jefferson from Kaskaskia (VSA-48: 109).

Account of soap delivered by Martin Carney by order of Col. Montgomery and Captain George at Fort Jefferson, to Sergeant Moore of Captain George's Company, 7 1/2 lbs (VSA-50: 50).

Captain Robert George's merchandise drawn out of the public store for which no returns or receipts have been issued or passed: five skeins thread per order (VSA-48: 93).

September 26, 1780/Tuesday

Robert George requests the quartermaster issue Sergeant Anderson one lb gunpowder and two lbs lead (VSA-13; 50: 10).

John Bailey and Robert George sign a request for one lb gunpowder and two lbs lead for two men of Bailey's Company that came from the Illinois (VSA-13; 50: 10).

Francis Bredin signs her mark she received 19 1/2 yards of linen to make shirts for the troops and six skeins of thread. F. Bredin acknowledged to have made six shirts and receive 1/2 yard linen and four yards flannel for making six shirts (VSA-13).

September 27, 1780/Wednesday

Richard Clark and Robert George sign a request to the quartermaster for 1/2 lb sugar out of the public store to Richard Underwood of Worthington's Company, who is sick (VSA-13).

Robert George requests Martin Carney issue one lb gunpowder and two lbs lead to two men of Captain Brashears' Co (VSA-13; 50: 10).

John Bailey and Robert George sign a request to the quartermaster for one lb sugar out of the public store, to two men of Bailey's Company who are sick (VSA-13; 50: 25).

Account of ammunition delivered by Martin Carney by Captain George's order: to a man of Captain George's Company, 1/4 lb gunpowder and 1/2 lb lead (VSA-50: 10).

Windsor Pipes is paid twelve yards white linen, two gallons of tafia, two check handkerchiefs, and 27 yards osnaburgs for 50 bushels Indian corn per receipt (VSA-48: 85).

September 28, 1780/Thursday

Abraham Kellar and Robert George sign a request for two lbs sugar for Kellar's own use (VSA-13).

Account of sugar delivered by Martin Carney by order of Captain George to one man of Captain Worthington's Company, 1/2 lb (VSA-50: 25).

Overdrawn by Captain Richard Brashears: one ivory comb, one horn comb, 3 1/2 gallons rum, eight weight sugar, four weight coffee, and six weight soap (VSA-48: 14).

William Robeson dies. He was a member of Worthington's Company (Harding 1981: 47 & 53).

John Swordin is discharged. He was a member of Worthington's Company (Harding 1981: 47, 53).

September 29, 1780/Friday
Sundry Articles overdrawn by Major John Williams above the clothing allowed him by law: eight weight coffee, six weight soap, and five weight sugar per order and receipt (VSA-48: 4).

September 30, 1780/Saturday
John Montgomery signs a provision return for two men for four days [30 September through 3 October] (VSA-13).

Robert George requests John Dodge issue four yards flannel to bury a soldier in, belonging to Captain Kellar's Company. Abraham Kellar signed he received the within contents (VSA-13).

Francis Bredin receives four yards flannel for work as a seamstress [See Sept. 15, 80] (VSA-13).

John Alison is paid thirty yards osnaburg for 25 bushels of corn (VSA-48: 85).

John Alison is paid two check handkerchiefs for carting 25 bushels of corn (VSA-48: 85).

John Gils is paid ten lbs soap per order of Captain Brashears (VSA-48: 43).

Captain Robert George's merchandise drawn out of the public store for which no returns or receipts have been issued or passed: four yards white flannel per order (VSA-48: 93).

Issued to Ensign Slaughter for Captain Bailey's Company by order of Col. Montgomery: two shirts (VSA-48: 42).

October, 1780/Miscellaneous
Sugar issued at Fort Jefferson by waste book by order of Robert George, 64 1/2 lbs (VSA-19; filed as May 2, 1781).

October 1, 1780/Sunday
John Montgomery requests John Dodge pay Ian Batist Lecroix for one pirogue purchased for hauling corn to Fort Jefferson from Kaskaskia. Lecroix signed he received 15 ells of linen in full of his demand from John Dodge (VSA-13).

Account of sugar delivered by Martin Carney by order of Captain George at Fort Jefferson: to Captain Kellar for his own use, two lbs; to Edward Murray, a soldier in Captain Bailey's Company, 1/2 lb (VSA-50: 25).

October 2, 1780/Monday
Robert George requests Martin Carney issue three men of George's Company, 3/4 lb gunpowder (VSA-13).

Abramham Kellar and Robert George sign a request to Martin Carney to issue Kellar 1/2 lb gunpowder and one lb lead for his journey to Cohos [Cahokia] (VSA-13; 50: 11).

Lt. Col. John Montgomery attests that the following provisions were delivered to different persons between September 2, 1779 and April 17, 1780: [Name not legible] 30 lbs pork, 28 lbs beef; to Joseph Hunter, 591 lbs flour and 152 bushels salt; to Micajah Mayfield, 439 lbs beef, 170 lbs meal, 670 lbs flour, 61 lbs pork; to an Indian, 228 lbs flour and 1/4 bushels salt; and to Mr. Shaw, 103 lbs flour and 70 lbs fresh beef. Total of 182 lbs Indian meal; 3,366 lbs flour; 187 lbs pork; 632 lbs fresh beef; seven lbs bears meat; one bushel peas; 21 and 26/32 bushels salt (VSA-13).

To Lt. Dalton 40 lbs flour, 16 lbs pork, "voyage to the post" Captain Leonard Helm 12 lbs meal, 80 lbs flour, 80 lbs pork, 95 lbs fresh beef, Lawrence

Slaughter 1,654 lbs flour "sent to Fort Patrick Henry, 6 1/2 bushels salt (VSA-13).

Account of ammunition delivered by Martin Carney by Captain George's orders: to Sergeant Hazard of Captain George's Company, 3/4 lb gunpowder and 1 1/2 lbs lead (VSA-50: 11).

Private Mark Foley deserts. He was a member of Captain Brashears' Company (Harding 1981: 51-52).

Sundry Articles overdrawn by Major Williams above the clothing allowed him by law: 5 1/2 quarts tafia (VSA-48: 4).

October 3, 1780/Tuesday

John Montgomery from Kaskaskia requests John Dodge issue 230 lb flour and two bags for the use of the troops at Fort Jefferson (VSA-13).

Henry Cruther is paid three India handkerchiefs, 1 1/2 ells camlet, five fine combs, six ells white linen, one romal handkerchief, and two check linen handkerchiefs for 37 bushels corn per receipt (VSA-48: 86).

John Holloway is paid thirty ells osnaburgs, 16 ells black calamanco, ten ells white linen, and five check linen handkerchiefs for 110 bushels of corn (VSA-48: 85).

John Holloway four paper pins and two ells camlet for 110 bushels of corn (VSA-48: 85).

Matross Lazurus Ryan is discharged from Captain Robert George's Co. of Artillery (Harding 1981: 30).

Sundry articles overdrawn by Major Williams above the clothing allowed him by law: 3 3/4 gallons rum (VSA-48: 4).

October 4, 1780/Wednesday

Robert George requests one lb gunpowder and two lbs lead for Joseph Thornton, Richard Bredin, and James Bryant of Worthington's Co. (VSA-13).

Account of ammunition delivered by Martin Carney by Captain George's orders: to three men of Captain Worthington's Company, 3/4 lb gunpowder and 1 1/2 lbs lead (VSA-50: 11).

Account of ammunition delivered by Martin Carney by order of Captain George: to Sergeant Pittman of Captain McCarty's Company, 1/2 lb gunpowder, one lb lead (VSA-50: 18).

Private James Brown is killed. He was a member of Worthington's Company (Harding 1981: 47).

Jacob Ditterin is listed as deceased. He was a member of George's Company (Harding 1981: 32).

Joseph Thornton is killed. He was a member of Worthington's Company (Harding 1981: 53).

October 5, 1780/Thursday

Pay Abstract for a Company of Militia commanded by Captain George Owens of the District of Clarksville states Ensign Edward Wilson was killed on this date (GRC, I: 464).

John Montgomery writes Oliver Pollack [Merchant in New Orleans] to tell him to pay Perrault $8940, 3 bitts and 3 quarters for all the goods delivered (VSA-13).

John Montgomery at Kaskaskia requests John Dodge to replace the 61 lbs flour borrowed from Thomas Kirk for the troops on their way from Fort Jefferson to Kaskaskia. Thomas Kirk signs his mark he received the replacement from John Dodge (VSA-13).

Account of ammunition delivered by Martin Carney by order of Captain George: to the militia at this place, five lbs gunpowder and ten lbs lead; to eight men of Captain George's Company, four lbs gunpowder and eight lbs lead (VSA-50: 18).

October 6, 1780/Friday

Col. John Bailey and Robert George sign a request to the quartermaster to issue Edward Murray 1/2 lb sugar (VSA-13).

John Bailey and Robert George sign a return to the quartermaster for 1/2 lb sugar for a sick man of Bailey's Co. (VSA-13).

Robert George requests the quartermaster issue Peter Wagoner of George's Company 1/2 lb sugar (VSA-13; 50: 26).

Major John Williams in Kaskaskia, requests John Dodge deliver to Sergeant W. Keeses for the use of Fort Jefferson, 121 bushels corn, 265 lbs flour, and three bags by order of Col. Montgomery (VSA-13). Sergeant Keeses deserted with the cargo (VSA-48: 109).

Account of sugar delivered by Martin Carney by order of Captain George at Fort Jefferson: to William Carr of Captain Bailey's Company, 1/2 lb (VSA-50: 25).

Account of soap delivered by Martin Carney by order of Col. Montgomery and Captain George at Fort Jefferson: to Lt. Dalton for his use, 5 1/2 lbs; to Captain Leonard Helm, for his own use, two lbs (VSA-50: 50).

October 7, 1780/Saturday

Robert George requests the quartermaster issue Lt. Dalton six lbs soap (VSA-13).

Leonard Helm, Superintendent of Indian Affairs, and Robert George sign a request to the quartermaster for two lbs sugar and two lbs soap for Helm's own use (VSA-13).

Private Jacob Decker dies. He was a member of Captain Kellar's Company (Harding 1981: 24).

October 9, 1780/Monday

John Bailey and Robert George sign a request to the quartermaster to issue Bailey eight lbs soap out of the public store (VSA-13; 50: 50).

Robert George requests the quartermaster issue George, 12 lbs soap out of the public store for George's own use (VSA-13; 50: 50).

One sick man of Captain Brashears' Company is issued 1/2 weight sugar (VSA-48: 110).

Account of soap delivered by Martin Carney by order of Col. Montgomery and Captain George at Fort Jefferson: to Mr. Donne, Commissary for his own use, four lbs; to Carney for his own use, eight lbs (VSA-50: 50).

Two shirts and three linen handkerchiefs issued by order Captain Rogers to Commissary Crutchfield per receipt (VSA-48: 110).

Paid Doctor Rey [Ray] two weight coffee and two weight sugar for the use of the sick (VSA-48: 110).

One weight sugar and 1/2 pound coffee to one sick man of Captain Worthington's (VSA-48: 110).

October 10, 1780/Tuesday

John Donne signs he received 496 lbs beef from Samuel Allen to be paid at current rate; given for all beef laid in by the public this fall and winter for the use of the troops (VSA-13).

John Montgomery at Fort Clark signs a request to [com]mandant at Fort Jefferson or whom it may [concern]: you are ordered to deliver to Mr. Bentley 73 lbs good gunpowder (VSA-13).

John Montgomery requests the quartermaster issue the within gunpowder to Mr. Israel Dodge on behalf of Bentley. Bentley received the within mentioned gunpowder from quartermaster Carney (VSA-13).

John Montgomery's letter addressed to all whom it may concern speaks of the troops at Fort Jefferson not having any provisions during June and July. Tells that a party of Kaskaskia Indians hunted and scouted about the garrison, because the troops were not able to and would have suffered if the Indians had not hunted. Most of Montgomery's men are at Cahokia, and are sick and could not give immediate relief, which is why he called upon the assistance of the Savages (VSA-48: 133).

John Crawley dies. He was a member of Kellar's Company (Harding 1981: 24).

Francis Villier is killed. He was a member of McCarty's Company (Harding 1981: 27).

October 11, 1780/Wednesday

Robert George requests the quartermaster issue six lbs soap out of the public store to Lt. Richard Clark (VSA-13; 50: 50).

Captain Robert George's sundry merchandise drawn out of the public store for which no returns or receipts have been issued or passed: six shirts per order. Robert George signs he received the six shirts (VSA-13; 48: 93).

Account of ammunition delivered by Martin Carney by order of Captain George: to Major Harlan of Militia for his own use, 1/4 lb gunpowder and 1/2 lb lead; to John Ash, a soldier in Captain George's Company, 1/4 lb gunpowder and 1/2 lb lead (VSA-50: 18).

October 12, 1780/Thursday

Thomas Jefferson in Richmond, writes George Rogers Clark in Louisville: some provisions [clothing] at Fort Pitt have become available; Major Moore at Fort Pitt will deliver them to Maj. Slaughter at the Falls (GRC, I: 459).

Charles Charleville writes he sold one large pirogue to Col. Montgomery for the use of transporting corn from Fort Clark to Fort Jefferson and was paid 128 livres (VSA-13).

Robert George requests the quartermaster issue to Francis Little one lb soap (VSA-13).

Robert George requests Martin Carney issue John Ash one lb soap (VSA-13).

John Bailey and Robert George certify that Mrs. Johnes [E. Jones] made five shirts for the use of Bailey's Co., and is to be paid in goods from the Public Store. Mrs. Johnes [Jones] signs she received three yards flannel for making the shirts from Israel Dodge (VSA-13).

October 13, 1780/Friday
Robert George requests the quartermaster issue Ensign Jarret Williams four lbs soap out of the public store (VSA-13; 50: 50).

Leonard Helm, Superintendent of Indian Affairs, and Robert George sign a request to the quartermaster to issue six lbs soap for Helm's use (VSA-13; 50: 50).

Robert George requests John Dodge issue John Hazzard of George's Company, one yd flannel to line a waistcoat. John Hazzard signed he received the flannel (VSA-13).

Captain Robert George's merchandise drawn out of the public store for which no returns or receipts have been issued or passed: one yard flannel per order (VSA-48: 93).

October 14, 1780/Saturday
Robert George requests John Dodge issue Samuel Allen 12 yards flannel and six skeins thread for 496 lbs beef delivered by Allen to the Commissary. Samuel Allen signed he received the within contents out of the public store in part of pay for said beef (VSA-13).

Account of ammunition delivered by Martin Carney by order of Captain George: to Sergeant Allen of Captain Brashears' company, 1 1/2 lbs gunpowder and three lbs lead (VSA-50: 18).

Captain Robert George's merchandise drawn out of the public store for which no returns or receipts have been issued or passed: 12 yards flannel and six skeins thread per order (VSA-48: 93).

Private Francis Hardin dies. He was a member of Captain Bailey's Company (Harding 1981: 46).

Matross Philip Long, Gunner William Poston, and Sergeant John Riley desert. They were members of Captain George's Co. (Harding 1981: 29-30).

October 15, 1780/Sunday
John Bailey and Robert George sign a request to John Dodge to issue Levi Theel and John Clark of Bailey's Co., cloth and trimmings for a suit of clothes each, to which they are entitled by law for enlisting three years. Levi Theel and John Clark sign they received seven yards blue cloth, six yards flannel, 12 skeins thread, and 10 dozen buttons (VSA-13).

Captain Robert George's merchandise drawn out of the public store for which no returns or receipts have been issued or passed: seven yards blue cloth, six yards flannel, and 12 skeins thread per order (VSA-48: 94).

Private George Hois deserts. He was a member of Captain Kellar's Company (Harding 1981: 23).

October 16, 1780/Monday
Account of ammunition delivered by Martin Carney by order of Captain George: to Frank Little of Captain George's Company, 1/4 lb gunpowder and 1/2 lb lead; to Sergeant Elms of Captain Brashears' Company, 1/2 lb gunpowder and one lb lead (VSA-50: 18).

Private John Clark deserts. He was a member of Captain Kellar's Company (Harding 1981: 46).

October 17, 1780/Tuesday
John Montgomery writes the Treasury of the State of Virginia and tells them to pay $2,000 to John Rogers for provisions supplied the troops at Fort Jefferson.

John Dodge signs he received the $2,000 from John Rogers to purchase provisions for the troops (VSA-13).

Private James Davies dies. He was a member of Captain Kellar's Co. (Harding 1981: 24).

October 18, 1780/Wednesday

Lt. Col. John Montgomery certifies he was with John Dodge and witnessed the accidental drowning of a brown horse while the troops were crossing the Ohio on their trip from Fort Jefferson to Kaskaskia (VSA-13).

John Montgomery at Kaskaskia requests John Dodge issue 200 lbs flour and 1/2 barrack of tafia for the use of the troops at Fort Jefferson. John Montgomery signed he received the goods from John Dodge (VSA-13).

John Montgomery, at Kaskaskia, requests John Dodge issue two bags for the transporting flour for the use of the troops at Fort Jefferson (VSA-13).

Two bags are issued to transport flour to Fort Jefferson per order of Lt. Col. Montgomery (VSA-48: 110).

Account of ammunition delivered by Martin Carney by order of Captain George: to two men of Captain Bailey's Company, 1 1/2 lbs gunpowder and one lb lead (VSA-50: 18).

October 19, 1780/Thursday

Account of ammunition delivered by Martin Carney by order of Captain George: to Sergeant Moore of Captain George's Company, 2 1/2 lbs gunpowder and five lbs lead (VSA-50: 18).

Overdrawn by Ensign Slaughter: one comb, one knife, ten weight sugar, three weight coffee, six lbs soap, one deer skin, and one bottle rum. Per order of Lt. Col. Montgomery, one ink holder, ten weight sugar, and 10 weight soap in error (VSA-48: 26).

Thirty-seven bushels corn sent to Fort Jefferson per receipt of John Donne, Deputy Conductor (VSA-48: 109).

Sometime after this date, the following were issued: one dressed deer skin and five weight soap, for Captain Kellar's Company; (some of these issues were probably made at Kaskaskia); one lb soap and one pair moccasins, for one man of Captain Bailey's Company; two dressed deer skins for Captain Kellar's Company; two lbs sugar and 1/2 coffee, delivered to two sick of Captain Brashears' Company; two lbs soap to David Glen, express; three lbs soap to three men of Captain George's Company; three weight sugar to David Wallis; two weight soap to one man of Captain Brashears' Company; four weight sugar to four sick of Captain Brashears' Company; five weight soap to James Wiley for liquor for the fatigue; one weight soap for one of Captain Kellar's Company; two dressed deer skins for Captain George's Company; five dressed deer skins for Captain Brashears' Company; two weight coffee and four weight sugar for two sick of Captain Kellar's Company; one pint tafia, one weight sugar, and 1/2 weight coffee for a sick man of Captain Bailey's Company; three weight sugar and 1 1/2 weight coffee for three sick of Captain Brashears' Company; three weight sugar and 3/4 weight coffee for three sick of Captain Brashears' Company; two dressed skins, 20 weight sugar, and 10 weight coffee for Captain Worthington's Company (VSA-48: 111).

Sometime after this date, the following were issued (some of these issues were probably made at Kaskaskia): one pair mockisons and one weight soap for Brashears' Company; 20 weight sugar and nine weight lead to Patrick McClosky for use of the hospital; paid Dr. Ichabod Camp for medicines for the light horse men per account; John Rogers Commander, 332 livres in peltry; paid Dr. Ichabod Camp two check handkerchiefs for a pickle cask; paid Dan Murray two check handkerchiefs, one horn comb, and four skeins thread for writing paper; paid Ichabod Camp 11 yards linnen and three yards chintz for making an Indian coat, 30 bags, and 20 shirts; paid Nicholas Smith 7 1/2 bushels corn for carting public goods; paid Sergeant Meriwither one qt tafia for assisting to load a boat; one qt tafia to two of Captain George's Company per order; five gallons tafia for use of Captain Rogers' Company; 1 1/2 weight coffee and one weight sugar to Captain Brashears for his Company per his order; three weight sugar and 1 1/2 coffee to the hospital per order Doctor Rey; one bottle tafia and one lb sugar for Brashears' Company; one bottle tafia for Captain Kellar's Company (VSA-48: 112).

Sometime after this date, the following were issued (some of these issues were probably made at Kaskaskia): 2 1/2 gallons and 1 1/2 pints tafia replaced to Thomas Hutchins; one qt tafia for men on fatigue; paid Major Bosron 1018 livres peltry for sundries for use of the savages and troops per his account and receipt; ten bags and 20 ells osnaburg issued to the commissary per order Major Williams, Commander; two bags and four ells osnaburg issued per order Major Williams, Commander for public use; 224 weight flour, two bags, and four ells osnaburg sent by Giles to Fort Jefferson by order of Captain John Rogers, Commandant; 2 1/2 yards toile gris, 1 1/4 yards calender, one yd coarse white linen, one skein thread, one English blanket, and one scalping knife issued to Israel Dodge in lieu of sundry articles lost by him in the Ohio March 27, 1780 when accompanying Joseph Lindsay Esquire on public business; 125 weight pork issued per receipt Major Williams, 125 livres peltry; 149 weight tobacco delivered Martin Carney, quartermaster for use of the troops per his receipt (VSA-48: 113).

Sometime after this date, the following were issued (some of these issues were probably made at Kaskaskia): to cash paid Ezekiel Johnson for sundry articles delivered to quartermaster Carney for the use of Fort Jefferson per receipt livres 13.17 hard money and 3040 continental dollars; paid sundry inhabitants at Kaskaskia for 5438 weight flour and 535 bushels corn, not yet delivered and whose obligations Dodge has delivered to Mr. Donne, Deputy Conductor, per his receipt; 519 weight lead, 17 1/2 bushels salt, and one pickle cask, 30 continental dollars, delivered to Patrick Kennedy, per his receipt; three yards toile gris, one skein fine thread, five yards osnaburg, and one stick twist paid John Donne for assisting in public business with the accounts while hurried; four bags and eight ells osnaburg delivered to Deputy Conductor Donne per his receipt; 25 yards white flannel, one weight twine, 12 skeins thread, two paper pins, four skeins thread, one yd linen, one yd blue cloth paid John Donne for assisting in adjusting public accounts; paid the sheriff 800 continental dollars for a cow sold at auction per receipt (VSA-48: 114).

Sometime after this date, the following were issued (some may have been issued at Kaskasia): delivered John Dodge for sundry articles taken with him to bear his expenses while on public business: 12 yards calamanco, 3 3/4 yards camblet, 11 check handkerchiefs, three check handkerchiefs George Slaughter, ten papers of pins, three papers George Slaughter; four razors; three horse phlegms; seven snaffle bridles; two paper ink holders, 9/12 dozen coarse horn combs, seven fine combs, two bolts gartering; four weight coarse thread (VSA-48: 115).

Sometime after this date, the following were issued (some of these issues may have been made at Kaskaskia): for sundry articles delivered to Israel Dodge, Deputy Agent, for the use of the troops: one piece blue cloth, three remnants blue cloth, 64 yards, and two remnants white cloth, 2 3/4 yards--good; eight remnants blue cloth, 95 1/2 yards and one remnant grey cloth, 4 1/2 yards--damaged; five peices flannel; three remnants five yards flannel; nine pieces linen; eight remnants linen containing 50 yards; one remnant fine linen, 82 yards, damaged; nine remnants linen, 158 1/2 yards, damaged; 20 3/4 yards toile gris; two yards brown holland, damaged; 8 1/2 yards osnaburg; eight papers of pins; 30 weight thread; 35 weight twine; two boxes brass buttons; 131 dozen Captain buttons; 30 looking glasses; 30 yards tinsel lace; 208 gunworms; 23 yards camblet; 1 1/2 yd calamanco; 3/4 yd camblet; four check handkerchiefs; two combs; two clasp knives; and six plain shirts (VSA-48: 117).

Sometime after this date, the following were issued (some of the issues may have been made at Kaskaskia): 3 1/3 dozen mohair buttons; two pair knee garters; one brass cork; three pair drawers; six yards toile gris; one large chest; six yards black calomancoe paid for a table for public use; one large chest for Col. Clark to contain public papers, 401 continental dollars; 400 continental dollars advanced Captain Bailey for the recruiting service; paid Ezekiel Johnston 2000 continental dollars for one horse drowned in the Ohio by the soldiers; six quire writing paper used in the Agent's office; one pair steelyards bought of Mark Ker and delivered to John Donne for use of the Commissary Department, eight dollars; 225 weight flour at 50 livres peltry, one cask at 24 livres peltry, and 96 weight salt pork at two livres peltry, 13 1/2 yards oznabrig made into hunting shirts for use of our friendly Indian Chiefs; 20 weight thread issued at sundry times for public use; 400 needles issued to the shirt makers-three dollars; 240 skeins silk issued to the officers and soldiers for their clothing; two boxes wafers used for public use, five dollars; 41 dozen metal buttons issued to the officers for their clothing at nine reals per dozen (VSA-48: 118).

Sometime after this date, the following were issued (some of the issues may have been made at Kaskaskia): 35 1/2 ells holland used for stocks for the troops; 57 3/4 ells muslin, brittanies, cambric and lawn for ruffling; six check handkerchiefs, two yards check, and 18 livres peltry issued to Captain Worthington and 3 3/4 fine white thread issued for making shirts for the troops (VSA-48: 119).

Sometime after this date, the following were issued: by a cross cut saw, per receipt Martin Carney, Deputy quartermaster; received per receipt John Donne, Deputy Conductor, 5,013 buffalo beef, 745 venison, and 58 bear meat; by one piece ribbon, chargeable to John Dodge; by an error in 482 1/2 ells linen, 12.05 dollars (VSA-48: 137).

October 20, 1780/Friday
Account of ammunition delivered by Martin Carney by order of Captain George: to Bryan a soldier in Captain Worthington's Company, 1/4 lb gunpowder and 1/2 lb lead; to four men of Captain Bailey's Company, one lb gunpowder and two lbs lead (VSA-50: 18).

Private James Thompson dies. He was a member of Captain Kellar's Company (Harding 1981: 24).

Matross Peter Wagoner dies. He was a member of Captain George's Company (Harding 1981: 30 & 32).

October 22, 1780/Sunday
Account of soap delivered by Martin Carney by order Captain George at Fort Jefferson: to John Ash, a soldier in Captain George's Company, one lb; to Frank Little, a soldier in Captain George's Company, one lb (VSA-50: 50).

October 23, 1780/Monday
Captain John Williams arrives at Fort Jefferson by order of Lt. Col. John Montgomery to take command of the fort (GRC, I: 463); however Captain George refuses to relinquish command without authorization from Col. Clark (see George to Clark letter, Oct. 28, 1780).

Robert George requests John Dodge issue the following men of George's Co., cloth and trimmings for a suit of clothes each, and linen for two shirts for William Pursley (VSA-13):

1. John Andrewson
2. Matthew Murray
3. William Fevers
4. James Ramsey
5. Patrick Marr
6. John Gilbert
7. Patrick Rogers
8. Francis Little
9. William Pursley

Robert George signed he received 31 1/2 yards cloth, 27 yards flannel, 58 skeins thread, 45 dozen buttons, 6 1/2 yards linen for the nine men (VSA-13).

October 24, 1780/Tuesday

Joshua Archer, John Johnson, James Perzzell, and Joseph Hunter sign a document stating that the beans and other goods grown in Thomas Phelps corn field are worth half the amount of the corn raised in the same field (Draper Manuscripts 1M8; VSA-20).

Zephaniah Blackford writes to Valentine T. Dalton that he received 3,228 1/2 lb of beef [$33 1/3 per lb], 943 lb dried beef [$66 2/3 per lb], 25 quarts salt [$6 per 1/4 quart] (VSA-13).

Zephaniah Blackford signs that the goods were delivered but no pay has been received. John Montgomery writes to Oliver Pollack to pay Valentine T. Dalton $1,860 1/6 for the provisions (VSA-13).

John Montgomery writes from Fort Jefferson requesting Valentine T. Dalton be paid 188 silver dollars for the following account (VSA-13): for 10 gal tafia at four silver dollars per gal [$40], for one deer skin [$1], for one horse and cart for 26 days at $1 per day [26], for 30 days on haul with horse at $1/2 per day [$15], for horse hired for 30 days on express [$15], for hire of three horses for 35 days at $1/2 per day [$52 1/2], for making four [set?] of colors for Indian chief [$4], for hire of a horse [$30], for candles [$5]. Total $188 1/2. All at Fort Patrick Henry. Valentine T. Dalton signed he received the above list of goods at New Orleans (VSA-13).

John Montgomery requests the Treasurer of Virginia give $1,760 to Jarret Williams for recruiting service. Jarret Williams signed he received of Col. Montgomery $1,760 in full (VSA-13).

Ensign Slaughter signed he received $400 from Col. Montgomery for recruiting services (VSA-13).

John Montgomery requests the quartermaster issue Montgomery ten lbs gunpowder for his use on his trip to New Orleans (VSA-13; 50: 15).

John Montgomery requests Israel Dodge to issue Lt. Dalton four yards linen for a hunting shirt and charge it to Dalton's account. Valentine T. Dalton signed he received the linen (VSA-13).

John Montgomery [Commandant of the Western Department in Col. Clark's absence] requests Israel Dodge to pay $108 out of the public store for an order given by John Dodge (VSA-13).

Mrs. Hannah Dalton requests $325 [one silver dollar per day] for her services as Indian Interpreter for the Wabash district. John Montgomery requests Oliver Pollock pay her. Valentine T. Dalton signs he received the within in full at New Orleans (VSA-13).

Mr. Valentine T. Dalton wants $650 [$2/day] for his services as Agent for Indian Affairs of the Wabash district. John Montgomery requests Oliver Pollock to pay him. Dalton signs he received the within in full at New Orleans (VSA-13).

Richard Winston at Kaskaskia writes the following letter to Robert Todd. Mr. Lindsay took goods from New Orleans and gave them to Captain Dodge at Fort Jefferson; Col. Montgomery left Kaskaskia to go to Fort Jefferson on 19 September with Brooks, and family, and Captain Brashears; Montgomery left with large quantities of provisions (boats deeply loaded) and five black slaves. Also, Captain Brashears has left the service, he married Brook's daughter; de Blame had been at Kaskaskia before leaving on an expedition against Detroit (Seineke 1981: 463-465).

Account of ammunition delivered by Martin Carney by order of Captain George: to Lt. Dalton for his journey to New Orleans, one lb gunpowder and ten lbs lead (VSA-50: 18).

October 25, 1780/Wednesday
Abramham Kellar, at Fort Jefferson, received $1,000 from John Montgomery for recruiting services. John Donne attests (VSA-13).

Abraham Kellar and Robert George sign a request to Martin Carney to issue two lbs soap for Kellar's own use (VSA-13; 50: 50).

Lt. Col. John Montgomery requests Oliver Pollack and the Treasurer of Virginia to repay Abraham Kellar $2,000 that was earlier borrowed from him by Montgomery, for public purposes (VSA-13).

Private John Allen deserts. He was a member of Captain Kellar's Company (Harding 1981: 24).

Private John Johnston moves away from Fort Jefferson. He was a member of Captain Owens' Company of Militia (GRC, I: 465; Harding 1981: 49).

Sundry articles overdrawn by Captain John Rogers: seven lbs sugar per order and receipt (VSA-48: 8).

October 26, 1780/Thursday
Robert George requests Captain Dodge pay Francis Bredin 25 shillings or the value in merchandise for making two suits for soldiers in Captain McCarty's Co. (VSA-13).

Montgomery requests the quartermaster issue a quantity of gunpowder to Israel Dodge. John Dodge signs that Israel Dodge received 73 lbs gunpowder [on Thomas Bentley's account] from Martin Carney (VSA-13; 50: 15).

Private David Shaffer deserts. He was a member of Captain Bailey's Company (Harding 1981: 46).

October 27, 1780/Friday
Israel Dodge receives the following items from John Dodge at Fort Jefferson (VSA 13): one piece blue cloth, three remnants cloth, 64 yards; 2 remants worsted cloth, 2 3/4 yards; eight remants blue cloth, 95 1/2 yards, 1 remnant grey cloth 4 1/2 yds; fives pieces flannel; 1 cherry table; three remnants flannel, 39 yds; nine pieces linen, 72 yards; nine remnants linen, 158 1/2 yards damaged; 20 3/4 yards toil gris; two yards brown holland; 8 1/2 yards oznaburg; eight papers pin; 30 lbs thread; 10 bunches twine; two boxes brass buttons; 30 looking glasses; 30 yards tinsel lace; 208 gun worms; 23 yards camblet; and 6 plain shirts.

Letter from Captain Robert George at Fort Jefferson to Captain John Rogers. George wants Rogers to assist Lt. Clark in sending a boat of provisions and men to Fort Jefferson, as they are in great distress. The boat at Fort Jefferson is on dry ground and they are not able to put any in the river (Draper Manuscripts 50J72; GRC, I: 462-463; Seineke 1981: 465).

Richard Brashears and Robert George sign a request for two skeins of thread to Micajah Mayfield to be used to mend his clothes (VSA-13).

Robert George requests Captain Dodge to issue Samuel Allen 1/2 yd stroud in part of pay for beef delivered to the commissary. He has already received 12 yards flannel out of the public store from William Clark. Allen signed he received the stroud from Israel Dodge (VSA-13).

Account of ammunition delivered by Martin Carney by order of Captain George: to Ensign Slaughter's own use, 1/2 lb gunpowder and one lb lead; to Captain Abraham Kellar for his own use, two lbs lead (VSA-50: 18).

Robert George writes a letter to George Rogers Clark that Valentine T. Dalton might go down river with Montgomery (GRC, I: 461-463; Seineke 1981: 465-466).

October 28, 1780/Saturday

Captain Robert George at Fort Jefferson writes to George Rogers Clark at the Falls of Ohio and tells him that the fort is being reduced to a very small garrison by famine, desertion and dying. There is a very small quantity of provisions. Mentions Montgomery stopping by on his way to Orleans and tells them that Dodge has purchased 1,000 bushels of corn and 10,000 lbs of flour. George is expecting provisions from New Orleans via Pollack any day. Majority of Inhabitants went down river. Those who remain are in a distressed state. Williams and Montgomery arrived and wanted to assume command but George refused until he receives further orders from Clark. Harlan is out hunting and in need of horses (GRC, I: 461-462; Seineke 1981: 465-466).

Captain John Williams writes from Fort Jefferson to George Rogers Clark. Williams arrived at Fort Jefferson on Oct. 23, 1780 by order of Col. John Montgomery to take command. He was formerly at Cohos [Cahokia] and in command there. He mentions a lack of food caused by low water preventing delivery; informs Clark that he did not take command from Robert George due to circumstances. He will await the arrival of George Rogers Clark (GRC, I: 463).

Robert George signs that he gave Dan Crump 10 cartridges for the use of a two lb swivel belonging to the blockhouse on the hill (VSA-13).

John Montgomery requests Martin Carney to send by the first boat going to Kaskaskia, 50 lbs gun gunpowder to Captain Rogers for the use of his command stationed there. Richard Clark signs he received 20 lbs gunpowder of from Martin Carney (VSA-13).

Account of ammunition delivered by Martin Carney by Col. Montgomery's orders: to Captain Rogers for the use of his men by Lt. Clark, 20 lbs gunpowder and 12 lbs lead (VSA-50: 15).

Account of ammunition delivered by Martin Carney by order of Captain George: to Sergeant Vaughan of Captain Bailey's Company, 1/4 lb gunpowder and 1/2 lb lead; to Anderson going express to the Falls of Ohio, 1 1/4 lbs gunpowder and three lbs lead (VSA-50: 18).

Articles purchased by Martin Carney for the State of Virginia by order of Col. Clark: purchased of the Widow Hughes, hard money price to one iron pick for keeping the hand mills in order, value 1/2 pound; purchased this same date of Archibold Lockard at the same price, value 1/2 pound (VSA-50: 2).

John Donne attests that Abraham Kellar received $1,000 from John Montgomery for recruiting work (VSA-13).

October 29, 1780/Sunday

Letter from Leonard Helm at Fort Jefferson to George Slaughter. Helm tells that he is sitting by Captain George's fire eating buffalo ribs. He congratulates Slaughter on his success against the Shawnees, and sends his compliments to Mrs. Slaughter (GRC, I: 466).

October 31, 1780/Tuesday

Account of ammunition delivered by Martin Carney by order of Captain George: to Captain John Williams, one lb gunpowder and two lbs lead; to Israel Dodge, Deputy Agent, 1/2 lb gunpowder and one lb lead (VSA-50: 18).

November 1, 1780/Wednesday
Matross William Moore deserts. He was a member of George's Company (Harding 1981: 29-30).

November 2, 1780/Thursday
John Bailey and Robert George sign request to Captain Dodge to issue Robert Whitehead two yards damaged cloth for a blanket and Nicholas Burt cloth with trimmings for a suit of clothes. Both men are of Bailey's Company, enlisted for three years (VSA-14).

John Bailey signs he received 3 1/2 yards good cloth, three yards flannel, five dozen buttons and six skeins of thread, and two yards damaged cloth from John Dodge (VSA-14).

Account of ammunition delivered by Martin Carney by order of Captain George: to Mr. Sherlock for the use of the Kaskaskia Indians, 80 lbs gunpowder and 89 lbs lead; to Captain Helm for his own use, two lbs gunpowder and two lbs lead; to three men of Captain Brashears' Company, 1 1/2 lbs gunpowder and three lbs lead (VSA-50: 18).

Richard Harrison dies. He was a member of Captain Richard Brashears' Company (Harding 1981: 51).

November 3, 1780/Friday
Robert George requests Mr. Dodge issue Mr. Sherlock, 1 1/2 yards cloth for leggings and flap in order he may go hunting with the Indians, and one yd flannel for swivel cartridges. James Sherlock signed he received 1 1/2 yards cloth and one yd flannel from Israel Dodge (VSA-14).

Account of ammunition delivered by Martin Carney by order of Captain George: to one man of Captain Brashears' Company, 1/2 lb gunpowder and one lb lead (VSA-50: 18).

Paid Frogget for thrashing per receipt, two gallons tafia and four lbs sugar (VSA-48: 87).

Thirty-two lbs twine issued for making a fish net for use of the garrison at Fort Jefferson (VSA-48: 87).

November 5, 1780/Sunday
Robert George requests Israel Dodge issue to Silas Harlan 13 yards linen, four yards. flannel, 3/4 yd cloth, and five skeins thread out of the public store. Silas Harlan signs he received 13 yards linen, four yards flannel, 3/4 yd cloth and six skeins of thread from Israel Dodge (VSA-14).

Robert George requests Israel Dodge issue Captain George Owens 3 1/2 yards linen, and four yards flannel for a hunting shirt as he had undertaken to hunt for this garrison. George Owens signs his mark he received 3 1/2 yards linen and four yards flannel from Israel Dodge (VSA-14).

Account of Ammunition delivered by Martin Carney by order of Captain George: to Simon Burney in lieu of 380 lbs of beef, six lbs gunpowder; to Major Harlan for hunting, one lb gunpowder and two lbs lead (VSA-50: 18).

November 6, 1780/Monday
Account of ammunition delivered by Martin Carney by order of Captain George: to two men of Captain George's Company, one lb gunpowder and two lbs lead (VSA-50: 18).

November 8, 1780/Wednesday
Robert George requests Israel Dodge issue Mr. Williams enough white cloth for a pair of leggings and a flap out of the public store. Jarret Williams signed he received the cloth from Israel Dodge (VSA-14).

Robert George requests Mr. Dodge issue John McGarr of George's Company four skeins of thread out of the public store. John McGarr signed his mark he received the thread from Israel Dodge (VSA-14).

Account of soap delivered by Martin Carney by order of Col. Montgomery and Captain George at Fort Jefferson: to Mr. John Garr, a soldier in Captain George's Company, one lb; to Joseph Thornton, artificer for public works, two lbs (VSA-50: 50-51).

November 9, 1780/Thursday
Richard Brashears and Robert George sign a request to John Dodge for Thomas Snellock of Brashears' Company, who is going with Major Harlan hunting, one pair of leggings. Thomas Snellock signed he received the leggings from Israel Dodge (VSA-14).

Richard Clark signs he received of John Dodge 126 3/4 bushels and three pecks corn at 40 quarts per bu, 600 lbs flour with five bags, 68 lbs brass kettles, 15 in number, seven large dressed deer skins, one cask sugar, one case soap, all for the use of the troops at Fort Jefferson. John Dodge signs that the within mentioned kettles were purchased from Mr. Bartley (VSA-14).

James Snellock and John Dodge sign a document stating John Oiler has died. His rifle gun was valued at $800 and it is being held the sheriff of Clarksville. Attested by Leonard Helm and Joseph Hunter (VSA-14).

Silas Harlan [Sheriff], signs he received the above bond and assigned it to Captain James Piggot. James Piggot signs he received from John Dodge 2 1/2 yards blue cloth and one yd flannel which is in full of Piggot's demand and obligation. John Donne signed that John Dodge paid for one milk cow for the use of the troops which was slaughtered at time of need (VSA-14).

Account of ammunition delivered by Martin Carney by order of Captain George: to two men of Captain Bailey's Company, one lb gunpowder and two lbs lead; to two men of Captain Brashears' Company, one lb gunpowder and two lbs lead; to two men of Captain Kellar's Company, one lb gunpowder and two lbs lead (VSA-50: 18-19).

Private Daniel Williams dies. He was a member of Captain Worthington's Company (Harding 1981: 47).

November 10, 1780/Friday
Robert George requests Israel Dodge issue Boston Demore of his company, one pair leggings out of the public store. Boston Demore signs his mark that he received 1/2 yd and half quarter blue cloth (VSA-14).

Captain Benjamin Roberts and George Slaughter sign a request for provisions for 35 men and two washwomen of Captain Roberts' Company, for four days beginning the 10th and ending the 13th (VSA-14).

November 11, 1780/Saturday
Abraham Kellar and Robert George request Israel Dodge issue Philip Doodle, David Russel, and Joseph Panter of Kellar's Company, six yards damaged cloth for blankets. Abraham Kellar signs he received the cloth from Israel Dodge (VSA-14).

Robert George requests Israel Dodge pay John Grimshaw 45 shillings in hard money or merchandise for making three suits of clothes for the troops. John Grimshaw signed he received nine yards white flannel in full of his demands from Israel Dodge (VSA-14).

November 12, 1780/Sunday
Jon Allin deserts. He was a member of Captain Brashears' Company (Harding 1981: 51).

James Morris dies. He was a member of Brashears' Company (Harding 1981: 51).

November 13, 1780/Monday
Robert George requests the quartermaster issue 11 lbs sugar from the public store to John Wilson (VSA-14).

Sugar received at Fort Jefferson from John Dodge per Lt. Richard Clark, one case (VSA-19).

November 14, 1780/Tuesday
Abraham Kellar and Robert George sign a request to Israel Dodge to issue Elizabeth Jones the fair price for making one suit of clothes. Elizabeth Jones signs her mark she received three yards white flannel in full of her demand (VSA-14).

Account of sugar delivered by Martin Carney by orders of Captain George: to three men carrying the sugar, three lbs (VSA-50: 26).

November 15, 1780/Wednesday
Robert George requests the quartermaster issue three brass kettles from the public store for George's own use. George signed he received the kettles (weighing 12 lbs) from Martin Carney (VSA-14; 50: 49).

Ensign Slaughter and Robert George sign a request to the quartermaster to issue a woman of Bailey's Company, one lb sugar for her sick child (VSA-14).

Robert George requests the quartermaster issue one brass kettle out of the public store to John Harry, armourer. John Harris signed he received the kettle from Martin Carney (VSA-14; 50: 49).

John Williams and Robert George sign a request of Martin Carney to issue one kettle and two hatchets for the use of Williams' mess. John Williams signed he received one brass kettle and two hatchets from Martin Carney (VSA-14).

Account of sugar delivered by Martin Carney by orders of Captain George: to Nelly Lewis, a soldiers widow, one lb; to five sick men of Captain Bailey's Company, five lbs; to 11 sick men of Captain George's Company, 11 lbs; to a sick woman of Captain Bailey's company, one lb (VSA-50: 26).

Account of brass kettles delivered by Martin Carney by order of Captain George at Fort Jefferson: to Ensign Lawrence Slaughter for Captain Bailey's Company, two kettles; to Captain Richard Brashears, one kettle; to Captain Leonard Helm for his use, one kettle; to Captain Abraham Kellar and Company, two kettles; to Major John Williams for his use, one kettle; to Lt. Richard Clark for Captain Worthington's Company, two kettles; for Carney's own use, one kettle (VSA-50: 49).

Reference to letter from Lt. Col. Montgomery to Robert George advising George to purchase Barbours cargo. Montgomery met Barbour while Montgomery was enroute to New Orleans (GRC, I: 314).

November 16, 1780/Thursday
Robert George requests Israel Dodge issue John Bryan, tailor, pay out of the public store, for making two suits of clothes for soldiers of George's Company. John O'Brion signs his mark he received three yards linen from Israel Dodge (VSA-14).

Account of sugar delivered by Martin Carney by orders of Captain George: to a sick man of Captain Worthington's Company, one lb; to Joseph Thornton, artificer, two lbs (VSA-50: 26).

November 17, 1780/Friday
Account of sugar delivered by Martin Carney by orders of Captain George: to Andrew Johnston and family of Captain Worthingtons, 1 1/2 lbs; to a soldier of Captain Bailey's Company, one lb; to two men of Captain Brashears' Company, two lbs; to a sick woman and child of Captain Brashears' Company, two lbs (VSA-50: 26).

November 18, 1780/Saturday
Account of sugar delivered by Martin Carney by orders of Captain George: to George Owens, Captain of Militia, three lbs; to Captain Kellar for his own use, two lbs (VSA-50: 26).

Account of soap delivered by Martin Carney by order of Captain George at Fort Jefferson, to Mr. Blackford, commissary, three lbs (VSA-50: 51).

Account of soap delivered by Martin Carney by order of Captain George at Fort Jefferson, to eight men of Captain Worthington's Company, eight lbs; to Sergeant Morgan for Captain George's Company, 15 lbs (VSA-50: 52).

November 19, 1780/Sunday
Account of ammunition delivered by Martin Carney by order of Captain George: to four men of Captain Kellar's Company, one lb gunpowder, two lbs lead (VSA-50: 19).

Account of sugar delivered by Martin Carney by orders of Captain George: to John Burks, a sick militia man, one lb (VSA-50: 26).

Account of soap delivered by Martin Carney by order of Captain George at Fort Jefferson, to Captain Bailey's Company, 12 lbs; to Captain Brashears' Company, 4 1/2 lbs; to Captain McCarty's Company, 1 1/2 lbs (VSA-50: 52).

Matross's Pat McAuley, James McDonell, and John O'Bryan desert. They were members of Captain George's Company (Harding 1981: 29-30).

Matross Richard Turpin dies. He was a member of Captain George's Company (Harding 1981: 29-30).

November 20, 1780/Monday
Account of sugar delivered by Martin Carney by order of Captain George: to three men of Captain George's Company, three lbs; to two men of Captain George's Company, two lbs; to a sick woman and child of Captain Worthington's, one lb; to Col. Clark's negro, sick, one lb (VSA-50: 26).

Privates Francis Benoit, John Lamarine, Alexis larishardie, Peter Pepin, Joseph Plant, and John Saintive desert. They were members of McCarty's Company (Harding 1981: 27).

November 21, 1780/Tuesday
Account of ammunition delivered by Martin Carney by order of Captain George: to Major Harlan for hunting, 2 1/4 lbs gunpowder and 4 1/2 lbs lead (VSA-50: 19).

Account of sugar delivered by Martin Carney by orders of Captain George: to Mr. Phelps, for his sick family [individual voucher for sugar issue to Phelps mentions family being six in number], two lbs; to Mrs. Hughes, a widow of militia, two lbs; to Carney for his use, six lbs; to John Wilson, Captain Worthington's servant, one lb (VSA-50: 26).

November 22, 1780/Wednesday
John Allen's status was changed from deserted to killed (VSA-14).

Account of ammunition delivered by Martin Carney by order of Captain George: to eight men going hunting with Harlan, three lbs gunpowder and six lbs lead (VSA-50: 19).

Account of soap delivered by Martin Carney by order of Captain George at Fort Jefferson, to Captain Abraham Kellar's Company, six lbs (VSA-50: 52).

November 23, 1780/Thursday
John Bailey and Robert George sign a request to the agent to pay Francis Bredin three yards flannel for making a suit of clothes for a man in Bailey's Company. Sergeant John Vaughan signed he received the flannel from Israel Dodge (VSA-14).

Robert George requests Israel Dodge issue 1 1/4 yards cloth to Joseph Hunter for helping transport provisions from Kaskaskia to Fort Jefferson. Joseph Hunter signed he received the cloth from Israel Dodge (VSA-14).

John Bailey and Robert George sign a request to Israel Dodge to issue John Vaughan two yards damaged cloth for making a blanket. John Vaughan signed he received the cloth contents from Israel Dodge (VSA-14).

John Donne signs he received meat from the Kaskaskia savages; 5,013 lb buffalo beef, 745 lbs venison 58 lbs bear meat, for the use of the troops at Fort Jefferson. John Dodge signs the meat was killed by the Savages while scouting about the garrison (VSA-14).

Account of sugar delivered by Martin Carney by orders of Captain George: to Captain George's mess, three lbs; to a soldier of Worthington's, one lb (VSA-50: 26).

Account of soap delivered by Martin Carney by order of Captain George at Fort Jefferson: to Major Harlan for his own use, three lbs; to James Sherlock, Interpreter for his use, six lbs (VSA-50: 52).

November 25, 1780/Saturday
John Bailey and Robert George sign a request to Israel Dodge by order of Col. Clark, to issue four skeins thread to Levi Theel of Bailey's Company, enlisted for three years. George Shephard signed he received four skeins of thread from Israel Dodge (VSA-14).

Account of sugar delivered by Martin Carney by orders of Captain George: to a sick woman of Captain George's Company, one lb; to Joshua Archer of militia, one lb (VSA-50: 26-27).

November 26, 1780/Sunday
Robert George requests Mr. Dodge [Deputy Agent] issue Martin Carney 3 1/4 yards linen out of the public store, for a hunting shirt. Carney signed he received the linen from Israel Dodge (VSA-14).

Account of sugar delivered by Martin Carney by orders of Captain George: to Mr. Donne, Commissary, six lbs (VSA-50: 27).

Account of ammunition delivered by Martin Carney by order of Captain Robert George at Fort Jefferson: to Jesse Piner for two dressed dear skins for the use of the soldiers at this post, 1 1/4 lbs gunpowder, two lbs lead; to Mr. William Clark, for his use, one lb gunpowder; to Mr. Archer, a militia man, one lb gunpowder (VSA-50: 29).

November 27, 1780/Monday
Robert George requests Mr. Dodge pay to Mrs. Murray for making eight shirts for Captain Kellar's Company. Mary Murray signs her mark she received four yards white flannel from Israel Dodge (VSA-14).

Account of sugar delivered by Martin Carney by orders of Captain George: to Mr. Lunsford and family, sick, five lbs; to the widow Meredith's family sick, three lbs (VSA-50: 27).

Account of soap delivered by Martin Carney by order of Captain George at Fort Jefferson: to Mr. Donne, Commissary, six lbs; to Mr. Israel Dodge, six lbs (VSA-50: 52).

November 28, 1780/Tuesday
Robert George requests Israel Dodge issue James Sherlock linen for one shirt, toile gris for a pair of trousers, blue cloth for a pair of leggings and flap. He has been hunting with the Indians for meat. James Sherlock, Indian Interpreter, signed he received 3 1/2 yards linen, 2 1/2 yards toil greys, and 1 1/2 yards cloth from Israel Dodge (VSA-14).

Account of sugar delivered by Martin Carney by orders of Captain George, to Captain Bailey and Mr. Slaughter, 12 lbs (VSA-50: 27).

November 29, 1780/Wednesday
John Bailey and Robert George sign a request to Israel Dodge to issue 1/4 and 1/2 quarter lining for Bailey's own use. Nicholas Burk signs his mark he received the line from Israel Dodge (VSA-14).

Account of sugar delivered by Martin Carney by orders of Captain George: to Mr. Israel Dodge, Deputy Agent, four lbs; to Joseph Hunters family, two lbs; to Captain Brashears for his use, six lbs; to Major Williams for his own use, six lbs (VSA-50: 28).

Account of ammunition delivered by Martin Carney by order of Captain Robert George at Fort Jefferson: to Mr. Donne, Commissary man, one lb gunpowder and three lbs lead; to Lt. Richard Clark, 1/2 lb gunpowder and one lb lead; to two men of Captain Bailey's Company, 1/2 lb gunpowder and one lb lead; to eleven men going on command to the Illinois, 2 3/4 lbs gunpowder and 5 1/2 lbs lead (VSA-50: 29).

Account of soap delivered by Martin Carney by order of Captain George at Fort Jefferson, to Captain Brashears for his own use, six lbs; to Major Williams for his own use, six lbs (VSA-50: 52).

Stores issued by order of Captain Robert George, to Lt. Richard Clark, three tomahawks (VSA-50: 40).

Patrick Marr enlists for three years by Lt. Valentine T. Dalton into Captain Robert George's Company of Artillery (MHS: B1, F23).

November 30, 1780/Thursday
John Todd, Jr., in Lexington, writes Thomas Jefferson that he has heard of a cargo of goods that arrived at Fort Jefferson from Mr. Pollack (GRC, I: 466-467; VSA-14).

Robert George requests Mr. Dodge issue enough thread to make four suits soldiers clothes for Captain George's Company. Matthew Sohas signs his mark he received 12 skeins thread from Israel Dodge (VSA-14).

Account of sugar delivered by Martin Carney by order of Captain George at Fort Jefferson: to a woman and two children of Worthington's Company, two lbs; to Captain Abraham Kellar for his use, two lbs (VSA-50: 28).

Private William enlists on this date in Captain John Bailey's Company of the Illinois Regiment in the Virginia State Service (Harding 1981: 45-46).

December, 1780/Miscellaneous
Sugar issued at Fort Jefferson by Waste Book by order of Captain Robert George, 137 lbs (VSA-19).

December 1, 1780/Friday
John Dodge and John Donne sign [Joseph Hunter attests], that they will see that the sheriff of Clarksville, his successor, or their assigns be paid $554 Continental currency within six months of this date for the debt owed by the deceased John Oiler (VSA-14).

James Piggot signs he received nine yards flannel and nine skeins thread (VSA-14).

John Donne certifies that John Dodge paid money for corn, cornfields and sundry other merchandise for the use of the Savages (VSA-14).

Lt. Richard Clark and Robert George sign a request to the quartermaster to issue Clark, 10 lbs sugar for Clark's own use out of the public store (VSA-14).

Account of sugar delivered by Martin Carney by order of Captain George at Fort Jefferson: to Lt. Richard Clark for his use, six lbs; to Captain Leonard Helm for his use, six lbs; to Mr. Harris, armourer at this place, two lbs; to Ensign Williams and Major Harlan, 12 lbs (VSA-50: 28).

Stores issued by order of Captain Robert George: to Captain Brashears' Company, two tomahawks (VSA-50: 40).

December 2, 1780/Saturday
Robert George requests Israel Dodge to pay Mary McAuley out of the public store for making six soldier shirts for George's Company. Mary McAuley signs her mark she received from Israel Dodge, three yards white flannel in full of her demand for making six shirts (VSA-14).

Stores issued by order of Captain Robert George: to Captain Helm, one tomahawk (VSA-50: 40).

December 3, 1780/Sunday
Silas Harlan and Robert George sign a request to Israel Dodge to issue John McGarr, eight yards of linen for hunting with Harlan for one month. John McGar signs hīs "mark" he received the eight yards of linen from Israel Dodge (VSA-14).

John Dodge [from Kaskaskia], certifies that the State of Virginia is indebted to an Indian one stroud blanket for coming express from Fort Jefferson on public business (VSA-14).

John Bailey and Robert George sign a request to Israel Dodge to issue Levi Theel of Bailey's Company, two yards damaged blue cloth for enlisting for three years. Levi Theel signed he received the blue cloth (VSA-14).

Account of soap delivered by Martin Carney by order of Captain George at Fort Jefferson, to John Hazzard of Captain George's Company, one lb (VSA-50: 52).

Issued to Captain John Rogers for his company, one check handkerchief to Sergeant Merriwether per order (VSA-48: 44).

December 4, 1780/Monday
Lt. Richard Clark and Robert George sign a request to Israel Dodge to issue two yards flannel for Clark's use. Richard Clark signed he received the two yards of flannel from Israel Dodge (VSA-14).

Robert George requests Martin Carney to issue four lbs gunpowder and eight lbs lead to Major Harlan and his hunting party as they are going to hunt meat for Fort Jefferson. Reverse is signed by Captain Leonard Helm in favor of Major Harlan (VSA-14; 50: 29).

Account of ammunition delivered by Martin Carney by order of Captain Robert George at Fort Jefferson: to the soldiers going with Major Harlan, two lbs gunpowder and four lbs lead (VSA-50: 29).

Account of soap delivered by Martin Carney by order of Captain George at Fort Jefferson, to Captain Helm for his use, six lbs (VSA-50: 52).

Stores issued by order of Captain Robert George: to Captain McCarty's Company, one tomahawk (VSA-50: 40).

December 5, 1780/Tuesday

Robert George requests the quartermaster issue two lbs gunpowder and four lbs lead for the party going with Major Harlan, because yesterday's draw was insufficient (VSA-14; 50: 29).

Letter from John Donne at Fort Jefferson to George Rogers Clark. Donne writes to inform Clark of the situation at Fort Jefferson. Donne talks of attack made by Indians on August 27 and tells that three of Captain George's men left after the attack for the Falls. Tells that the most useful inhabitants have deserted, being struck with panic. The Indians destroyed the cornfields and anything that they could. All that remains of the settlers are those who are sick and weak. The remains of the cornfields were appraised for use by the troops. A small part of the corn was stored. Donne speaks of Mr. Harlan hunting for meat at the beginning of last month [November]. He tells that Harlan had brought in 14 and 15,000 weight, and the Kaskaskia Indians had brought 3,000 weight and 1,000 weight to the fort. He also tells that 8,000 weight was eaten last month [November]. Captain Rogers has been ordered from Illinois to reinforce Fort Jefferson and will add 1,000 weight to the monthly issue. Donne believes Captain George has done all in his power to issue the provisions with frugality to the inhabitants. Supplies come from the Illinois. John Dodge has been there for some time. The greatest difficulty is transporting provisions from the Illinois to Fort Jefferson. The trip takes about 15 to 20 days. Dodge fears there will be a revolt in the Illinois. Mr. Blackford arrived after Clark's departure and will be attending to the issues in Donne's absence. Donne suggests that Col. Montgomery might have done more to save Fort Jefferson. Donne hopes to return to Fort Jefferson before Major Harlan departs for the Falls (MHS: B1, F23).

Account of soap delivered by Martin Carney by order of Captain George at Fort Jefferson: to a man of Captain McCarty's Company, 1/2 lb [manuscript torn]; to a man of Captain George's Company, one lb (VSA-50: 52).

December 6, 1780/Wednesday

Account of soap delivered by Martin Carney by order of Captain George at Fort Jefferson: to Mr. Harris, armourer at this place, two lbs (VSA-50: 52).

December 7, 1780/Thursday

John Montgomery at Fort Jefferson orders the quartermaster to issue John Ash one gill tafia for every man belonging to the garrison. Reverse states: "Number of soldiers belonging to the out posts and garrison to draw liquor, seventy-eight quarts and six gills" (VSA-14).

Robert George requests Israel Dodge to issue and charge Mr. William Clark for four yards osnaburg for a hunting shirt. William Clark signed he received the osnaburg from Israel Dodge (VSA-14).

Captain Abraham Kellar and Robert George sign a request to Israel Dodge to pay Mrs. Frances Bredin out of the public store for making four soldier coats for

Kellar's Company. Francis Bredin "marks" she received from Israel Dodge eight yards white flannel in full of her demands for making the coats (VSA-14).

Robert George requests Israel Dodge issue two ounces thread fit to make a pair of leather breeches to Zephaniah Blackford and charge it to his account. Blackford signed he received six skeins of thread from Israel Dodge (VSA-14).

Letter from Captain Richard Harrison at the Falls to Col. Clark in Richmond. Harrison is planning to leave on the 9th to go to Fort Jefferson; he is taking all his artillery and "her stores." He mentions that Captain Shannon is taking a quantity of corn with him. Harrison hopes that Fort Jefferson will soon be relieved. He also mentions that Captain Barbour is expected to bring a very large cargo. Harrison states that Captain Worthington is at Harrodsburgh and feels he has no intention of going to Fort Jefferson during the winter. Harrison hopes to return to the Falls in February (GRC, I: 468-469).

Account of ammunition delivered by Martin Carney by order of Captain Robert George at Fort Jefferson: to one man of Captain John Bailey's Company, 1/4 lb gunpowder and 1/2 lb lead; to two men of Captain John Bailey's Company, 1/2 lb gunpowder and two lbs lead (VSA-50: 29).

Account of soap delivered by Martin Carney by order of Captain George at Fort Jefferson, to Ensign Slaughter for his use, six lbs (VSA-50: 52).

Stores issued by order of Captain Robert George: to Captain George, one sword (VSA-50: 40).

Stores issued by order of Captain Robert George: to Captain Kellar, one axe (VSA-50: 37).

December 8, 1780/Friday

Letter from George Slaughter in Louisville to Thomas Jefferson in Virginia. Slaughter has enclosed letters from Captains George and Williams at Fort Jefferson for Clark, and also a letter by Leonard Helm. Helm will tell of the situation of the officers. Slaughter tells that he has ordered the remains of the country store for the use of the State. He also tells that many complaints have been made against Captain Dodge due to his "shameful misapplication of the Goods in his care" (GRC, I: 472).

December 9, 1780/Saturday

Robert George requests Israel Dodge pay John Anderson out of the public store for making one suit of clothes for a soldier of George's Company. John Anderson signed he received three yards flannel and a skein of thread in full of Anderson's demands for making a suit of clothes from Israel Dodge (VSA-14).

Sergeant John Giles signs his "mark" he received of John Dodge the following: 150 lbs flour, 45 bushels corn at 40 quarts per bushel, and 16 bags. The corn and flour are for the use of the troops at Fort Jefferson. The bags are to be returned to Giles. Five files and 15 lbs steel are received by Giles for the use of the armourer (VSA-14).

Robert George requests Israel Dodge pay Elizabeth Jones for making four suits of soldiers clothes for George's Company. Elizabeth Jones signs her "mark" she received of Israel Dodge, six yards white linen which is in full of her demands for making four suits of clothes (VSA-14).

John Montgomery requests Captain Owens make out a general return of men intending to stay and one of those who are planning to leave from Fort Jefferson. Montgomery also requests any man who can be spared from duty to help bring in corn from the fields (VSA-14).

Stores issued by order of Captain Robert George: to Captain Brashears' Company, two tomahawks (VSA-50: 37).

December 10, 1780/Sunday
George Slaughter at the Falls of Ohio writes a letter to George Rogers Clark in Richmond telling him that he is forwarding letters from the Mouth of Ohio, which will provide Clark with a full account of the affairs of the whole country (MHS: B1, F23).

Account of soap delivered by Martin Carney by order of Captain George at Fort Jefferson: to Captain George for his use, 15 lbs; to Negro Ceaser, artificer, 1 1/2 lbs; to Mr. William Clark, six lbs; to Ensign Williams, six lbs; to Carney, quartermaster, six lbs; dried away and wasted, 13 lbs (VSA-50: 52).

Robert George signs a return for men enlisted by Lt. Valentine T. Dalton for the artillery service from November 18, 1779 to December 10, 1780 for the term of three years or during the war:

1. Jeremiah Horn	November 18, 1779
2. Thomas Laney	November 29, 1779
3. Patrick Marr	November 29, 1779
4.x Samuel Coffy	November 29, 1779
5. John Anderson	November 29, 1779
6. Benjamin Lewis	December 11, 1779
7. Thomas Bolton	January 1, 1780
8. Paul Quibea	January 10, 1780
9. James McDonald	January 31, 1780
10.x Patt MCulty	March 10, 1780
11. Andrew Conore	March 20, 1780
12. John Hazard	March 28, 1780
13.x Francis Puccan	April 12, 1780
14.x John Bowden	April 20, 1780
15. Jacob Ditterin	June 13, 1780
16. Anthony Montroy	June 18, 1780
17.x James Mulboy	July 10, 1780
18.x Joseph Lonion	December 10, 1780

The above six men marked with x's are not included in George's pay roll because Lt. Dalton neglected to give an account of what had become of them or when and how their time expired (MHS: B1, F23).

December 11, 1780/Monday
William Shannon at Louisville writes a letter to Thomas Jefferson. Shannon speaks of the distressed situation at Fort Jefferson and many who have deserted because of it. Shannon is expecting a boat to come down river daily, and he intends to purchase flour which he will send to Fort Jefferson; he has already sent corn and salt (GRC, I: 473-474).

December 12, 1780/Tuesday
Martin Carney attests to a memorandum of weights and stores brought to Fort Jefferson from New Orleans: one Spanish musket and bayonette, one cartridge box and bayonette belt, one arms chest, one belt chest, and one large trunk. Also a list of articles brought by Captain Barbour as public store property: 12 cases of arms or chests, 120 stand muskets, three cases of cartridge boxes and belts, one trunk of cartridge boxes and belts, 261 cartridge boxes, 422 bayonette belts, 300 lbs of damaged gungunpowder, 14 oil cloths or Spanish tents and an eight lb bar of steel (VSA-14).

Account of ammunition received by Martin Carney at this post Clarksville: received of Captain Philip Barbour, 472 lbs gunpowder 300 lbs damaged gunpowder (VSA-50: 5).

Account of arms received by Martin Carney in this Department, the property of the Commonwealth of Virginia: received of Captain Barbour, 120 muskets with bayonets and belts (VSA-50: 16).

December 13, 1780/Wednesday
William Clark, Secretary, requests the quartermaster send him one quart rum (VSA-14).

December 14, 1780/Thursday
Matross Richard Hopkins and Gunner Lawrence Keinan [Keenan] desert from Captain Robert George's Company of Artillery (Harding 1981: 30).

December 15, 1780/Friday
Israel Dodge writes that the following merchandise was received of Robert George for the use of the troops in the Illinois Department belonging to the State of Virginia. Robert George certified that the following is a true copy of the invoice delivered to Israel Dodge: one bail of cloth in different colors; 16 3/4 ells brown cloth; 15 3/4 ells brown cloth; 14 1/4 ells blue cloth; 18 ells pompedore; one piece of linen, 36 1/2 ells; two pieces of linen, 50 1/2 ells; four lbs vermillion; 29 1/2 ells white flannel; eight bunches of thread; 17 pounds of thread in different colors; 34 skeins silk; 24 dozen large buttons; 24 dozen small buttons; four dozen large buttons; 5 1/2 dozen small buttons; 104 skeins mohair; 105 pair shoes; 15 ells of topsail duck; 18 small bags; 53 bunches of capwire; one brass ink stand; 16 [illeg.] needles; four papers of pins; one [illeg.] pin (VSA-14).

Statement in which Captain George had an inventory of a quantity of tafia delivered to Martin Carney and another for a quantity of broad cloth with a receipt signed by Israel Dodge. It was witnessed by Captain John Bailey and Leondard Helm (GRC, II: 315).

December 17, 1780/Sunday
Letter from Col. John Gibson at Fort Pitt to George Rogers Clark at Louisville. Gibson had been asked to deliver a quantity of clothing to Captain Moore for the use of the troops on the Ohio. Gibson says he cannot comply with the order because his men are "quite naked" (GRC, I: 474).

December 18, 1780/Monday
Silas Harlan and Robert George sign a request to Israel Dodge to issue Thomas Snellock, Nicholas Tuttle, and Thomas Hays eight yards linen each for 31 days of assistance to Harlan on a hunting trip for Fort Jefferson. Thomas Snellock, Nicholas Tuttle, and Thomas Hays signed they received the material from Israel Dodge (VSA-14).

Account of ammunition delivered by Martin Carney by order of Captain Robert George at Fort Jefferson: to Captain Bailey, 1/2 lb gunpowder and one lb lead (VSA-50: 29).

December 19, 1780/Tuesday
Abraham Kellar and Robert George sign a request to Israel Dodge to issue Mrs. Nancy Hunter pay for making a coat, two waistcoats, and a pair of overalls for Kellar's Company. Nancy Hunter signs her "mark" she received 3 3/4 yards white flannel in full of her demands for the within order (VSA-14).

Robert George requests Israel Dodge issue Silas Harlan cloth and trimmings for one suit of clothes, one pair of shoes, cloth for a capote, and linen for two shirts. Silas Harlan signs he received 3 1/2 yards superfine broad cloth, two dozen and seven large buttons, two dozen and four small buttons, one skein of mohair, two yards broad cloth for the capote, one pair of shoes, six yards linen, and two yards flannel from Israel Dodge (VSA-14).

Account of ammunition delivered by Martin Carney by orders of Captain Robert George at Fort Jefferson: to Abraham Taylor, militia man, 1/4 lb gunpowder and 1/2 lb lead (VSA-50: 29).

December 20, 1780/Wednesday

Israel Dodge requests Martin Carney issue one gallon "spirits" for Dodge's own use (VSA-14).

Robert George requests the agent issue Captain Benjamin Roberts his full quota clothing as allowed by law (VSA-14).

John Dodge signs that 4 1/2 yards of cotton sacque, and 2 1/2 yards of scarlet calamanco, were taken out of the public store to bear Dodge's expenses (VSA-14).

Account of ammunition expended by the artillery at sundry times by order of Captain Robert George, Commandant at Fort Jefferson: at Captain Harrison and Captain Roberts' arrival from the Falls of Ohio per verbal orders, six lbs gunpowder, two lbs lead, and one yd flannel (VSA-50: 33).

December 21, 1780/Thursday

Pay abstract of a Company of Militia commanded by Captain George Owens of the District of Clarksville in the State of Virginia. Service ended on this date for Captain George Owens, Sergeant John Wilson, and Sergeant Joseph Hunter (GRC, I: 464-465).

Captain Richard Brashears and Robert George sign a request to Israel Dodge to issue eight pair of shoes to eight men in Brashears' Company. Richard Brashears signed he received the shoes from Israel Dodge (VSA-14).

Richard Brashears and Robert George sign a request to Israel Dodge to issue two shirts each to 13 men of Brashears' Company. Richard Brashears signs that he received 84 1/2 yards linen agreeable to the within order from Israel Dodge (VSA-14).

Robert George requests Israel Dodge issue 40 pair of shoes for men in Captain George's Company. Richard Harrison signed he received the shoes from Israel Dodge for Captain George's Company (VSA-14).

Abraham Kellar and Robert George sign a request to Israel Dodge to issue 11 pairs of shoes for 11 men in Kellar's Company. Abraham Kellar signed he received the shoes from Israel Dodge (VSA-14).

Robert George requests Israel Dodge issue two shirts each for 40 men of George's Company for the ensuing year. Richard Harrison signed he received 260 yards linen for the use of Captain Robert George's Company of Artillery from Israel Dodge within order (VSA-14).

Abraham Kellar and Robert George sign a request to Israel Dodge to issue enough linen to make two shirts each for 11 men of Captain Kellar's Company for the ensuing year. Abraham Kellar signed he received 71 1/2 yards linen from Israel Dodge for the use of Kellar's Company (VSA-14).

Robert George requests Israel Dodge issue 3/4 yd cloth to Major Harlan for a waistcoat. Silas Harlan signed he received the material from Israel Dodge (VSA-14).

December 22, 1780/Friday

John Williams and Robert George sign a request to the quartermaster for three lbs loaf sugar (VSA-14).

Silas Harlan and Robert George sign a request to the quartermaster for Abraham Taylor, Hugh Montgomery, John Levrig, and John Wilson, 1/2 lb gunpowder and one lb lead for each man (VSA-14).

Stores issued by order of Captain Robert George: to Captain Benjamin Roberts, two tents or oil cloths (VSA-50: 39).

December 23, 1780/Saturday
William Shannon and George Slaughter sign a request to the Treasurer of the State of Virginia to pay Mr. George Wilson 2,500 pounds, being for sundries furnished the Illinois Department (VSA-14).

Abraham Kellar and Robert George sign a request to Israel Dodge to issue thread for making two shirts each for seven men of Kellar's Company. Kellar signed he received 22 skeins of thread from Israel Dodge (VSA-14).

Robert George requests two bags for Captain Benjamin Roberts to carry necessities to Col. Slaughter at the Falls of Ohio. Benjamin Roberts signed he received the bags from Israel Dodge (VSA-14).

Robert George requests the quartermaster issue Maj. Silas Harlan one barrel rum, three lbs coffee, and six lbs sugar. Silas Harlan signed he received the contents from Martin Carney (VSA-14).

Robert George requests Mr. Dodge to issue Captain Roberts the use of the troops, and to Col. Slaughter at the Falls of Ohio: 157 3/4 yards linen, 23 1/2 yards fine linen, eight yards toile gris, two yards flannel, six skeins colored thread, 46 skeins white thread, and two papers of pins (VSA-14).

Robert George requests Israel Dodge issue Captain Roberts, 1 1/2 yards blue cloth, two yards course flannel, four skeins thread, and one skein silk thread. Benjamin Roberts signed he received the items from Israel Dodge (VSA-14).

Robert George requests Mr. Dodge issue Captain Roberts three dozen coat buttons and three dozen small buttons. Benjamin Roberts signed he received the buttons (VSA-14).

Account of ammunition delivered by Martin Carney by order of Captain Robert George at Fort Jefferson: to four militia men, two lbs gunpowder and four lbs lead (VSA-50: 29).

December 24, 1780/Sunday
Letter from Robert George at Fort Jefferson to George Rogers Clark. George states he has received letters from Oliver Pollock and Col. Montgomery. He says that the greatest part of a cargo sent to Clark for the use of the State was lost in a hurricane. The remainder of Captain Barbour's goods were purchased as a result. Captain Harrison informed George that it is Clark's intent to evacuate Fort Jefferson and erect another fortification at the Iron Banks. George states that his "yellow locks" will turn gray if Clark does not arrive soon to clarify his intentions. George also states that Captain Helm is of infinite service and comfort to George at Fort Jefferson (MHS: B1, F23; Seineke 1981: 468-469).

Robert George requests Israel Dodge issue William Freeman of George's Company, one full suit of clothes which he is entitled to for having enlisted during the present war. William Freeman signed his "mark" he received the clothes from Israel Dodge (VSA-14).

John Bailey and Robert George sign a request to Israel Dodge to issue linen to make two shirts each for 25 men of Captain Bailey's Company for the ensuing year. John Bailey signed he received from Israel Dodge, 162 1/2 yards linen (VSA-14).

Account of ammunition delivered by Martin Carney by order of Captain Robert George at Fort Jefferson: to Captain Benjamin Roberts, 24 flints (VSA-50: 31).

December 25, 1780/Monday
Account of ammunition delivered by Martin Carney by order of Captain Robert George at Fort Jefferson: to Captain Bailey's Company, six lbs gunpowder and 12 lbs lead (VSA-50: 29).

Account of ammunition expended by the artillery at sundry times by order of Captain Robert George, Commandant at Fort Jefferson: by five swivels and one four pounder both in town and garrison, per verbal orders, 60 lbs gunpowder, seven lbs lead, and six yards flannel (VSA-50: 33).

Joshua Archer should be paid ten shillings and four pence for buffalo and bear meat furnished Captain George's troops (GRC, II: 334).

Pay Abstract of a Company of Militia commanded by Captain George Owens of the District of Clarksville in the State of Virginia. Privates John Burk, Joshua Archer, George Phelps, Anthony Phelps, Peter Hellebrant, John McCormack, Robert Craten, and William Reid end their service on this date (GRC, I: 464-465).

December 26, 1780/Tuesday
Robert George requests John Dodge issue Captain Richard Harrison sky blue cloth and good trimmings for a coat, and pompedore broad cloth for facing and edging. Richard Harrison signs he received from Israel Dodge 1 1/2 yards sky blue cloth, 38 large buttons, six small buttons, two skeins mohair, one skein silk, two yards white flannel, 3/4 yd linen, 1/8 yd pompedore, and one skein white thread (VSA-14).

Abraham Kellar and Robert George sign a request to Israel Dodge to pay William Pritchet for making four suits of clothes for Kellar's Company. William Pritchet signed he received six yards toile gris from Israel Dodge (VSA-14).

Matross Jeremiah Horn dies. He was a member of Captain Robert George's Company (Harding 1981: 29-30, 32).

December 27, 1780/Wednesday
Richard Brashears and Robert George sign a request to Israel Dodge to issue 12 needles to John Boiles for making clothes. John Boiles signs his "mark" he received the 12 needles from Israel Dodge (VSA-14).

Robert George requests Mr. Dodge to issue Ensign Slaughter a set of buttons and mohair to make a suit of clothes. Slaughter signed he received from Israel Dodge, two dozen and eleven large buttons, 2 1/2 dozen small buttons, and three skeins of mohair (VSA-14).

Account of ammunition delivered by Martin Carney by order of Captain Robert George at Fort Jefferson: to Captain George's Company, ten lbs gunpowder and 20 lbs lead (VSA-50: 31).

December 28, 1780/Thursday
Account of ammunition delivered by Martin Carney by order of Captain Robert George at Fort Jefferson: to Ensign Williams and his hunting party, 22 flints; to Captain George's Company, 28 men, two flints each, equals 56 flints (VSA-50: 31).

Stores issued by order of Captain Robert George: to three men of Captain Worthington's Company, one rifle and two muskets (VSA-50: 37).

December 29, 1780/Friday
William Clark and Robert George sign a request for one lb sugar for Clark's own use (VSA-14).

John Bailey and Robert George sign a request for two yards flannel for Bailey's own use. Bailey signed he received from Dodge, the two yards of flannel (VSA-14).

Account of ammunition delivered by Martin Carney by order of Captain Robert George at Fort Jefferson: to Captain Brashears' Company, 20 flints; to Captain Worthington's Company, 32 flints; and to Captain Bailey's Company, 36 flints (VSA-50: 31).

Stores issued by order of Captain Robert George: to two men of Captain Bailey's Company, two muskets (VSA-50: 37).

December 30, 1780/Saturday

John Bailey and Robert George sign a return for one kettle for Captain Bailey's Company (VSA-14; 50: 37).

Account of ammunition delivered by Martin Carney by order of Captain Robert George at Fort Jefferson: to two men of Captain Brashears' Company, one lb gunpowder and two lbs lead; to Captain Roberts, [of Col. Slaughter's Company, 100 lbs gunpowder and 200 lbs lead had been written but was crossed out]; to Captain Brashears, one lb gunpowder and four lbs lead; to two men of Captain Rogers' Company, 1/2 lb gunpowder and one lb lead; and to Captain Harrison's, four lbs gunpowder and eight lbs lead (VSA-50: 30).

December 31, 1780/Sunday

Robert George requests Mr. Dodge to issue Phillip Orbin of George's Company, a coat, waistcoat, and pair of overalls for enlisting for three years. Orbin signed his "mark" he received the clothing from Israel Dodge (VSA-14).

Martin Carney signs he received from Israel Dodge, three yards super fine broad cloth to complete an order given John Dodge to deliver to Martin Carney (VSA-14).

The following individuals received a pair of shoes from Israel Dodge by certificate from John Dodge (VSA-14): Ensign Slaughter, Martin Carney, Leonard Helm, Lt. John Girault, Major John Williams, Ensign Jarrett Williams, Captain Richard Brashears, Captain Richard Harrison, Richard Clark, and Captain John Bailey.

Account ammunition delivered by Martin Carney by order of Captain Robert George at Fort Jefferson: to Captain Kellar's Blockhouse, eight lbs gunpowder and five lbs lead (VSA-50: 30).

Stores issued by order of Captain Robert George: to Captain Brashears', one tent or oil cloth; to Captain Harrison, one tent or oil cloth (VSA-50: 37).

January, 1781/Miscellaneous

Sometime between January 1, 1781 and January 19, 1781, a letter was written from John Donne at Fort Jefferson to George Rogers Clark in Richmond. Reference is made to another letter written by Donne to George Rogers Clark on December 5. In the December 5 letter, Donne mentioned he would be taking a trip to Kaskaskia. He had expected to obtain a large quantity of goods which had been purchased, but found instead a quantity unpaid. The quantity on hand in the Illinois consists of about 200 bushels of corn in stow, and a large quantity of flour said to have been purchased. While Donne was away, Captain Barbour arrived from New Orleans with a quantity of goods, part of which Captain George intends to use for the purchase of the Kaskaskia provisions (MHS: B1, F23).

Robert George signs a request to Martin Carney to issue Mr. Guion two gallons tafia in lieu of 50 pounds tallow delivered to the deputy conductor by Guion. John Donne signs he has received the two gallons of tafia (VSA-15).

Ensign Jarrett Williams and Robert George sign a request to the quartermaster to issue three gallons of tafia for Williams' use (VSA-15).

Jarrett Williams signs a request to the quartermaster to issue one pound sugar for Williams' use (VSA-15).

Samuel Kirby signs he received from John Donne, $600 in full amount for liquor for use of the fatigue, attested by Martin Carney (VSA-15). Note added after signature: Kirby was also paid $115 more for the same purpose, not having had the opportunity to obtain the rest when setting off for Fort Jefferson [probably written by John Donne] (VSA-15).

January 1, 1781/Monday

Captain Robert George at Fort Jefferson writes to Oliver Pollock at New Orleans. Letter sent with two sets of exchange for $237,320 in favor of Captain Philip Barbour who furnished a large cargo of liquors and dry goods which George says saved the post. George states he called a council of officiers, consulted them about the sum, and then paid Barbour's inflated price. The council and George felt it was a reasonable amount considering the difficulties Barbour encountered getting the cargo to Fort Jefferson. George begs Pollock to pay for the cargo in gold or silver coin so Barbour can supply Fort Jefferson in the future (GRC, I: 496-497).

Robert George requests Oliver Pollock [Agent at New Orleans] to pay Captain Philip Barbour 5,000 Spanish milled dollars for liquor and clothing furnished George for use of the troops of the Illinois Department (VSA-15).

Laurence Slaughter requests the quartermaster issue two quarts tafia for Slaughter's own use (VSA-15).

Jarritt Williams requests the quartermaster issue two quarts tafia for Williams' own use (VSA-15).

Laurence Slaughter requests the quartermaster issue one pound sugar for Slaughter's own use (VSA-15).

Buckner Pittman signs he received from Martin Carney, three barges and painters, 120 oars, one iron grapple, one pittaugree, one canoe, and 12 fathon new cable rope. John Donne attests (VSA-15).

Leonard Helm and Robert George sign a request to the quartermaster to issue each of 25 Indians going to war against the Chickasaws, 1/2 pound gunpowder, one pound lead, and two flints each (VSA-15).

John Williams requests the quartermaster issue three quarts tafia for Williams' own use (VSA-15).

Buckner Pittman and Robert George sign a request to the quartermaster to issue tafia for 16 men on fatigue (VSA-15).

Richard Brashears and Robert George sign a request to the quartermaster to issue two pairs overalls for two men of Brashears' Company, who enlisted for three years. Captain Brashears signs he received from Israel Dodge the two pair overalls(VSA-15).

Sergeant Prockter [Procter] Ballard and George Slaughter sign a request for provisions for 26 men and one washer woman of Captain Roberts' Company for four days [Jan. 1 - Jan. 4] (VSA-15).

Reverse lists: 112 pounds beef, 112 pounds flour, and 14 gills salt (VSA-15). George Slaughter signs a request for provisions for Ensign Asher's widow for four days [Jan. 1 - Jan. 4] (VSA-15).

Leonard Helm and Robert George sign a request to Martin Carney to issue James Sherlock six pounds tobacco to deliver to the Indians. John Sherlock signed he received the tobacco from Martin Carney (VSA-15).

John Donne, Deputy Conductor, signs he received from Captain John Dodge, Agent, three quarts tafia for use of the Commissary Department, also two quarts spirits for use of a fatigue party on command going for provisions purchased from Mr. Thomas Bentley in Kaskaskia at John Donne's desire (VSA-48: 135).

Edward Worthington and George Slaughter sign a request for rations for 21 men of the Illinois Regiment for two days commencing January 1 through the 2nd, 1781. [This issue takes place in Louisville and is in preparation for Worthington's travel to Fort Jefferson.] (VSA-15).

January 2, 1781/Tuesday

Lieutenant Jarrett Williams requests Martin Carney issue two quarts of rum (VSA-15).

Robert George requests Martin Carney issue guns for three men of Robert George's Company of artillery (VSA-15).

Stores issued by order of Captain Robert George: to three men of Captain George's Company, three muskets (VSA-50: 37).

Lieutenant Richard Clark and Robert George sign a request to the quartermaster for six pounds sugar and six pounds coffee for Lieutenant Clark's own use (VSA-15).

Robert George requests the quartermaster issue six quarts tafia for George's own use (VSA-15).

Robert George requests the quartermaster issue John LaRichardy [?], a soldier in Captain McCarty's Company, one pound sugar (VSA-15).

Robert George requests Mr. Dodge issue Ensign Slaughter two yards of the best kind of flannel to make a pair of stockings for George. Slaughter signed he received the flannel from Israel Dodge (VSA-15).

Matross George Smith, a soldier in Captain George's Company, dies (Harding 1981: 29-30, 32).

January 3, 1781/Wednesday

John Williams requests Martin Carney issue 12 pounds sugar for Williams' use (VSA-15).

John Williams requests the quartermaster issue one bottle tafia for Williams' use (VSA-15).

Leonard Helm and Robert George sign a request to the quartermaster for two gallons rum for Helm's use (VSA-15).

Silas Harlan and Robert George sign a request to the quartermaster for four pounds sugar and two pounds coffee for Harlan's use (VSA-15).

Robert George requests the quartermaster issue three quarts rum for George's use (VSA-15).

Robert George requests the quartermaster issue one sergeant and seven men on fatigue, eight gills tafia (VSA-15).

January 4, 1781/Thursday
Robert George requests Martin Carney issue Ensign Williams six pounds sugar and three pounds coffee (VSA-15).

Israel Dodge requests the quartermaster issue three pints of rum for Dodge's use (VSA-15).

Silas Harlan and Robert George sign a request to the quartermaster issue Joseph Hunter 1/4 pound gunpowder and one pound lead (VSA-15; 50: 31).

Captain George Slaughter at Louisville writes a letter to Thomas Jefferson. Slaughter has given orders to Captain George to send 100 weight gunpowder and 400 weight lead to Kaskaskia. Slaughter also tells that complaints have been made against Captain Dodge concerning his misapplication of public goods. Orders have been given to Captain George to make an inquiry into his conduct (GRC, I: 493).

January 5, 1781/Friday
William Clark signs a request to Martin Carney to issue one bottle tafia for Clark's use (VSA-17 misfiled).

Slaughter signs a request to the quartermaster for 1/2 gallon spirits for Slaughter's use (VSA-15).

Robert George signs a request to Martin Carney to issue Sergeant John Walker of George's Company one quart tafia (VSA-15).

Leonard Helm and Robert George sign a request to Martin Carney to issue 14 flints for the friendly Indians (VSA-15).

Robert George signs a request to Martin Carney to issue five quarts rum to Captain George Owens for Owens' own use (VSA-15).

Robert George signs a request to the quartermaster to issue three gallons tafia for George's use (VSA-15).

Leonard Helm and Robert George sign a request to the quartermaster to issue Helm five pounds sugar (VSA-15).

Captain Benjamen Roberts requests the quartermaster issue three pints tafia for Roberts' use (VSA-15).

Robert George requests Israel Dodge to issue Mr. Donne, two pairs of shoes "being naked footed." John Donne signed he received the shoes from Israel Dodge (VSA-15).

Leonard Helm requests Mr. Dodge issue two yards flannel to make two pair stockings for Helm's own use. Leonard Helm signed he received the flannel from Israel Dodge (VSA-15).

Robert George signs a request to Mr. Dodge to issue Martin Carney two yards fine flannel out of the state store to make two pair stockings. Martin Carney signed he received the fine flannel from Israel Dodge (VSA-15).

Robert George signs a request to Israel Dodge to issue Matthew Murray, a soldier in George's Company, two skeins of thread. Matthew Murray signed his "mark" he received the thread from Israel Dodge (VSA-15).

January 6, 1781/Saturday
Richard Clark signs a request to the quartermaster to issue one quart tafia for Clark's use (VSA-15).

Lieutenant Richard Clark and Robert George sign a request for one bottle tafia for Clark (VSA-15).

Leonard Helm and Robert George sign a request to the quartermaster to issue 23 gills rum to a number of friendly Indians (VSA-15).

Robert George signs a request to Martin Carney to issue three quarts rum for George's use (VSA-15).

Robert George signs a request to the quartermaster to issue one sergeant and nine men on fatigue, one gill tafia per man (VSA-15).

Captain John Bailey and Robert George sign a request to Israel Dodge to issue 50 skeins of thread for making 25 shirts for Bailey's Company. John Bailey signed he received the items from Israel Dodge (VSA-15).

Robert George requests Israel Dodge issue Mrs. Sarah Trent, 17 yards white linen for making clothing for the soldiers. Sarah Trent signed she received the items from Israel Dodge (VSA-15).

Robert George requests Israel Dodge issue four yards white flannel to John Williams. John Williams signed he received the flannel from Israel Dodge (VSA-15).

John Thruston and Robert George sign a request to Mr. Dodge to issue trimmings for a suit of clothes and one pair shoes for Thruston's use. John Thruston signed he received from Israel Dodge: one pair shoes, two dozen and 10 large buttons, two dozen and six small buttons, one skein silk, and one skein mohair (VSA-15).

January 7, 1781/Sunday

Robert George requests breech cloths and leggings of such cloth as they should choose for Captain Bailey and Captain Owens in order to go express to the Falls (VSA-15).

Captain John Bailey requests the quartermaster issue two pounds sugar for Bailey's use (VSA-15).

Israel Dodge requests the quartermaster issue three quarts tafia for Dodge's own use (VSA-15).

Lieutenant Richard Clark requests Martin Carney to issue one bottle tafia for Clark's own use (VSA-15).

Captain Benjamin Roberts requests the quartermaster issue three pints tafia for Roberts' use as he is being called on for beverage for Roberts' coat [assume Roberts may be giving his tailor tafia for making his coat] (VSA-15).

John Bailey and Robert George sign a request to the quartermaster to pay Edward Murray of Bailey's Company, six quarts tafia as Murray had furnished Bailey with that quantity at different times at Cahokia for the use of Bailey's Company (VSA-15).

Israel Dodge and Robert George sign a request to Mr. Carney to issue 1 1/2 quire of paper for use of the Agents Department (VSA-15).

John Bailey requests the quartermaster issue two quarts tafia for Bailey's use (VSA-15).

James Sherlock and Robert George sign a request to Mr. Carney to issue one quart tafia for Sherlock's use (VSA-15).

Edward Worthington and George Slaughter sign a request to the issuing commissary to issue rations for ten days for 21 men under Worthington's command belonging to the Illinois Regiment commencing the 7th day of January and ending the 16th (VSA-15).

January 8, 1781/Monday

Letter from John Montgomery at New Orleans to Thomas Jefferson. Montgomery writes to represent the distressed situation at Fort Jefferson. The inhabitants are leaving the settlement for want of subsistence. The soldiers are deserting for want of provisions. Montgomery also states that if the "late" attack [Aug-Sept, 1780] had held a few days longer, all the stores and ammunition would fall into the hands of the enemy. There was nothing but corn in the garrison, and no more than what would have lasted for six days. Montgomery states that it is well-known how impossible it is to transport provisions to the fort in time of an invasion (GRC, I: 497-498).

Leonard Helm and Robert George sign a request to Martin Carney to issue two gallons tafia for 25 of the friendly Indians (VSA-15).

Leonard Helm requests the quartermaster issue one gallon tafia for Helm's use (VSA-15).

Robert George requests the quartermaster issue ten quarts and one pint rum for George's use (VSA-15).

John Bailey and Robert George sign a return to the quartermaster for one pound gunpowder and two pounds lead for three men of Bailey's Company (VSA-15; 50: 31).

John Bailey and Robert George sign a return to the quartermaster for one day's ration tafia for 26 men of Bailey's Company (VSA-15).

Patrick Kennedy requests the quartermaster let Edward Murray have two quarts tafia for Kennedy's use (VSA-15).

Account of ammunition delivered by Martin Carney by order of Captain Robert George at Fort Jefferson: to friendly Indians going to war, 12 1/2 pounds gunpowder, 25 pounds lead, and 50 flints; to Captain Bailey and Owens going express to the Falls, 1 1/2 pounds gunpowder and four pounds lead; to Captain Rogers' Company, three pounds gunpowder and six pounds lead (VSA-50: 31).

January 9, 1781/Tuesday

Patrick Kennedy and Robert George sign a request to Martin Carney to issue the bearer one bottle tafia and one pound sugar (VSA-15).

Lieutenant Richard Clark requests the quartermaster issue three pints tafia for Clark (VSA-15).

Robert George requests Martin Carney issue Patrick Kennedy, Assistant Conductor, 12 pounds sugar and six pounds coffee for Kennedy's use (VSA-15).

John Williams requests the quartermaster issue three quarts tafia for Williams' use (VSA-15).

John Donne requests Martin Carney issue four gallons tafia for Donne's use (VSA-15).

Ensign Jarret Williams requests the quartermaster issue 1/2 gallon tafia for Williams' use (VSA-15).

Ensign Jarret Williams and Robert George sign a request to the quartermaster to issue 78 gills rum for 78 men on fatigue (VSA-15).

Robert George requests the quartermaster issue ten sick men of the garrison ten pounds sugar and five pounds coffee (VSA-15).

James Sherlock and Robert George sign a request to Martin Carney to issue three pints tafia for Sherlock's use (VSA-15).

Robert George requests Martin Carney issue 1/2 gallon tafia to Mr. Guion in lieu of a like quantity by Guion furnished a party of troops on fatigue transporting provisions in bad weather. John Donne certifies Mr. Guion received 1/2 gallon of liquor agreeable (VSA-15).

Robert George requests Mr. Dodge issue Mrs. Owens 4 1/2 yards flannel, 1 1/2 yards pompadore, one paper of pins, and 25 sewing needles, and charge it to the State of Virginia as her husband has gone express to the Falls of Ohio. Charaty Owens signs her "mark" she received from Israel Dodge the contents plus three skeins thread (VSA-15).

January 10, 1781/Wednesday
John Williams signs a request to the quartermaster to issue three pints tafia for his use (VSA-15).

Robert George signs a return to the quartermaster for four pounds gunpowder and eight pounds lead for 15 men going on command to the Illinois (VSA-15; 50: 31).

Buckner Pittman signs a request to Martin Carney to issue two quarts rum for his use (VSA-15).

John Thruston and Robert George sign a return for three pounds gunpowder and six pounds lead for the use of Captain Roger's Company (VSA-15).

John Williams signs a request to the quartermaster to issue 13 quarts and a pint for the use of your very humble and most devoted servant (VSA-15).

Robert George signs a request to the quartermaster to issue Ensign Slaughter ten pounds sugar and four pounds coffee for his use (VSA-15).

Lieutenant Richard Clark and Robert George sign a request to Martin Carney to issue Captain James Piggott, two gallons tafia being for so much advanced by Mr. Piggott for the use of the boat crew under Clark's command transporting provisions from Kaskaskia (VSA-15).

Ensign Slaughter requests the quartermaster issue 1/2 gallon tafia for his use (VSA-15).

Robert George signs a request to Israel Dodge to issue James Sherlock 1 1/2 yards cloth and trimmings for a waistcoat and breeches. James Sherlock signed he received from Dodge, 1 1/2 yards broad cloth, two dozen small buttons, one skein mohair, and two skeins thread (VSA-15).

Ensign Slaughter and Robert George sign a request to Mr. Dodge to issue George Shepperd of Bailey's Company one dozen needles to work for the use of the troops at this post. George Sheppard signed his "mark" he received the pins from Israel Dodge (VSA-15).

Robert George requests Martin Carney issue James Sherlock, 80 pounds gunpowder, 40 pounds lead, and 80 flints to deliver to the Kaskaskia Indians. John Sherlock signed he received munition supplies from Martin Carney (VSA-15).

Edward Worthington writes, he received of William Shannon, quartermaster in the Illinois Department, one flat bottomed boat, five oars and a pump which Worthington intends to deliver to the quartermaster at Fort Jefferson, the danger of the enemy and water excepted. Willis Green attested (VSA-15).

Robert George requests Mr. Dodge issue six bags to Major John Williams for bringing provisions from Kaskaskia to Fort Jefferson. John Williams signed he received the bags from Israel Dodge (VSA-15).

Stores issued by order of Captain Robert George: to Patrick Kennedy, one musket and one bayonet with belt (VSA-50: 37).

Captain Worthington signs he received from George Wilson, Deputy Conductor of Issues at the Falls of Ohio, 15 barrels flour containing 3,478 pounds; and 46 1/2 gallons of good whiskey in five kegs which Worthington intends to deliver to the commanding officer or commissary at Fort Jefferson, the danger of the enemy and water excepted (VSA-15).

Martin Carney signs he received from Mr. James Piggott, 757 feet poplar plank, for which Carney is to pay Piggott ten dollars and 1/2 the old way [barter for commodities]. Captain Robert George requests the quartermaster pay the order in tafia at four shillings per gallon, sugar at 18 pence per pound, and coffee at one shilling and charge to the State of Virginia (VSA-15).

James Piggott signed he received 14 gallons tafia, four pounds sugar, and one pound coffee on the above order from Martin Carney (VSA-15).

<u>January 11, 1781/Thursday</u>

Coronet John Thruston and Captain Robert George sign a request to the quartermaster to issue two pounds sugar and one pound coffee for his use (VSA-17).

Leonard Helm and Robert George sign a request to the quartermaster to issue one quart tafia to the friendly Indians and charge to the State of Virginia (VSA-15).

Robert George signs a request to Martin Carney to issue six pounds sugar for Georges use (VSA-15).

Robert George signs a request to Martin Carney to issue John Williams 10 gallons tafia for Williams' trip to the Illinois (VSA-15).

Robert George signs a request to Martin Carney to issue Captain Roberts, 10 gallons tafia for Roberts' trip up the river (VSA-15).

Israel Dodge signs a request to Martin Carney to issue three quarts tafia for Dodge's own use (VSA-15).

Robert George signs a request to Martin Carney to issue Sergeant John Walker of George's Company, one quart tafia (VSA-15).

Leonard Helm and Robert George sign a request to Martin Carney to issue Joseph, a friendly Indian, two quarts tafia and charge it to the State of Virginia (VSA-15).

John Donne signs a request to Martin Carney to fill Donnes' keg with five quarts liquor (VSA-15).

Robert George signs a request to Israel Dodge to issue Mr. Kennedy four yards fine cloth to make him clothes, 10 1/2 yards linen to make him shirts, and 3 1/2 yards blue cloth to make a cape and overalls as Kennedy is going on public Service (VSA-15).

Robert George requests two hogheads and two barrels tafia out of the country store for Patrick Kennedy together with two empty hogheads for Mr.Girrault to purchase provisions for the fort. Patrick Kennedy signed he received from Martin Carney, four hogsheads and two half hogsheads of tafia for the purpose of purchasing provisions agreeable to the within order (VSA-15).

Leonard Helm and Robert George sign a request to Israel Dodge to issue two pounds vermilion to James Sherlock for the Indians. James Sherlock signed he received the vermillion from Israel Dodge the within contents (VSA-15).

Account of ammunition expended by the artillery at sundry times by order of Captain Robert George, Commandant at Fort Jefferson: expended at other different times, 17 pounds gunpowder and 3 1/2 yards flannel; issued Captain Bailey for the use of the artillery at the O'Post, three yards flannel (VSA-50: 33).

Stores issued by order of Captain Robert George: to a soldier of Captain Bailey's Company, one musket and one bayonet with belt; Major Williams, eight tents or oil cloths [amount appeared to be eight but was crossed out]; to Major Williams, [one swivel had been listed but appears to have been crossed out] (VSA-50: 37).

January 12, 1781/Friday

Robert George signs a request to the quartermaster to issue George's Company one brass kettle (VSA-20; 50: 37).

William Clark signs a request to Martin Carney to issue one quart tafia for Clark's use (VSA-17).

Joseph Hunter and Robert George sign that Hunter received one broad sword from Martin Carney, which Hunter promises to return the danger of the Indians excepted (VSA-15; 50: 37).

Slaughter signs a request to the quartermaster to issue 1/2 gallon tafia for Slaughters own use (VSA-15).

Robert George signs a request to the quartermaster to issue Mr. Hunter three quarts tafia being "one of our late magistrates" (VSA-15).

Robert George signs a request to the quartermaster to issue three gallons tafia for George's own use (VSA-15).

Richard Brashears and Robert George sign a request to the quartermaster to issue two pounds sugar to a sick man of Brashears' Company (VSA-15).

Robert George signs a request to Mr. Dodge to issue Maj. Silas Harlan 2 1/2 yards toil greys and charge Harlan with the same (VSA-15).

Captain Benjamin Roberts and Robert George sign a request to Mr. Dodge to pay Mrs. Hughes for making eight shirts for men of Captain Roberts' Company and charge it to the State of Virginia (VSA-15).

Richard Clark and Robert George sign a request to the quartermaster to issue 1/2 pound gunpowder, one pound lead, and two flints for Clark's own use (VSA-15; 50: 31).

Robert George signs a request to the quartermaster to issue James Sherlock a sword (VSA-15; 50: 37).

Ensign Slaughter and Robert George sign a request to Mr. Carney to issue 23 swords for 23 men of Captain John Bailey's Company. Ensign Slaughter signed he received the swords from Martin Carney (VSA-15; 50: 37).

Richard Clark and Robert George sign a request to the quartermaster to issue 17 swords to Lieutenant Richard Clark for the use of Captain Edward Worthington's Company stationed at the blockhouse (VSA-15; 50: 37).

Robert George signs a request to Mr. Dodge to issue to Paul Quibea of George's Company a coat, waistcoat, and pair of overalls. Paul Quibea signs his "mark" he received othe clothing from Israel Dodge (VSA-15).

Ensign Slaughter and Robert George sign a request to Mr. Dodge to issue cloth and trimmings for a suit of clothes in part of Slaughter's clothing for this year. Slaughter signed he received from Israel Dodge three yards broad cloth, 3 1/2 yards linen, three skeins mohair, one skein silk, and six skeins thread (VSA-15).

Godfrey Linctot at O'Post writes to George Rogers Clark at the Falls of Ohio, pleading for gunpowder and lead. He expects a British attack. He adds he is going to Fort Jefferson (MHS, B2, F1).

Account of ammunition delivered by Martin Carney by order of Captain Robert George at Fort Jefferson: to Majr. Williams, six cartridges for swivel, four pounds gunpowder and six pounds lead; to Captain Bailey's Company, six flints (VSA-50: 31).

January 13, 1781/Saturday

Leonard Helm signs a request to the quartermaster to issue three gallons tafia for Helm's own use (VSA-15).

Leonard Helm and Robert George sign a request to the quartermaster to issue three pints tafia for five friendly Indians (VSA-15).

Leonard Helm and Robert George sign a request to Mr. Carney to issue one bottle tafia to an Indian (VSA-15).

Israel Dodge signs a request to Mr. Carney to issue three pints tafia for Dodge's own use (VSA-15).

Edward Worthington and George Slaughter sign a request to the issuing commissary at the Falls of Ohio to issue 10 gallons whiskey for the officers of Colonel Clark's regiment on their way to Fort Jefferson (VSA-15).

Edward Worthington and George Slaughter sign a request to the issuing commissary at the Falls of Ohio to issue 30 pounds beef and 25 pounds flour for the officers of Clark's regiment going to Fort Jefferson (VSA-15).

January 14, 1781/Sunday

George Slaughter at Louisville writes a letter to Thomas Jefferson at Richmond regarding Slaughter's orders to Captain George to send Kaskaskia 100 lbs gunpowder and 400 lbs lead, and to have Captain George look into inappropriate behavior of Captain Dodge (GRC, I: 493-494).

Jarrit Williams and Robert George sign a request to the quartermaster for one pound sugar and 1/2 pound coffee, to one man of Captain Brashears' Company (VSA-15).

Mr. Donne, Captain John Bailey, and Lieutenant Richard Clark were all delivered one padlock (VSA-15).

Robert George signs a request to the quartermaster to issue three case bottles tafia at three pints each (VSA-15).

Lieutenant Richard Clark signs a request to Mr. Carney to issue one quart tafia for Clark's own use (VSA-15).

John Bailey signs a statement to the quartermaster, "good for two quarts tafia" (VSA-15).

Edward Worthington at the Falls signs he received one axe from William Shannon for the use of the troops under Worthington's command ordered to Fort Jefferson (VSA-15).

January 15, 1781/Monday

Sergeant John Young and Robert George sign a request to the quartermaster to issue six men of Captain Roberts' Company on fatigue, their allowance of tafia for one day (VSA-15).

Ensign Slaughter signs a request to the quartermaster to issue 1/2 gallon tafia for Slaughter's use (VSA-15).

Israel Dodge signs a request to the quartermaster to issue three gallons tafia for Dodge's use (VSA-15).

Robert George signs a request to Mr. Carney to issue three pints tafia for George's use (VSA-15).

Leonard Helm and Robert George sign a request to the quartermaster to issue one quart tafia to the friendly Indians (VSA-15).

Martin Carney signs that Joseph Thornton worked as an artificer from 1/15/81 to 2/15/81 at $15 per day (VSA-15).

Robert George signs a request to the quartermaster to issue George Smith of George's Company two pounds sugar and one pound coffee as Smith is sick (VSA-15).

Leonard Helm and Robert George sign a request to Mr. Carney to issue five pints tafia for the friendly Indians (VSA-15).

Leonard Helm and Robert George sign a request to Mr. Carney to issue four pounds gunpowder and four pounds lead to the friendly Indians (VSA-15).

Silas Harlan and Robert George sign a request to Martin Carney to issue a sword for Harlan's use (VSA-15).

Ensign Jarret Williams and Robert George sign a request to Mr. Carney to issue 10 swords for 10 men of Captain Brashears' Company (VSA-15).

George Owens and Robert George sign a request to the quartermaster to issue 12 men on fatigue three pints tafia (VSA-15)

Israel Dodge and Robert George sign a request to Martin Carney to issue four pounds sugar for Dodge's use (VSA-15).

Robert George requests the quartermaster issue three pints tafia for George's use (VSA-15).

Leonard Helm and Robert George sign a request to the quartermaster to issue one quart tafia to the friendly Indians (VSA-15).

Lieutenant Richard Clark and Robert George sign a request to Israel Dodge to issue 3 1/4 yards cloth and trimmings for a suit of clothes in part of Clark's draft of clothing for this year. Richard Clark signed he received from Israel Dodge 3 1/4 yards broad cloth, eight large buttons, six small buttons, two skeins mohair, 16 skeins thread, and one skein silk (VSA-15).

Matross William Fever, a member of Captain Robert George's Company, is killed (Harding 1981: 32).

January 16, 1781/Tuesday
Ensign Jarret Williams signs a request to Mr. Carney to issue one quart tafia for Williams' use (VSA-15).

Israel Dodge requests three pint bottle of tafia (VSA-15).

Leonard Helm and Robert George sign a request to Mr. Carney to issue the friendly Indians five quarts and one pint tafia (VSA-15).

Sergeant Charles Morgan and Robert George sign a request to the quartermaster to issue 34 swords and carriages for the use of Captain George's Company (VSA-15).

Robert George signs a request to Martin Carney to issue seven gills rum to the militia for service they have done (VSA-15).

Ensign Jarret Williams signs a request to the quartermaster for two gallons tafia for Williams' use (VSA-15).

Ensign Slaughter requests the quartermaster issue 1/2 gallon tafia for Slaughter's use (VSA-15).

Stores issued by order of Captain Robert George: to Captain George's Company, 32 swords (VSA-50: 37).

January 17, 1781/Wednesday
William Clark signs a request to Mr. Carney for one quart tafia for Clark's use (VSA-17).

Jarret Williams and Robert George sign a request to Mr. Dodge to issue three yards cloth and trimmings for a suit of clothes in part of Williams' draft of clothing for this year (VSA-15).

Israel Dodge signs a request to Martin Carney for three quarts tafia for Dodge's own use (VSA-15).

Robert George signs a request to Israel Dodge for 3 1/2 yards linen for George's own use (VSA-15).

Ensign Slaughter signs a request to the quartermaster for 1/2 gallon tafia for Slaughter's own use (VSA-15).

John Bailey signs a statement to Martin Carney, "Good for two Quarts taffia" (VSA-15).

Israel Dodge requests Mr. Carney to issue 1 1/2 gallons tafia and two pounds sugar for Dodge's own use (VSA-15).

Jarret Williams and Robert George sign a request to the Agent to pay Mrs. Burks for making two shirts for men of Captain Brashears' Company. Elizabeth Burks signs her "mark" she received 15 skeins thread (VSA-15).

Jarret Williams and Robert George sign a request to Israel Dodge for one yard linen, one skein mohair, and six needles for Williams' use. John Williams signed he received the items from Israel Dodge (VSA-15).

Jarret Williams and Robert George sign a request to Israel Dodge for 20 skeins thread to make that many shirts for Captain Brashears' Company. Jarret Williams signed he received the thread from Israel Dodge (VSA-15).

January 18, 1781/Thursday
Abraham Kellar and Robert George sign a request to the quartermaster for 54 gills tafia for that many men on fatigue (VSA-15).

Robert George signs a request to the quartermaster for three gallons and three quarts tafia for George's use (VSA-15).

James Sherlock, Leonard Helm, and Robert George sign a request to the quartermaster for six pounds sugar and three pounds coffee for Sherlock's use (VSA-15).

Ensign Slaughter signs a request to the quartermaster for issue 1/2 gallon tafia for Slaughter's use (VSA-15).

Robert George signs a request to the quartermaster for three pints tafia for George's use (VSA-15).

Captain Abraham Kellar and Robert George sign a return to the quartermaster for tafia for three men on fatigue (VSA-15).

Israel Dodge and Robert George sign a request to the quartermaster to issue one sword for Dodge's use (VSA-15).

Jarret Williams signs a request to the quartermaster for 1/2 gallon tafia for Williams' use (VSA-15).

Lieutenant Richard Clark signs a request for three pints tafia for Clark's own use (VSA-15).

Israel Dodge signs a request to the quartermaster for three quarts tafia for Dodge's use (VSA-15).

Captain John Bailey and Robert George sign a request to Mr. Dodge to pay Mrs. Nancy Hunter for making eight shirts for Bailey's Company. Nancy Hunter "marks" she received from Israel Dodge five yards camblet (VSA-15).

Robert George signs a request to Mr. Dodge to pay Mrs. Merrideth for making three soldiers' shirts for men of George's Company. Luvana Merideth signed she received two yards flannel from Israel Dodge (VSA-15).

Robert George signs a return to the quartermaster for one gun for one man in Captain George's Company. Sergeant Jesse Piner signed his "mark" he received the gun with bayonet and belt [attested by W. Clark] (VSA-15).

Captain John Bailey and Captain Robert George sign a request to Israel Dodge to pay Mrs. Kennedy for making seven shirts for Bailey's Company. Rachel Kennedy signs her "mark" she received 1 1/2 yards toile gris, two papers of pins, and 12 skeins thread from Israel Dodge (VSA-15).

John Bailey and Robert George sign a request to Mr. Dodge to pay Mrs. Phelps for making eight shirts for Bailey's Company. Elizabeth Phelps signs her "mark" that she received 4 3/4 yards from Israel Dodge (VSA-15).

Robert George signs request to Mr. Dodge to issue Martin Carney two dozen needles and two skeins thread for making [illeg.] (VSA-15).

Leonard Helm and Robert George sign a request to Mr. Dodge to issue cloth for a coat, and waistcoat and trimmings for a suit of clothes in part of Helm's draft of clothing for this year. Leonard Helm signed he received three yards cloth, one skein silk, two skeins mohair, and five skeins thread from Israel Dodge (VSA-15).

Captain Abraham Kellar and Robert George sign request to Mr. Dodge to issue three yards cloth in part of Kellars draw of clothing for this year (VSA-15).
Leonard Helm and Robert George sign a request to Mr. Dodge to issue 1 1/4 yards cloth for Helm's use. Helm received the cloth (VSA-15).

Captain John Bailey and Robert George sign a request to Israel Dodge to issue three yards cloth and trimmings for a suit of clothes in part of Bailey's draw of clothing for this year. Bailey signed he received three yards cloth from Israel Dodge (VSA-15).

Benjamin Roberts, Colonel Slaughter, and Captain George sign a request to Mr. Dodge to issue Sergeant John Young of Roberts' Company, cloth for a pair of trousers and thread to make them. John Young signs his "mark" he received 1 1/4 yards cloth and three skeins thread (VSA-15).

Jarrit Williams certifies Mrs. Elms made three coats and two pairs of overalls for three men of Captain Brashears' Company (VSA-15).

Leonard Helm signs request to the quartermaster to issue three quarts tafia for Helm's use (VSA-15).

Stores issued by order of Captain Robert George: to Captain George's Company, one musket and one kettle (VSA-50: 37).

Abraham Kellar and Robert George sign a request to the quartermaster to issue five gills tafia for so many men on fatigue (VSA-15).

Captain Robert George signs a request to the quartermaster for three gallons and three quarts tafia for George's use (VSA-15).

James Sherlock, Leonard Helm and Robert George sign a request to the quartermaster to issue six pounds sugar and three pounds coffee for Sherlock's use (VSA-15).

Lawrence Slaughter signs a request to the quartermaster to issue 1/2 gallon tafia for Slaughter's use (VSA-15).

Captain Robert George signs a request to the quartermaster to issue three pints tafia for George's use (VSA-15).

<u>January 19, 1781</u>/<u>Friday</u>
Robert George signs a request to Mr. Dodge to issue one coat, three waistcoats, and one pair overalls for part of Captain Worthington's Company and also five dozen and four metal buttons for one Sergeant (VSA-15).

Robert George signs a request to Mr. Dodge to issue to Captain John Bailey 30 skeins thread, six dozen buttons, and three suits of clothes readymade for the use of Bailey's Company (VSA-15).

Robert George signs a request to Mr. Dodge to issue 9 1/2 yards cloth to Captain Bailey for the use in Bailey's Company (VSA-15).

Robert George signs a request to Israel Dodge to issue three yards cloth, 12 skeins thread, and one skein mohair for one sergeant in Worthington's Company (VSA-15).

Robert George signs a request to Israel Dodge to issue five coats, five waistcoats, two pair trousers, and five dozen and five metal buttons for part of George's Company (VSA-15).

Robert George signs a request to Israel Dodge to issue three yards cloth, 12 skeins thread, two sticks mohair for part of George's Company (VSA-15).

John Bailey and Robert George sign a request to the quartermaster to issue 58 gills of tafia for 50 men on fatigue (VSA-15).

Israel Dodge signs a request to the quartermaster to issue three quarts tafia for Dodge's use (VSA-15).

Lieutenant Richard Clark and Robert George sign a request to the quartermaster to issue 1/2 pound gunpowder and one pound lead each to three men belonging to the blockhouse (VSA-15).

John Bailey signs a statement to Martin Carney, "Good for four Qts. taffia" (VSA-15).

Robert George signs a request to the quartermaster to issue one pound sugar for David Kennedy, a soldier of Captain George's Company, who is sick (VSA-15).

Buckner Pittman, boatmaster, signs a request to the quartermaster for two quarts rum for Pittman's use (VSA-15).

Robert George signs a request to Mr. Carney to issue Mr. Donne one sword and two [doc. torn], for the use of Donne's house it being a convenient [doc. torn] Captain Bailey's redoubt. John Donne signs he received from Martin Carney, two belts with bayonets and one sword [doc. torn] (VSA-15; 50: 37).

Robert George signs a request to Israel Dodge to issue Buckner Pittman cloth and trimmings for a suit of clothes. Pittman signed he received three yards cloth, five dozen and four buttons, two skeins mohair, 12 skeins thread, and two skeins silk (VSA-15).

John Bailey and Robert George sign a request to Israel Dodge to issue cloth and trimmings for two suits of clothes for two sergeants in Bailey's Company. Bailey signed he received six yards cloth, 10 dozen and eight buttons, 25 skeins thread, two skeins mohair, and two skeins silk (VSA-15).

Account of ammunition delivered Martin Carney by order of Captain Robert George at Fort Jefferson: to three men of Captain Worthington's Company, 1 1/2 pounds gunpowder and three pounds lead (VSA-50: 31).

Stores issued by order of Captain Robert George: to Mr. Donne, Commissary, two muskets (VSA-50: 37).

Letter from John Donne at Fort Jefferson to Colonel Clark. Speaks of Mr. Dodge being universally hated and despised among the Illinois inhabitants. Also mentions that Captain Barbour arrived from New Orleans while Donne was gone (MHS B1, F23).

January 20, 1781/Saturday

Sergeant William Elms and Robert George sign a request to the quartermaster to issue three pounds tobacco for men belonging to Captain Brashears' Company (VSA-15).

Israel Dodge signs a request to Martin Carney for three pints tafia for Dodge's own use (VSA-15).

Lieutenant Richard Clark and Robert George sign a request to the quartermaster to issue two gallons and one pint tafia for the fatigue (VSA-15).

Matthew Murray a member of Captain Robert George's Comany, deserted (Harding 1981: 31-33).

January 21, 1781/Sunday

Leonard Helm signs a request to the quartermaster for three quarts tafia for Helm's use (VSA-15).

John Bailey and Robert George sign a request to Martin Carney to issue Beverly Trent's wife, who is sick, one pound coffee and two pounds sugar (VSA-15).

Robert George signs a request to Martin Carney to issue Sergeant John Walker of George's Company, two quarts tafia (VSA-15).

Captain John Bailey and Robert George sign a return to the quartermaster for William Karu of Bailey's Company, who is very sick, one pound sugar and 1/2 pound coffee (VSA-15).

John Donne signs a request to Martin Carney saying, "Good for five quarts taffia" (VSA-15).

Lieutenant Richard Clark signs a request to the quartermaster to issue one quart tafia to Clark (VSA-15).

January 22, 1781/Monday
William Clark signs a request to Martin Carney for seven quarts tafia for Clark's use (VSA-15).

Robert George signs a request to Israel Dodge for four yards cloth and six skeins thread for part of Captain Brashears' Company (VSA-15).

Robert George signs a request to Israel Dodge for three coats, three waistcoats, one pair overalls and four dozen metal buttons for part of Captain Brashears' Company (VSA-15).

Lieutenant Jarret Williams signs a request to the quartermaster for three pints rum for Williams' use (VSA-15).

Buckner Pittman signs a request to Mr. Carney for two quarts tafia for Pittman's use (VSA-15).

Sergeant Elms and Robert George sign a request to the quartermaster for one pound tobacco to four men of Captain Brashears' Company (VSA-15).

Leonard Helm signs a request for three pints tafia for Helm's use (VSA-15).

Leonard Helm signs a request to the quartermaster for two quarts tafia for Helm's use (VSA-15).

Richard Clark and Robert George sign a request to Mr. Dodge to issue seven yards cloth, 12 skeins thread and six dozen buttons for the use of Captain Worthington's Company. Richard Clark signed he received the items from Israel Dodge (VSA-15).

Robert George signs a request to Israel Dodge to issue ten yards cloth, ten skeins thread and three dozen buttons for George's Compnay. Lieutenant Martin Carney signed he received the within contents from Dodge (VSA-15).

Captain Abraham Kellar and Robert George sign a request to Mr. Dodge to issue 4 1/2 yards cloth and trimmings for two suits of clothes for Kellar's Company. Kellar signed he received the items and also 18 skiens thread from Israel Dodge (VSA-15).

Abraham Kellar and Robert George sign a request to Israel Dodge to issue two coats, three waistcoats, and one pair overalls for part of Kellar's Company. Kellar signed he received the contents from Israel Dodge (VSA-15).

Captain Robert George signs a request to direct Martin Carney to issue the troops at Fort Jefferson, 93 gallons whiskey that Captain Worthington will deliver to

George for that purpose; and it is to be issued in the same manner as tafia (VSA-15).

January 23, 1781/Tuesday
Robert George at Fort Jefferson receives a letter from George Slaughter at Louisville [probably communication Slaughter referenced to Jefferson on 1-8-81] regarding abundance of supplies (GRC, I: 506-507).

Robert George signs a request to the quartermaster to issue 100 weight sugar for George's use (VSA-15).

Ensign Slaughter and Robert George sign a request to the quartermaster to issue 58 gills tafia to that many men on fatigue for unloading a boat that came from the Falls of Ohio (VSA-15).

Israel Dodge signs a request to Martin Carney for three pints tafia for Dodge's use (VSA-15).

Robert George signs a request to Martin Carney to issue rations of tafia for four men on fatigue (VSA-15).

Israel Dodge signs a request to Martin Carney for three pints tafia for Dodge's use (VSA-15).

Maj. Silas Harlan and Robert George sign a request to Martin Carney for ten pounds sugar and three pounds coffee for Harlan's use (VSA-15).

John Donne signs a request to Martin Carney saying, "Good for five Quarts Taffia" (VSA-15).

Ensign L. Slaughter signs request to the quartermaster to issue 1/2 gallon tafia for Slaughter's use (VSA-15).

Robert George signs a request to Martin Carney to issue 12 pounds sugar to Mr. Donne to celebrate a festival at Donne's (VSA-15).

George Slaughter at Louisville signs a request to the quartermaster to issue Bartlit Searcy a canoe and paddles to go express to Fort Jefferson. Bartlit Searcy signed he received from William Shannon, one canoe and two paddles. Searcy promises to deliver the canoe to the quartermaster at Fort Jefferson (VSA-15).

Robert George signs a request to Mr. Dodge to issue two pair overalls for two men of George's Company. Martin Carney signed he received the overalls from Mr. Dodge (VSA-15).

January 24, 1781/Wednesday
Captain Edward Worthington signs a request to Mr. Carney to issue Mr. John Wilson one quart tafia (VSA-15).

Ensign L. Slaughter signs a request to the quartermaster to issue 1/2 gallon tafia for Slaughter's use (VSA-15).

Robert George signs a request to Mr. Carney to issue Ensign Williams two pounds gunpowder and four pounds lead for the use of Williams' hunting trip (VSA-15).

Sergeant Jesse Pinere and Robert George sign a request to the quartermaster to issue 55 gills tafia for men on fatigue (VSA-15).

Lieutenant Joseph Calvit and Robert Geroge sign a request to the quartermaster to issue liquor to ten men on fatigue (VSA-15).

Lieutenant Joseph Calvit and Robert George sign a request to the quartermaster to issue four pounds coffee and six pounds sugar for Calvit's use (VSA-15).

Robert George signs a request to the quartermaster to issue 1/2 pound gunpowder and one pound lead to two men of George's Company (VSA-15).

[Illeg. signature] requests the quartermaster issue rations of tafia to 34 men of Captain George's Company (VSA-15).

George Slaughter signs a request to the commissary to issue one keg whiskey, and send it to Fort Jefferson by Captain Worthington for the use of Captain Roberts and Slaughter's men under Roberts' command, who were ordered to Fort Jefferson. Worthington signed he received of George Wilson, Commissary of Issues at the Falls, one keg good whiskey containing 11 gallons which Worthington will deliver to Captain Roberts at the Mouth of the Ohio, the dangers and the enemy excepted (VSA-15).

Robert George signs a request to Israel Dodge to issue three yards cloth and trimmings for a suit of clothes in part of George's draw of clothes for Lieutenant Calvit. Calvit signed he received three yards cloth, 12 skeins thread, two skeins mohair, two skeins silk, and three dozen buttons from Israel Dodge (VSA-15).

Account of ammunition delivered by Martin Carney by order of Captain Robert George at Fort Jefferson: to two men of Captain George's Company, 1/4 pound gunpowder (VSA-50: 31).

Private William Carr dies. He was a member of Captain John Bailey's Company (Harding 1981: 46).

January 25, 1781/Thursday

Robert George signs a request to Mr. Dodge to issue one suit of clothes and 323 buttons to Lieutenant Calvit's party (VSA-15).

Robert George signs a requests to Mr. Dodge to issue 21 1/2 yards cloth and 40 skeins thread for Lieutenant Calvit's party (VSA-15).

Israel Dodge signs a request to Mr. Carney stating, "Good for one Quart Taffia" (VSA-15).

Lieutenant Joseph Calvit signs a request to Mr. Carney to issue four quarts liquor for Calvit's use (VSA-15).

Leonard Helm signs a request to the quartermaster to issue three pints tafia for Helm's use (VSA-15).

Edward Worthington signs a request to Mr. Carney to issue Edward Murray one quart tafia (VSA-15).

Lieutenant Joseph Calvit and Robert George sign a request to Mr. Dodge to issue six skeins thread out of the public store for Calvit's use (VSA-15). Calvit signed he received items from Israel Dodge (VSA-15).

Lieutenant Calvit and Robert George sign a request to Mr. Dodge to let the bearer have four dozen needles. George Vickpale(?) signs his "mark" he received the needles from Israel Dodge (VSA-15).

Captain Edward Worthington and Robert George sign a request to Mr. Dodge to issue three yards cloth and trimmings for a suit of clothes for Worthington's use. Worthington signed he received from Israel Dodge, three yards cloth, two skeins silk, two skeins mohair, 12 skeins thread, and three dozen and two large buttons (VSA-15).

George Slaughter signs a request for flour for four days for nine men from the 25th-28th of January (VSA-15).

Stores issued by order of Captain Robert George: to Captain Brashears' Company, ten swords (VSA-50: 39).

January 26, 1781/Friday
Ensign L. Slaughter and Robert George sign a request to Israel Dodge to issue 3/4 yard camblet, one knife and two skeins silk for Slaughter's use (VSA-15). Note written on reverse: the within knife and silk belong to Captain Barbour's abstract of goods, and therefore the camblet is only charged in this abstract.

January 27, 1781/Saturday
Lieutenant Joseph Calvit signs a request to Mr. Carney to issue three pints rum for Calvit's use (VSA-15).

Lieutenant Calvit and Robert George sign a request to the quartermaster to issue three swords, one brass kettle, and one pair flat irons for Calvit's use. Calvit signed he received the items from Martin Carney (VSA-15).

Stores issued by order of Captain Robert George: one kettle (VSA-50: 39).

Robert George signs a request to Mr. Dodge to issue two pair trousers for two men in George's Company. Lieutenant(?) Martin Carney signed he received the within contents (VSA-15).

Lieutenant Calvit and Robert George sign a request to Mr. Dodge to issue cloth and trimmings for a coat, three waistcoats, and two pair overalls for Michael Miles, Page Partwood, and Andrew Ryon under Calvit's command. Calvit signed he received (?) yards cloth, 78 buttons, and seven skeins thread (VSA-15).

Captain Edward Worthington at Fort Jefferson certifies Pattrick Shirke [Sharkey] has enlisted in Worthington's Company for three years (MHS: B2, F1).

Account of ammunition delivered by Martin Carney by order of Captain Robert George at Fort Jefferson: to two men of Captain George's Company, 1/2 pound gunpowder and one pound lead (VSA-50: 31).

January 28, 1781/Sunday
Robert George signs a request to the quartermaster to issue two pounds sugar to two men of George's Company (VSA-15).

Lieutenant Richard Clark and Robert George sign a request to the quartermaster to issue two pounds tobacco for Clark's own use (VSA-15).

January 30, 1781/Tuesday
William Clark and Robert George sign a request to the quartermaster to issue six pounds sugar for Clark's use (VSA-15).

Leonard Helm signs a request to the quartermaster to issue three pints tafia for Helm's use to give to the men on fatigue (VSA-15).

John Donne signs a request to Carney to send Donne, by the bearer, five quarts tafia (VSA-15).

Lieutenant Joseph Calvit signs a request to the quartermaster to issue one quart tafia on Calvit's account (VSA-15).

Robert George signs a request to the quartermaster to issue one days ration of tafia to 110 men of the Illinois Regiment (VSA-15).

January 31, 1781/Wednesday
Jarret Williams signs a request to the quartermaster to issue two quarts and a pint tafia for Williams' use (VSA-15).

Lieutenant Richard Clark and Robert George sign a request to Israel Dodge to issue one waistcoat and one pair overalls to Pattrick Shirkia [Sharky] who is engaged for the war in Captain Worthington's Company. Clark signed he received the items from Israel Dodge (VSA-15).

Captain John Bailey and Robert George sign a request to Mr. Dodge to issue three pair trousers for Bailey's Company. Bailey signed he received the items from Israel Dodge (VSA-15).

February, 1781/Miscellaneous
Jacob Pyatte signs that he received 3,333 1/3 dollars for going express to Fort Jefferson in February (VSA-16).

February 1, 1781/Thursday
Leonard Helm signs a request to the quartermaster to issue three pints tafia for Helm's use (VSA-16).

Lieutenant Joseph Calvit signs a request to Mr. Carney, to send by the bearer, four quarts tafia (VSA-16).

Buckner Pittman and Robert George sign a request to the quartermaster to issue eight gills tafia for eight men on fatigue (VSA-16).

Abraham Kellar and Robert George sign a request to the quartermaster to issue 1/2 pound gunpowder and one pound lead for two men of Kellar's Company (VSA-16; 50: 31).

Edward Worthington signs a request to the quartermaster to issue one quart tafia for Worthington's use (VSA-16).

Joseph Calvit signs a request to the quartermaster let the bearer have one quart liquor (VSA-16).

Leonard Helm signs a request to the quartermaster to issue three quarts rum for Helm's use (VSA-16).

John Bailey and Robert George sign a request to Israel Dodge to issue Mrs. Bredin pay for making 10 shirts for Bailey's Company (VSA-16).

Lieutenant Jarret Williams signs a request to the quartermaster to issue three pints tafia for Williams' use (VSA-16).

Joseph Calvit signs a request to the quartermaster let the bearer have one quart whiskey (VSA-16).

John Donne signs a request to Martin Carney to send Donne five quarts tafia (VSA-16).

Robert George signs a request for one pound sugar to David Kennedy (VSA-15).

John Donne signs a request to Martin Carney to send three quarts tafia for the first, second, and third of February, according to regulations (VSA-16).

February 2, 1781/Friday
Captain John Bailey signs a request to the quartermaster stating, "Good for two quarts taffia" (VSA-16).

Ensign Jarrett Williams and Robert George sign a request to Martin Carney to issue five pounds sugar for Williams' own use (VSA-16).

Robert George signs a request to Martin Carney to issue one quart tafia to sergeant John Walker of George's Company (VSA-16).

Lieutenant Joseph Calvit and Robert George sign a request to Martin Carney to issue 41 gills whiskey for men on fatigue (VSA-16).

Joseph Calvit signs a request to Martin Carney to send seven quarts liquor [a week's ration] to Calvit (VSA-16).

Lieutenant Richard Clark and Robert George sign a request to Israel Dodge to pay Mrs. Martin Hunter for making four soldiers' shirts for Worthington's Company. Marah Hunter signed she received five yards osnaburg and two bunches of cap wire for the within order (VSA-16).

February 3, 1781/Saturday

Leonard Helm and Robert George sign a request to Martin Carney for two quarts rum for the friendly Indians (VSA-16).

Edward Worthington signs a request to the quartermaster for three pints tafia for Worthington's use (VSA-16).

Robert George signs a request to Martin Carney for 1 1/2 gallons rum for George's use (VSA-16).

Richard Clark signs a request to the quartermaster for one quart tafia for Clark (VSA-16).

Leonard Helm and Robert George sign a request to Martin Carney for two quarts tafia for the friendly Indians (VSA-16).

John Bailey signs a request to the quartermaster stating, "Good for two quarts taffia" (VSA-16).

Beverly Trent and Robert George sign a request to the quartermaster to issue rations of whiskey for 104 men of the Illinois Department (VSA-16).

Edward Worthington and Robert George sign a request to the quartermaster to issue 13 gills of whiskey for the fatigue under George's command (VSA-16).

Israel Dodge signs a request to Martin Carney stating, "Good for three pints of taffia" (VSA-16).

Joseph Calvit and Robert George sign a request to the quartermaster to issue liquor [one gill per man] for seven men of Calvit's Company on fatigue (VSA-16).

Jarret Williams signs a request to the quartermaster to issue four quarts and a pint of rum for Williams, being a week's allowance (VSA-16).

Leonard Helm and Robert George sign a request to the quartermaster to issue one quart rum for the friendly Indians (VSA-16).

Leonard Helm signs a request to the quartermaster to issue three quarts tafia for Helm's use (VSA-16).

Joseph Calvit and Robert George sign a request to Martin Carney to issue 1/2 pound gunpowder and one pound lead for Calvit's use (VSA-16; 50: 31).

Joseph Calvit and Robert George sign a request to the quartermaster to issue two axes for Calvit's Company (VSA-16; 50: 38).

Michael Wolf signed his "mark" he received $18 from John Donne for one rasp and two staples from the provision store house door (VSA-16).

Account of ammunition delivered by Martin Carney by order of Captain Robert George at Fort Jefferson: to Lieutenant Clark for his use, 1/2 pound gunpowder (VSA-50: 31).

Stores issued by order of Captain Robert George: to Lieutenant Calvit, three swords (VSA-50: 38).

February 4, 1781/Sunday

Joseph Calvit signs a request to Martin Carney to issue Sergeant Miles one quart tafia and charge it to Calvit (VSA-16).

Beverly Trent and Robert George request the quartermaster issue rations of whiskey for 100 men of the Illinois Regiment (VSA-16).

Leonard Helm and Robert George request the quartermaster issue quarts of tafia for the Kickapoo Indians (VSA-16).

Zephaniah Blackford and Robert George request the quartermaster issue 1/4 pound gunpowder, 1/2 pound lead, and two flints to Blackford, and charge it to Blackford's account (VSA-16).

Edward Worthington requests the quartermaster issue three pints tafia for Worthington's use (VSA-16).

Ensign L. Slaughter requests the quartermaster issue 1/2 gal tafia for Slaughter's use (VSA-16).

Lieutenant Richard Clark and Robert George request from the quartermaster 1/2 pound tobacco for one man in Worthington's Company (VSA-16).

Richard Clark and Robert George sign a request to the quartermaster, for ammunition for two men of Worthington's Company (VSA-16).

Richard Clark and Robert George sign a request to the quartermaster for 1/2 pound gunpowder for Clark's own use (VSA-16).

Leonard Helm and Robert George sign a request to the quartermaster for Paul, a soldier, one quart rum for acting as interpreter (charge to the Indian Department) (VSA-16).

Lieutenant Richard Clark and Robert George sign a request to Israel Dodge to pay Mrs. Lunsford in goods from the public store for making two shirts for Worthington's Company. Anthony Lunsford signed over the order to Mrs. Breden by consent of Lunsford's wife (VSA-16).

Account of ammunition delivered by Martin Carney by order of Captain Robert George at Fort Jefferson: to two men of Captain Worthington's Company, one pound gunpowder and two pounds lead (VSA-50: 31).

Stores issued by order of Captain Robert George, to a soldier of Captain Bailey's: one musket and one bayonet with belt (VSA-50: 38).

February 5, 1781/Monday

Ensign Slaughter and Robert George sign a request to Martin Carney to issue gills of tafia to men on fatigue under Slaughter's command (VSA-16).

Captain George Owens and Robert George sign a request to the quartermaster to issue 1/4 pound gunpowder and 1/2 pound lead to Abraham Taylor (VSA-16; 50: 31).

Lieutenant Richard Clark signs a request to Martin Carney for three quarts tafia for Clark's own use (VSA-16).

Leonard Helm and Robert George sign a request to the quartermaster for one gallon tafia for the Kickapoo Indians (VSA-16).

Edward Worthington and Robert George sign a request to the quartermaster for three pounds coffee for his use (VSA-16).

Leonard Helm and Robert George request two quarts tafia for the Kickapoo Indians (VSA-16).

Edward Worthington and Robert George sign a request to Martin Carney for six gallons tafia for Worthington's use (VSA-16).

Robert George signs a request to the quartermaster for three pounds sugar to Miss Phelps (VSA-16).

Edward Worthington and Robert George sign a request to the quartermaster for six pounds sugar for Worthington's use (VSA-16).

Robert George signs a request to the quartermaster for 1/2 gallon rum for George's use (VSA-16).

Robert George signs a request to the quartermaster for Bartlit Searcy for one quart tafia for being on express (VSA-16).

Israel Dodge signed a statement to the quartermaster, "good for one quart taffia" (VSA-16).

Richard Clark signs a request to Martin Carney for one quart tafia for Clark's own use (VSA-16).

Lieutenant Joseph Calvit and Robert George sign a request to Israel Dodge to issue 3/4 yard cloth for Calvit's own use and in part of Calvit's draw of clothing for this year (VSA-16).

Martin Carney and Robert George sign a request to Mr. Dodge to issue three yards cloth and as much mohair and silk as necessary for a suit of clothes which is part of Carney's draw of clothes for this year. Carney signed he received three yards cloth, two skeins silk, three skeins mohair, and five skeins thread from Israel Dodge (VSA-16).

John Bailey and Robert George sign a request to Israel Dodge to pay Mrs. Trent for making nine shirts, two coats, one waistcoat, and two pair breeches for Bailey's Company. John Williams signs in behalf of Sarah Trent; he received of Israel Dodge nine yards flannel and eight looking glasses for the within order (VSA-16).

February 6, 1781/Tuesday

Robert George signs a request to the quartermaster for one day's ration of whiskey for 110 men of the Illinois Regiment (VSA-16).

Beverly Trent and Robert George sign a request to the quartermaster for rations of whiskey for 109 men of the Illinois Regiment (VSA-16).

John Bailey and Robert George sign a request to the quartermaster for one carot tobacco for Bailey's use (VSA-16).

John Bailey signs a statement to Carney, "Good for two quarts taffia" (VSA-16).

Leonard Helm and Robert George sign a request to Martin Carney to issue one gallon tafia for the friendly Indians (VSA-16).

Lieutenant Richard Clark and Robert George sign a request to the quartermaster for 17 gills whiskey for 17 men on fatigue (VSA-16).

Captain Robert George signs a return to the quartermaster for 1/2 pound gunpowder and one pound lead to Jesse Piner and William Pursley of George's Company (VSA-16).

Account of ammunition delivered by Martin Carney by order of Captain Robert George at Fort Jefferson: to two men of Captain George's Company, one pound gunpowder and two pounds lead (VSA-50: 31).

February 7, 1781/Wednesday

Beverly Trent and Robert George sign a request to the quartermaster to issue rations of whiskey for 109 men of the Illinois Regiment (VSA-16).

Major Silas Harlan and Robert George sign a request for 1 1/2 pounds gunpowder and three pounds lead for three men on command to the Falls (VSA-16).

Lieutenant Joseph Calvit and Robert George sign a request to the quartermaster for two gallons tafia for Calvit's use (VSA-16).

Leonard Helm, Superintendent of Indian Affairs, and Robert George sign a request to the quartermaster for five gallons tafia for the Kickapoo Indians to carry to their ration (VSA-16).

Ensign Slaughter signs a request to Martin Carney for 1/2 gallon tafia for Slaughter's use (VSA-16).

Lieutenant Joseph Calvit and Robert George sign a request to Martin Carney for three pounds sugar for Calvit's use (VSA-16).

Sergeant Edward Parker and Robert George sign a request for rations of tafia for 15 men on fatigue (VSA-16).

Leonard Helm and Robert George sign a request to the quartermaster for Paul Soldier [?] one quart tafia for being an interpreter (VSA-16).

Lieutenant Richard Clark signs a request to the quartermaster for one quart tafia for Clark's use (VSA-16).

Captain Robert George requests the quartermaster issue 1/4 pound gunpowder and 1/2 pound lead to three men of Captain George's Company (VSA-16; 50: 31). Israel Dodge signs a statement to Martin Carney, "good for three pints of taffia" (VSA-16).

Lieutenant Richard Clark and Robert George sign a request to Israel Dodge for six skeins thread and one dozen needles for the use of Captain Worthington's Company. Lieutenant Clark signed he received the items from Israel Dodge (VSA-16).

Account of ammunition delivered by Martin Carney by order of Captain Robert George at Fort Jefferson: to the Kickapoo Indians, seven pounds gunpowder and four pounds lead; to two militia men going to the Falls, two pounds gunpowder and one pound lead (VSA-50: 31).

February 8, 1781/Thursday

Captain John Bailey signs a statement to Martin Carney, "good for two quarts taffia" (VSA-16).

Jerrit Williams signs a request to Martin Carney for seven quarts tafia for Williams' weeks ration (VSA-16).

Leonard Helm signs a request for three quarts tafia for Helm's use (VSA-16).

Abraham Kellar and Robert George sign a request to the quartermaster for 23 gills tafia for 23 men on fatigue (VSA-16).

John Bailey and Robert George sign a request to the quartermaster for one pound sugar and 1/2 pound coffee to Anthony Lunsford of Bailey's Company, who is sick (VSA-16).

Richard Clark signs a request to the quartermaster for one quart tafia to the bearer (VSA-16).

Robert George signs a request to the quartermaster for eight pounds gunpowder and 16 pounds lead for men going hunting (VSA-16).

Account of ammunition delivered by Martin Carney by order of Captain Robert George at Fort Jefferson: to Captain Bailey's hunting party, 12 pounds gunpowder and 24 pounds lead (VSA-50: 31).

Robert George signs a request to Martin Carney for one quart tafia to Sergeant John Walker of George's Company (VSA-16).

February 9, 1781/Friday
Captain John Bailey and Robert George sign a request to the quartermaster pay Mrs. Johnston for making one shirt and three pairs of overalls for Bailey's Company (VSA-16).

John Bailey signs statement to the quartermaster, "Good for two quarts taffia" (VSA-16).

Captain Robert George signs a request to the quartermaster to issue 2 1/2 gallons whiskey to Mr. Moses Henry (VSA-16).

Robert George signs a request to the quartermaster to issue one quart rum to the express from the Falls of Ohio (VSA-16).

Captain Edward Worthington and Robert George sign a request to the quartermaster for six pounds sugar for Worthington's use (VSA-16).

John Donne signs a request to Martin Carney to send five quarts tafia to Donne (VSA-16).

Lieutenant Richard Clark signs a request to the quartermaster for three pints tafia for Clark's own use (VSA-16).

Captain Edward Worthington signs a request to the quartermaster for five quarts tafia for Clark's own use (VSA-16).

Robert George signs a request to Israel Dodge for Bartlet Searcey, 2 3/4 yards cloth and 12 skeins thread for arriving express from the Falls of Ohio (VSA-16).

February 10, 1780/Saturday
William Clark signs a request to the quartermaster for one gallon tafia for Clark's use (VSA-16).

Captain John Bailey and Robert George sign a request to the quartermaster for one gun to Edward Murray, a soldier in Bailey's Company (VSA-16).

John Bailey signs a request to the quartermaster for one pound tobacco for Bailey's use (VSA-16).

Captain Edward Worthington signs a request to Martin Carney for five quarts tafia for Worthington's use (VSA-16).

Beverly Trent and Robert George sign a request to the quartermaster for rations of whiskey for 109 men of the Illinois Regiment (VSA-16).

Ensign Slaughter signs a request to the quartermaster for 1/2 gallon tafia for Slaughter's use (VSA-16).

Ensign Slaughter signs a request to the quartermaster for one quart tafia for Slaughter's use (VSA-16).

Leonard Helm signs a request to the quartermaster for three pints tafia for Helm's use (VSA-16).

Leonard Helm and Robert George sign a request to the quartermaster for three pounds sugar for Helm's use (VSA-16).

Patrick Kennedy signed at Kaskaskia that the following were received from Israel Dodge for the use of the troops at Fort Jefferson: 519 pounds lead; 17 1/2 bushels salt; one large pickle cask; eighteen stone plates, and two salt sellers issued for Colonel Clark's own use (VSA-16).

February 11, 1781/Sunday
Leonard Helm and Robert George sign a request to Israel Dodge for a friendly Indian, one shirt (VSA-16).

Captain John Bailey signs statement to Martin Carney, "Good for quart taffia" (VSA-16).

Israel Dodge signs a request to the quartermaster for three quarts tafia for Dodge's use (VSA-16).

Major Linctot signs a request to the quartermaster for 100 pounds gunpowder in two kegs, 100 pounds lead, and 150 flints for the use of the Indian Department (VSA-16).

Lieutenant Richard Clark signs a request to the quartermaster for three pints tafia for Clark's own use (VSA-16).

Sergeant Beverly Trent and Robert George sign a request for rations of whiskey for 109 men of the Illinois Regiment (VSA-16).

February 12, 1781/Monday
Sergeant Beverly Trent and Robert George sign a request to the quartermaster for rations of whiskey for 110 men of the Illinois Regiment (VSA-16).

Ensign Slaughter signs a requests to Martin Carney for 1/2 gallon tafia for Slaughter's use (VSA-16).

Captain Edward Worthington signs a request to Martin Carney for one quart tafia for Worthington's use (VSA-16).

Lieutenant Richard Clark signs a request to the quartermaster for one quart tafia for Clark's use (VSA-16).

Sergeant William Elms and Captain Robert George sign a request to the quartermaster for ten gills whiskey, for so many men on fatigue (VSA-16).

Robert George signs a request to the quartermaster for one pound tobacco to the express from the Falls of Ohio (VSA-16).

Edward Worthington signs a request to Martin Carney for three pints tafia for Worthington's use (VSA-16).

Robert George signs a request to Israel Dodge for two pounds vermilion for the use of the friendly Savages; charge the same to the state of Virginia (VSA-16).

Lieutenant Joseph Calvit and Robert George sign a request to Martin Carney for 1 1/2 pounds sugar for Sergeant Mills' sick wife (VSA-16).

Account of ammunition delivered by Martin Carney by order of Captain Robert George at Fort Jefferson: to Z. Blackford, 1/4 pound gunpowder and 1/2 pound lead (VSA-50: 32).

February 13, 1781/Tuesday

Lieutenant Richard Clark signs a return to the quartermaster for whiskey for 13 men of Captain Worthington's Company (VSA-16).

Captain Edward Worthington signs a request to the quartermaster for one quart tafia for Worthington's use (VSA-16).

Captain Robert George signs a request to Israel Dodge for 15 1/2 pounds white thread and 1,000 needles to Major Linctot for the use of the Indian Department (VSA-16).

Israel Dodge signs a request to the quartermaster for three quarts rum for Dodge's use (VSA-16).

Leonard Helm and Robert George sign a request to the quartermaster for eight pounds tobacco to the Peorian Indians (VSA-16).

Captain Robert George signs a request to Mr. Dodge for Major Linctot 12 pounds twine, five pounds colored thread, 4 1/2 pounds white thread, and 1/4 pound cambric thread for use of the Indian Department (VSA-16).

Captain John Bailey signs statement to Martin Carney, "Good for two quarts taffia" (VSA-16).

John Bailey and Robert George sign a request to the quartermaster for 30 pounds coffee for Bailey and Ensign Slaughter's use (VSA-16).

Robert George signs a request to Israel Dodge to issue 3 1/2 yards cloth for Major Linctot's own use. Linctot signed he received the cloth from Israel Dodge (VSA-16).

Stores issued by order of Captain Robert George: to Captain Bailey, one axe; to a soldier of Captain Brashears, one musket and one bayonet with belt; to Peorian Indians, seven swords; to Buckner Pittman, Boatmaster, one kettle; to Captain Worthington's Company, two muskets; and to Captain Worthington for his use, one kettle (VSA-50: 38).

February 14, 1781/Wednesday

Sergeant Beverly Trent and Robert George sign a request to the quartermaster for rations of whiskey for 109 men of the Illinois Regiment (VSA-16).

John Bailey and Robert George sign request to Martin Carney to issue one terijohn of tafia a piece for Captain Bailey and Ensign Slaughter's own use as rations going to St. Vincent [O'Post] (VSA-16).

William Clark signs a request to Martin Carney for one quart tafia for Clark's use (VSA-16).

William Clark signs a request to the quartermaster for one quart tafia; charged to Clark's account (VSA-16).

Robert George signs a request to the quartermaster for 13 1/2 gallons rum for George's use (VSA-16).

Leonard Helm signs a requests to Martin Carney for two gallons and one quart tafia for Helm's use (VSA-16).

Leonard Helm signs a request to the quartermaster three pints tafia for Helm's use (VSA-16).

Leonard Helm signs a request to the quartermaster for five pints tafia for Helm's use (VSA-16).

Robert George requests Mr. Dodge issue Major Linctot three yards broad cloth, five skeins thread, and three skeins mohair for Linctot's use (VSA-16).

John Bailey signs a statement to Martin Carney, "Good for two, one quarts taffia" (VSA-16).

Robert George signs a request to the quartermaster for 2 1/2 pounds gunpowder, five pounds lead, and three flints to the express from the Falls of Ohio (VSA-16).

Account of ammunition delivered by Martin Carney by order of Captain Robert George at Fort Jefferson: to B. Scarcy, express, 2 1/2 pounds gunpowder, and five pounds lead (VSA-50: 32).

Robert George signs a request to Israel Dodge for five dozen and ten buttons for Major Linctot's use (VSA-16).

Ensign Jarret Williams and Robert George sign a request to the quartermaster for one musket to a soldier of Brashears' Company. John McMichael signed his "mark" he received the within musket with bayonet and belt from Martin Carney (VSA-16).

Robert George signs a request to Israel Dodge for three yards broadcloth, five skeins thread and three skeins mohair to Captain Robert Todd. Ensign L. Slaughter signed he received the items from Israel Dodge on behalf of Captain Todd (VSA-16).

Leonard Helm writes to Colonel George Slaughter from Fort Jefferson (MHS B2,F1).

Captain John Bailey signs statement to the quartermaster, "Good for two quarts taffia" (VSA-16).

Captain Richard Brashears received the following on this date: 1/2 yd scarlet cloth, 7/4 wide; 1/2 yd broadcloth; 2 1/2 yds shalloon; two yds calander; four yds toile gris; eight yds toile gris; three yds grey cloth 7/8 wide; 19 1/2 yds white linen; 3/4 yd fine holland; two yds muslin; ten skeins thread; 2 1/2 yds check; 2 1/2 yds coarse linen; one pair thread hose; one silk handkerchief; four linen handkerchiefs; four skeins silk; one hat; 2 3/4 yds calamanco; three yds blue broadcloth; one English blanket; one ivory and one horn comb; 3 1/2 gallons rum; eight lbs sugar; six lbs soap; four lbs coffee; 11 gallons, three quarts and a pint rum; ten lbs sugar; three lbs coffee; four gallons, one quart and a pint of rum; 60 lbs sugar; five lbs tobacco; one pair shoes and 22 white shirts (VSA-16).

Captain John Bailey receives the following issues on this date: 1 1/2 yds brown broadcloth, 7/4 wide; 1 1/2 yds scarlet cloth; one stick silk twist; eight skeins silk; 2 1/4 yds thickset; two yds toile gris; 4 1/2 yds check linen; 3 1/8 yds calender; 5/8 yd sycee; two yds toile gris; two yds chintz; 19 1/2 yds white linen; two yds muslin; 2 1/2 yds shalloon; 3/4 yd fine Holland; nine skeins white thread; one silk handkerchief; one India handkerchief; four linen handkerchiefs; two pair thread hose; 3 1/2 yds coarse linen; three yds broad cloth 7/4 wide; 2 3/4 yd calamanco; 3/4 yd spotted flannel; four yds osnaburg; 5/8 strouding; one blanket; and five yds white flannel (VSA-16).

February 15, 1781/Thursday

Letter from Captain Robert George at Fort Jefferson to George Slaughter. George states he received Slaughter's letter of January 23, 1781. He received a small amount of supplies; they were very helpful and he wishes for more. George states that Major Harlan will give Slaughter news about Fort Jefferson. Captain George is sending with Harlan, 100 weight sugar, 12 lbs soap, and 50 weight coffee. George also tells of sending men and supplies to O'Post (GRC, I: 506-507).

Ensign L. Slaughter signs a request to the quartermaster for one gallon tafia for Slaughter's use (VSA-16).

Robert George signs a request to the quartermaster for 1/2 hogshead tafia to Major Linctot for his own use (VSA-16).

John Bailey and Captain Robert George sign a request to the quartermaster for one axe from the public store for Bailey's use (VSA-16).

Ensign L. Slaughter signs a request to the quartermaster for ten gallons tafia for Slaughter's use (VSA-16).

Robert George signs a request to the quartermaster for 15 pounds coffee for Major Linctot (VSA-16).

Robert George signs a request to the quartermaster for five hogsheads tafia to Linctot for use of the Indian Department (VSA-16).

Buckner Pittman, boatmaster, and Robert George, sign a request to the quartermaster for three gills tafia for three men on fatigue (VSA-16).

Captain John Bailey signs a statement to Martin Carney, "Good for one quart taffia" (VSA-16).

Zephaniah Blackford and Robert George sign a request to the Department Agent of Stores for one dozen sewing needles for Blackford's; charge to Blackford's account (VSA-16).

Lieutenant Joseph Calvit and Robert George sign a request to Martin Carney for six pounds sugar for Calvit's use (VSA-16).

Edward Worthington signs a request to Martin Carney for three pints rum for Worthington's use (VSA-16).

Lieutenant Richard Clark signs a request to the quartermaster issue two quarts and one pint tafia for Clark's use (VSA-16).

Michael Miles and Robert George sign a request to the quartermaster for rations of whiskey for 109 men of Illinois Regiment (VSA-16).

Robert George signs a request to the quartermaster for Ensign Slaughter 1/2 pound gunpowder and one pound lead for Slaughter's use in going on command to the O'Post (VSA-16; 50: 34).

Leonard Helm signs a request to the quartermaster for three pints tafia for Helm's use (VSA-16).

Sergeant John Young and Robert George sign a request to the quartermaster for 2 1/4 pounds gunpowder for nine men of Captain Roberts' Company (VSA-16).

Sergeant John Young and Robert George sign a request to the quartermaster for two pounds tobacco for nine men of Captain Roberts' Company (VSA-16).

Israel Dodge signs a request to Martin Carney for three pints rum for Dodge's use (VSA-16).

Robert George signs a request to the quartermaster for Major Linctot 300 pounds gunpowder, 100 pounds lead, and 150 gun flints for the Indian Department and inhabitants of St. Vincent [Vincennes] (VSA-16).

Jerrit Williams signs a request to Martin Carney for seven quarts tafia for Williams' use (VSA-16).

Israel Dodge signs a request to the quartermaster for three quarts and a pint of tafia for Dodge's use (VSA-16).

Captain Robert George at Fort Jefferson writes to George Rogers Clark. George encloses a previously written letter to Clark that had not been delivered because Captain Roberts was driven back by Indians. Mentions Maj. Linctot's arrival from O'Post with chiefs of the Ottawas and Piankashaws. They had been given permission to "lift" the tomahawks against the enemy. George also mentions that Captain Bailey and Ensign Slaughter have been sent to the O'Post with 20 men. George has sent a quantity of liquor and salt to purchase provisions for support of the O'Post. Also sent by Major Linctot were a quantity of liquor and half of what ammunition George could spare for the use of the inhabitants at the O'Post (MHS, B2: F1).

Account of ammunition delivered by Martin Carney by order of Captain Robert George at Fort Jefferson: to Captain Roberts' Company, going on command, 2 1/4 pounds gunpowder (VSA-50: 32).

<u>February 16, 1781</u>/<u>Friday</u>
Robert George signs a request to Martin Carney to issue Captain John Bailey 150 pounds gunpowder, 100 pounds lead, and 100 flints to take to St. Vincent [Vincennes], for the defense of that post (VSA-16; 50: 34).

Captain John Bailey signs a request to Israel Dodge for 3/4 yd camblet for Bailey's use (VSA-16).

Captain John Bailey signs a statement to Martin Carney, "Good for three quarts taffia" (VSA-16).

Lt. Joseph Calvit signs a request to the quartermaster for seven quarts tafia for Calvit's use (VSA-16).

Buckner Pittman, boatmaster, and Robert George sign a request to the quartermaster for three pints rum for Pittman's use (VSA-16).

Ammunition delivered by order of Captain George: to Majr. Linctot for the Indian Department, 400 pounds gunpowder, 212 pounds lead and 300 flints; to Lt. Calvit, 1/2 pound gunpowder; to Lt. Clark's Company, 3 3/4 pounds gunpowder and 7 1/2 pounds lead (VSA-50: 34).

Major Geofrey Linctot signs he received from Martin Carney, the following for the Indian Department: 400 pounds gunpowder; 212 pounds lead; 300 flints; 15 pounds coffee; two axes; 5 1/2 hogsheads; 48 1/2 gallons tafia or Spanish rum; two pounds pitch; two pounds tallow; 35 nails; and eight pounds steel (VSA-16).

Leonard Helm signs a request to the quartermaster for three pints tafia for Helm's use (VSA-16).

Robert George signs a request to the quartermaster to issue Major Silas Harlan three pounds sugar and charge it to account (VSA-16).

Sergeant John Young and Robert George sign a request to the quartermaster for ten gallons whiskey to a command going by water to the Falls of Ohio (VSA-16).

Robert George signs a request to the quartermaster to issue Major Linctot's party three gallons tafia (VSA-16).

Robert George signs a request to the quartermaster to issue Major Harlin six pounds coffee (VSA-16).

Robert George signs a request to the quartermaster for one gallon tafia to Bartly [Sic] Searcy an express; charge it to Searcy's account (VSA-16).

Robert George signs a request to the quartermaster to issue three gallons and three pints rum for George's use (VSA-16).

Robert George signs a request to the quartermaster to issue Captain John Bailey three yards flannel, one stick [illeg.] and [doc. torn], for the use of Bailey's command (VSA-16).

Captain John Bailey and Robert George sign a request to the quartermaster for eight pounds tobacco for the use of Captain Bailey's Company (VSA-16).

Leonard Helm signs a request to the quartermaster for three pints tafia for Helm's use (VSA-16).

Buckner Pittman, boatmaster, and Robert George sign a request to Martin Carney for rations of tafia for 16 men on fatigue (VSA-16).

Leonard Helm signs a request to the quartermaster for one quart tafia for Helm's use (VSA-16).

Michael Miles and Robert Geroge sign a request to the quartermaster for one ration whiskey to 109 men belonging to the Illinois Regiment (VSA-16).

Lt. Richard Clark signs a request to the quartermaster for three quarts tafia for Clark's own use (VSA-16).

Robert George signs a request to Israel Dodge to issue Major Harlan six skeins thread for Harlan's use. Harlan signed he received from Israel Dodge six skeins of thread (VSA-16).

Lt. Joseph Calvit and Robert George sign a request to Mr. Dodge to pay Mrs. Lunsford for making two pairs overalls for two men under Calvit's Command. Sarah Lunsford signs her "mark" she received one pound twine from Israel Dodge (VSA-16).

Captain John Bailey and Robert George sign a request to Israel Dodge to pay George Shepard for making one pair overalls for the use of Bailey's Company. Shepard signed his "mark" he received four skeins thread (VSA-16).

Account of ammunition expended by the artillery at sundry times by order of Captain Robert George, Commandant at Fort Jefferson: expended by the arrival and setting off of some French batus, five pounds gunpowder and 1/2 yd flannel (VSA-50: 33).

The Commonwealth of Virginia in account with Abraham Kellar: to cash paid Mary Lunsford as per receipt, 72 pounds (VSA-19).

February 17,1781/Saturday
Robert George signs a request to Martin Carney to issue one quart tafia to Sergeant John Walker of George's Company (VSA-16).

John Bailey signs a statement to the quartermaster, "Good for three quarts taffia" (VSA-16).

Israel Dodge signs a request to Martin Carney to issue three pints tafia for Dodge's use (VSA-16).

Lt. Richard Clark and Robert George sign a request to the quartermaster to issue 15 men, under Clark's command, 1/4 pound gunpowder and 1/2 pound lead each (VSA-16).

Sergeant Boston Deamier and Robert George sign a request to the quartermaster for rations of tafia for 12 men on fatigue (VSA-16).

Edward Worthington signs a request to the quartermaster for one quart rum for Worthington's use (VSA-16).

Lt. Richard Clark and Robert George sign a request to the quartermaster for four pounds sugar and three pounds coffee for Clark's use (VSA-16).

Quartermaster Sergeant Michael Miles and Robert George sign a request to the quartermaster for rations of whiskey to 77 men of the Illinois Regiment (VSA-16).

Robert George signs a request to the quartermaster for nine pounds sugar and 4 1/2 pounds coffee to four sick men, two women and three children (VSA-16).

Major Silas Harlan signs a request to Martin Carney for one quart tafia, Harlan because he had left that amount on the Island (VSA-16).

February 18, 1781/Sunday
Sergeant Michael Miles and Robert George sign a request to the quartermaster for rations of liquor for 77 men of the Illinois Regiment (VSA-16).

Major Silas Harlan signs a request to Martin Carney for three quarts tafia for Harlan's use (VSA-16).

Buckner Pittman, boatmaster, and Robert George sign a request to the quartermaster for rations of whiskey for 31 men on fatigue (VSA-16).

Leonard Helm signs a request to the quartermaster for three pints tafia for Helm's use (VSA-16).

Israel Dodge signs a request to the quartermaster for three pints tafia for Dodge's use (VSA-16).

Captain Edward Worthington signs a request to the quartermaster for three pints tafia (VSA-16).

Ensign William Roberts and George Slaughter sign a request for provisions for 16 men and one washer woman of Captain Roberts' Company for eight days, beginning the 18th and ending the 25th of February (VSA-16).

February 19, 1781/Monday
Thomas Jefferson at Richmond writes George Rogers Clark regarding abuses in the "Western quarter" and suggests that Clark make subtle inquiry about them. Mentions that they do not know what to do with the bills Major Slaughter refers to, and hopes that an inquiry would take care of every bill (GRC, I: 507-508).

Captain John Bailey signs a return to the commissary for 14 days [Feb 19-Mar 4], for rations of salt for 25 men, three women and two children of Bailey's Company (VSA).

Ensign Jarrit Williams and Robert George sign a return to the quartermaster for one pound gunpowder and one pound lead each to two men of the hunting party (VSA-16).

Leonard Helm signs a request to the quartermaster to issue three pints tafia for Helm's use (VSA-16).

Robert George signs a request to Mr. Dodge to issue 4/3 yd of coarse blue cloth for leggings for the express from the Falls of Ohio and charge the same to the express (VSA-16).

Quartermaster Sergeant Michael Miles and Robert George sign a request to the quartermaster to issue liquor for one day for 73 men of the Illinois Regiment (VSA-16).

Robert George signs a request to the quartermaster to issue Buckner Pittman 1/2 pound gunpowder and 1/2 pound lead (VSA-16).

Captain Edward Worthington signs a request to the quartermaster to issue three pints rum for Worthington's use (VSA-16).

Lt. Joseph Calvit and Robert George sign a request to the quartermaster to let the bearer have two quarts tafia (VSA-16).

Ammunition delivered by order of Captain George: to Lt. Williams' hunting party, one pound gunpowder and two pounds lead (VSA-50: 34).

Zephaniah Blackford and John Bailey sign a provision return for ten days commencing the 19th and ending the 28th of February, both days included on a march [10 rations] (VSA-16).

February 20, 1781/Tuesday
William Clark signs a request to the quartermaster for one quart tafia for Clark's use (VSA-16; misfiled).

Sergeant Michael Miles and Robert George sign a request to the quartermaster to issue one day ration of liquor to 60 men belonging to the Illinois Regiment (VSA-16).

Leonard Helm signs a request to the quartermaster for one case bottle tafia for Helm's use (VSA-16).

Captain Robert George signs a request to the quartermaster for two quarts tafia for the friendly Indians and charge it to the Indian Account (VSA-16).

Captain Edward Worthington signs a request to the quartermaster to issue two quarts and a pint of tafia for Worthington's use (VSA-16).

John Donne signs a request to Martin Carney to issue one quart tafia for Donne's use (VSA-16).

Lt. Richard Clark and Robert George sign a request to the Agent to pay Mrs. Bredin in goods out of the public store for making seven shirts for Worthington's Company (VSA-16).

Leonard Helm signs a request to the quartermaster to issue three pints tafia being for a particular occassion (VSA-16).

Israel Dodge, Deputy Agent, signs a request to Martin Carney to issue three pints tafia for Dodge's use (VSA-16).

Captain Abraham Kellar and Robert George sign a request to the quartermaster for 18 gills tafia for so many men on fatigue (VSA-16).

John Williams and Robert George sign a request to Israel Dodge to for 1 1/4 yds white flannel, four skeins fine thread, and 16 skeins course (VSA-16).

February 21, 1781/Wednesday

Leonard Helm signs a request to the quartermaster for three pints tafia for Helm's use (VSA-16).

Lt. Richard Clark signs a request to Martin Carney for five gallons and three quarts tafia for Clark's use (VSA-16).

Captain Robert George signs a request to the quartermaster for 50 pound coffee for the use of George's family (VSA-16),

Lt. Richard Clark signs a request to the quartermaster for three pints tafia for Clark's use (VSA-16).

Leonard Helm and Robert George sign a request to the quartermaster for two quarts rum for the friendly Indians (VSA-16).

Quartermaster Sergeant Martin Miles and Robert George sign a request to the quartermaster for liquor rations for one day for 50 men of the Illinois Regiment (VSA-16).

Lt. Richard Clark and Robert George sign a request to the quartermaster for two pounds tobacco for Clark's use (VSA-16).

Captain Edward Worthington and Robert George sign a request to the quartermaster for three pounds coffee for Worthington's use (VSA-16).

Captain Edward Worthington signs a request to the quartermaster for one pint tafia for Worthington's use (VSA-16).

Captain Robert George signs a request to Israel Dodge for one skein silk out of the public store to Lt. Richard Clark (VSA-16).

February 22, 1781/Thursday

Leonard Helm and Robert George sign a request to the quartermaster for 30 pounds gunpowder and 30 pounds lead for the friendly Indians (VSA-16).

Captain Edward Worthington signs a request to the quartermaster for three pints tafia for Worthington's use (VSA-16).

Ensign Jerrit Williams signs a request to Martin Carney for seven quarts tafia for Williams' use (VSA-16).

Leonard Helm signs a request to the quartermaster for two gallons rum for Helm's use (VSA-16).

Captain Robert George signs a request to the quartermaster for three quarts tafia for the friendly Indians (VSA-16).

Captain Edward Worthington signs a request to the quartermaster for two quarts and one pint tafia for Worthington's use (VSA-16).

Captain Edward Worthington and Robert George sign a request to the quartermaster for 16 gills of tafia for the fatigue (VSA-16).

Lt. Joseph Calvit signs a request to the quartermaster for seven quarts tafia for Calvit's use (VSA-16).

Robert George signs a request to the quartermaster for two quarts tafia for James Sherlock, Indian Interpreter (VSA-16).

John Donne signs a request to Martin Carney for three quarts tafia for February 23, 24, and 25 Donne can begin anew with the week on Monday (VSA-16).

Lt. Joseph Calvit signs a request to Mr. Kennedy, Assistant Conductor, for his party on fatigue under Calvit's command, 127 lbs flour transporting provisions from the Illinois to Fort Jefferson (VSA-13).

Ammunition delivered by order of Captain George: to Peorian [Peoria] Indians, 30 pounds gunpowder, 30 pounds lead, and 80 flints; to two men going with Majr. Harlan to the Falls of Ohio, 1 1/2 pounds gunpowder and three pounds lead; to Buckner Pittman, boatmaster, 1/2 pounds gunpowder and one pound lead; to Mr. Kennedy, one pound gunpowder; to three men of Captain Bailey's Company, 1 1/2 pounds gunpowder and three pounds lead (VSA-50: 34).

February 23, 1781/Friday

Buckner Pittman, boatmaster, and Robert George sign a request to the quartermaster to issue one kettle for Pittman's use (VSA-20).

Captain Robert George signs a request to Mr. Dodge to issue 100 sewing needles to the friendly Indian allies (VSA-16).

Robert George signs a request to Mr. Dodge to issue two pounds twine for use of the friendly Indians (VSA-16).

Sergeant William Crump and Robert George sign a return for tafia for 16 men belonging to the fatigue (VSA-16).

Israel Dodge signs a request to Martin Carney to issue one gallon tafia for Dodge's use (VSA-16).

Robert George signs a request to Martin Carney to issue one quart tafia to Sergeant John Walker of George's Company (VSA-16).

Leonard Helm and Robert George sign a request to Martin Carney to issue three quarts tafia for the Indians now at this place (VSA-16).

Leonard Helm and Robert George sign a request for 20 gallons tafia to the Peorian Fort as they are now on duty on the Mississippi (VSA-16).

Leonard Helm and Robert George sign a request to the quartermaster to issue three pounds coffee for Helm's use (VSA-16).

James Sherlock and Robert George sign a request to the quartermaster to issue one quart tafia for Sherlock's use (VSA-16).

Captain Edward Worthington signs a request to the quartermaster to issue three pints tafia for Worthington's use (VSA-16).

John Dodge signs a request to Israel Dodge to issue one riding saddle for John Dodge's use. John Dodge signed he received the saddle (VSA-16).

Captain John Rogers signs a request to Martin Carney to issue rations of flour for 21 men of Rogers' Company for two days commencing the 23rd and ending the 24th, both days included on a march (VSA-16).

Leonard Helm signs a request for three pints tafia for Helm's use (VSA-16).

Robert George signs a request to Martin Carney that Joseph Hunter be issued four pounds sugar (VSA-16).

February 24, 1781/Saturday
Captain Edward Worthington signs a request to the quartermaster for three pints tafia for Worthington's use (VSA-16).

Robert George signs a request to the quartermaster for one quart tafia to the quartermaster sergeant (VSA-16).

Leonard Helm and Robert George sign a request to the quartermaster for seven swords and 80 flints to the Peoria Indians (VSA-16).

Lt. Richard Clark signs a request to the quartermaster for two quarts and one pint tafia for Clark's use (VSA-16).

Lt. Richard Clark signs a request to the quartermaster for one quart tafia for Clark's use (VSA-16).

Robert George signs a request to the quartermaster for ten pounds gunpowder to Mr. Datcherut. Datcherut is to replace this amount upon his return from New Orleans (VSA-16).

Leonard Helm and Robert George sign a request to the quartermaster for three pints tafia for Helm's use (VSA-16).

Leonard Helm and Robert George sign a request to the quartermaster for two gallons rum for the friendly Indians (VSA-16).

Leonard Helm signs an exchange to Oliver Pollock for 175 livres in peltry for Monsieur Datcherut as an advance for the Indian Department and charge to the State of Virginia (VSA-16).

February 25, 1781/Sunday
Robert George signs a request for one quart rum for the use of Mr. James Sherlock (VSA-16).

Captain John Rogers signs a request to the quartermaster for one quart tafia for Rogers' use (VSA-16).

Lt. Joseph Calvit and Robert George sign a request to the quartermaster for four quarts of tafia for Calvit's use (VSA-16).

Leonard Helm and Robert George sign a request to the quartermaster for three quarts tafia for the friendly Indians (VSA-16).

Leonard Helm signs a request to the quartermaster for three pints tafia for Helm's use (VSA-16).

Captain Edward Worthington signs a request to the quartermaster for three pints tafia for Worthington's use (VSA-16).

Sergeant Robert Davis and Robert George sign a request to the quartermaster for liquor to one Sergeant and 16 men [one gill per man] being on fatigue (VSA-16).

Girault signs a request to the quartermaster for one quart tafia for Girault (VSA-16).

Lt. Richard Clark and Robert George sign a request to Mr. Dodge to pay Mrs. Jones for making four pairs of overalls for Captain Worthington's Company. Elizabeth Jones signs her "mark" she received of Israel Dodge, one yd broad cloth (VSA-16).

Account of ammunition received by Martin Carney at this post, Clarksville: received from Pattrick Kennedy, 340 pounds lead (VSA-50: 5).

February 26, 1781/Monday
Robert George signs that the following shall be present at a Court of Inquiry to inspect alligations (retailing liquors, disobedience of orders, gambling with soldiers) against Captain Worthington by Major George Slaughter (Draper Manuscripts 56J27-28; VSA-16):

1. Captain Roberts
2. Captain Kellar
3. Lieut Giralt
4. Captain Rogers - Pres.
5. Lieut Calvit
6. Lieut Clark
7. Cornet Thruston

Robert Davis has no rank or affiliation given, but he collaborated testimony of Sergeant Miles and Lt. Calvit at Fort Jefferson during Board of Inquiry regarding Captain Worthington (Draper Manuscripts 56J28).

Robert George signs a request to the quartermaster to issue Mr. Dejean, three pints rum (VSA-16).

Lt. Richard Clark signs a request to the quartermaster for one gallon tafia for Clark's own use (VSA-16).

John Williams signs a request to Martin Carney to "let" him have one bottle for this day (VSA-16).

Leonard Helm and Robert George sign a request to the quartermaster for three pints tafia for the friendly Indians (VSA-16).

Leonard Helm and Robert George sign a request to the quartermaster for three quarts tafia to the Peorian Indians who are friendly allies (VSA-16).

Lt. Richard Clark signs a request to the quartermaster for three pints tafia for Clark's use (VSA-16).

Robert George signs a request to the quartermaster for nine gallons rum for George's use (VSA-16).

Buckner Pittman, boatmaster, and Robert George sign a request to the quartermaster for one quart tafia for Pittman's use (VSA-16).

John Williams signs a request to the quartermaster for two gallons tafia, (VSA-16).

John Donne and Robert George sign a request to Mr. Carney for four gallons tafia to be charged to Donne as rations (VSA-16).

John Williams signs a note to Mr. Carney, asking him for one more bottle as Captain George has come to visit, and Williams has none to offer him (VSA-16).

Robert George signs a request for three pints rum to Philip Dejean for Dejean's use (VSA-16).

John Donne signs a request to Mr. Carney to issue seven quarts tafia for Donne's allowance from the 26th to the 4th of March (VSA-16).

Robert George signs a request to Israel Dodge to issue one coat and seven pairs of trousers out of "your" store for George's Company. Lt. Martin Carney signed he received the trousers from Israel Dodge (VSA-16).

February 27, 1781/Tuesday
Lt. Richard Clark signs a request to the quartermaster for three pints tafia for Clark's use (VSA-16).

Buckner Pittman, Boatmaster, and Robert George sign a request to the quartermaster for rations of tafia for 11 men on fatigue (VSA-16).

Leonard Helm signs a request to Mr. Carney to let the bearer have three pints tafia (VSA-16).

Captain Edward Worthington signs a request to the quartermaster for one quart tafia for Worthington's use (VSA-16).

John Thruston signs a requests to the quartermaster for one bottle tafia for Thruston's use (VSA-16).

Beverly Trent and Robert George sign a request to the quartermaster for rations of whiskey for 109 men of the Illinois Regiment (VSA-16).

February 28, 1781/Wednesday
William Clark signs a request to the quartermaster for four gallons tafia for Clark's use (VSA-16).

Lt. Richard Clark signs a request to the quartermaster for three pints tafia for Clark's use (VSA-16).

Leonard Helm signs a request to the quartermaster for three pints tafia for Helm's use (VSA-16).

Buckner Pittman and Robert George sign a request to the quartermaster for one quart rum for Pittman's use (VSA-16).

Captain Edward Worthington signs a requests to the quartermaster for one quart tafia for Worthington's use (VSA-16).

Lt. Richard Clark signs a request to Martin Carney for three pints tafia for Clark's own use (VSA-16).

Robert George signs a request to Mr. Carney for one quart tafia to Sergeant John Walker of George's Company (VSA-16).

Captain John Rogers signs a request to the quartermaster for three pints tafia for Rogers' use (VSA-16).

Captain John Rogers and Robert George sign a request to the quartermaster for one quart tafia for a sick man to exchange for molasses (VSA-16).

John Williams signs a request to Martin Carney for a bottle of tafia stating "Lord, how dry I am" (VSA-16).

William Crump, sergeant of fatigue, and Robert George, sign a request to the quartermaster for tafia for 14 men belonging to the fatigue (VSA-16).

John Williams signs a request to Mr. Carney for a bottle of "the best" to make Williams' "heart glad" (VSA-16).

Court of Inquiry to look into charges laid against Captain Richard McCarty regarding his being disrespectful to the Service/State of Virginia. Charges brought by Captain John Dodge. Court heard statements adjourned until tomorrow, Thursday, March 1, 1781. The following individuals sat on the Board of the Court of Inquiry (Draper Manuscripts 56J29):

1. Captain Robert George, President
2. William Clark, Judge Advocate
3. Captain Keller
4. Captain Roberts
5. Lieutenant Girault
6. Lieutenant Calvit
7. Lieutenant Clark
8. Cornet Thruston

March, 1781/Miscellaneous
John Rogers is ordered to Fort Jefferson [he had been in charge at Kaskaskia] (VSA-17).

John Rogers is later dispatched to Louisville, possibly with his troops (VSA-17).

March 1, 1781/Thursday
Court of Inquiry continues: James Finn, John Rogers, James Sherlock, and [Samuel?] Watkins provide testimony. Court adjourns, but will meet tomorrow at 8 a.m. (Draper Manuscripts 56J31-33).

Captain Worthington and Robert George sign a request to the quartermaster for one kettle for Worthington's use (VSA-17).

James Sherlock and Robert George sign a request to the quartermaster for one bottle for Sherlock's use (VSA-17).

Sergeant Michael Miles and Robert George sign a request to the quartermaster for nine gills liquor to nine men on fatigue (VSA-17).

Lt. Calvit signed a request to the quartermaster for two quarts tafia for Calvit's use (VSA-17).

Leonard Helm signs a request to the quartermaster for three quarts rum for Helm's use (VSA-17).

Robert George signs a request to the quartermaster to issue Mr. Sherlock three quarts tafia (VSA-17).

Leonard Helm signs a request to Martin Carney to let the bearer have three pints tafia (VSA-17).

Document with no signature, addressed to the issuing commissary for ten lbs flour for John Daughterty (VSA-17).

Captain Edward Worthington signs a request to the quartermaster for three pints tafia for Worthington's use (VSA-17).

Buckner Pittman and Robert George sign a request to Martin Carney for one quart tafia for Pittman's use (VSA-17).

James Finn signs a request to the quartermaster to send Finn one bottle of rum (VSA-17).

Joseph Calvit signed a request to Martin Carney for one case bottle of tafia for Calvit's use (VSA-17).

March 2, 1781/Friday
Court of Inquiry reconvenes at eight a.m. regarding Richard McCarty. Court hears testimony from John Rogers and Cornet Thruston, then adjourns until eight a.m. tomorrow (Draper Manuscripts 56J33-34).

James Finn and Robert George sign a request to the quartermaster to send one pint of rum (VSA-17).

Edward Worthington signs a request to the quartermaster for two days rum ration for Worthington's use [one quart] (VSA-17).

Captain Edward Worthington signs a request to the quartermaster for three pints tafia for Worthington's use (VSA-17).

Robert Todd signs a request for one [illeg.] of stocking and one shirt, so Todd will not "run naked" (VSA-17).

Robert George signs a request for three bushels corn (VSA-17).

John Rogers signs a request to the quartermaster for two carabins for two men of Rogers' Commissary (VSA-17).

Leonard Helm signs a request to the quartermaster for three pints tafia for Helm's use (VSA-17).

Richard Clark signs a request to the quartermaster for three pints tafia for Clark's use (VSA-17).

Robert George signs a request to the quartermaster for one quart tafia to John Walker of George's Company (VSA-17).

Richard Clark signs a request to the quartermaster to send one quart tafia to Clark (VSA-17).

George Owens and Robert George sign a request for three pints tafia, charged to Owens (VSA-17).

Stores issued by order of Captain Robert George: to Captain Brashears' Company, three muskets or smoothed guns; to Captain Robert George's Company, one musket or smoothed gun; to Captain Robert George's company, no voucher not delivered to Captain George, one kettle (VSA-50: 39).

March 3, 1781/Saturday
Court of Inquiry reconvenes at eight a.m. regarding Captain Richard McCarty. Court hears testimony from Louis Gagnia and Abraham Keller; adjourns until Monday, March 5, 1781 (Draper Manuscripts 56J34).

During Court of Inquiry, Lt. Calvit was ordered by Captain Robert George to leave and go to the Illinois for provisions for Fort Jefferson (Draper Manuscripts 56J34-35).

Edward Worthington signs a request to the quartermaster for three pints tafia for Worthington's use (VSA-17).

Edward Worthington and Robert George sign a request to the quartermaster for two guns for two men of Worthington's Company (VSA-17).

Robert George signs a request to Mr. Dodge to pay Mary Damewood for making two shirts for George's Company. Mary Damewood signs her "mark" she received 1/2 lb twine from Israel Dodge 1/2 lb twine (VSA-17).

James Sherlock and Robert George sign a request to the quartermaster for one quart tafia for Sherlock's own use (VSA-17).

John Vaughan and Robert George sign a request to the quartermaster for 1 1/2 lbs gunpowder and three lbs lead for three men of Captain Bailey's Company (VSA-17).

Israel Dodge signs a request to Mr. Carney for three quarts tafia for Dodge's use (VSA-17).

Richard Clark signs a request to the quartermaster for three pints tafia for Clark's own use (VSA-17).

Leonard Helm and Robert George sign a request to the quartermaster for one gallon [document illeg.] for the friendly Indians (VSA-17).

Robert George signs a request to the quartermaster for three quarts tafia for men going on fatigue to the Illinois (VSA-17).

James Sherlock and Robert George sign a request to the quartermaster for one bottle tafia for the use of Sherlock (VSA-17).

Leonard Helm signs a request to the quartermaster for three pints tafia for Helm's use (VSA-17).

Buckner Pittman and Robert George sign a request to the quartermaster for liquor to four men on fatigue, one gill each (VSA-17).

Israel Dodge signs a request to Martin Carney for one gallon tafia for Dodge's use (VSA-17).

John Rogers signs a request to Martin Carney for three pints rum for Rogers' use (VSA-17).

John Williams signs a request to the quartermaster for one quart tafia for use of the "poor" soldiers (VSA-17).

John Rogers signs a request to Martin Carney for two quarts tafia for Rogers' Company (VSA-17).

John Williams signs a request to the quartermaster for one bottle tafia for Williams' use (VSA-17).

John Donne and Robert George sign a request to the quartermaster for one quart tafia from the company store for eight days work (VSA-17).

Matross Francis Little and Philip Orbin of Captain George's Company deserted (Harding 1981: 29-33).

March 4, 1781/Sunday

Leonard Helm signs a request to the quartermaster for three pints tafia for Helm's use (VSA-17).

Patrick Kennedy certifies the common price of corn in the Illinois Country is ten lbs peltry per bushel, and flour 30 lbs peltry per hundred or more. John Donne signs the within amounts are just (VSA-17).

Joseph Calvit signs a request to Martin Carney to let the bearer have one pint tafia out of Calvit's rations (VSA-17).

Israel Dodge signs a request to Martin Carney for one quart tafia for Dodge's use (VSA-17).

James Finn and Robert George sign a request to the quartermaster to send Finn one bottle taifa (VSA-17).

Patrick Kennedy signed he received of John Dodge, 127 lbs flour for the use of the troops going on command from Kaskaskia to Fort Jefferson (VSA-17).
John Donne signed he received of John Dodge, 270 lbs flour for the use of the troops at Fort Jefferson (VSA-17).

Robert George signs a request to the quartermaster for one quart tafia to John Walker of George's Company (VSA-17).

Lt. Girault signs a request to the quartermaster to issue six quarts tafia for Girault's use (VSA-17).

Robert George signs a request to the quartermaster for three quarts rum for George's Company (VSA-17).

Richard Clark signs a request to the quartermaster for two quarts and one pint tafia for Clark's own use (VSA-17).

Lt. Joseph Calvit signs a request to Martin Carney for two quarts tafia for Calvit's use (VSA-17).

March 5, 1781/Monday
Court of Inquiry reconvenes regarding Captain Richard McCarty. Court hears testimony from Fred Guion and Patick Kennedy and adjourns. Will meet again tomorrow at eight a.m., March 6, 1781 (Draper Manuscripts 56J36-37).

Captain Edward Worthington signs a request to the quartermaster for three pints tafia for Worthington's use (VSA-17).

Robert George signs a request to the quartermaster for seven gallons rum for George's use (VSA-17).

Joseph Calvit signs a request to the quartermaster for two quarts tafia for Calvit's use (VSA-17).

William Clark requests one gallon tafia for Clark's use from the quartermaster (VSA-17).

Buckner Pittman and Robert George sign a request to the quartermaster for liquor for six men on fatigue (VSA-17).

Benjamin Roberts signs a request to the quartermaster for three quarts and one pint tafia for Roberts' use (VSA-17).

Richard Clark signs a request to the quartermaster for one gallon tafia for Clark's use (VSA-17).

Richard Clark signs a request to the quartermaster for three pints tafia for Clark's own use (VSA-17).

Buckner Pittman and Robert George sign a request to the quartermaster for two quarts tafia for Pittman's use (VSA-17).

Pattrick Kennedy signs a request to Martin Carney for the bearer to have one bottle tafia for Kennedy (VSA-17).

John Rogers and Robert George sign a request to the quartermaster for one quart tafia for one man, who is sick (VSA-17).

Benjamin Roberts signs a request to the quartermaster for one quart tafia for Roberts' use (VSA-17).

James Finn and Robert George sign a request to the quartermaster for three pints tafia (VSA-17).

William Clark signs a request to the quartermaster for one quart tafia for Clark's use (VSA-17).

March 6, 1781/Tuesday
Court of Inquiry regarding Captain Richard McCarty, reconvenes, does not hear any testimony, then adjourns until tomorrow March 7, 1781 [Wednesday] (Draper Manuscripts 56J37).

Captain McCarty signs a request to the quartermaster for one case bottle tafia on McCarty's rations (VSA-17).

Edward Worthington signs a request to the quartermaster for three pints tafia for Worthington's use (VSA-17).

Edward Worthington and Robert George sign a request to Israel Dodge for one lb twine thread for Worthington's use (VSA-17).

Richard Clark signs a request to the quartermaster for three pints tafia for Clark's use (VSA-17).

John Williams signs a request to the quartermaster for one bottle tafia for Williams (VSA-17).

Joseph Calvit signs a request to the quartermaster for one quart tafia for Calvit's use (VSA-17).

Joseph Calvit and Robert George sign a request to Israel Dodge for two dozen and 11 large buttons, two dozen and six small [buttons], and nine skeins thread for Calvit's use (VSA-17).

Robert George signs a request to the quartermaster for six flints for three men of Captain Bailey's Company (VSA-17).

Leonard Helm signs a request to the quartermaster for three pints tafia for Helm's use (VSA-17).

Robert George signs a request to the quartermaster to send one bottle tafia to George (VSA-17).

Israel Dodge signs a request to Martin Carney for three pints tafia for Dodge's use (VSA-17).

Jarrit Williams signs a request to Martin Carney for two quarts tafia for Williams' use (VSA-17).

March 7, 1781/Wednesday
Court of Inquiry reconvenes at eight a.m. regarding Captain Richard McCarty. Court hears defense testimony from Captain McCarty then passes verdict. Guilty of first offense (threatening to leave the military service and Virginia) and recommends general court martial. Second offense (insulting a fellow officier), guilty, and shall make concessions to Captain Rogers for his insults. Other charges against McCarty are dismissed (Draper Manuscripts 56J39).

Captain Edward Worthington signs a request to the quartermaster for three pints tafia for Worthington's use (VSA-17).

John Dodge signs a request to the quartermaster for three quarts tafia for the use of the Savages (VSA-17).

George Slaughter and Robert George sign a request to the quartermaster for eight gills tafia for so many men on fatigue (VSA-17).

Joseph Calvit signs a request to Martin Carney for seven quarts tafia for Calvit's use (VSA-17).

John Williams signs a request to the quartermaster to let Williams have one bottle tafia (VSA-17).

Michael Miles and Robert George sign a request to the quartermaster for liquor for men of the Illinois Regiment at one gill each (VSA-17).

Leonard Helm signs a request to the quartermaster for three pints tafia for Helm's use (VSA-17).

Robert George signs a request to the quartermaster for one bottle tafia (VSA-17).

Leonard Helm and Robert George sign a request to the quartermaster for one gallon tafia for the friendly Indians (VSA-17).

Richard Clark signs a request for three pints tafia for Clark's own use (VSA-17).

Benjamin Roberts signs a request to the quartermaster for ten quarts tafia for Roberts' use (VSA-17).

Captain McCarty signs a request to the quartermaster for one quart rum for McCarty's use (VSA-17).

Patrick Kennedy signs a request to Martin Carney for the bearer for one bottle of tafia (VSA-17).

James Finn and Robert George sign a request to the quartermaster to send one bottle tafia (VSA-17).

Leonard Helm and Robert George sign a request to the quartermaster for three pints tafia for the Indian Department (VSA-17).

Lt. Calvit issued seven quarts tafia at Fort Jefferson from Quartermaster Carney (VSA-17).

March 8, 1781/Thursday
Captain Edward Worthington signs a request to the quartermaster for three pints tafia for Worthington's use (VSA-17).

Captain Edward Worthigton signs a request to the quartermaster for three pints tafia for Worthington's use (VSA-17).

Leonard Helm and Robert George sign a request to Israel Dodge for two lbs paint [vermilion] for the friendly Indians (VSA-17).

John Walker and Robert George sign a request to Martin Carney for one quart tafia for John Walker (VSA-17).

James Finn and Robert George sign a request to the quartermaster to send three pints tafia (VSA-17).

Leonard Helm and Robert George sign a request to the quartermaster for four quarts tafia for the Indian allies (VSA-17).

Robert George signs a request to the quartermaster for two lbs gunpowder and four lbs lead for Ensign Williams' hunting party (VSA-17).

Leonard Helm and Robert George sign a request to the quartermaster for three pints tafia for friendly Indians (VSA-17).

Robert George signs a request to the quartermaster for three pints tafia for George's use (VSA-17).

Ammunition delivered by order of Captain George: to Ensign Williams' hunting party, one pound gunpowder and two pounds lead (VSA-50: 34).

March 9, 1781/Friday

A Court of Inquiry was held by order of Captain Robert George to look into Captain John Rogers Conduct during his command at Kaskaskia. The following individuals participated:

Captain Abraham Keller, President
William Clark, Judge Advocate
Captain Roberts
Lieutenant Richard Clark
Lieutenant John Girault
Lieutenant Martin Carney

The Court met, found no proof of any misconduct, and aquitted Captain Rogers (Draper Manuscripts 56J45).

Edward Worthington signs a request to the quartermaster for three pints tafia for Worthington's use (VSA-17).

Robert George signs a request to Martin Carney to deliver 100 weight gunpowder for the support of the inhabitants of Kaskaskia by way of Mr. Patrick Kennedy (VSA-17).

Ammunition delivered by order of Captain George: to Patrick Kennedy for the inhabitants of the Illinois, 100 lbs gunpowder (VSA-50: 34).

John Rogers and Robert George sign a request to Martin Carney to let Patrick Kennedy have 2 1/2 gallons tafia (VSA-17).

Robert George signs a request to Martin Carney to issue Patrick Kennedy 1/2 lb gunpowder and one lb lead for Kennedy's voyage to the Illinois [Kaskaskia] (VSA-17).

Ammunition delivered by order of Captain George: to Patrick Kennedy for his use, 1/2 lb gunpowder and one lb lead (VSA-50: 34).

Robert George signs a request to Martin Carney to deliver four [illeg.] tafia for the purpose of purchasing provisions for Patrick Kennedy (VSA-17).

Joseph Calvit and Robert George sign a request to Martin Carney for ammunition for 15 men under Calvit's command to Kaskaskia, 1/4 lb gunpowder and 1/2 lb lead per man (VSA-17).

Joseph Calvit and Robert George sign a request to Martin Carney for three gallons tafia for Calvit's use (VSA-17).

Lt. Richard Clark signs a request to the quartermaster for three pints tafia for Clark's use (VSA-17).

Leonard Helm and Robert George sign a request to the quartermaster for two quarts tafia for the friendly Indians (VSA-17).

Leonard Helm and Robert George sign a request to the quartermaster for one quart tafia to the chief of the Kaskaskia Indians (VSA-17).

Robert George signs a request to the quartermaster to send one bottle tafia to George (VSA-17).

Richard McCarty and Robert George sign a request to the quartermaster for one demijohn of tafia for McCarty's use (VSA-17).

John Williams signs a request to the quartermaster for nine bottles tafia for Williams' use (VSA-17).

John Thruston signs a request to the quartermaster for one bottle tafia for Thruston's use (VSA-17).

Leonard Helm and Robert George sign a request to Mr. Carney for six quarts tafia for the friendly Indians (VSA-17).

Benjamin Roberts and Col. Slaughter sign a request to the quartermaster for 4 1/2 gallons tafia for Roberts' use (VSA-17).

Richard Clark signs a request to the quartermaster for three pints tafia for Clark's own use (VSA-17).

Abraham Kellar and Robert George sign a request to the quartermaster for 1/4 lb gunpowder and 1/2 lb lead for the use of hunting for the garrison (VSA-17).

Robert George signs a request to the quartermaster for one lb gunpowder for Captain McCarty (VSA-17).

Robert George signs a request to the quartermaster for one quart tafia for eight men on fatigue (VSA-17).

Leonard Helm signs a request to the quartermaster to have one bottle tafia sent to Helm (VSA-17).

Leonard Helm signs a request to the quartermaster for one quart tafia for Helm's use (VSA-17).

Leonard Helm and Robert George sign a request to the quartermaster for three quarts tafia for the Kaskaskia Indians (VSA-17).

Joseph Calvit signs a request to Martin Carney for seven quarts tafia for Calvit's use, being "next week's" rations (VSA-17).

John Rogers signs a request to Martin Carney for three pints tafia for Rogers' use (VSA-17).

John Rogers signs a request to Martin Carney for three pints tafia as Rogers has "not been troublesome" (VSA-17).

James Finn and Robert George sign a request to the quartermaster for one case bottle tafia (VSA-17).

James Finn and Robert George sign a request to the quartermaster for one case bottle tafia "as it is a cold morning" (VSA-17).

John Williams signs a request to the quartermaster for one bottle tafia for Williams' throat (VSA-17).

Ammunition delivered by order of Captain George: to Captain McCarty for his use, one lb gunpowder (VSA-50: 34).

Ammunition delivered by order of Captain George: to John Burks, a militia man, 1/4 pound gunpowder (VSA-50: 34).

Ammunition delivered by order of Captain George: to Lt. Calvit command to the Illinois, 3 3/4 lbs gunpowder and 7 1/2 lbs lead (VSA-17).

March 10, 1781/Saturday
Martha Hughes signs "her mark" that she was issued at Fort Jefferson, two small looking glasses and two paper pins for attending soldiers clothing. Attested by John Donne (VSA-17).

John Dodge signs a request to Israel Dodge for 3 1/2 [not specified] pompedore cloth; 6 1/2 yds white linen; two pair shoes; three skeins worsted; three skiens silk; 2 1/2 [illeg.] buttons; 23 [not specified] white flannel; 16 skeins thread; one stick black ball for Dodge's use as part of his clothing issue for the year. John Dodge signs he received the items from Israel Dodge (VSA-17).

John Dodge signs a request to Israel Dodge to issue eighteen bunches capwire and 300 needles for Dodge's expenses on public service (VSA-17).

Captain Robert George signs a request to the quartermaster to let David Kennedy have a pint of tafia (VSA-17).

Leonard Helm and Robert George sign a request to the quartermaster 20 lbs gunpowder and 40 lbs lead to the friendly Indians (VSA-17).

John Thruston and Robert George sign a request to Israel Dodge for two shirts in part of Samuel Watkins' clothing allowed him by law as a member of Captain Rogers' Company (VSA-17).

Robert George signs a request for a smoothing iron for Patrick Kennedy (VSA-17).

Robert George signs a request to the quartermaster for one bottle tafia for George's use (VSA-17).

Robert George signs a request to the quartermaster for one pint tafia for Ann Elms (VSA-17).

Ammunition delivered by order of Captain George: to Captain Kellar for hunting, 1/4 pound gunpowder and 1/2 pound lead; to the Kaskaskia Indians, 20 pounds gunpowder, 40 pounds lead, and 50 flints (VSA-50: 34).

Stores issued by order of Captain Robert George: to Lt. Calvit's Command [four tents or oil cloths had been listed but were crossed out] (VSA-50: 39).

March 11, 1781/Sunday
Leonard Helm and Robert George sign a request to the quartermaster for three pints of tafia for Helm's use, as he is very sick (VSA-17).

Leonard Helm and Robert George sign a request for five gallons tafia for the friendly Indians (VSA-17).

March 12, 1781/Monday
Silas Harlan signed at "Camp Jefferson" that he recieved of George Rogers Clark, 3,440 dollars for goods delivered to the Falls. Attested by William Clark (VSA-10).

John Donne signed that he received from John Dodge, one small packet of medicine for use of the troops at Fort Jefferson (VSA-17).

Leonard Helm and Robert George sign a request to the quartermaster for three pints tafia to the friendly Indians (VSA-17).

Leonard Helm and Robert George sign a request to the quartermaster for two quarts tafia for the friendly Indians (VSA-17).

Leonard Helm and Robert George sign a request to the quartermaster for six lbs tobacco for the friendly Indians (VSA-17).

March 13, 1781/Tuesday

Edward Worthington and Robert George sign a request to the quartermaster for one [illeg.] of tobacco for Worthington's use (VSA-17).

Richard Clark and Robert George sign a request to John Dodge for four skeins thread for Clark's own use (VSA-17).

Robert George signs a request to the quartermaster for five quarts tafia for George's use (VSA-17).

Benjamin Roberts and Robert George sign a request to the quartermaster for one carot tobacco for Roberts' use (VSA-17).

Martin Carney signed he received from John Dodge, 149 lbs tobacco; one fish seine; and one cross cut saw for the use of the troops at Fort Jefferson (VSA-17).

Leonard Helm and Robert George sign a request to the quartermaster for three pints tafia for Helm's use to put with Jesuit Bark to cure a fever (VSA-17).

John Williams signs a request to the quartermaster for three quarts tafia for Williams' use, as there are several sick persons at his house (VSA-17).

John Williams signs a request to the quartermaster for five gills and a quart of tafia for Williams' use (VSA-17).

Leonard Helm and Robert George sign a request to the quartermaster to furnish the Kaskaskia Indians with two swords from the public store (VSA-17).

March 14, 1781/Wednesday

John Rogers and Robert George sign a request to the quartermaster for three gallons tafia for Rogers' use (VSA-17).

Michael Miles and Robert George sign a request to the quartermaster for tobacco for 50 men of the Illinois Regiment at 1/2 lb per man (VSA-17).

Robert George signs a request to Martin Carney for one quart tafia for Sergeant Miles, as his wife is sick (VSA-17).

Robert George signs a request to the quartermaster for three pints tafia for George's health (VSA-17).

March 15, 1781/Thursday

Edward Worthington signs a request to the quartermaster for one quart tafia for Worthington's use as he is "unwell" (VSA-17).

William Clark and Robert George sign a request to Martin Carney for three lbs tobacco for Clark's use (VSA-17).

Robert George signs a request to the quartermaster for three sick people, three lbs sugar, and 1/2 lb coffee (VSA-17).

Ammunition delivered by Martin Carney by order of Captain George, to two men going with Major Harlan to the Falls of the Ohio, 1 1/2 pounds gunpowder, three pounds lead (VSA-50).

March 16, 1781/Friday
Robert George signs a request to the quartermaster to issue three pints tafia (VSA-17).

Jarrett Williams signs a request for seven quarts and one pint [unspecified] for Williams' use (VSA-17).

John Williams signs a request to the quartermaster for nine quarts tafia and 28 lbs sugar (VSA-17).

Robert George signs a request to Mr. Dodge to issue Mr. Finn three skeins thread and one stick mohair for Finn's use (VSA-17).

John Williams signs a request to the quartermaster for one bottle tafia for Williams, as he is very sick (VSA-17).

Robert George signs a request to Mr. Dodge to issue Mr. Finn, 2 1/2 dozen large and one dozen small buttons for Finn's use (VSA-17).

Stores issued by order of Captain Robert George: to Mr. Kennedy, one tent or oil cloth (VSA-50: 39).

March 17, 1781/Saturday
Edward Worthington signs a request to the quartermaster for one quart tafia to Saint Patrick, who is "almost dead" (VSA-17).

Edward Worthington signs a request to the quartermaster for one quart tafia for Worthington's use (VSA-17).

Michael Miles and Robert George sign a request to the quartermaster for liquor for 90 men of the Illinois Regiment at one gill each (VSA-17).

Leonard Helm and Robert George sign a request to the quartermaster for three pints tafia for "the sake of St. Patrick" (VSA-17).

Lt. Girault signs a request to the quartermaster for one quart tafia for "the use of St. Patrick" (VSA-17).

Lt. Girault signs a request to Martin Carney to let Girault have a bottle of tafia (VSA-17).

Robert George signs a request to Israel Dodge for three dozen buttons for Lt. Richard Clark, for Clark's own use (VSA-17).

Lt. Richard Clark signs a request to the quartermaster for one quart tafia for Clark's own use (VSA-17).

John Rogers signs a request to the quartermaster for one quart tafia for Rogers' use (VSA-17).

John Rogers signs a request to Martin Carney for three pints tafia for Rogers' use (VSA-17).

James Sherlock and Robert George sign a request to the quartermaster for one quart tafia, for Sherlock's use to "drink to St. Patrick's health" (VSA-17).

John Bailey certifies he received from Zephaniah Blackford, 17 bushels Indian corn; and 1,280 lbs beef for two officers, 26 men, three women, and two children on command from Fort Jefferson to Fort Partick Henry, a 27 day journey (VSA-17).

John Donne signs he received from Ensign Jarrit Williams, 1,652 lbs buffalo beef and 188 lbs bear meat for the use of the troops belonging to the Illinois Department stationed at Fort Jefferson (VSA-17).

March 18, 1781/Sunday

James Sherlock and Robert George sign request to the quartermaster for one quart tafia for Shealy's sake; she being the wife of St. Patrick (VSA-17).

Edward Worthington signs a request to the quartermaster for three pints tafia for Worthington's use (VSA-17).

Michael Miles and Robert George sign a request to the quartermaster for 10 3/4 lbs gunpowder and 21 1/2 lbs lead, to 43 men of the Illinois Regiment (VSA-17).

Lt. Richard Clark signs a request to the quartermaster for two quarts tafia for Clark's own use (VSA-17).

Abraham Kellar and Robert George sign a request to Israel Dodge for five dozen capped buttons and five skeins coarse thread for Kellar's use (VSA-17).

James Finn signs a request to Martin Carney for three quarts and one pint tafia for Finn's use (VSA-17).

Benjamin Roberts signs a request to the quartermaster for one bottle tafia for Roberts' use (VSA-17).

Leonard Helm signs a request for an issuance of seven quarts tafia for Helm's use (VSA-17).

Lt. Girault signs a request to Martin Carney for one bottle tafia for the use of "a poor fellow" (VSA-17).

John Rogers signs he received of John Dodge, 225 lbs flour for the use of Rogers' Company on their way from Fort Jefferson to the Falls of Ohio (VSA-17).

John Rogers signs he received from John Dodge, 96 lbs pickled pork for the use of Rogers' Company on their way from Fort Jefferson to the Falls of Ohio (VSA-17).

March 19, 1781/Monday

Edward Worthington requests Martin Carney issue one quart tafia for Worthington's use, as he is unwell (VSA-17).

John Donne requests Martin Carney issue one bottle tafia on Donne's account, for an unnamed individual who has made a pair of shoes for Mrs. Donne. Donne also states the quantity of tafia received from Carney yesterday was insufficient, because Donne had several visitors (VSA-17).

Donne signs he received three quarts tafia on the above and a prior order (VSA-17).

Richard Clark signs he received from John Dodge, one large walnut chest and one iron mortar which was purchased by Dodge for Col. Clark. Attested by John Donne (VSA-17).

Reverse of above receipt for the chest and iron mortar is initialed J.D. [John Donne or John Dodge] and states it is for Major Williams to show General Clark (VSA-17).

John Thruston and Robert George sign a request to the quartermaster for six lbs coffee for Thruston's use (VSA-17).

Richard Clark and Robert George sign a request to the quartermaster for one gun to Sergeant [doc. torn], for the Sergeant's use as he does not have a gun (VSA-17).

Benjamin Roberts and Robert George sign a request to the quartermaster to furnish Roberts with one demijohn and one pair of flat irons for Roberts' use (VSA-17a).

Martin Carney and Robert George sign a request to Mr. Dodge to issue eight skeins thread for making cartridges for the swivels (VSA-17).

Captain George requests Israel Dodge issue Captain Roberts one yd brown holland for Roberts' use (VSA-17).

Robert George requests Mr. Dodge issue Captain Roberts two skeins silk, four skeins, thread, 12 needles, four skeins mohair, and 1/2 yd cloth for Roberts' use (VSA-17).

John Rogers, Benjamin Roberts, and Robert George sign a request to the quartermaster for five gallons tafia for Rogers and Roberts' use on their passage to the Falls (VSA-17).

Jarrit Williams requests the quartermaster issue one quart tafia for Williams' use (VSA-17).

John Rogers and Robert George request the quartermaster issue six lbs coffee for Rogers' use (VSA-17).

No signature on document certifying Andrew Clark worked as an artificer from February 3rd to September 7th, 1780 (VSA-17).

Robert George requests Israel Dodge issue Captain Rogers, 24 gun worms for the use of Rogers' Company (VSA-17).

Leonard Helm requests from the quartermaster, one quart tafia for Helm's health, as he is very sick (VSA-17).

Leonard Helm and Robert George request the quartermaster issue two swords for two Indian chiefs (VSA-17; 50: 39).

Robert George signs a request to the quartermaster to furnish William Clark with 1/2 lb gunpowder and 2 1/2 lbs lead (VSA-17).

Robert George signs a request to the quartermaster to issue Captain Rogers 25 lbs gunpowder for the use of his men going on command to the Falls (VSA-17).

James Finn and Robert George sign a request to the quartermaster for one quart tafia for Finn's use (VSA-17).

Robert George signs a request to Israel Dodge to issue John Rogers 16 skeins thread for the use of Rogers' soldiers who are mending their shirts (VSA-17).

Robert George signs a request to the quartermaster to furnish Captain John Dodge with one spade and two mattocks to help purchase a quantity of balls for the protection of Fort Jefferson. John Dodge signed he received the spade and mattocks (VSA-17).

Martin Carney signed he received of John Dodge, 166 lbs of ball for the protection of Fort Jefferson (VSA-17; 50: 5).

Letter from Lt. Girault of Fort Jefferson to Col. Clark. Girault requests to go on any expedition with the troops from Fort Jefferson. Girault feels he could be of greater service in any other place other than Fort Jefferson. Girault mentions there have been several disputes since Clark's departure (MHS, B2: F2).

Letter from Captain Edward Worthington at Fort Jefferson to George Rogers Clark. Letter is very incomplete and torn (MHS, B2: F2).

"Phlegm, phlegm question phlegm, may be propounded by a fool, for no wise man can Answer for his soul." Anonymous (VSA-17).

Ammunition delivered by order of Captain George: to the Kaskaskia Indians, 1 1/2 pounds gunpowder and three pounds lead; to Captain Rogers going to the Falls of Ohio, 25 pounds gunpowder and 20 pounds lead; to the Regiment, 10 3/4 pounds gunpowder and 21 1/2 pounds lead (VSA-50: 34).

Stores issued by order of Captain Robert George: to Mr. Miles, quartermaster Sergeant, one musket or smoothed gun; to Captain Rogers going to the Falls of Ohio, two muskets or smoothed guns and five tents or oil cloths (VSA-50: 39).

March 20, 1781/Tuesday

Robert George signs a request to the quartermaster for 32 lbs Jesuit Bark to Captain Roberts for the use of Col. Slaughter's Company. Benjamin Roberts signs he received the within contents from Martin Carney (VSA-17b).

John Donne signs a statement that Israel Dodge appeared before him and made an oath that Dodge delivered to Captain George at Fort Jefferson one receipt for George to sign for merchandise that was issued out of the Commercial Agent's store. George refused to sign the receipt stating his order was equally as good (VSA-17).

Robert George signs a request to the quartermaster to furnish Captain Rogers with 20 lbs ball for use on Rogers' voyage up the river (VSA-17).

Benjamin Roberts and Robert George sign a request to Israel Dodge for four guns for four men of Roberts' Company (VSA-17).

Robert George signs a request to the quartermaster for three pints tafia for George (VSA-17).

Robert George signs a request to the quartermaster for two quarts and one pint tafia for George (VSA-17).

Richard Clark and Robert George sign a request to the quartermaster for 1/2 lb gunpowder and one lb lead for Clark's own use (VSA-17).

John Williams signs a request to the quartermaster for one bottle tafia to drink with a friend before departing (VSA-17).

Court Martial Hearings for David Allen and James Taylor. Court convened at 10 a.m. by order of Captain Robert George, Fort Commandant. Court members include Captain Keller, President; Lt. John Girault, Judge Advocate; Captain Roberts; Lt. Carney; Lt. R. Clark; and Cornet Thruston (Draper Manuscripts 56J40-41).

Charges brought against Allen and Taylor include: robbing Major Williams' kitchen, beating his servants, and verbally abusing an officer.

Valentine Balsinger gave testimony at Fort Jefferson during Court Martial Proceedings. While he was sentry of the guard house he heard one of the prisoners speak disrespectfully of Maj. Williams. Mrs. Damewood was mentioned during testimony. She was the person who also harassed Rachel Yeats (throwing bones at her through a window). John Daughterty provided testimony in defense of James Taylor saying he was with Taylor throughout the "fray." Philip Hupp testified he saw Boston Damewood make darts and shoot them through a window at

Rachel Yeats. Jones (possibly Matthew) is mentioned during the testimony by Elizabeth Watkins. Mr. and Mrs. Watkins and James Taylor stayed at Jones' lodge. Rachel Kennedy testified she heard derogatory language directed toward Major Williams, stating either David Allen, James Taylor or both had said what she heard. Elizabeth Watkins provided testimony stating she went to lay [sleep?] at Jones' where Taylor [James] lodges, but had forgotten her bedding so she sent her husband after it at Major Williams'. Unfortunately, he returned with the wrong blanket.

After hearing the testimony, the Court acquitted James Taylor. The Court also acquitted David Allen of robbery and participating in the fray; however, the Court found Allen guilty of speaking disrespectfully of Major Williams, and ordered 50 lashes on Allen's bare back. The Court adjourned (Draper Manuscripts 56J40-41).

John Donne certifies that a number of charges have been entered by him and are agreeable to a number of vouchers produced by Captain John Dodge; that the said charges are a true abstract of the aforesaid vouchers (VSA-48: 120).

March 21, 1781/Wednesday

Edward Worthington signs a request for one quart tafia for Worthington's use (VSA-17).

John Dodge signs a request to Israel Dodge for 3/4 yd white cloth and 1/2 yd blue cloth for John Dodge's use for leggings and flap (VSA-17).

Leonard Helm and Robert George sign a request to Martin Carney for one quart tafia to "drive away all sorrow" (VSA-17).

John Bailey signs a request to the "commandant" for three days rations for 29 men, three women, and two children of Bailey's Company (VSA-17).

Israel Dodge requests Martin Carney for three pints tafia for Dodge's use (VSA-17).

Jarrit Williams signs a request to the quartermaster for one quart tafia for Williams' use (VSA-17).

Benjamin Roberts signs a request to the quartermaster for three pints tafia for Roberts' use (VSA-17).

Robert George signs a request to the quartermaster for six lbs sugar to Mr. Dejean, a prisoner of war (VSA-17).

Robert George signs a request to the quartermaster for six gallons tafia to Mr. Dejean, a prisoner of war (VSA-17).

March 22, 1781/Thursday

Richard Clark and Robert George sign a request to the quartermaster for one carot tobacco for Clark's own use (VSA-17).

Jarrit Williams and Robert George sign a return to the quartermaster for 1 1/2 lb gunpowder and three lbs lead for five men going hunting (VSA-17).

Israel Dodge and Robert George sign a request to Martin Carney for 1/2 lb gunpowder and 1 1/2 lbs lead for Dodge's own use (VSA-17).

Michael Miles and Robert George sign a request to the quartermaster for tobacco for nine men at 1/2 lb each (VSA-17).

Robert George signs a request to the quartermaster for one quart tafia for the use of Miles' wife, who is sick (VSA-17).

Ammunition delivered by order of Captain George: to Mr. Dodge, 1/2 lb gunpowder and one lb lead (VSA-50: 34).

Ammunition delivered by order of Captain George to Mr. William Clark, 1/2 pound gunpowder and 2 1/2 pounds lead (VSA-50: 35).

March 23, 1781/Friday
William Clark and Captain John Dodge left Fort Jefferson. Clark was going to Louisville to procure supplies. Dodge was going to Lexington and then Richmond to settle his accounts (MHS: B1, F15; VSA-18).

John Donne signs a request to Martin Carney to send the shoemaker one quart tafia and to send Donne one quart for the day (VSA-17).

Leonard Helm signs a request to the quartermaster for four days rations of tafia for the 23rd-25th of March (VSA-17).

Ammunition delivered by order of Captain George to Mr. Archer, 1/2 lb gunpowder (VSA-50: 35).

Ammunition delivered by order of Captain George to Ensign Williams' hunting party, 1 1/2 pounds gunpowder and three pounds lead (VSA-50: 35).

March 24, 1781/Saturday
Robert Davis signs he received from Patrick Kennedy, six days rations for 14 men of the Illinois Regiment who are transporting provisions to Fort Jefferson (VSA-17).

Israel Dodge signs a request to the quartermaster for three pints tafia for Helm's use (VSA-17).

Richard Clark signs a request to the quartermaster for three pints tafia for Clark's use (VSA-17).

Jarrit Williams signs a request to the quartermaster for two quarts and a pint rum for Williams' use

Israel Dodge signs a request to the quartermaster for two quarts and one pint rum for Dodge's use (VSA-17).

Ammunition delivered by order of Captain George to one man of Captain George's Company, 1/4 pound gunpowder and 1/2 pound lead (VSA-50: 35).

William Clark and Captain John Dodge left Fort Jefferson. Clark was going to Louisville and Dodge was going on to Lexington (MHS: B1, F15).

March 25, 1781/Sunday
Joseph Calvit signs a request to the quartermaster for one quart tafia for Calvit's use (VSA-17).

Leonard Helm and Robert George sign a request to the quartermaster for one quart tafia for George's use (VSA-17).

Robert George signs a request to the quartermaster for three quarts tafia for George's use (VSA-17).

Robert George signs a request to the quartermaster for one quart tafia for Sergeant Miles, as he is taking charge of the boat (VSA-17).

Leonard Helm and Robert George sign a request to the quartermaster for three quarts tafia for use of the friendly Indians (VSA-17).

Leonard Helm and Robert George sign a request to the quartermaster for one quart tafia for the friendly Indians (VSA-17).

March 26, 1781/Monday
John Rogers signs a request to the quartermaster for one pint tafia for a sick man in Rogers' Company (VSA-17).

Richard Clark signs a request to the quartermaster for five days provisons for Clark's own use (VSA-17).

Robert George signs a request to the quartermaster for three pints tafia for George's own use (VSA-17).

Robert George signs a request to Martin Carney for one quart tafia for Sergeant John Walker of George's Company (VSA-17).

John Williams signs a request to the quartermaster for two bottles tafia to "make my host glad and give contentment to my friend" (VSA-17).

March 27, 1781/Tuesday
Edward Worthington signs a request to the quartermaster for three pints tafia for Worthington's use (VSA-17).

Robert George signs a request to Israel Dodge to issue Mr. Finn, one lb twine to make a pair of stockings (VSA-17).

Robert George signs a request to issue one lb coarse thread to Mr. Donne for purchasing 30 lbs salted buffalo beef for the use of the troops at Fort Jefferson. John Donne signs he received the beef and issued it to Thomas Quirk (VSA-17).

James Finn signs a request to the quartermaster to send one bottle tafia (VSA-17).

Leonard Helm and Robert George sign a request for three pints tafia for the friendly Indians (VSA-17).

Leonard Helm and Robert George sign a request to the quartermaster for two quarts tafia to the friendly Indians (VSA-17).

Leonard Helm and Robert George sign a request to the quartermaster to issue two quarts tafia to the friendly Indians (VSA-17).

Jarrit Williams signs a request to the quartermaster for one quart tafia (VSA-17).

Leonard Helm and Robert George sign a request to the quartermaster for three pints tafia for the friendly Indians (VSA-17).

Robert George signs a request to the quartermaster to issue 1/2 lb gunpowder and one lb lead to John Walker of George's Company (VSA-17).

John Williams signs a request to the quartermaster for three pints tafia for Williams' use (VSA-17).

Robert George signs a request for 3 1/2 gallons tafia, eight lbs tobacco, and one lb gunpowder for the purpose of purchasing 256 lbs beef for the use of the troops. John Donne signed he received the above from Martin Carney, and issued agreeable to order (VSA-17).

Ammunition delivered by order of Captain George to Sergeant Walker, 1/2 pound gunpowder and one pound lead (VSA-50: 35).

Captain Helm, Superintendent of Indian Affairs, is issued three pints tafia for use of friendly Indians at Fort Jefferson, from the quartermaster per Captain George's order (VSA-17).

Ensign Williams was issued one quart tafia from the quartermaster (VSA-17).

Captain Helm, Superintendant of Indian Affairs, was issued two quarts tafia for the use of the friendly Indians (VSA-17).

Captain Helm, Superintendant of Indian Affairs, was issued two quarts tafia for the use of friendly Indians (VSA-17).

Captain Helm, Superintendant of Indian Affairs, was issued three pints tafia for use of friendly Indians (VSA-17).

Commissary Officer Finn is issued one bottle tafia (VSA-17).

George Rogers Clark at Yohogania writes to Thomas Jefferson regarding the agreement with Thomas Jefferson over inquirying into the conduct of Montgomery and Dodge (GRC, I: 516-517).

March 28, 1781/Wednesday

Ensign Jarret Williams and Robert George sign a return to the quartermaster for two guns, two bayonets, and belts for two men of Captain Brashears' Company (VSA-17).

Jarret Williams and Robert George sign a request to the quartermaster for two lbs coffee for Williams' own use (VSA-17).

Richard Clark requests two lbs [item not specified] (VSA-17).

Robert George signs a request to issue Mr. Donne four lbs coffee (VSA-17).

Robert George and Lt. Girault sign a request to the quartermaster for 1/2 lb gunpowder and lead equivalent for Girault's use (VSA-17).

Robert George signs a request to the quartermaster for one quart tafia for Buckner Pittman (VSA-17).

Robert George signs a request for one pound gunpowder and lead equivalent to one man of George's Company (VSA-17).

Robert George and James Finn sign a request to the quartermaster for four lbs coffee for Finn's use (VSA-17).

George Owens and Robert George sign a request to Martin Carney for 2 1/2 lbs gunpowder and five lbs lead to ten men of the militia (VSA-17).

Israel Dodge and Robert George sign a request to Martin Carney for four lbs coffee for Dodge's use (VSA-17).

John Bailey signs a request to the quartermaster for two lbs gunpowder, four lbs lead, and five flints for a hunting party, who are getting meat for the garrison (VSA-17).

Robert George signs a request to Martin Carney to issue Mr. Donne four gallons tafia to pay for 240 lbs salted beef for use of the troops stationed at Fort Jefferson (VSA-17).

Leonard Helm signs a request to the quartermaster for three lbs tafia for Helm's use (VSA-17).

Jarret Williams and Robert George sign a request to the quartermaster to issue one gun to one man of Captain Brashears' Company (VSA-17).

Robert George signs a request to Martin Carney to issue Mr. Donne 1/2 lb gunpowder for the protection of Donne's house, as it is on the frontier and flanking the blockhouse (VSA-17).

Ammunition delivered by order of Captain George: to Mr. Donne, 1/2 lb gunpowder; to militia at Clarksville, 2 1/2 lbs gunpowder and five lbs lead (VSA-50: 35).

John Williams signs a request to the quartermaster for two bottles tafia, two lbs sugar, and one cask to make vinegar (VSA-17).

Robert George and Lt. Girault sign a request to the quartermaster for four lbs coffee for Girault's use (VSA-17).

Ammunition delivered by order of Captain George: to Lt. Richard Clark, 1/2 pound gunpowder and one pound lead; to Lt. Girault, 1/2 pound gunpowder and one pound lead (VSA-50: 35).

Ammunition delivered by order of Captain Rbt. George at Fort Jefferson: to Lt. Calvit and Bowman, one pound gunpowder (VSA-50: 36).

Private Jess Piner is killed. He was a member of Captain Richard McCarty's company (Harding 1981: 27).

March 29, 1781/Thursday
Edward Worthington signs a request to the quartermaster for one bottle tafia, for a poor sick Hibernian (VSA-17).

Robert George signs a request to the quartermaster for one bottle tafia for Mr. Archer (VSA-17).

John Dodge signs a request to Martin Carney for three pints tafia for Dodge's use (VSA-17).

Leonard Helm signs a request to the quartermaster for one lb tobacco for Helm's use (VSA-17).

Joseph Calvit signs a request to Martin Carney to send one quart tafia to Calvit (VSA-17).

Robert George signs a request for 1/4 lb gunpowder to John Burks (VSA-17).

March 30, 1781/Friday
Leonard Helm and Robert George sign a request to Israel Dodge for one shirt for a friendly Indian Chief that has been warring against the Chickasaws (VSA-17).

John Donne signs a request to Martin Carney for one quart tafia, because Donne is "extremely unwell" (VSA-17).

Leonard Helm and Robert George sign a request to Israel Dodge for one paper pins for Helm's use (VSA-17a).

John Williams signs a request to the quartermaster for one bottle tafia for Williams' use (VSA-17).

Robert George signs a request to Martin Carney for three pints tafia for George's own use (VSA-17).

James Finn signs a request to Martin Carney for one bottle tafia for Finn's use (VSA-17).

Robert George signs a request to the quartermaster for three pints tafia for George's use (VSA-17).

Lt. Girault and Robert George sign a request to the quartermaster for two lbs tobacco for Girault's use (VSA-17).

Leonard Helm and Robert George sign a request to Israel Dodge for two lbs vermillion to give to the friendly Indians (VSA-17).

April, 1781/Miscellaneous
Edward Worthington signs a request to the quartermaster to issue three pints tafia for Worthington's use (VSA-18).

Sometime between April 1 and April 14, Captain John Rogers and his Company of Light Dragoons arrived at Sullivan's Station in Central Kentucky. With him were Dodge, Dejean, Bentley, Bapttist and other Indians (GRC, I: 554-555).

April 1, 1781/Sunday
Jarret Williams signs a request to the quartermaster for one quart tafia for Williams' use (VSA-18).

George Owens and Robert George sign a request to the quartermaster for one bottle tafia for Owens' use (VSA-18).

April 2, 1781/Monday
Edward Worthington signs a request to the quartermaster for three gallons tafia for Worthington's use (VSA-18).

John Walker and Robert George sign a request for two quarts tafia for Walker's use. Martin Carney signed he received the contents (VSA-18).

Jarret Williams signs a request to Martin Carney for two gallons tafia for the use of Buckner Pittman (VSA-18).

Robert George signs a request to the quartermaster for one gallon rum to Sergeant Miles (VSA-18).

Robert George signs a request to the quartermaster for one gallon tafia for the use of John Walker (VSA-18).

Leonard Helm signs a request to Martin Carney for two gallons tafia (VSA-18).

Richard Clark signs a request to Martin Carney for two gallons tafia for Clark's own use (VSA-18).

Buckner Pittman and Robert George sign a request to the quartermaster for two quarts tafia for Pittman's use (VSA-18).

John Donne receives two gallons tafia delivered to Donne from Martin Carney (VSA-18).

Robert George signs a request to the quartermaster for two gallons rum for George's use (VSA-18).

April 3, 1781/Tuesday
Edward Worthington signs a request for 1/2 gallon tafia for Worthington's use (VSA-18).

Richard Clark signs a request to Martin Carney for two quarts tafia for Clark's own use (VSA-18).

John Donne signs he received one quart tafia from Martin Carney (VSA-18).

Captain Helm received seven lbs tobacco for the use of the Indian allies. Order issued by Martin Carney (VSA-18).

April 6, 1781/Friday
Edward Worthington and Robert George sign a request to the quartermaster for six lbs coffee for Worthington (VSA-18).

Robert George signs a request to Israel Dodge for two lbs twine to make a drum cord for the use of this garrison. Martin Carney signed he received the twine from Mr. Dodge (VSA-18).

Robert George signs a request to Israel Dodge to issue Mr. Pittman, two dozen and eight buttons for Pittman's own use (VSA-18).

John Williams and Robert George sign a request to the quartermaster for one mahogeny case with 11 bottles for Williams' use (VSA-18).

Leonard Helm and Robert George sign a request for one pair of flat irons for Helm's use (VSA-18).

Leonard Helm and Robert George sign a request to the quartermaster for seven lbs tobacco for the friendly Indians (VSA-18).

Robert George signs a request to the quartermaster for one carot of tobacco for George's use (VSA-18).

Robert George signs a request to Israel Dodge for one skein silk for Martin Carney for his use (VSA-18).

April 7, 1781/Saturday
Robert George signs a request to the quartermaster for tafia for 58 men of the Illinios Regiment at 1/2 lb per man (VSA-18).

Tobacco issued to Sundry persons per order of Captain George, Commandant: to five men of Captain George's Company, 2 1/2 pounds (VSA-50: 13).

April 8, 1781/Sunday
Richard Clark signs a request to Martin Carney for 1 1/2 gallon tafia for Clark's own use (VSA-18).

April 9, 1781/Monday
William Clark certifies he measured sundry pieces of cloth and flannel of the same cargo which Clark delivered to Captain John Dodge, and held out about 32 yards per piece (VSA-18).

April 10, 1781/Tuesday
Leonard Helm and Robert George sign a request to the quartermaster for three lbs tobacco for Helm's use (VSA-18).

April 11, 1781/Wednesday
Thomas Jefferson signs a request to issue George Wilson for William Shannon a warrant for 2,500 lbs on account [item not specified] (VSA-18).

Letter to George Rogers Clark at Fort Pitt from William Clark at Louisville. William Clark left Fort Jefferson on March 23rd and he was hoping to see George Rogers Clark in Louisville. William Clark came up with Captain John Dodge, who is on his way to Virginia. William Clark will be in Louisville for a while and hopes to see George Rogers Clark before he leaves. William Clark and Captain John Dodge met Mr. Jacob Pyatte a little below the Mouth of Salt River with packets from George Rogers Clark. William Clark wants to see Col. Todd and try to make a settlement with him for goods that had been delivered to him (MHS: B2, F15).

April 12, 1781/Thursday
Private Joseph Cooper dies. He was a member of Captain Kellar's Company (Harding 1981: 23).

April 13, 1781/Friday
Robert George signs a request to Martin Carney to issue Mr. Donne, one carot tobacco (VSA-18).

Richard Clark and Robert George sign a request to Israel Dodge for one lb twine for making fishing lines for the men at Clark's station. Page Certain signs he received the twine from Israel Dodge (VSA-18).

Robert George signs a request to Israel Dodge to issue one lb twine thread for making fishing lines for the soldiers in the upper block house under Captain Worthington's command (VSA-18).

Tobacco issued to sundry persons per order Captain George: to John Donne, three lbs (VSA-50: 13).

Tobacco issued to sundry persons per order of Captain George, Commandant: to Martin Carney, three pounds (VSA-50: 13).

Ammunition delivered by order of Captain Robert George at Fort Jefferson: to Captain Owens of militia, one lb gunpowder; to Mr. Finn, Commissary, 1/2 lb gunpowder and one lb lead (VSA-50: 36).

April 15, 1781/Sunday
Captain James Sullivan at Beargrass Station [near the Falls], writes to George Rogers Clark at Steward's Crossing, stating he sent the letters that Clark had given him to Fort Jefferson by express (GRC, I: 528-529).

April 17, 1781/Tuesday
Benajamin Roberts signs a request for provisions for nine men in Captain Roberts' Company for eight days (VSA-18).

Robert George signs a request to Israel Dodge to issue Sergeant Miles six skeins brown thread (VSA-18).

Robert George signs a request to Israel Dodge for one lb twine thread for David Kennedy to make a fishing line. David Kennedy signed he received the twine from Israel Dodge (VSA-18).

Robert George signs a request to Mr. Donne for 1/2 lb twine to make a fishing line for the use of his family this scarce time. John Donne signed he received the twine from Israel Dodge (VSA-18).

Abraham Kellar and Robert George sign a request to the quartermaster for 2 1/2 lbs tobacco for five men of Kellar's Company (VSA-18).

Tobacco issued to sundry persons per order of Captain George, Commandant: to Captain Kellar's Company, two pounds; to Jacob Pyatte, three pounds (VSA-50: 13).

Ammunition delivered by order of Captain Robert George at Fort Jefferson, to Captain Robert George's Company, one lb gunpowder and two lbs lead (VSA-50: 36).

April 18, 1781/Wednesday
Jarret Williams and Robert George sign a request to the quartermaster for two flat irons for Williams' use (VSA-18).

Robert George signs a request to Israel Dodge for one lb twine for the use of men in Captain George's Company to make fishing line. Charles Morgan signs he received the twine from Israel Dodge (VSA-18).

April 20, 1781/Friday
Letter from Joseph Hunter at Fort Jefferson to George Rogers Clark. Hunter mentions the loss of all stock and grain. He has released some grain to the troops, and they have used it all. He mentions that Captain George has done his part as a "good officer," and the other officers have treated Hunter with esteem (GRC, I: 539).

Letter from Edward Worthington at Fort Jefferson to George Rogers Clark. Worthington is pleased to know that Clark may take the officers and soldiers at Fort Jefferson on an expedition [Detroit?]. Worthington mentions soldiers have deserted due to lack of provisions. An express took the last "dependance" from the public store on the 15th of April (MHS, B2: F2).

Captain Benjamin Roberts and George Slaughter certify by receipt from Captain William Shannon, one large bateau and 13 oars taken from Fort Jefferson on public service. The bateau was lost through an "unavoidable accident." William Shannon signed he received 316 2/3 dollars for the bateau (VSA-18).

April 21, 1781/Saturday
James Finn and Robert George sign a request to the quartermaster for one carot tobacco for Finn's use (VSA-18).

Joseph Calvit and Robert George sign a request to Israel Dodge for one lb twine for making fishing line for Calvit's own use (VSA-18).

Ammunition delivered by order of Captain Robert George at Fort Jefferson: to express from Falls of Ohio, two lbs gunpowder and four lbs lead; to Captain George's Company, 2 1/2 lbs gunpowder and five lbs lead; to Captain Worthington's Company, 1/2 lb gunpowder and one lb lead (VSA-50: 36).

April 22, 1781/Sunday
Letter from Martin Carney to George Rogers Clark. Carney states he has been stationed at Fort Jefferson too long and would like to leave had it not been for "you" [Clark?]. Carney wishes to be relieved of his post at Fort Jefferson (MHS, B2: F2).

Letter from Leonard Helm at Fort Jefferson to George Rogers Clark. Helm mentions the serious circumstances at Fort Jefferson. Major Linctot had been at Fort Jefferson with some of the Piankashaw Indians and some inhabitants from Vincennes, requesting ammunition to carry out an expedition against the Omia [Miami Indians]. Captain George gave them what he could. He mentions that Mr. Sherlock and Captain Dodge have gone to "government" (MHS, B2: F2).

Robert George signs a request to Israel Dodge to issue two lbs thread for making cartridges for the swivels at Fort Jefferson (VSA-18).

April 23, 1781/Monday
Robert George signs a request to Israel Dodge for a pair of cotton drawers to Mr. Pyatt, express from the Falls of Ohio. Jacob Pyatt signed he received the drawers from Israel Dodge (VSA-18).

Jacob Pyatt [Pyatte] and Robert George sign a request to the quartermaster for one carot tobacco for Mr. Pyatt (VSA-18).

Robert George signs a request to the quartermaster for three carots tobacco for George's use (VSA-18).

Ammunition delivered by order of Captain Robt. George at Fort Jefferson: to Mr. Pyatte going on command to the Falls, 12 flints (VSA-50: 36).

To Captain Robert George, per order, three lbs tobacco (VSA-49: 3).

April 24, 1781/Tuesday
Robert George signs a request to the quartermaster to furnish Mr. Pittman with one blunder buss, two lbs gunpowder, four lbs lead, and two tents or oil cloths for Pittman's command to the Falls of Ohio. Buckner Pittman signed he received the within contents from Martin Carney (VSA-18).

Stores issued by order of Captain Robert George: to Buckner Pittman, Boat master [two tents or oil cloths had been listed but appear to have been crossed out] (VSA-50: 39).

Joseph Calvit and Robert George sign a request to Israel Dodge to issue 26 skeins thread for making soldier clothes. Joseph Calvit signed he received the contents from Israel Dodge (VSA-18).

Tobacco issued to sundry persons per order of Captain George, Commandant: to six men going to the Falls of Ohio, six pounds (VSA-50: 13).

April 25, 1781/Wednesday
Robert George signs statement to the quartermaster that due to high water, the troops and stores have been moved out of the garrison. Robert George requests one hogshead tafia for the officers and soldiers at Fort Jefferson (VSA-18).

Tafia issued at Fort Jefferson to the officers, troops, and Indians by order of Captain Robert George, one hogshead tafia (VSA-19).

Tafia received at Fort Jefferson from Captain Philip Barbour, left in store by Barbour, one hogshead tafia (VSA-19).

April 26, 1781/Thursday
Joseph Calvit and Robert George sign a request to the Quartermater for 62 gills liquor for the use of the fatigue (VSA-18).

Michael Miles and Robert George sign a request to the quartermaster for tobacco for 43 men of the Illinois Regiment at 1/2 lb per man (VSA-18).

Tobacco issued sundry persons per order of Captain George: to the Illinois Regiment, 21 1/2 lbs (VSA-50: 13).

April 28, 1781/Saturday
Michael Miles and Robert George sign return to the quartermaster for one lb tobacco for two men belonging to Captain Rogers' Company for hunting (VSA-18).

Tobacco issued to sundry persons per order of Captain George, Commandant: to one man of Captain George's Company, one pound (VSA-50: 13).

April 29, 1781/Sunday
Letter from John Rogers at Harrodsburg to Thomas Jefferson. States that Captain McCarty has been under arrest since September for treason. He mentions that several of Col. Montgomery's men were left under Rogers' care; and some have died (GRC, I: 545-546).

May, 1781/Miscellaneous
James Finn and Robert George sign a request to the quartermaster for five gallons and three quarts tafia to purchase 577 weight [doc. torn] for the use of the troops at Fort Jefferson (VSA-19).

Leonard Helm signs a request to the quartermaster for three quarts tafia for Helm's use (VSA-19).

Leonard Helm and Robert George sign a request to the quartermaster for one quart tafia for Helm (VSA-19).

Leonard Helm and Robert George sign a request to the quartermaster for three lbs tafia for Helm's use (VSA-19).

Sugar issued at Fort Jefferson by an abstract settled with Captain George by order of Col. Montgomery, six cases (VSA-19).

May 1, 1781/Tuesday
Abraham Kellar and Robert George sign a request to the quartermaster for three pints tafia for Kellar's use (VSA-19).

Letter from John Montgomery at Falls of the Ohio to Governor Thomas Nelson. The letter is dated August 10, 1781, but mentions Montgomery's arrival at Fort Jefferson on May 1, 1781. Montgomery mentioned that the troops were in a low and starving condition, and there were no goods or other property to purchase. No assistance could be expected from the Illinois, either (GRC, I: 585-586).

May 2, 1781/Wednesday
Joseph Calvit and Robert George sign a request to the quartermaster for eight lbs sugar for Calvit's use (VSA-19).

Martin Carney signed he received from Captain Robert George six cases sugar, four tureens tafia, and 240 carots tobacco for the use of the officers and soldiers (VSA-19).

Account of sugar received at Fort Jefferson: Captain Robert George provided six cases sugar (VSA-19).

Leonard Helm and Robert George sign a request to the quartermaster for two quarts tafia for Helm's use (VSA-19).

John Williams and Robert George sign a request to the quartermaster for ten lbs sugar for Williams' use (VSA-19).

Robert George signs a statement to Oliver Pollock as his first exchange for 5,062 Spanish milled dollars for sundries furnished for the subsistance of the garrison (VSA-19).

Robert George signs a statement to Oliver Pollock as his second exchange for 5,062 Spanish milled dollars for sundries furnished for the subsistance of the garrison (VSA-19).

Robert George signs a statement to Oliver Pollock as his first exchange for 358 Spanish milled dollars for sundries furnished the garrison (VSA-19).

Robert George signs a statement to Oliver Pollock as his second exchange for 358 Spanish milled dollars for sundries furnished for the use of the garrison (VSA-19).

Tafia issues at Fort Jefferson: Captain Robert George requests four tureens tafia for officers, troops, and Indians (VSA-19).

Account of tafia received at Fort Jefferson: Captain Robert George provided four tureens tafia (VSA-19).

Ammunition delivered by order of Captain Robert George at Fort Jefferson: to Captain Kellar's hunting party: two lbs gunpowder and four lbs lead; to six men on command, 1 1/2 lbs gunpowder and three lbs lead (VSA-50: 36).

May 3, 1781/Thursday
To militia of Clarksville, Mr. Archer per orders, three lbs sugar and one carot tobacco (VSA-49: 65).

Michael Miles and Robert George sign a request to the quartermaster for sugar to 76 men, nine women, and ten children belonging to the Illinois Regiment. The men received two lbs each, the women and children, one lb each (VSA-19).

Joseph Calvit and Robert George sign a request to Martin Carney for one musket and cartridge box to Andrew Ryan, a soldier in Calvit's company (VSA-19).

Martin Carney signs a request to let Andrew Ryon [Ryan], have a gun out of the country store, a soldier belonging to "my" company (VSA-19).

John Walker and Robert George sign a request to the quartermaster for one quart tafia for Walker's use (VSA-19).

Richard Brashears signs a request to the quartermaster for sugar for children of Brashears' Company (VSA-19).

Abraham Kellar and Robert George sign a request to the quartermaster for three lbs sugar for Kellar's own use (VSA-19).

Joshua Archer and Robert George sign a request to the quartermaster for one carot tobacco for Archer's use (VSA-19).

Richard Brashears signs a request to Martin Carney to let Brashears have six case bottles tafia and five lbs sugar for Brashears' own use (VSA-19).

James Finn and Robert George sign a request to the quartermaster to let Finn have one quart tafia (VSA-19).

Richard Brashears requests the quartermaster to let the bearer have one quart tafia (VSA-19).

Joshua Archer and Robert George request the quartermaster issue three lbs sugar for Archer's use (VSA-19).

Abraham Kellar and Robert George request the quartermaster issue three pints tafia for Kellar's use (VSA-19).

Tobacco issued to sundry persons per order Captain George: to Joshua Archer, three lbs (VSA-50: 13).

Incomplete document: "Personally appeared before me one of the magistrates for the Borrough of Clarksville, and was duly sworn according to law. John Moor said that Edward Matthews had command of a boat from the Falls. He loaded about 150 bushels of corn, and a cask of whiskey containing 30 gallons. Moor said Matthews inquired" [ms torn] (VSA-19).

To Captain Richard Brashears, per orders from day book, four gallons, one quart, one pint rum, and five lbs sugar (VSA-49: 7).

To Lt. Joseph Calvit, per orders from day book, two gallons, one quart rum, and eight lbs sugar (VSA-49: 17).

To Martin Carney, quartermaster, per orders, three gallons and three quarts rum (VSA-49: 47).

To Lt. Richard Clark, per orders brought from day book, three gallons, one quart rum (VSA-49: 19).

To Mr. Israel Dodge, Deputy Agent, per orders from day book, three gallons, one quart rum, and eight lbs sugar (VSA-49: 43).

To Mr. Donne, Deputy Conductor, per orders from day book, three gallons rum (VSA-49: 37).

To Mr. Finn, Issuing Commissary, per orders from day book, two gallons, three quarts, one pint rum (VSA-49: 45).

To Illinois Regiment, rations and fatigue, per order to four men of Captain George's Company, eight lbs sugar (VSA-49: 67).

To Lt. John Girault, per order from day book, one gallon, one quart, and one pint rum (VSA-49: 15).

To Captain Leonard Helm, per orders from day book, three gallons, one quart, and one pint rum (VSA-49: 27).

To Captain Abraham Kellar, per orders from day book, three gallons, two quarts, one pint rum, and three lbs sugar (VSA-49: 49).

To Mr. John Walker, Sergeant Major, per order from day book, two quarts, one pint rum (VSA-49: 59).

To Ensign Jarrett Williams, per orders from day book, one gallon, one pint rum (VSA-49: 33).

To Major John Williams, per orders from day book, one gallon, one quart, one pint rum, and ten lbs sugar (VSA-49: 5).

To Illinois Regiment, rations and fatigue, per order to regiment, 171 lbs sugar (VSA-49: 67).

May 4, 1781/Friday
Edward Worthington signed a request to the quartermaster for one bottle tafia, for a sick Hibernian (VSA-19).

James Finn and Robert George signed a request to the quartermaster for one bottle tafia for Finn's use (VSA-19).

Abraham Kellar signed a request to the quartermaster to let Kellar have a case bottle tafia (VSA-19).

Joseph Calvit signed a request to the quartermaster to let Calvit have one quart tafia for Calvit's use (VSA-19).

Israel Dodge and Robert George sign a request to the quartermaster for eight lbs sugar for Dodge's own use (VSA-19).

Israel Dodge signs a request to Martin Carney for one gallon tafia for Dodge's use (VSA-19).

Israel Dodge and Robert George sign a request to Martin Carney for three quarts tafia for Dodge's own use (VSA-19).

To Lt. Valentine Thomas Dalton, per order from day book, one gallon rum (VSA-49: 21).

May 5, 1781/Saturday
Edward Worthington and Robert George sign a request for two lbs sugar for one man of Captain Worthington's Company. Reverse states that this is a certification that Edward Matthews was confined in [doc. torn and illeg.] (VSA-19).

Leonard Helm and Robert George sign a request to the quartermaster for one quart tafia for Helm's use (VSA-19).

Robert George signs a request to the quartermaster to issue Mr. Williams eight lbs sugar for Williams' use (VSA-19).

James Finn and Robert George sign a request to the quartermaster for eight lbs sugar for Finn (VSA-19).

Richard Clark and Robert George sign a request to the quartermaster for eight lbs sugar for Clark's own use (VSA-19).

Leonard Helm and Robert George sign a request to the quartermaster for eight lbs sugar for Helm's use (VSA-19).

To Martin Carney, quartermaster, two lbs sugar (VSA-49: 47).

To Lt. John Girault, per order, two lbs sugar (VSA-49: 15).

To militia of Clarksville, per Captain Owens order, six lbs sugar (VSA-49: 65).

To Illinois Regiment, rations and fatigue, per order to one man of Captain Worthington's Company, two lbs sugar (VSA-49: 67).

May 6, 1781/Sunday

Joseph Calvit signs a request to Martin Carney for one quart tafia for Calvit's use (VSA-19).

Ammunition delivered by order of Captain Robert George at Fort Jefferson: to one man of Captain George's, 1/2 lb gunpowder and one lb lead; to two men of Captain George's, one lb gunpowder, 1/2 lb lead, and eight flints (VSA-50: 36).

May 7, 1781/Monday

George Owens and Robert George sign a request to the quartermaster for six lbs sugar for Owens' use (VSA-19).

To Illinois Regiment, rations and fatigue, per orders, nine carots of tobacco (VSA-49: 67).

May 8, 1781/Tuesday

James Finn and Robert George sign a request to the quartermaster for 11 gallons and two quarts tafia to Barnard Bassackland, for the purchase of 1,152 weight meat, allowing one gallon per 100 weight for the use of the troops. James Finn signed he received the within from Martin Carney (VSA-19).

To Mr. Finn, Issuing Commissary, per orders for purchasing provisions for the use of the troops at Fort Jefferson, 17 gallons and one quart rum (VSA-49: 45).

James Finn and Robert George sign a request to the quartermaster for 1/2 lb gunpowder for Finn's use (VSA-19).

May 9, 1781/Wednesday

Israel Dodge signs a request to Martin Carney for three pints tafia for Dodge's own use (VSA-19).

May 10, 1781/Thursday

James Finn and Robert George sign a request for three lbs tobacco for purchasing provisons for the troops at Fort Jefferson (VSA-19).

Joseph Calvit signs request to Martin Carney for one quart tafia for Calvit's use (VSA-19).

Leonard Helm and Robert George sign a request to the quartermaster for 1/2 gallon tafia for Helm's use (VSA-19).

James Finn and Robert George sign a request to the quartermaster to let Finn have one bottle tafia (VSA-19).

John Montgomery and Robert George sign a request to the quartermaster for 12 lbs sugar for Montgomery's use (VSA-19).

Account with Abraham Kellar, to cash paid Mary Morgan as per receipt, 90 pounds (VSA-19).

Tobacco issued by order of Captain George: to James Finn, three lbs (VSA-50: 16).

To Martin Carney, quartermaster, six lbs sugar (VSA-49: 47).

To Mr. Finn, per orders, for Finn's use, eight lbs sugar and one carot tobacco (VSA-49: 45).

Ammunition delivered by order of Captain George at Fort Jefferson: to one man of Captain George's Company, 1/4 lb gunpowder and 1/2 lb lead (VSA-50: 36).

To Col. John Montgomery, per order from day book, 12 lbs sugar (VSA-49: 1).

May 11, 1781/Saturday

Robert George signs a request to the quartermaster for tafia for 25 men of the Illinois Regiment on fatigue at one gill each (VSA-19).

Ammunition delivered by order of Captain Robert George at Fort Jefferson: to Lt. Dalton, one lb lead; to one man of Captain Worthington's, 1/2 lb gunpowder and one lb lead (VSA-50: 36).

To Illinois Regiment, rations and fatigue, per order for rations, two gallons, one quart, and 1/4 pint rum; per order for fatigue, three quarts and 1/4 pint rum (VSA-49: 67).

May 12, 1781/Saturday

Michael Miles and Robert George sign a request to the quartermaster for rations tafia for 75 men of the Illinois Regiment (VSA-19).

Abraham Kellar and Robert George sign a request to the quartermaster for one quart tafia for Kellar's own use (VSA-19).

To the Illinois Regiment, rations and fatigue, per order for fatigue, three quarts and 1/4 pint rum; per order for fatigue, one quart and 1/4 pint rum (VSA-49: 67).

May 13, 1781/Sunday

Robert George signs a request to Martin Carney to issue Mr. Donne two quarts and one pint tafia and eight lbs sugar for the use of Donne's family (VSA-19).

Michael Miles and Robert George sign a request to the quartermaster for liquor for 30 men of the Illinois Regiment on fatigue at one gill each (VSA-19).

May 14, 1781/Monday

Edward Worthington signs a request to the quartermaster for four case bottles tafia for Worthington's use (VSA-19).

Edward Worthington and Robert George sign a request to the quartermaster for ten lbs sugar for Worthington's use (VSA-19).

Edward Worthington and Robert George sign a request for one bottle tafia, for a sick Hibernian (VSA-19).

Mary Helebrant and Robert George sign a request to the quartermaster for four lbs sugar in behalf of Harry the Smith (VSA-19; 49: 65).

Robert George signs a request to the quartermaster for three gallons tafia for George's use (VSA-19).

Robert George signs a request to the quartermaster for nine gills taifa, to so many men of fatigue (VSA-19).

Joseph Calvit and Robert George sign a request to the quartermaster for three pints tafia for Calvit's use (VSA-19).

Richard Clark signs a request to the quartermaster for 2 1/2 gallons tafia for Clark's own use (VSA-19).

Abraham Kellar and Robert George sign a request to the quartermaster for one quart tafia for Kellar's use (VSA-19).

James Finn signs a request to the quartermaster for three quarts tafia for Finn's use (VSA-19).

Richard Clark and Robert George sign a request to the quartermaster for one lb sugar for Clark's use (VSA-19).

John Montgomery signs a request to Martin Carney for one bottle tafia (VSA-19).

Tobacco issued by order of Captain George, Commandant, to Illinois Regiment, 27 pounds (VSA-50: 16).

Ammunition delivered by order of Captain Robert George at Fort Jefferson: to Lt. Calvit, 1/2 lb gunpowder and one lb lead (VSA-50: 36).

To Lt. Valentine T. Dalton, per order, ten lbs sugar (VSA-49: 21).

Ammunition delivered by order of Captain Robert George at Fort Jefferson: to Captain Owens of Militia, 1/2 lb gunpowder; to Captain Kellar, 1/2 lb gunpowder and one lb lead (VSA-50: 36).

To Mr. John Walker, Sergeant Major, per order, three lbs sugar (VSA-49: 59).

To Captain Edward Worthington, per orders from day book, four gallons, one quart, one pint rum, and ten lbs sugar (VSA-49: 9).

May 15, 1781/Tuesday

Richard Brashears signs a request to the quartermaster to issue three quarts tafia for Brashears' use (VSA-19).

John Walker and Robert George sign a request to the quartermaster for three lbs sugar for Walker's use (VSA-19).

James Finn and Robert George sign a request to the quartermaster for one bottle tafia for Finn's use (VSA-19).

Jarret Williams and Robert George sign a request to the quartermaster for three pints tafia for Williams' use (VSA-19).

Ammunition delivered by order of Captain Robert George at Fort Jefferson: to Captain Brashears, 1/2 lb gunpowder and 1/2 lb lead; to Lt. Clark's Blockhouse, 5 1/2 lbs gunpowder and 11 lbs lead; to Ensign Williams, 1/2 lb gunpowder and one lb lead; to Col. Montgomery, 1/2 lb gunpowder and one lb lead; to the Regiment, 113 lbs gunpowder and 23 lbs lead (VSA-50: 36).

May 16, 1781/Wednesday
Leonard Helm and Robert George sign a request to the quartermaster for three pints tafia for Helm's use (VSA-19).

Israel Dodge and Robert George signed a request to Martin Carney for three pints tafia for Dodge's use (VSA-19).

Leonard Helm and Robert George sign a request to the quartermaster for three pints tafia for Helm's use (VSA-19).

Robert George signs a request to the quartermaster to let Lt. Dalton have ten lbs sugar on Dalton's account (VSA-19).

May 17, 1781/Thursday
Richard Clark and Robert George sign a request to the quartermaster to furnish William Cann with one gun, as he accidently lost his own in the Mississippi. Sergeant Page Partwood signed he received one gun from Martin Carney (VSA-19).

Robert George signs a request to the quartermaster for three case bottles tafia for George's own use (VSA-19).

Abraham Kellar and Robert George sign a request to the quartermaster for one bottle tafia for Kellar's use (VSA-19).

Michael Miles and Robert George sign a request to the quartermaster for ten gills tafia to one sergeant and nine men on fatigue (VSA-19).

John Montgomery and Robert George sign a request to the quartermaster for tobacco for 53 men of the Illinois Regiment at 1/2 lb each (VSA-19).

Joseph Calvit and Robert George sign a request to the quartermaster for three pints tafia for Calvit's use (VSA-19).

Richard Clark signs a request to the quartermaster for three pints tafia for Clark's own use (VSA-19).

John Donne signs a request to Martin Carney for "another" bottle tafia, Donne having company. Donne also states he plans to join Carney in the morning to provide him with assistance (VSA-19).

Tobacco issued by order of Captain George, Commandant, to Captain Worthington, three pounds (VSA-50: 16).

To Illinois Regiment, rations and fatigue, per order for fatigue, one quart and 1/4 pint rum (VSA-49: 67).

To Col. John Montgomery, per order ten lbs sugar (VSA-49: 1).

Captain Edward Worthington and Robert George sign a request to Martin Carney for three pints taffia for Worthington's use.

May 18, 1781/Friday
Edward Worthington and Robert George sign a request to the quartermaster for one carot tobacco for Worthington's use (VSA-19).

Abraham Kellar signs a request to the quartermaster for three pints tafia for Kellar's use (VSA-19).

Richard Clark signs a request to the quartermaster for three pints tafia for Clark's use (VSA-19).

Leonard Helm signs a request to the quartermaster for three pints tafia for Helm's use (VSA-19).

Robert George signs a request to Martin Carney to issue two quarts and one pint tafia to Mr. Donne (VSA-19).

Robert George signs a request to the quartermaster for three quarts tafia for George's use (VSA-19).

Abraham Kellar signs a request to the quartermaster for three pints tafia for Kellar's use (VSA-19).

John Montgomery signs a request to the quartermaster to send a bottle tafia to "save his life" (VSA-19).

Tobacco issued by order of Captain George, Commandant, to Martin Carney, three pounds (VSA-50: 16).

To Martin Carney, quartermaster, one carot of tobacco (VSA-49: 47).

To Col. John Montgomery, per order, two gallons rum (VSA-49: 1).

May 19, 1781/Saturday
Edward Worthington and Robert George sign a request to the quartermaster for two lbs sugar for Worthington's use (VSA-19).

James Finn and Robert George sign a request to the quartermaster for one lb sugar for Finn's use (VSA-19).

Richard Brashears and Robert George sign a return to the quartermaster for two lbs sugar for one man in Captain Brashears' Company (VSA-19).

Israel Dodge and Robert George sign a request to Martin Carney for six lbs sugar for Dodge's use (VSA-19).

Robert George signs a request to Israel Dodge for one small looking glass for Lt. Calvit's use (VSA-19).

Buckner Pittman and George Slaughter sign a request to the issuing commissary for six days rations of corn and beef for five men on command from Fort Jefferson (VSA-19).

To Mr. Israel Dodge, Deputy Agent, per orders, six lbs sugar (VSA-49: 43).

To Illinois Regiment, rations and fatigue, per order to a man of Captain Brashears' Company, two lbs sugar (VSA-49: 67).

May 21, 1781/Monday
Letter from William Shannon at Sullivans Station to George Rogers Clark. Shannon states he has learned through letters from Fort Jefferson that they are in a starving condition and he does not feel he will be able to relieve them. He states that Major Slaughter has used the provisions purchased for Fort Jefferson, and it injured the credit. Shannon now finds it impossible to purchase anything. Shannon hopes to purchase one or two hundred bushels of corn for the relief of Fort Jefferson and will send the corn along with eight or ten thousand weight beef. John Rogers arrived six or seven weeks ago from the Illinois with his whole company; Dodge, Dejean, and Bentley were also with him (GRC, I: 554-555).

Michael Miles and Robert George sign a request to the quartermaster for sugar for 69 men, eight women, and ten children of the Illinois Regiment. The men should draw two lbs each; the women and children draw one lb each (VSA-19; 49: 67).

Abraham Kellar and Robert George sign a request to the quartermaster for four lbs sugar for Kellar's own use (VSA-19).

Tobacco issued by order of Captain George, Commander, to Mr. Hunter, three pounds (VSA-50: 16).

May 22, 1781/Tuesday
Robert George signs a request to Martin Carney for one carot tobacco for Mr. Hunter (VSA-19).

Richard Brashears and Robert George sign a request to Israel Dodge for three skeins thread for one man of Brashear's Company. William Elms signed he received the thread from Israel Dodge (VSA-19).

Letter from John Floyd at Beargrass Station to George Rogers Clark. He mentions corn being plentiful in the upper counties and suggests sending some down to the Iron Bank Station [Fort Jefferson], because of their starving condition (GRC, I: 556-558).

May 23, 1781/Wednesday
Robert George signs a request to the quartermaster to pay Mrs. Burks for making eight shirts for George's company. Elizabeth Burks signed she received five lbs sugar for her work (VSA-19; 49:74).

Joseph Calvit and Robert George signed a request to the quartermaster for eight lbs sugar for Calvit's use (VSA-19).

Tobacco issued by order of Captain George, Commander, to Captain Helm, three pounds (VSA-50: 16).

May 24, 1781/Thursday
Edward Worthington and Robert George sign a request to Israel Dodge to issue 4 3/4 yds linen, 16 skeins thread, and four paper framed pocket glasses for Worthington's use (VSA-19).

John Donne signs a request to Israel Dodge for one paper pins, six dozen large buttons, six dozen small buttons, and three gun worms for Donne's use (VSA-19).

Martin Carney and Robert George sign a request to Israel Dodge for two pocket glasses for Carney's use (VSA-19).

May 25, 1781/Friday
John Donne signs a request to Israel Dodge for eight small bunches of capwire, one skein silk, and three sticks worsted for Donne's use (VSA-19).

Richard Clark and Robert George sign a request to the quartermaster for one carot tobacco for Clark's own use (VSA-19).

Israel Dodge signs a request to Martin Carney for three quarts tafia for Dodge's use (VSA-19).

John Montgomery signs a request to the quartermaster for three quarts tafia for Montgomery's use (VSA-19).

Michael Miles and Robert George sign a request to the quartermaster for tafia for 64 men of the Illinois Regiment at one gill per man (VSA-19).

Richard Clark signs a request to Martin Carney for three quarts tafia for Carney's own use (VSA-19).

Robert George signs a request to the quartermaster for three quarts tafia for George's use (VSA-19).

John Walker and Robert George sign a request to the quartermaster for three pints tafia for Walker's use (VSA-19).

Joseph Calvit signs a request to the quartermaster for three quarts tafia for Calvit's use (VSA-19).

Richard Brashears signs a request to the quartermaster for three quarts tafia for Brashears' own use (VSA-19).

Robert George signs a request to Martin Carney to issue Mr. Donne, three quarts tafia for the use of Mr. Donne and his family (VSA-19).

Abraham Kellar signs a request to the quartermaster for three quarts tafia for Kellar's use (VSA-19).

Edward Worthington signs a request to the quartermaster for three quarts tafia for Worthington's use (VSA-19).

To Lt. Richard Clark, per order, one carot of tobacco and six lbs sugar (VSA-49: 19).

To Captain Robert George, per order from day book, five gallons, two quarts, and one pint of rum (VSA-49: 3).

To Illinois Regiment, rations and fatigue, per order for rations, two gallons rum (VSA-49: 67).

To Captain Leonard Helm, per orders, eight lbs sugar and one carot of tobacco (VSA-49: 27).

May 26, 1781/Saturday
Edward Worthington and Robert George sign a request to the quartermaster for ten lbs sugar for Worthington's use (VSA-19).

Robert George signs a request to the quartermaster to let Lt. Dalton have three quarts tafia (VSA-19).

Richard Brashears and Robert George sign a request to the quartermaster for ten quarts sugar for Brashears' own use (VSA-19).

To Captain Richard Brashears, per order, 10 lbs of sugar (VSA-49: 7).

Leonard Helm and Robert George sign a request to the quartermaster for eight lbs sugar for Helm's use (VSA-19).

To Lt. Valentine Thomas Dalton, per order, six lbs sugar (VSA-49: 21).

May 27, 1781/Sunday
Robert George signs a request to the quartermaster to have a soldier and some men search the soldiers camps in the town and garrison. Some ammunition may have possibly been stolen from the public store (VSA-19).

Stores issued by order of Captain Robert George: to William Carr, soldier, conductor to Lt. Richard Clark, one musket or smoothed gun and one bayonet with belt (VSA-50: 39).

May 28, 1781/Monday
Jarret Williams signs a request to the quartermaster for three quarts tafia for Williams' use (VSA-19).

May 29, 1781/Tuesday
Deputy Agent Israel Dodge issued ten lbs sugar from the quartermaster (VSA-19; 49:43).

Received one bolt slow match from Patrick Kennedy for the use of the artillery, as acknowledged by Martin Carney, quartermaster (VSA-19).

Israel Dodge and Robert George sign a request to the quartermaster for ten lbs sugar for Dodge's use (VSA-19).

May 30, 1781/Wednesday
John Montgomery signs a request to the quartermaster for five lbs sugar for Montgomery's use (VSA-19; 49:1).

Robert George signs a request to the quartermaster for 24 lbs sugar for George's use (VSA-19; 49:1).

Robert George signs a request to the quartermaster to let Lt. Dalton have six lbs sugar on Dalton's account (VSA-19).

May 31, 1781/Thursday
Buckner Pittman and George Slaughter sign a request to the quartermaster for two lbs gunpowder and four lbs lead, and one lb gunpowder and two lbs lead for four men in command at Fort Jefferson (VSA-19).

George Slaughter at the Falls signs a request to the commissary for 18 gallons whiskey for the use of the party going with provisions to Camp Jefferson (VSA-19).

To Major John Williams, per orders, one carot tobacco (VSA-49: 5).

June 1781/Miscellaneous
Valentine Dalton and Robert George request the quartermaster issue arms for two men of Captain George's Company, who were formerly in Captain Rogers' Company (VSA-20).

June 1, 1781/Friday
Lt. Girault and Robert George sign a request to the quartermaster for ten lbs sugar for Girault's use (VSA-20).

Lt. Girault and Robert George sign a request to Martin Carney for one lb gunpowder and two lbs lead for Girault's use (VSA-20).

Account of ammunition delivered by Martin Carney by order of Captain Robert George and Col. Montgomery: to Lt. Girault, one lb gunpowder and two lbs lead (VSA-50: 42).

John Walker and Robert George sign a request to the quartermaster for six lbs sugar for Walker's use (VSA-20; 49: 59).

Account of ammunition delivered Martin Carney by order of Captain George and Col. Montgomery: to Major Williams, one lb gunpowder (VSA-50: 42).

To Mr. Finn, Issuing Commissary, per orders, ten lbs sugar (VSA-49: 45).

To Illinois regiment, rations and fatigue, per order for one man of Captain George's Company, three lbs sugar (VSA-49: 67).

To Illinois Regiment, rations and fatigue, per orders to James McMullin, Gunner, three lbs sugar (VSA-49: 67).

To hospital or sick accounts per order to two men of Worthington's company, four lbs sugar (VSA-49: 63).

June 2, 1781/Saturday
John Williams and Robert George request the quartermaster to issue one lb gunpowder for Williams' use (VSA-20).

Edward Worthington and Robert George request the quartermaster issue four lbs sugar for two men of Worthington's company, who have returned from fatigue (VSA-20).

Michael Miles and Robert George sign a request to the quartermaster to issue tobacco to 58 men of the Illinois Regiment, allowing 1/2 lb per man (VSA-20; 50: 16).

To Lt. John Girault, per order, ten lbs sugar (VSA-49: 15).

Richard McCarty, who was not at Fort Jefferson at this time, was killed (Harding 1981: 27).

June 4, 1781/Monday
Richard Clark and Robert George request the quartermaster to issue six lbs sugar for Clark's own use (VSA-20).

Reuben Kemp signs he received of Martin Carney four lbs sugar for helping saw, 700 feet poplar plank. Attested by Michael Miles (VSA-20; 49: 74).

Israel Dodge and Robert George request Martin Carney issue ten lbs sugar for Dodge's use (VSA-20).

James Finn and Robert George request the quartermaster issue ten lbs sugar for Finn's use (VSA-20; 49: 43).

John Grimshaw signs his mark he received of Martin Carney four lbs sugar and four bushels charcoal (VSA-20).

June 5, 1781/Tuesday
Valentine T. Dalton and Robert George sign a return to the quartermaster for sugar for one man of Captain George's Company (VSA-20).

Edward Worthington and Robert George sign a return to the quartermaster for ammunition for three men belonging to Captain Worthington's Company (VSA-20).

Edward Worthington and Robert George sign a return to the quartermaster for four lbs sugar for two men belonging to Captain Worthington's Company (VSA-20).

Robert George signs a request for two carots tobacco for Patrick Kennedy's voyage to the Falls of Ohio (VSA-20).

Robert George requests 12 lbs sugar from Martin Carney for Mr. Joseph Hunter, as he is one of the late magistrates (VSA-20).

Joshua Archer and Robert George request Martin Carney to let Joshua Archer have 12 lbs sugar (VSA-20).

Abraham Kellar and Robert George request the quartermaster issue one lb gunpowder and two lbs lead for the use of hunting for the troops on their route to the Falls (VSA-20).

Abraham Kellar and Robert George request the quartermaster issue 24 lbs sugar for Kellar's use (VSA-20).

Robert George requests the quartermaster to issue 12 lbs sugar to Captain George Owens (VSA-20).

Joshua Archer and Robert George request the quartermaster to let Archer have one lb gunpowder and one lb lead (VSA-20).

Lt. Girault and Robert George request Martin Carney issue three lbs sugar for Girault's use (VSA-20).

Lt. Girault and Robert George request the quartermaster issues five lbs sugar for Girault's use (VSA-20).

Robert George requests the quartermaster issue three lbs sugar to James McMullen, being on fatigue (VSA-20).

Robert George requests the quartermaster issue four lbs sugar to Michael Miles for Miles' own use (VSA-20; 49:61).

Patrick Kennedy and Robert George request to let the bearer have 20 lbs sugar (VSA-20).

Robert George requests Patrick Kennedy to have one lb gunpowder, two lbs lead, and six flints for his voyage to the Falls of Ohio (VSA-20).

Account of ammunition delivered by Martin Carney by order of Captain Robert George and Col. Montgomery: to Mr. Kennedy for his voyage to the Falls, one lb gunpowder, two lbs lead and six flints; to Mr. Archer, one lb gunpowder and one lb lead; to Captain Kellar for the use of hunting for the troops going to the Falls, one lb gunpowder and two lbs lead (VSA-50: 42).

To Lt. Thomas Dalton, per order, 25 lbs sugar (VSA-49: 21).

Issued to Mr. Pattrick Kennedy, Deputy Conductor, per order from day book, 12 lbs sugar (VSA-49: 39).

To Captain Abraham Kellar, per orders, 24 lbs sugar (VSA-49: 49).

To militia of Clarksville, Mr. Archer per orders, to 12 lbs sugar (VSA-49: 65).

To militia of Clarksville, Joseph Hunter, per orders to, 12 lbs sugar (VSA-49: 65).

To Captain Richard Brashears, per order, 20 lbs sugar (VSA-49: 7).

To militia of Clarksville, John Burks per orders to, six lbs sugar (VSA-49: 65).

To Lt. Joseph Calvit, per orders, 20 lbs sugar (VSA-49: 17).

Account of ammunition delivered by Martin Carney by order of Captain Robert George and Col. Montgomery: to Lt. Clark, 1/2 lb gunpowder and one lb lead; to three men of Lt. Clark's 1 1/2 lbs gunpowder and three lbs lead; to three men of Captain Worthington's Company, 3/4 lbs gunpowder and 1 1/2 lbs lead (VSA-50: 42).

To Illinois regiment, rations and fatigue per order, to three men of George's Company, eight lbs sugar (VSA-49: 67).

To militia of Clarksville, Miles Hart per orders, to 12 lbs sugar (VSA-49: 65).

To militia of Clarksville, Mrs. Hellebrant per orders, to three lbs sugar (VSA-49: 65).

To Col. John Montgomery, per order, six lbs sugar and 20 lbs (VSA-49: 1).

Edward Murray dies. He was a member of Captain Bailey's Company (Harding 1981: 46).

To militia of Clarksville, per orders to Captain Owens, one carot tobacco, six lbs sugar, and 12 lbs sugar (VSA-49: 65).

To State of Virginia, per order exchanged for fatigue, liquor with Mr. Pyatte, 50 lbs sugar (VSA-49: 74).

To Ensign Jarrett Williams, per orders, 20 lbs sugar (VSA-49: 33).

To State of Virginia, per order to a soldier for burning four bushels of sharkcoal [charcoal], four lbs sugar (VSA-49: 74).

To State of Virginia, per order for a militia man rowing 16 days up the Ohio, 16 lbs sugar (VSA-49: 74).

To Lt. John Girault, per order, five lbs sugar (VSA-49: 15).

To Illinois Regiment, rations and fatigue, per orders to one of Captain Worthington's Company, four lbs sugar (VSA-49: 67).

June 6, 1781/Wednesday
George Owens and Robert George request the quartermaster to issue four lbs gunpowder and eight lbs lead to the militia (VSA-20).

James Finn and Robert George request the quartermaster issue one carot tobacco for Finn's use (VSA-20).

George Owens and Robert George request the quartermaster issue one carot tobacco to Captain Owens for Owens' own use (VSA-20).

John Donne and Robert George request the quartermaster issue one carot tobacco for Donne's use (VSA-20).

Robert George requests the quartermaster issue three lbs sugar for Mrs. Helebrand and family, as she is upon sufferance (VSA-20).

Lt. Girault and Robert George request the quartermaster issue two carots tobacco for Girault's use (VSA-20; misfiled).

Jarret Williams and Robert George request Martin Carney issue 20 lbs sugar for Williams' use (VSA-20).

William Shannon certifies that Edward Daughtery went express from the Falls of Ohio to Fort Jefferson in April, 1781, with dispatches from General Clark and returned. Daughterty is entitled to receive 1,000 pounds Virginia Currency (VSA-20).

Robert George signs a return to the quartermaster for two lbs sugar for one man of Captain George's Company (VSA-20).

Richard Clark and Robert George request the quartermaster issue 1/2 lb gunpowder and one lb lead for Clark's use (VSA-20).

Lt. Girault and Robert George request the quartermaster issue six lbs sugar for John Daughterty and his children for their journey to the Falls (VSA-20).

Robert George requests Martin Carney issue six lbs sugar for the use of John Burks' family (VSA-20).

John Williams and Robert George request the quartermaster stating: "for Gods sake let me have two pounds of shuger for use" (VSA-20).

John Walker and Robert George request the quartermaster issue six lbs sugar for Walker's use (VSA-20).

Jarret Williams and Robert George request the quartermaster issue one kettle for Williams' use (VSA-20).

Richard Brashears and Robert George request the quartermaster issue four lbs sugar for one woman and three children belonging to Brahsears Company (VSA-20).

Jarret Williams and Robert George request Israel Dodge issue two looking glasses for Williams' use (VSA-20).

John Williams and Robert George request Martin Carney issue six carots tobacco to purchase moccasins for detatchment to the Falls of Ohio (VSA-20).

Miles Heart signs his mark and Robert George requests the quartermaster issue 12 lbs sugar for Hearts' use, being for provisions delivered in the country store (VSA-20).

Stores issued by order of Captain George: to Ensign Williams, one kettle (VSA-50: 39).

Account of ammunition delivered Martin Carney by order of Captain Robert George and Col. Montgomery: to Captain Owens Militia, four lbs gunpowder and eight lbs lead (VSA-50: 42).

Account of ammunition delivered by Martin Carney by order of Captain Robert George and Col. Montgomery: to Col. Montgomery, one lb gunpowder, two lbs lead, and two flints; to Mr. Finn, 1/2 lb gunpowder (VSA-50: 42).

To Captain Robert George, per orders, 150 lbs sugar (VSA-49: 3).

Stores issued by order of Captain Robert George: to Col. Montgomery, one kettle (VSA-50: 39).

To Major John Williams, per orders, two lbs sugar and six carots of tobacco (VSA-49: 5).

June 7, 1781/Thursday
James Finn signes he received from Mr. Phelps, 103 lbs pork and veal for use of the troops belonging to the Illinois Regiment stationed at Fort Jefferson (VSA-20).

Robert George requests the quartermaster issue four lbs sugar to Joseph Thornton for Thornton's own use (VSA-20).

Robert George requests the quartermaster issue two lbs lead and one lb gunpowder to Daniel Whitegar, who is hunting for the troops going to the Falls (VSA-20).

Robert George requests the quartermaster issue two lbs lead and one lb gunpowder to Patrick Callaghan, who is hunting for the troops going to the Falls (VSA-20).

Valentine Dalton and Robert George request the quartermaster issue two lbs sugar for three of Captain George's Company (VSA-20).

Leonard Helm and Robert George request the quartermaster issue 12 lbs sugar for Helm's use (VSA-20).

Robert George signs a return to the quartermaster for three lbs sugar for one man of Captain George's Company (VSA-20).

Martin Carney initials he received from Sergeant Crump, 444 lbs lead (VSA-20).

Martin Carney initials he received from Sergeant Crump, one small canoe which is state property that Crump brought from the Illinois (VSA-20).

Robert George request the quartermaster issue 20 lbs sugar for George's use (VSA-20).

Robert George requests the quartermaster issue 150 lbs sugar for George's use (VSA-50).

Michael Miles and Robert George request the quartermaster issue tobacco to 57 of the Illinois Regiment at 1/2 lb each (VSA-20).

Robert George requests Martin Carney issue 12 lbs sugar to Mrs. Meredith, for the use of Sergeant Miles' child who's in distress (VSA-20; 49: 61).

Valentine Dalton and Robert George sign a return to the quartermaster for three lbs sugar for one man of Captain George's Company, who is sick (VSA-20).

Patrick Kennedy and Robert George certify that Captain Helm gave one cow and calf to the troops at Fort Jefferson (VSA-20).

Joseph Calvit and Robert George request Martin Carney issue two carots tobacco for Calvit's use (VSA-20).

Account of ammunition delivered by Martin Carney by order of Captain Robert George and Col. Montgomery: to Patrick Callahan, one lb gunpowder and two lbs lead; to Daniel Whitegar, one lb gunpowder and two lbs lead (VSA-50: 42).

To Captain Leondard Helm, per orders, 12 lbs sugar (VSA-49: 27).

To Col. John Montgomery, per order, one carot of tobacco (VSA-49: 1).

To hospital or sick accounts, per order to one woman of Captain Brashears, four lbs sugar; per order to one man and two children of Captain George's Company, six lbs sugar; per order to one man and woman of Captain George's Company, three lbs sugar; per order to one man of Captain George's, two lbs sugar (VSA-49: 63).

To Lt. Joseph Calvit, per orders, two carots of tobacco (VSA-49: 17).

To Martin Carney, quartermaster, 12 lbs sugar (VSA-49: 47).

Account of ammunition delivered by Martin Carney by order of Captain Robert George and Col. Montgomery: to six men going to the Falls by land, three lbs gunpowder and six lbs lead (VSA-50: 42).

To Mr. Donne, per orders, 12 lbs sugar and one carot of tobacco (VSA-49: 37).
To Mr. Finn, Issuing Commissary, per orders, one carot of tobacco (VSA-49: 45).

To Captain Robert George, per orders, 12 lbs sugar (VSA-49: 3).

To Lt. John Girault, per order, two carots of tobacco and three lbs sugar (VSA-49: 15).

To Mr. Patrick Kennedy, Deputy Conductor, 20 lbs sugar and two carots of tobacco (VSA-49: 39).

To Mr. John Walker, Sergeant Major, per order, six lbs sugar (VSA-49: 59).

To Captain Edward Worthington, per orders, ten lbs sugar (VSA-49: 9).

To Regiment, per order to a man of Captain George's, three lbs sugar; per order to the regiment, 9 1/2 carots of tobacco (VSA-49: 70).

To Captain Richard Brashears, per order, one carot of tobacco (VSA-49: 7).

June 8, 1781/Friday
Edward Worthington, Richard Brashears, and Abraham Kellar sign a statement to Martin Carney, ordered by Captain George, to determine whether the state wagon should be left at Fort Jefferson. The wagon was loaded heavily, and they determined it should be buried at the fort until the wagon can be converted to public use (VSA-20).

Abstract of work done by artificers at Fort Jefferson while commanded by Robert George from May 17, 1780 to June 8, 1781: helping to build a garrison, flooring and covering two bastions and setting three gates; building three storehouses and five dwelling houses for service; building and finishing three blockhouses, setting up a two pounder and three swivels in them; breaking 11 flat bottomed boats for public service; building eight huts or camps for the use of the soldiers in the garrison; making 38 coffins for men, women, and children; framing 12 feet of a well in the garrison and building a windless; sawing 1,800 feet of plank; building a necessary house framed with two rooms; repairing several boats at different times; making 176 oars for boats, and making a carriage for a six pounder. Abstract signed by Martin Carney and Robert George (VSA-20).

Martin Carney signs a memorandum of state property left at Fort Jefferson at the time of evacuation: seven hand mills, one wagon; one piece [illeg.] ordinance; fifty stand old arms [muskets], one grinding stone; two 56 weight and one 28 lb grinding stone, two canoes, one beek iron, one pair of bellows belonging to John Harris, armourer (VSA-20).

Robert George signs a statement certifying that at the time of evacuation there was not a sufficient way to transport the above items (VSA-20).

Valentine Dalton and Robert George sign a return to the quartermaster for three lbs sugar for one man of Captain George's Company (VSA-20).

Letter from John Montgomery at Falls of Ohio to Thomas Nelson dated August 10, 1781. Montgomery mentions that due to the loss of credit with the State and no supplies coming in, Fort Jefferson was evacuated on June 8, 1781, due to a lack of provisions (GRC, I: 585-586).

June 10, 1781/Sunday
Letter from George Rogers Clark at Yohogania Court House to Thomas Jefferson. Mentions that Captain Bently is desirious of supplying Fort Jefferson with provisions for a garrison of 100 men. If Jefferson will agree, Clark states that Bently would be the right person to accomplish such a task (GRC, I: 563-564).

June 13, 1781/Wednesday
Enroute to the Falls: Account of ammunition delivered by Martin Carney by order of Captain Robert George and Col. Montgomery: to 23 men at Elk Camp, 5 3/4 lbs gunpowder and 11 1/2 lbs lead (VSA-50: 42).

June 21, 1781/Thursday
Enroute to the Falls: Stores issued by order of Captain Robert George: to Captain Brashears' Company, three muskets or smoothed guns; to Captain George's Company, one musket or smoothed gun; to Captain Worthington's Company, one musket or smoothed gun; to Captain Worthington's Company, one musket or smoothed gun, and one bayonet with belt (VSA-50: 40).

June 24, 1781/Sunday
Enroute to the Falls: Captain Edward Worthington, per orders, ten lbs sugar (VSA-49: 9); Mr. Pittman, Boatmaster, per order brought from day book, six lbs sugar (VSA-49: 57); Mr. Miles, quartermaster Sergeant, per order, five lbs sugar (VSA-49: 61); hospital or sick accounts, per order to one man of Captain Worthington's, two lbs sugar (VSA-49: 63); Regiment, per order to regiment, 18 carots tobacco; per order to regiment, 95 lbs sugar (VSA-49: 70).

July 1, 1781/Sunday
James Finn and Robert George on the Ohio, sign they received from Joshua Archer, 1,068 lbs buffalo and bear meat for the use of the troops on their passage from Fort Jefferson to Falls of the Ohio (Louisville) (VSA-21).

To individuals, per order Mr. Archer, 15 lbs sugar (VSA-49: 68).

July 2, 1781/Monday
Martin Carney signed that Buckner Pittman, a sergeant in Captain George's Company was appointed boatmaster under Carney at Fort Jefferson, January 1, 1781, and acted in that capacity until July 2, 1781 (VSA-21).

July 4, 1781/Wednesday
Account of ammunition delivered by Martin Carney by order of Captain Robert George and Col. Montgomery, to Col. Slaughter for rejoining dragoons, 25 lbs gunpowder (VSA-50: 42).

July 6, 1781/Friday
To Mr. Meridith [Meredith] Price, per order from day book, ten lbs sugar (VSA-49: 25).

To Captain Abraham Kellar, per orders, ten lbs sugar (VSA-49: 49).

To Captain John Rogers, per orders from day book, 15 lbs sugar (VSA-49: 53).

Martin Carney issued to Captain John Rogers: 13 lbs sugar (VSA-21; filed as August 10, 1781).

July 7, 1781/Saturday
To Col. George Slaughter, per order, 100 lbs sugar (VSA-49: 11).

To Mr. Israel Dodge, Deputy Agent, per orders, ten lbs sugar (VSA-49: 43).

To hospital or sick accounts, per order to a man of Captain George's, two lbs sugar (VSA-49: 63).

Account of ammunition delivered by Martin Carney by order of Captain Robert George and Col. Montgomery: to a hunter by order of Col. Montgomery, two lbs gunpowder and four lbs lead; to a hunter by order of Captain George, 1/4 lb gunpowder and 1/2 lb lead (VSA-50: 42).

James Finn signed at Falls of Ohio, he received 440 lbs beef and 125 lbs bear meat for the troops on their way from Fort Jefferson to the Falls (VSA-21).

July 8, 1781/Sunday
To Lt. Richard Clark, per order, six lbs sugar (VSA-49: 19).

To Captain Mark Thomas, per orders from day book, ten lbs sugar (VSA-49: 31).

To Ensign Jarret Williams, per orders, ten lbs sugar (VSA-49: 33).

To hospital or sick accounts, per order to a man of Lt. Clark's, two lbs (VSA-49: 63).

Account of ammunition delivered by Martin Carney by order of Captain Robert George and Col. Montgomery: to Captain Owin [Owen] and Patt Calahan for hunting, one lb gunpowder and two lbs lead (VSA-50: 42).

July 9, 1781/Monday
To Captain Edward Worthington, per orders, ten lbs sugar (VSA-49: 9).

To Lt. Joseph Calvit, per orders, ten lbs sugar (VSA-49: 17).

To Captain Leonard Helm, per order, ten lbs sugar (VSA-49: 17).

To Ensign William Roberts, per order from day book, ten lbs sugar (VSA-49: 35).

To Mr. Donne, Deputy Conductor, per orders, ten lbs sugar (VSA-49: 37).

To Mr. Finn, Issuing Commissary, per order, six lbs sugar (VSA-49: 45).

To Martin Carney, quartermaster, ten lbs sugar (VSA-49: 47).

July 12, 1781/Thursday
To Cornet Thruston, per order from day book, 20 lbs sugar (VSA-49: 51).

To Mr. Pittman, boatmaster, per order, six lbs sugar (VSA-49: 57).

To Mr. Miles, Quartermaster Sergeant, per order, six lbs sugar (VSA-49: 61).

To hospital or sick accounts, per order to a man of Captain Brashears', two lbs; per order to a man of Captain Rogers', four lbs (VSA-49: 63).

To individuals, per order George Wilson, 20 lbs sugar (VSA-49: 68).

John Montgomery signs he received of George Wilson, 180 lbs fresh beef for the use of the detachment which arrived from Fort Jefferson (VSA-21).

Arrived at the Falls of the Ohio.

Glossary

Baize (also spelled baize, bays in the text): "A coarse woollen stuff, having a long nap" (OUD 1964:138). Also, "a loosely woven cotton or wool fabric in a plain weave made with soft twist filling yarns and closely napped to imitate felt. It is dyed in solid colors, usually green. It was originally made in Baza, Spain, with coarse woollen warp and filling yarns, heavily felted, and finished with a long nap on both sides; it was later made thinner and finer and used clothing, when warm knitted underwear was unknown" (FC 1959:41).

Bateau "A light river-boat, especially the long tapering boats with flat bottoms used by the French Canadians" (OUD 1964:153).

Bath coating (also blue bath and blue berth "coating" in text). During the 18th century, coating material consisted of a "thick double-raised baize, used for overcoats" (CC&B 1960:243). "A light weight, wide fabric with a long nap, bleached or colored. Originally used for coatings..." (FC 1959:52).

Binding (see also worsted, i.e., worsted binding). "A protective covering for the raw edges of a fabric, braid, etc." (OUD 1964:180).

Black ball or blackball. "A composition used by shoemakers, etc., and also for taking rubbings for brasses and the like; a heel ball (OUD 1964: 184). "To blacken with blackball" (OUD 1964:184). Made of beeswax, wax, and lamp-black.

Breech cloth. "A garment covering the loins and thighs (OUD 1964:219).

Broadcloth. "A fine woollen cloth of plain weave" (CC&B 1960: 245). "A term originally indicating a fabric made on a wide loom, specifically, wider than 27 inches" (FC 1959:82).

Calamanco or calimanco (in text also spelled calmanco, callimanco, calimango). "Of single worsted, glazed (CC&B 1960:246). "A glazed linen fabric with a pattern on one side only..." (FC 1959:96).

Calender (also spelled callendry, calandery, callardery, and callender in text). "To give linen a gloss, to smooth (WDEL 1970: 41). "A machine in which cloth, paper, etc., is pressed under rollers for the purpose of smoothing or glazing; also for watering or giving a wavy appearance" (OUD 1964:249).

Calico "Printed cotton cloth" (WDEL 1970:41). "From 1600 to 1773 the weft of cotton with ways of linen; since then entirely of cotton" (CC&B 1960:247).

Cambric (in text also cambrik, cambrick). "A kind of fine linen from Flanders" (WDEL 1970: 41). "A very fine quality of linen" (CC&B 1960: 247). "A kind of fine white linen, originally made at Cambry in Flanders" (OUD 1964:253). "A plain weave, soft cotton or linen fabric calendared with a slight luster on the fabric (FC 1959:97-98).

Camlet (in text also camelot, camblet, camlett, chamblet, chamblette). "Thought to have been a kind of mohair, later of various mixed materials. In 18th century sometimes of wool or silk or hair or mixtures...made plain or twilled (CC&B 1960:257). "In Britain the term referred to a fine, lightweight, plain weave fabric made with luster wools and generally dyed bright red" (FC 1959:99).

Capot (also capeau in text). "A French term for strong filled fabric with a napped face used for sailor's clothes, waterproof coats, etc., similar fabric is made in Great Britain with shoddy" (reclaimed wool)(FC 1959:103). French for "a great coat" (BFD 1827:99). Also meaning "long cloak, little cape, or riding hood" (BFD 1827:100).

Carabin (also carabine in text). "Is a firearm somewhat smaller than the firelocks (flintlocks) of the infantry, and used by all the horse (calvary). It carries a ball of 24 in the pound, its barrel is 3 feet long and the whole length including the stock is 4 feet" (UMD 1969:50).

Carat of Tobacco (also carotte and pigtail in text). "A sweet leaf, it was formed in long, thin rolls, treated with treacle, cut like modern pigtail...In the late 18th century, the best medium of exchange in Louisiana was the "carat" of tobacco. These had definite weight and value. They were sometimes prepared in the same manner as frontier plug tobacco. Snuff was made by grating tobacco from the end of a carat and was used by men and women of that time (TD 1940:27).

Cashmere. "A fine soft woollen fabric first imported from Cashmere. The original material was the wood of the Tibet goat" (RPC 1976:278). "A woollen fabric made in imitation of the true cashmere" (OUD 1964:271).

Cassimir (also cassimere in text). "Cassimir was a cloth patented in 1766, although some records use this term before that date. It apparently was a woollen cloth of a certain description (RPC 1976:278). "A thin twilled woollen textile of worsted warp and woollen weft in a diagonal twill weave ' (CC&B 1960:248).

Cask (i.e., pickle cask in text). "A wooden vessel of cylindrical form, made of curved staves bound together by hoops, with flat ends; a barrel (OUD 1964:271). "A barrel or wooden vessel used for liquor" (WDEL 1970:44).

Chacart. "French term meaning 'Indian cotton'" (BFD 1827:107). In the context of the issues, "Cotton Sachecque" is probably referring to Indian cotton. However, John Dodge's variation with phonetic spelling might indicate that "Casaque" or "Sachque" was the term specified indicating cotton materials issued for a campaign or upper coat. If Sachecque was the phonetic misspelling of Casaquin, then the cotton material issued by might have been for making a "short great coat" (BFD 1827:103). "An East Indian calico printed in bright, multicolored checks" (FC 1959:116).

Challis (also chalinet in text). "A thin twilled textile of silk and worsted; originally of silk and camel hair. Printed in color" (CC&B 1960:249). "A soft, supple, lightweight, plain weave fabric made of wool...cotton, or blends. Usually printed in small floral patterns" (FC 1959:117).

Check linen. " A striped or checked linen fabric used for dress and aprons. Generally in combination of blue and white and red and white. The term is now applied to similar but heavier fabrics used for table cloths (FC 1959:322).

Chintz (also chince in text). "Indian cottons, fine printed calico" (WDEL 1970:49). "The painted calicoes imported from India; now, a name for cotton cloths fast printed with designs of flowers, etc., in a number of colors, and usually glazed" (OUD 1964: 303). "Originally a glazed, plain weave cotton fabric, generally woven with a hard spun fine warp and coarser, slack twist filling; decorated with a brightly colored pattern of flowers, stripes, etc." (FC 1959:126).

Coating. "Clothing of the nature of a coat, 1798. Material for coats" (OUD 1964:332). "Any fabric used to make coats; usually a heavier weight wool. A British term for heavy fabric woven with a three up, and one down twill, dyed black, and given a lustrous finish. Also made in a satin weave and vertical cord effects" (FC 959:136).

Corduroy (also corderoy in text). "A kind of coarse thick-ribbed cotton stuff" (OUD 1964:394). "Thick cotton stuff, ribbed" (WDEL 1970: 67). In the 18th century, corduroy was a thick corded stuff of cotton, with a pile like velvet (CC&B 1960:250).

Cottonade. "A name for various coarse cotton fabrics"(OUD 1964:403). "A coarse heavy cotton fabric woven with a three harness, left hand, warp faced twill. Given a firm finish and sometimes napped on the back" (FC 1959:157).
Cross-cut (as in saw in text). "Adapted for cross-cutting, as a cross-cut saw" (OUD 1964:427).

Damask. "A rich silk fabric woven with elaborate designs and figures. A twilled linen fabric with designs which show up by opposite reflections of light from the surface" (OUD 1964:450). "Silk, woollen, & etc., woven into flowers" (WDEL 1970:76. "A figured fabric of silk or linen of which the woven pattern appears reversed on the back (CC&B 1960:252). "Originally a rich silk fabric with woven floral designs made in China and introduced into Europe...The fabric is similar to brocade but flatter" (FC 1959:171).

Dimity (also corded dimete, dimete, dimetty, dimithy, dimitty, dinitky, drinete in text). In the 17th century, dimity was, "a fine sort of fustian; a cotton stuff" (CC&B 1960:252). "A stout cotton cloth, woven with raised stripes and fancy figures; used undyed for beds and hangings, and sometimes for garments" (OUD 1964:511). "A kind of white fustian, a fine fustian (WDEL 1970:86). "A fine kind of fustian, or cloth of cotton" (JDEL 1785). "A range of lightweight, sheet cotton fabrics characterized by ways cords are made by bunching and weaving two, three, or more warp threads together...sometimes printed and plain finished" (FC 1959:181).

Ell. "A measure of length varying in different countries: (OUD 1964:594). "A measurement of length, seldom used today for cloth. The ell varied from about 24 to 48 inches, in different countries, i.e., Great Britain (45 inches), Flanders (27 inches), Scotland (37 inches), Denmark (24.7 inches)...The ell or el of the Netherlands today is the meter" (FC 1959:215).

Fathom (as in cable in text). "Originally denoted that space a man can reach when both his arms are extended; but now means a measure of six feet or two yards; equivalent to the French word toise" (UMD 1969:88).

Ferret (also ferreting, and ferreting in text). "A narrow ribbon of silk or cotton, a kind of tape (CC&B 1960:255). "A narrow binding tape of cotton, wool, or silk..." (FC 1959:215).

Ferriage. "The fare or price paid for the use of a ferry" (OUD 1964:690).

Flannel. "Originally a Welsh-made woollen material; made of woollen yarn slightly twisted with open texture-plain or twill weave. A soft nappy stuff or wool" (CC&B 1960:255). "A kind of soft woollen cloth" (WDEL 1970:118). "An open woollen stuff, of loose texture, usually without a nap" (OUD 1964:710). "A light or medium weight woollen fabric of plain or twill weave with a slightly napped surface...originated in Wales...usually identified by the fibre of which they are constructed such as wool flannel, cotton flannel, etc." (FC 1959:222-223).

Flax. "A slender annual plant, <u>Linum usitatissimum</u>, the bast fiber of which is called linen. The soft fiber is obtained from the stalks by retting, scutching and hackling; it is from 12 to 40 inches long, capable of fine subdivisions, flexible and very strong. It has a pronounced luster but is somewhat lacking in elasticity. The color of the best varieties of flax is a pale yellowish white. Other colors are silver gray, bluish green, brown. Flax is the oldest textile fiber known and is now produced mainly in USSR, Belgium, Holland, Italy, Ireland, France, and Egypt...Yarn and fabric made of flax are known as linen (FC 1959:243).

Phlegm (as in horse phlegm in text). "A surgical instrument for letting blood or for lancing the gums a lancet" (OUD 1964:713).

Fustian (also fustaine in text). "A coarse twilled textile with linen warp and cotton weft. The surface resembling velvet; hence the term 'Mock Velvet'" (CC&B 1960:256). "An old term for a class of closely woven, heavy cotton fabrics with cut pile or strong filling face, made with one set of warp and two sets of filling. Corduroy, moleskin, velveteen, etc., are included in this category. A term used in England in the 18th century for a printed fabric with linen warp and cotton filling (FC 1959:256). "Formerly a coarse cloth made of linen and cotton, and perhaps now of cotton only" (JDEL 1785). "Formerly, a coarse cloth made of cotton and flax. Now a thick, twilled cotton cloth with a short pile of nap, usually dyed of a dark color (OUD 1964:765).

Gatering. "A tie or band to keep the stocking in place on the leg and placed above or below the knee. In the...18th century some were like small decorative scarves, with fringed ends and tied in a bow on the outer side of the knee...Garters might be of wool, worsted, crewel, list, or ribbon, taffeta, cypress, and net...(CC&B 1960:92-93).

Gingham. "A kind of cotton or linen cloth, woven of dyed yarn, often in stripes or checks" (OUD 21964:794). "A cloth of cotton and linen striped and glazed" (OUD 1964 :794). "A medium or lightweight, plain weave, yarn dyed, cotton fabric, made with corded or combed yarn. It is woven on box looms, usually in a balanced check or plain pattern" (FC 1959:244).

Gris (also grees, gres, grese, and gresi in text). "A term used...for ray cotton goods..." (FC 1959:254).

Half-thicks (also called leggings in text). "A pair of outer coverings of leather or cloth to protect the legs in bad weather, reaching from the ankle to the knee, or sometimes higher" (OUD 1964:1126). "A term applied to a fabric similar to washwhiter, being white in color, but thinner and lighter in weight" (FC 1959: 261). "A woolen fabric, face finished with a highly lustrous, fine nap. It is filled more and has shorter nap than beaver, and about the same weight as mutton and beaver. Durable it is used for overcoating and uniforms" (FC 1959:301-302).

Handkerchief. "A square of linen or silk, often edged with lace, carried about the person and used for covering the face or nose; the non-elegant styles being used for display only...a neckcloth or neckerchief, the former term commonly used for the latter in the 18th century" (CC&B 1960:101).

Handmill. "A grinding mill consisting of one millstone turned upon another by hand, a quern" (OUD 1964:862).

Harrowing. "To draw a harrow over; to break up, crush, or pulverize with a harrow. To cut through as a harrow; to plough" (OUD 1964:869).

Heel-ball (see also blackball). "A ball of wax and lamp-black, used for polishing the sole-edges of new shoes" (OUD 1964:885).

Hemp. "An annual herbaceous plant...cultivated for its valuable fibre. The cortical fibre of this plant, used for making cordage, and woven into stout fabrics' (OUD 1964:890).

Holland (also hollond in text). "A fine linen first imported from Holland, later the name applied to any fine linen" (CC&B 1960:258-259). "When unbleached, called 'Brown holland'" (OUD 1964:912). "A plain weave cotton or linen fabric, usually a low count print cloth...a term formerly applied to all fine, plain weave, imported linen fabric and specifically to linen produced in Holland" (FC 1959:269).

Indian handkerchief. "Short for India silk" (OUD 1964:989).

Jesuit Bark. "Jesuit bark, Spanish bark, and China bark are terms for Chinchona Bark, a South American tree bark containing a quinine-like substance...to inhibit malarial symptoms" (BM 1974:76).

Lace. "An ornamental textile formed without the aid of a ground fabric...it is an open-work fabric produced by a network of threads, twisted together, and sometimes knotted, to form patterns. It is made by hand with bobbins and pins (bobbinet or pillow lace), with needles (needlepoint or point lace)_, with hooks (tatting), or by machinery" (FC 1959:339).

Lawn, as in Flowered Lawn in text. "A very fine semi-transparent linen cloth" (CC&B 1960:261). "A kind of fine linen, resembling cambric" (OUD 1964:115). "The term lawn originally was used for fine, plain weave linen fabric with an open texture" (FC 1959:317).

Leggings (see also Half--thicks): "An extra covering for the leg from ankle to knee and sometimes higher; the term leggings was not used in earlier centuries" (CC&B 1960:125). A pair of outer coverings (usually of leather or cloth) to protect the legs in bad weather, reaching from the ankle to the knee or sometimes higher" (OUD 1964:1126).

Linen (also spelled linnen in text; see also flax, hemp, and tow). "A woven textile made of flax; many varieties and qualities (CC&B 1960:262). "Cloth woven from fax (OUD 1964:1147). "Cloth of hemp or flax. The texture of linen varies from coarse to fine, depending on the number of warp threads used per inch, such as coarse, 40 to 43.5 threads per inch, medium, 44 to 47.5 per inch, and fine, 48 to 51.5 threads per inch"(WDEL 1970:177).

Mattocks. "An agricultural tool used for loosening hard ground, grubbing up trees, etc. It has a socketed steel head, having on one side an adze-shaped blade, and sometimes on the other a kind of pick": (OUD 1964:1219).

Merino. "A thin twilled woollen cloth, originally made of wool of the Spanish Merino sheep. A worsted plainback very soft to the touch. French merino indicated the better qualities, though made in England" (CC&B 1964: 1252).

Millstone. "One of a pair of circular stones used for grinding corn in a mill" (OUD 1964: 1252).

Mohair. "A kind of fine camlet made from the hair of the Angora goat, sometimes watered. Also, yarn made from this hair. Now often, an imitation of true mohair, made usually of a mixture of wool and cotton (OUD 1964:1269). "A thread or stuff made of goats hair (WDEL 1970:194). In the 18th century mohair was made "of silk, both warp and woof, having its grain wove very close" (CC&B 1960:264).

Muskets (also musquet in text). "The most useful and commodious fire-arm used by any army. They carry a ball of 29 ounces to 2 pounds. Its length is 3 feet and 8 inches from the muzzle to the pan" (UMD 1969:191). The 18th century firearm was a flintlock, a weapon that generates a spark when the flint strikes a frizzen, the spark landing in a pan with fine gunpowder which ignites and then touches off the main charge of powder in the barrel through a small hole. The smooth bore version, the musket, was quite inaccurate as a weapon, unlike its rifled counterpart. Battles with these weapons were often fought only during good weather as the musket was unreliable in windy or rainy conditions. The bayonet fixed on the end of the musket, it is said, caused more harm to the enemy than the charge in the musket.

Muslin Britannias. "A term applied to a larger group of firm, plain weave cotton fabrics in a wide range of quality and weight, which ranges from light weight sheer to heavy weight sheetings, and may be finished with a variety of finishes" (FC 1959:368). A fine cotton fabric having a downy nap on its surface" (CC&B 1960:265).

Nankeen (also nankin in text). "A kind of cotton cloth, originally made at Nanking, China from a yellow variety of cotton but now from ordinary cotton dyed yellow" (OUD 1964: 1309). "A species of cotton cloth from China" (WDEL 1970: 199). In the 18th century, Nankeen was, "A cotton cloth of a yellowish-brown color, originally from Nankin" (CC&B 1960:265). "An absolute, durable, firm textured cotton fabric...(made) from brownish yellow cotton...finished without any size or bleach...Imitations were made in France and usually dyed yellow to match the natural color of Nankeen cotton" (FC 1959:372).

Oakum. "A term applied to the coarse fiber of hemp and flax. It is mixed with tar and used for caulking. Term also applied to old ropes which are untwisted and pulled apart, mixed with tar, and used for caulking" (FC 1959:385).

Osnaburg (also ozenbrig in text). A German linen" (CC&B 1960: 267). "Also spelled ozenbridge, ossenbrigs, osnabrug, and was universally used for shirts, breeches, and jackets" (RPC 1976:284).

Paper pins. "A sheet or card of paper containing pins or needles stuck in it" (OUD 1964:1425).

Parit. French for "ruined or decayed" (BFD 1827:390).

Persian (also pertion in text). "A thin soft silk, used for linings" (OUD 1964:1478). "A thin soft silk, usually plain, much used for linings of coats, gowns, etc." (CC&B 1960:269). "A fine, light weight, plain weave silk lining fabric printed with large floral patterns. Used in England since the 18th century (FC 1959: 410).

Pigtail (as in pigtail of tobacco). "Tobacco twisted into a thick rope" (OUD 1964:1500). "Another name for spun, twist, or roll tobacco. The term usually applies to a roll weighing no more than one pound and generally cut no more than a quarter inch in diameter. Pigtail is dark hard spun leaf, favored in Britain" (TD 1940:125).

Pirogue. The French definition of a pirogue (BFD 1827:396) is, "a canoe with out-riggers." However, a pirogue or piragua may refer to "any kind of open, flat-bottomed schooner-rigged vessel" (OUD 1964: 1508).

Ravelled gartering. "To unweave, to unknit, as to ravel out a twist or piece of knit work" (JDEL 1785), "a string or ribbon by which the stocking is held upon the leg" (ibid.).

Rifle. "A fire-arm...having a spirally grooved bore 1775" (OUD 1964:1737). "Calibers averaged 0.55 to 0.60. Barrels were octagonal and relatively long with a blade front sight and an open V rear sight. Stocks were made of curly maple, and they ran to within a few inches of the muzzle. The stocks of these early rifles were not so sharply crescentic. Also the butts were quite thick, perhaps three inches though in a typical specimen. Mountings were almost always brass, and most characteristic of all was the hinged patch box cover on the right side of the stock" (BCS 1968:40).

Romal (also rumal in text). "A silk or cotton square or handkerchief; a thin silk or cotton fabric with a handkerchief pattern: (OUD 1964: 1749). "A plain or printed cotton, silk or cashmere fabric, usually square made in India and used for turbans and other head dresses and shawls, handkerchiefs, etc. " (FC 1959:515).

Romal handkerchief (also spelled rumal in text). A silk or cotton square or handkerchief; a thin silk or cotton fabric with a handkerchief pattern" (OUD 1964:1683). "A linen or cotton square in blue plaid patterns" (FC 1959:510).

Saltcellar. "A small vessel placed on the table for holding salt" (OUD 1964:1783).

Shalloon (also siloon, seloon, and shallon in text). "A loosely woven woollen stuff twilled on both sides" (CC&B 1960:274). "A light weight, loosely woven woollen fabric made with a two up, two down twill. Used for coat linings and dresses. A twilled worsted fabric with single warp made in England and France in the 18th century" (FC 1959:497).

Silk Twist. "A silk thread made by twisting a number of single silk yarns together often with a slack twist and then giving a reverse and often harder twist to two or more of these. Usually a fine, closely twisted thread" (FC 1959:496).

Skein (also skain in text). "A quantity of thread or yarn, wound to a certain length upon a reel, and usually put up in a kind of loose knot. (A skein of cotton consists of eighty turns of the thread upon a reel fifty-four inches in circumference [360 feet])" (OUD 1964:1905).

Snaffle (also snaffle bridle in text). "A simple form of bridle-bit, having less controlling power than one provided with a curb" (OUD 1964:1927). "A bridle that crosses the nose" (WDEL 1970:282).

Stroud. "A blanket manufactured for barter or sale in trading with the North American Indians. The material of which these blankets were made 1759" (OUD 1964:2047). "A coarse blanketing formerly used in trading with North American Indians" (FC 1959:531).

Sundries. "Small articles of miscellaneous kind; small items lumped together in an account as not needing individual mention" (OUD 1964:2079).

Superfine. In the 18th century, superfine meant "a superior quality of broadcloth, made of Spanish marine wool" (CC&B 1960:275).

Swivel. "A pivoted rest for a gun, especially on the gunwale of a boat [or in a blockhouse or fortification], enabling it to turn horizontally in any required direction (OUD 1964:2106). "The swivel gun was usually a 1- or possibly 2-pounder, similar in all respects to the pieces used for mounting on grasshopper carriages. In the instances when it was used as a swivel, however, it was equipped with an iron yoke similar to a huge oarlock. The trunnions fitted into loops on the upper extremities of the yoke, and the pintle was fitted into a socket in the gunwale of a boat or in a stout post set in the ground" (BCS 1968:128).

Sycee (also saysay, seysays, seysays, sysays, syseys as in the text). "Fine silk, so called because, if pure, it may be drawn into fine threads" (OUD 1964:2107).

Taffeta. "A name given to a fundamental group of fabrics made with plain weave and possessing a fine, smooth, crisp, and either lustrous or mat face, although most often lustrous" (FC 1959:540). "Originally a plain glossy silk textile; later a thin glossy silk with a wavy lustre" (CC&B 1960:276).

Tafia (also taffea, taffia in text). "A rum-like spirituous liquor obtained from the lower grade of molasses, refuse brown sugar, etc." (OUD 1964:2121).

Tape. "A narrow woven fabric not more than eight inches wide. Made in a wider variety of materials including cotton, linen, wool...often made in a broken twill weave but also in plain weave, twill, and even a satin weave. Used for trimming, binding, etc." (FC 1959:544). "A narrow flat woven braid of flax or later of cotton" (CC&B 1960:276).

Thickset. "A stout twilled cotton cloth with a short very close nap; a kind of fustian" (OUD 1964:2171). In the 18th century, thickset was considered, "a coarse fustian worn by the lower classes" (CC&B 1960:276). "A strong corduroy with short, thick pile and twill back made in Great Britain. Woven with high filling count per square unit. Used for work clothing. The pile was so thickly set as to somewhat resemble a coarse velveteen" (FC 1959:554).

Ticking (also ticken). "A strong cloth for bedcases" (WDEL 1970:310). "The case or cover containing feather, flocks, or the like, forming a mattress or pillow; also, applied to the strong hard linen or cotton material used for making such cases" (OUD 1964: 2188). "A general term for a strong, durable, closely woven fabric in plain, twill, or satin weave..." (FC 1959:556).

Toile gris (also toile grese, toille grise, toille gres, or toille grees as in text). Toile, a "cloth, linen-cloth (BFD 1827:503). Gris, "gray, gray color (BFD 1827:278)." Toile, "a French word for cloth or fabric, linen, sailcloth, canvas" (FC 1959:560).

Tow, a heavy and coarse fabric, handwoven of tow (FC 1959:564).

Twist. "The twisting of threads into a cord, etc., thread or cord composed of two or more fibers or filaments of hemp, silk, wool, cotton, or the like, wound round one another; in cotton spinning, warp yarn, which is more twisted in spinning, and stronger than weft; fine silk thread used by tailors, hatters, etc." (OUD 1964:2274). "Thread composed of filaments of textile material wound round one another" (CC&B 1960:278).

Velvet. "Silk with a short fur or pile on it" (JDEL 1785). "A warp pile fabric with short, closely woven cut pile which gives the fabric a rich, soft texture" (FC 1959:589). "A silk fabric having a short dense pile" (CC&B 1960:279).

Vermilion (also vermillion or vermillion in text). "Scarlet wool or fabric (OUD 1964:2347). "To color or paint with or as with vermilion, to give the color of vermilion to the face, etc. (<u>ibid</u>.). "A cotton cloth dyed scarlet" (CC&B 1960:279). "A fine medieval wool cloth dyed scarlet with natural dyes" (FCV 1959:591).

Waistcoat (also called shortcoat). "A shortcoat usually quilted and worn with or without sleeves...worn for warmth or if for display then of rich materials (CC&B 1960:231). "An undercoat, at front cut on similar lines to the coat, but without hip button and pleats, the sleeve being discarded around 1750,...becoming shorter, c. 1775, the front skirts were mere flaps which disappeared by 1790" (**ibid.**).

Worms (also gun worms). "A screw fixed on the end of a rod, used for withdrawing the charge or wad from a muzzel-loading gun" (OUD 1964:2451). "This corkscrew-like device was normally threaded to attach to the small end of the ramrod. With it the soldier withdrew the wad holding the bullets in his piece and so removed a charge that might have become damp and unfirable. The usual worm consisted of two prongs pointed at the ends and making two and a half turns" (BCS 1968:73).

Worsted (see also binding, i.e., worsted binding in text). "A cloth made of long-stapled wool combed straight and smooth before spinning" (CC&B 1960:280). "A woollen fabric or stuff made from well-twisted yarn spun of long-staple wool combed to lay the fibers parallel. A closely twisted yarn made of long-staple wool in which the fibers are arranged to lie parallel to each other. Later, a fine and soft woollen yarn used for knitting and embroidery" (OUD 1964:2453). "Term applied generally to fabric woven from yarn that has been spun from combed wool" (FC 1959:613).

References Cited for Glossary

Abbreviations	Reference
CC&B	Cunnington, C. Willett, Phillis Cunnington, Charles Beard 1960 A Dictionary of English Costume. Barnes & Noble, Inc., New York.
BFD	Fowle, William B. 1827 Boyer's French Dictionary. T. Bedlington, Bradford and Peaslee, Boston.
RPC	Gehret, Ellen J. 1976 Rural Pennsylvania Clothing. G. Shumway Publisher, york, Pennsylvania.
TD	John, Raymond, editor 1940 Tobacco Dictionary. Philosophical Library, New York.
JDEL	Johnson, Samuel 1785 A Dictionary of the English Language. 7th Edition, London.
OUD	Little, William, et al. 1964 The Oxford Universal Dictionary on Historical Principals. Third Edition, Oxford University Press, London.
FC	Marks, Steven S., editor 1959 Fairchild's Dictionary of Textiles. Fairchild Publications, Inc., New York.
BCS	Peterson, Harold L. 1968 The Book of the Continental Soldier. Stackpole Books, Harrisburg, PA.
UMD	Smith, George 1969 An Universal Military Dictionary. Originally published in 1779 by J. Millan, Whitehall, England. Reprinted by Museum Restoration Service, Ottawa, Ontario.
WDEL	Webster, Noah 1970 A Compendious Dictionary of the English Language: A facsimile of the first (1806) edition. Introduction by Philip B. Gove, Crown Publishers, Inc., New York.
BM	Wood, Peter H. 1974 Black Majority. W. W. Norton, New York.

FULLNAME INDEX TO PART ONE

Part II:

The Quartermaster Books of George Rogers Clark's Fort Jefferson, 1780-1781: An Inventory of Quartermaster Activities in the Western Department in Support of George Rogers Clark's Illlinois Battalion

Edited By
Kenneth Charles Carstens
Murray State Univesity

Table of Contents for Part II

The Quartermaster Books
of George Rogers Clark's Fort Jefferson,
1780-1781

Introduction

This is the second part of the Ft. Jefferson series. Like the Calendar, it is intended to supplement and complement the 1972 AMS reprint of James Alton James' George Rogers Clark Papers, 1771-1783. As noted previously, prior to James publishing the two volume set of GRC Papers between 1912 and 1926, another body of Clark papers, previously believed lost during the American Revolution, was found in the basement of the governor's house in Virginia, still bundled in their original bindings (Swem 1927). Amounting to more than 20,000 individual documents, these papers were removed to the Virginia State Library for preservation. There, they have remained virtually unstudied (Meeker 1976; Swem 1927).

Our understanding of the history of Fort Jefferson has been based for the most part upon a limited number of published documents. The presentation of a large collection of previously unpublished historical papers is very exciting because of its potential contribution to history. The Quartermaster Books from Fort Jefferson, which include John Dodge's book and Martin Carney's "1E" and "1F," provide very detailed data about the Illinois Battalion at Fort Jefferson for the 1780-1781 period. The contents of these ledgers add considerably to the previously published papers and letters of Clark and throw new light on the history of the frontier during the American Revolution.

John Dodge and Martin Carney were private citizens. Although more is known about Dodge than Carney, that which is known is controversial. Henry Hamilton, the infamous "hair buyer" dismissed Dodge as an "obscure person...unprincipled and [a] perjured renegado [sic]" (James, ed., 1972, I: 202).

John Dodge was born on July 12, 1751 in Connecticut. He was named after his father, who was a blacksmith. Dodge left Connecticut and began a trading business among the Indians around Sandusky, Ohio, prior to 1770 (Dodge 1779: 6). Along with an associate, William Tucker, he purchased a house and a lot in Detroit on April 4, 1776 (ibid.), where he apparently continued his trading activities among the Indians of the Detroit region. He was arrested by the British for allegedly spying and other non-loyal activities, and was imprisoned in Quebec, escaping in October of 1778 (ibid.). Fleeing to Boston, Dodge gave information to Generals Gates and Washington relevant to American operations against Canada (ibid.: 6-9; 56). In January, 1779, Dodge wrote a letter to John Montour detailing his plight, later expanding the detail and writing a Narrative of Mr. John Dodge During His Captivity at Detroit, which was first published in Philadelphia in 1779 and reprinted in England the following year. Dodge was subsequently recommended to Thomas Jefferson by Washington as a person who might be useful in the West (Alvord 1922:352).

It is probable that Dodge and George Rogers Clark first met at Fort Pitt, as both individuals spent time in that area. Dodge served Clark first as Indian Agent for the Western Department (ibid.), and later as quartermaster for the Illinois Battalion (Alvord 1907, II: xcv). Subsequent references to Dodge as "Captain" seem unfounded, however (see especially the discussion by Alvord 1907:xcv, n.1; cxii-cxiii), but may have been a courteous title applied to a person's name (Donald Carson, personal communication, September 19, 1999). Agents and quartermasters, however, were paid at the rate of six shillings per day, the same pay as a captain (Hening 1823, IX:14; X:256). Dodge may have extended the rationale of "rate of pay" to one of rank which would be in keeping with his personality as described by Alvord (op. cit., xcvi-xcvii, xcix, 620 ; 1909:156, 215, 219-220; 644) and James (ed., 1972, I:338, n. 1; 472), and as expressed by persons at Fort Jefferson (Draper Manuscripts, see especially 56J22; 56J29). Accusations challenging Dodge's character and honesty are found in surviving letters (Alvord 1922: 352-353; Seineke 1981: 474; 478; 480; 481). Military and civilians alike, at Kaskaskia, Vincennes, and Fort Jefferson, question Dodge and his associates (especially the double agent Thomas Bentley, and Dodge's lack of scruples (see previous references). No accusations against his younger brother, Israel, seem to exist, however, nor are there questions about Martin Carney's character. John Dodge, alone, appears to have played a questionable role at Fort Jefferson and Kaskaskia (Seineke 1981:68-75) during the occupation of Fort Jefferson and after. Indeed, a State of Illinois interpretative sign at Fort Gage (above Kaskaskia where John Dodge lived after 1781) refers to John Dodge as a "freebooter," that is to say, a person who pillages or plunders.

Little is known about Martin Carney. He worked as quartermaster in Dunmore county, Virginia, for the 8th Virginia Regiment (National Archives, Revolutionary Record Group, Item No. 16876, Voucher Receipt, Dated 4 November 1777). He may have come into contact with Clark or one of Clark's associates who recruited the Holston Valley of Virginia for the Illinois Battalion. Carney was in the Louisville area (Falls of the Ohio) by early March, 1780, purchasing equipment for Colonel Clark for Fort Jefferson. After Fort Jefferson's abandonment, Carney returned to Louisville, where he continued his quartermaster duties at Fort Nelson. It remains unclear what happened to Carney. John Dodge apparently lost track of Carney by 1785. Writing to William Clark (the cousin of GRC, not the brother) at the Falls of the Ohio, John Dodge asked, "Pray Let me Know if Mr. Carney is in that Quarter or whare (sic) the Little Heron is" (Alvord 1909:376). What Dodge meant by "Little Heron" is unclear, unless it referenced Carney as a slender, bird-like figure of a man. Although Carney was granted land after the war for his service to Virginia, the acreage was subsequently disallowed by the Western Commissioners at the end of the war (see English 1896, II:840; 1072; James, ed., 1972, II).

The Supply System of the Western Department[1]

According to the laws of Virginia (Hening IX:14; X:256), quartermaster positions were given to individuals who, in addition to posting a bond, could read, write, do simple arithmetic, and swear an oath that they would be honest with all accounting practices.

The quartermaster procurement and issuance system in the Western Department depended heavily upon both local and non-local sources for its supplies. Even on the frontier, settlements in the middle Mississippi Valley were tied to world markets through major port cities, such as New Orleans. The long-distance trade with New Orleans brought dry goods, fabrics, liquors, and equipment; more local trade provided perishable items (food supplies primarily). Products received from long-distance trade were often used to procure items from the more immediate markets (especially corn and flour).

The major frontier areas controlled by the Americans included Cahokia, Kaskaskia, Fort Jefferson, Vincennes, the Falls area, and the central Kentucky forts and stations of the Bluegrass region, like Boonesborough and Harrodsburg. Although French and Spanish assistance was available from the Mississippi and Wabash settlements, American credit, the devaluation of Virginian currency, and prior demands placed upon the French and Spanish settlements by Clark's forces, made it mandatory for the Virginian government to assist with the support of its western outposts.

Unfortunately, by 1780, Virginia was not in a position to provide support. Goods procured for the Western Department through long-distance trade were shipped from two principal sources, Fort Pitt and New Orleans, through the efforts of Oliver Pollock (Cummins 1988; James 1970). Local trade came from the French settlements of St. Genevieve, Kaskaskia, Cahokia, and Vincennes, and from other Anglo settlements: Harrodsburg, Boonesborough, and the Falls of the Ohio.

---

1 Portions of the following were taken from Carstens (1990:54-75), Issues at Fort Jefferson, 1780-1781: The Quartermaster Books of John Dodge and Martin Carney. Selected papers from the 1987 and 1988 George Rogres Clark Trans-Appalachian Frontier History Conferences. Edited by Robert J. Holden, Eastern National Parks & Monument Association and Vincennes University, Vincennes, Indiana.

Fort Jefferson's survival depended upon an unbroken flow of goods from these settlements to the mouth of the Ohio and the post reciprocated by providing the Illinois, Wabash, and Falls settlements with European and Caribbean goods it received from New Orleans (Figure 1).

Although seemingly sound on paper, the scheme did not work. The flow of supplies did not always follow the prescribed path (Randall 1921). Goods directed to Fort Jefferson from Fort Pitt were sometimes redirected enroute to the central Kentucky stations or were appropriated by officers at the Falls of the Ohio for their own use. Foods were often ill-cured and poorly packed, which also compounded the problem. On several occasions the inhabitants of Fort Jefferson initially overjoyed at the arrival of food from the Falls, were disappointed when the supplies turned out to be too ill-preserved to be consumed. In his February 15, 1781 letter from Fort Jefferson to George Slaughter, Commissary at the Falls of the Ohio, Captain Robert George, Commandant at Fort Jefferson, writes:

...The Small Supplies you have sent us, have been of infinite Service, & if you frequently repeat them they will be of singular advantage as we look to you for it, but the supplies I beg may be of a better Quality than what is yet come to hand. The Beef is really of the poorest kind --ill-cured, and not half salted-- the Barrels being bad, the pickle became wasted, if every any had been put in, and tho' the Meat does not absolutely stink, it wants little of it...'Twere well if all that you send was first inspected (James, ed. 1972, I:50-6).

Fort Jefferson's major source of supply was New Orleans (Figure 2). Unfortunately, most of the supplies reaching Fort Jefferson from that port were dry goods and liquor, which did little to compensate for the loss of foodstuffs from the Illinois settlements, Fort Pitt, or the Falls of the Ohio area. Even when the quartermaster at Fort Jefferson sent loads of dry goods and rum to other posts to trade for food, only small amounts of food were found (James, ed., 1972, I: 461-463; 473-475; 506-507); moreover, the Illinois towns were ready to revolt, because the French towns had grown tired of supporting the Americans.

Four individuals at Fort Jefferson occupied positions of authority associated with the distribution of goods and foods: John Dodge, Israel Dodge, Martin Carney, and John Donne. Occasionally Patrick Kennedy or James Finn from Fort Clark (Kaskaskia), or Zephaniah Blackford from Fort Patrick Henry

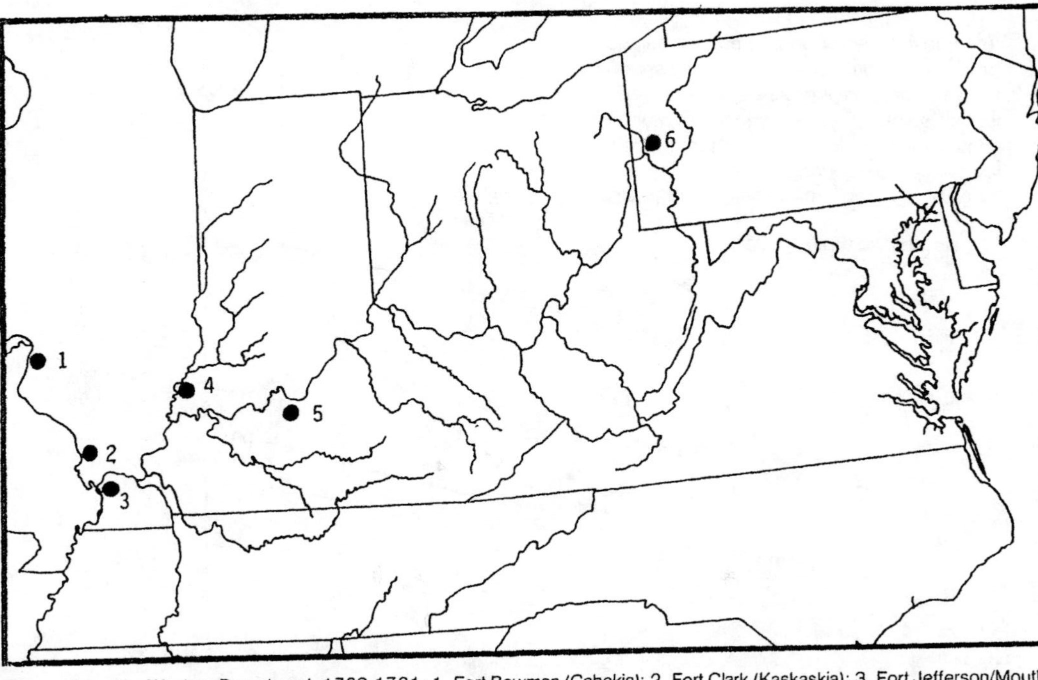

Figure One: The Western Department, 1780-1781: 1, Fort Bowman (Cahokia); 2, Fort Clark (Kaskaskia); 3, Fort Jefferson/Mouth of the Ohio; 4, Fort Patrick Henry (Vincennes); 5, Louisville (Falls of the Ohio); and 6, Fort Pitt (Pittsburgh).

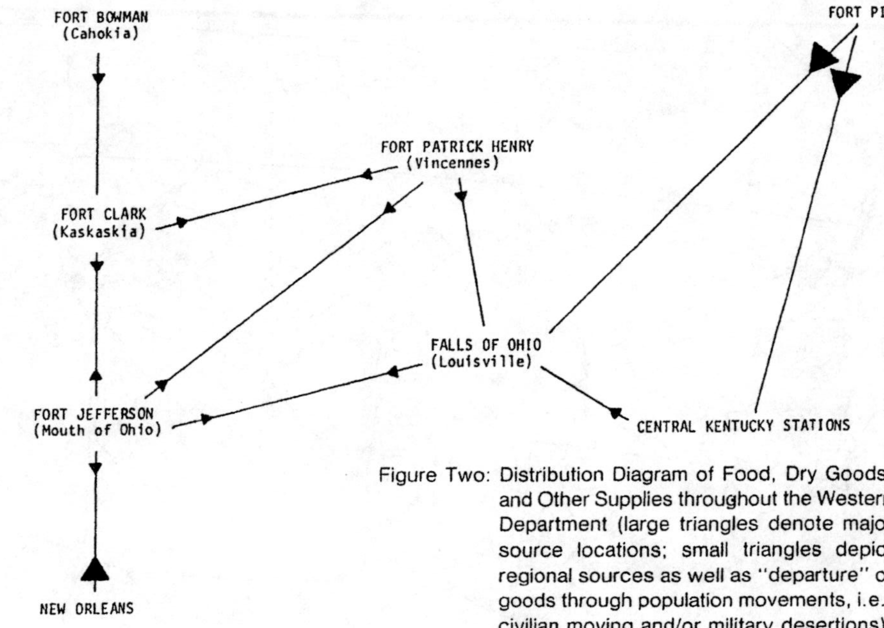

Figure Two: Distribution Diagram of Food, Dry Goods, and Other Supplies throughout the Western Department (large triangles denote major source locations; small triangles depict regional sources as well as "departure" of goods through population movements, i.e., civilian moving and/or military desertions).

(Vincennes), would arrive to assist or take over in the absence of one of the former purveyors. Except for Carney, the Dodge brothers and Donne appear to have been associates while at Fort Pitt in 1779 (National Archives, Revolutionary Record Group, Item No. 0113; and Butterfield 1972:746).

Despite the presence of numerous vouchers, letters, and other records belonging to Israel Dodge and John Donne in the Fort Jefferson papers, only John Dodge and Martin Carney left quartermaster books among the unpublished Clark papers (George Rogers Clark Papers, Virginia State Library, Archives Division).

The John Dodge quartermaster book (Box 48 of the GRC Papers, Virginia State Library, Archives Division), consists of 144 pages, each bound page measuring six inches wide by nine inches long. Each page was made from blank sheets of paper measuring six by eighteen inches. The pages of the book were hand-ruled by its owner to facilitate bookkeeping. The exterior of the Dodge book consists of a plain weave, coarse linen fabric that covers pressed pages of coarse paper. The binding of the book consists of a single loose stitch with a coarse linen thread (eleven stitches varying from one-quarter of an inch to one inch in length). The stitching bound the pages and cover together to form the book.

The majority of the pages in the Dodge book contain itemized charges, which are entered sequentially by the individual being charged. Each entry specifies whether or not the issue was due that person by law (i.e., clothing allowance by rank and time served), or if the individual had charged the purchase against his personal account (i.e., overdrawn). The quantity and price per item were given for supplies whose cost recovery was necessary.

Dodge's quartermaster book contains 1,718 separate entries. The number of entries varies per page. The book is organized into sections that list issues to officers (generally in order of rank), military companies, and different specialized departments (such as the Indian department, interpreters, and the surgeon among others). Dodge concludes his book with copies of letters, testimonies, and statements important to his career, such as his letter of appointment as Agent, and various inventories of goods that were lost during shipments to or from Fort Jefferson for which he would not take responsibility.

The entries of the John Dodge book, name 204 individuals including men, women, and children of the military, civilian, and Indian communities. The genealogical significance of that listing is very important. From an anthropological, economical, or historical perspective, the ultimate significance of the Dodge book lies in the completeness of the accounting record and the insight that information provides the researcher of late eighteenth century frontier life.

The Martin Carney quartermaster books consist of two volumes labeled "1E" and "1F" (Boxes 50 and 49, respectively, of the GRC Papers, Virginia State Library, Archives Division). Books "1A" through "1D" are, apparently, missing.

Carney's book "1E" measures six and one-half inches long by five and one-half inches wide. The cover and the first three numbered pages of the book are missing; fifty-two pages survive. The paper of the Carney book, like that of the Dodge book, is folded in half and sewn down the middle. Blank pages were hand-ruled as necessary. No apparent organization of Martin Carney's book "1E" exists other than individual page headings. Book "1E" records issues of ammunition (powder, lead, and flints), arms and accoutrements (muskets, swivels, rifles, bayonets with belts, swords, axes, kettles, and tents), and commodities (sugar, tobacco, and soap). In addition, Carney inventoried items he purchased for the establishment of Fort Jefferson and provides information in some cases as to how those items would be used (such as the flat-bottomed boats purchased in Louisville "for sake of the plank to build a garrison and barracks"). Lastly, in the 823 line entries of Carney's "1E," 74 additional individuals and families are identified at Fort Jefferson who are not named by Dodge in his quartermaster book.

Carney's book "1F" consists of 80 pages, each measuring five and one-half inches wide by seven and one-half inches long. Like the other quartermaster books, the pages of book "1F" were originally blank, but were hand-ruled to create forms necessary for accounting. The front and back covers are missing from this book.

The subject-matter of book "1F" consists almost entirely of commodities: rum, sugar, tobacco, and soap. Fifty-four individuals are named in its 190 entries (five persons listed were not previously named by Dodge or Carney). In total, the quartermaster books from Fort Jefferson contain 2,731 line item entries; they identify more than 283 persons; make reference to the comings and goings of various military companies; identify the Clarksville militia; name and specify quantities of arms, accoutrements, munitions, commodities and dry goods issued to officers, members of their companies, members of the militia, and the friendly Indian allies; and, they offer an approximation of family size and activities pursued by men, women, and children while serving in a support capacity at Fort Jefferson and the civilian community of Clarksville.

The quartermaster books also reflect major activities occurring within and without the fort area, and they provide very specific information about the presence and absence of certain structures associated with the fort and community, ownership of those buildings, building function, and, in several cases, even the type of wood used to build the structures, e.g. "cherry wood used for flooring."

The quartermaster books of John Dodge and Martin Carney are extremely significant. They provide a better understanding of life and activities at Fort Jefferson, and they enlighten our previous misconceptions about frontier history during the American Revolution.

References Cited

Alvord, Clarence W.

1907 Collections of the Illinois State Historical Library, Volume II: Cahokia Records, 1778-1790. Illinois State Historical Library, Springfield, Illinois.

1909 Collections of the Illinois State Historical Library, Volume V: The Kaskaskia Records, 1778-1790. Published by the Trustees of the Illinois State Historical Library, Springfield.

1922 The Illinois Country 1673-1818. Reprinted in 1965 in the American West Series By Loyola University Press, Chicago, edited by J. F. Bannon.

Butterfield, Consul W.

1972 History of George Rogers Clark's Conquest of Illinois and the Wabash Towns 1778 and 1779. Reprinted by Gregg Press, Boston.

Carstens, Kenneth C.

1990 Issues at Fort Jefferson, 1780-1781: The Quartermaster Books of John Dodge and Martin Carney, Pages 54-75. Selected Papers from the 1987 and 1988 George Rogers Clark Trans-Appalachian Frontier History Conferences, edited by Robert J. Holden. The Eastern National Park & Monument Association and Vincennes University, Vincennes, Indiana.

Cummins, Light T.

1988 Oliver Pollock and George Rogers Clark's Service of Supply: A Case Study in Financial Disaster, Pages 1-16. Selected Papers from the 1985 and 1986 George Rogers Clark Trans-Appalachian Frontier History Conferences, edited by Robert J. Holden. Eastern National Park & Monument Association and Vincennes University, Vincennes, Indiana.

Dodge, John

1779 Narrative of Mr. John Dodge During His Captivity at Detroit. Reproduced in facsimile from the second edition of 1780. Introductory note by Clarence Monroe Burton, Cedar Rapids, Iowa, 1909, The Torch Press.

Draper, Lyman C.

n.d. The Draper Manuscripts, Series J, Volume 56. State Historical Society of Wisconsin, Madison.

English, William H.

1896 Conquest of the Country Northwest of the River Ohio, 1778-1783 and Life of General George Rogers Clark, Vols. I and II. Reprinted in 1991 by Heritage Books, Inc., Bowie, Maryland.

Hening, William W.

1823 The Statutes at Large: Being a Collection of All the Laws of Virginia from the First Session of the Legislature in the Year 1619, Vols. I, IX, X. Reprinted in 1969 for the Jamestown Foundation by the University Press of Virginia, Charlottesville.

James, James Alton

1970 Oliver Pollock: The Life and Times of an Unknown Patriot. Originally published 1937, Books for Libraries Press, New York.

James, James Alton, editor

1972 George Rogers Clark Papers, 1771-1784, Vols. I and II. Reprinted by AMS Press, New York.

Meeker, Mary Jane

1976 Original Vouchers in the George Rogers Clark Bicentennial Exhibition. Indiana History Bulletin, June, Vol. 53, No. 6, Indianapolis.

National Archives
1777-1779 Documents 0113 and 16876 from the War Department Collection of Revolutionary War Record, National Archives, Washington, D.C.

Randall, J.G.
1921 George Rogers Clark's Service of Supply. Mississippi Valley Historical Review, Vol. 8, pp. 250-262.

Swem, E. G.
1927 The Lost Vouchers of George Rogers Clarke (sic). Virginia Journal of Education, Vol. XXII, June, p. 424.

Virginia State Library
n.d. The Unpublished Papers of George Rogers Clark, Boxes 48-50, Virginia State Library, Archives Division, Richmond.

Martin Carney's
Account of Issues of Ammunition and Arms
At Fort Jefferson & The Falls of Ohio,
1780-1781

N°- 1 E.

Articles purchased by me for the State of Virginia by order of Colonel Clark to Martin Carney

			L	S	D
April	5	Purchased one wagon, gears, and four gallons tar; purchased five flatbottomed boats for the plank to build a garrison and barracks at or near the mouth of the Ohio River......................	1148		
	6	Purchased one bateau to be paid by the State of Virginia from Eliasha Freeman....................	275		
	10	Purchased one large bateau to be paid by the State to John A. Johns...........................	1000		
April	7	Purchased from William Papo two muskets and a rifle..	300		
June	9	Purchased from Archibald Lockard five pairs mill stones for the State of Virginia to be paid by the said State....................................	300		
June	13	Purchased one hundred and sixty one pounds tobacco for the use of the troops at this post at 241 livre in peltry equal to......................	30	2	6
April	8	Had appraised one rifle gun, the property of Nathanal Randal valued at......................	180		
April	22	Taken into service, two horses the property of Captain Worthington, valued at....................	1800		
Sept.	6	~~Received from a French bateau from New Orleans~~			
April	8	[No entry given.]			
Oct.	28	Purchased from the Widow Hughes, hard money price, one iron pick to keep the handmills in order......	1/2		
		Purchased the same date of Achibald Lockard, at the same price................................	1/2		

Account of arms delivered by me to Cap[t] George's Company of Artillery of the Illinois Regiment

1780			Rifle Guns	Muskets	Carabines
April	12	Delivered to Sg[t] Walker	2		
April	26	Delivered to Cap[t] George	1		
May	2	Delivered to Cap[t] Lt. Harrison		4	3
June	20	Delivered to Cap[t] George at Camp Jefferson	1	1	
July	15	Delivered to Sg[t] Anderson		5	5
August	17	Delivered to Sg[t] Anderson for Sailor Worthington	1		
(See Ledger A. page 1---)			5	10	8

Account of arms delivered to Cap[t] John Bailey's Company

1780			Rifles	Carabines
April	12	Delivered Sg[t] Trent by Col[o] Clark's verbal order	2	
April	26	Delivered to Ensign Slaughter	1	
April	26	Delivered to Cap[t] John Bailey	1	
May	8	Delivered to Ensign Slaughter	1	
May	31	Delivered to Cap[t] John Bailey		1
See Arms Account Lib: A folio 1:			5	1

Account of ammunition received by me at this post (Clarksville), May the 1st 1780: M.C.

1780		Powder lbs	Lead lbs
May 1	Received from the French boats by order of Col[o] Clark, ten kegs gunpowder said to contain one hundred weight each	1000	
	Rec[d] the same day from Cap[t] George by Col[o] Clark's verbal order, three kegs said to contain one hundred weight each. None of them full	200	

(continued)

(continued)

1780		Powder lbs	Lead lbs
	Recd the same date from Captain Dodge twenty-one pig lead, said to be....................................		1600
May 19	Recd at Kaskaskia five pigs lead said to be...............		480
June 3	Recd at Kaskaskia, ten and one-half pigs, said to be...		1000
May 29	Recd at Kaskaskia, one keg powder.................	40	
Sepr 6	Recd from a French bateau, arrived from New Orleans, twelve kegs gunpowder sent by Mr Pollock, said to be..............................	1200	
Decr 12	Recd of Capt Philip Barbour......................	472	
	Received of Do Do Damaged.....................	300	
1781			
Feby 25	Recd from Patrick Kennedy......................................		340
Mar 19	Recd from Capt John Dodge, ball............................		166
Sepr 9	Recd of Lt Dalton, gunpowder and ball...........	23	15
	Transfrd to, & regularly entered in Ledger A, folio 2:	3235	3601

Account of sundry arms, tools, utensils, etc., received by me, Martin Carney, QMr at Fort Jefferson between 1st May 1780 & the 1st May 1781 ---Viz.---

1780		A	B	C	D	E	F	G	H	I	J
			Qmr		Engr	QMr	BtM	Engr			
Engr											
May 1st	Brot from the Falls	X	X	X	X	X	X	X	X	X	X
Dec 20	Recd of Capt Ben Roberts....................................										20
Sepr 8	Recd of John Dodge							1	1	1	....
Nov 13	Recd of John Dodge							1	1		....
May 26	Recd at Kaska........................					10	26				....
Sep 9	Recd of Lt Dalton			1 whip							....
1781											
May 2	Recd of C George 6 Cases 240.........................								6	4 tierces	
Apl 25	Recd of Phil Barbour									1Hkd..	

(continued)

(continued)

	K	L	M	N	O	P	Q	R	S	T	U	V*
Brot from the Falls	X	5	X	X	7	32	X	Military Stores	X	X	X	X
July 12 Recd Lt Wilson						5						
Decr 12 Recd of Capt P. Barbour						120	120	14	1200	120	120	
Decr 20 Recd of Capt Ben Roberts	7	1										
1781												
Mar 19 Recd of Capt John Rogers						8						
1780												
June 13 Recd of Jos. Lindsay												161
Nov 13			14									
May 26 Recd Kaska	2											
1781												
Mar 13 Recd C. J.Dodge												149

WHERE:
A=Crock Raisins; B=Carrots of Tobacco; C=Cross-cut Saw; D=Fish Seine; E=Fathoms of Cable Rope; F=Tomahawks; G=Case of Soap; H=Case of Sugar; I=Hogsheads of Tafia; J=Mattocks; K=Axes; L=Pairs of Hand Millstones; M=Brass Kettles; N=Pounds Lead; O=Rifle Guns; P=Muskets; Q=Bayonets; R=Oil Cloths; S=Gun Flints; T=Bayonet Belts; U= Cartridge Boxes; and V=Pounds of Tobacco.

Account of ammunition delivered by me by order of Col^{o} Clark --M.C.

1780	Delivered	Powder lbs	Lead lbs
May 19	To Capt Richard Harrison at Kaskaskia	23 1/2	
"	To Silas Harlan, Major of Militia at ~~Do Clarksville~~..................................	3	6
"	To John Bailey, Capt of Regulars at D^{G} Kaskaskia......................................	9 1/2	19
"	To Mr Perault Lieu^{t} D^{o} at D^{o}................	1/2	
"	To Doctor [?] and Lieu^{t} Girault D^{o} at D^{o}...	1	2
May 26	To Richard Brashears, Capt D^{o} at Cahokia......	4 3/4	9 1/2
"	To D^{o} D^{o} D^{o} D^{o} at D^{o}.............	5	11
"	To Capt John Rogers D^{o} at D^{o}.................	6	
"	To Capt Richard Harrison, D^{o} at Cahokia.......	136	
"	To John Bailey Capt at Cahokia...............	4 1/2	9
"	To Mr Brady for Indians at Cahokia............	3	4
"	To John Duff, Spy at D^{o}..........................	1/4	1/2
"	To John Bailey, Capt at D^{o}....................	9 1/2	19
"	To Capt Mc Carty at D^{o}..........................	4 3/4	9 1/2
"	To Jarrit Williams, Ensign at D^{o}..............	3 1/2	7
"	To Capt Richard Harrison at D^{o}..........................		21
May 31	To Capt of Militia at D^{o}....................	34	56
"	To Daniel Flanery, at D^{o}......................	5	
June 3^{d}	To John Rogers, Capt at D^{o}..................	80	
5	To D^{o} D^{o} D^{o} at D^{o}....................	40	
"	To Richard Winston at Kaskaskia...............	50	
8	To Major Harlan at Camp Jefferson.............	13	26
9	To Herman Consola at D^{o}.......................	1/2	
	Amount of issues transferred to Lib: A. fol:2	437 1/4	199 1/2

Account of ammunition delivered by me by order of Capt Robert George at Camp Jefferson -- M.C.

1780		Powder	Lead	Flints
June 10	To Capt Lt Richard R. Harrison.................		1 1/2	40
13	To Josiah Phelps and John Montgomery...........		1	2
13	To Capt Harrison................................		1/2	
"	To D^o D^o to take to the Falls of Ohio................................	500	1000	
"	To Capt George for the use of the Troops...............................	3/4	1 1/2	
14	To Capt George's men going to the Falls of Ohio.........................	2		
21	To Mr Donne, Commissary................	1	2	
"	To Thomas Wilson L^t	2	4	
"	To Capt George for the troops at Camp Jefferson........................	2 1/4	4 1/2	
"	To Indians going to Kaskaskia..........	1	2	6
23	To Capt George for the troops at this place...........................	3/4	1 1/2	
"	To Sergeant Anderson...........................		1/2	1
29	To Daniel Bolton, gunner..............	15		
30	To Lieu^t Wilson for a party of men going hunting.........................	2 1/4	4 1/2	
"	To Michael Hacketon, a soldier in Capt George's Company..........................		1	
"	To Sergeant Anderson for the use of the garrison............................	4 1/2	9	8
July 3	To Mr. Kennedy, Conductor.............	1	2	
5	To the militia at this place..........	1 3/4	3 1/2	46
8	To Lt Wilson going on command.........	1 1/4	2 1/2	
12	To Capt Abra^m Kellar going to Cahokia.	1/2	1	
14	To Capt John Rogers D^o D^o......	1	1	
15	To Martin Carney, QM in lieu of meat..	1		
17	To Sergeant Anderson for the defense of this place........................	22	104	
29	To one of the militia soldiers at this place...........................	1/2	1	
Aug 1	To Francis Little, a soldier at this place............................	1/2	1	
	See folio 2, Lib. A	562 1/2	1150 1/2	[not added]

Account of ammunition delivered by me by Captain George's order -- M.C.

1780		Pwd^{r}	Lead	Flints
Aug 1st	To Sgt Vaughan of Captain Bailey's Company......	7	14	Two
"	To James Sherlock, Interpreter for the Kaskaskia Indians..............................	10	20	and one
"	To Mr. Jacob Pyatte on his way to the Falls of Ohio..	1/2	1	half yards
3	To Sergeant Anderson for the use of some of the soldiers..................................	1	2	flan^{l}
9	Capt George Owens' Company Militia..............	11 1/2	46	
14	To Sg^{t} Anderson, for a hunter at this place.....	1/2	1	
"	To Lawrence Keinan, gunner at this place........	13 1/2		
16	To Lt Richard Clark............................	1/2	1	1
17	To Lt Richard Clark, for a man of Capt Worthington's..........................	1/4	1/2	
21	To Captain Leonard Helm for his own use.........	1/2	1	
"	To a French man in Captain George's Company.....	1/4		
24	To a man of Capt Bailey's Company.............	1/4	1/2	
"	To a soldier in Capt George's Company...........	1/4	1/2	
26	To Thomas Leny, gunner at the blockhouse........	1	2	
27	To the soldiers and inhabitants at this place...	22	44	
"	To the artillery men at this place..............	25	50	and
Sep^{t} 6	To John Dodge, Agent for Indians................	5	10	six
	To D^{o} D^{o} for a French boat going to Pancore (St. Louis)...........................		20	yards flan^{l}
15	To Capt Bailey's Company........................	5 1/2	11	
"	To John Hazard of artillery.....................	1/4	1/2	
"	To two men of Captain McCarty's Company.........	1	2	
"	To the artillery at this place..................	16	32	
26	To Sg^{t} Anderson of Capt George's Company........	1	2	
"	To two men of Capt Bailey's Company.............	1	2	
27	To two D^{o} of Capt Brashears' Company............	1	2	
"	To a man of Capt George's Company...............	1/4	1/2	
Oct 2	To Sg^{t} Hazard of Capt George's Company..........	3/4	1 1/2	
"	To Capt Keller..................................	2	1	
4	To three men of Capt Worthington's Company......	3/4	1 1/2	
	See Lib: A: Fol: 2	127	269 1/2 * [Not totaled]	

Account of tobacco delivered by me by order of Captain Robert George at this place. -- M.C.

1780			Carrots	Pounds
June	13	To Capt Lieut Harrison going up the Ohio......	6	18
June	20	To Mr. Donne, Commissary.....................	1	3
July	21	To Lawrence Keinan by Capt George's order.....	2/3	2
	25	To Thornton, a soldier in Capt Worthington's Company by order of Captain George..........	1/3	1
	28	To Sgt Anderson in Capt George's Company......	3	9
	28	To Sgt Mains in Capt Worthington's Compy......	2	6
	28	To Mr. Clark, Secretary to Colonel Clark......	1	3
	28	To Andrew Clark, Artificer....................	1/2	1 1/2
August	3	To Sgt Anderson...............................	1 1/2	4 1/2
	"	To Mr. Sherlock, Interpreter, to the Indians..	2	6
	"	To Sgt Elms for Capt Brashears' Company.......	1	3
	"	To Mr. Sherlock, Interpreter, for the Kaskaskia Indians.............................	1	3
Do	4	To Matthew Murray, a soldier in Capt Abraham Keller's Company............................	1/2	1 1/2
	5	To Sergeant Vaughan of Captain Bailey's Company	3 1/3	10
		To Francis Little for taking care of the State boats.................................	1	3
	8	To Martin Carney, Qmstr, for his own use......	1	3
	8	To Capt Leonard Helm for his own use..........	1	3
	24	To Reubin Kemp, Sgt of Worthington's Co.......	1/2	1 1/2
Aug	24	Thornton, a soldier in Capt Worthington's Comy	1	3
	"	To Lt Richard Clark for his own use...........	1	3
	26	To Joseph Anderson, sergeant, for his own use	1/2	1 1/2
	28	To Mr. Sherlock, interpreter for the Indians..	1	3
Sept	1	To John Grimshaw, gunner......................	1/2	1 1/2
	2	To Richard Hopkins for corking and paying public boats................................	2	6
	3	To Sgt Vaughan for Capt Bailey's Company......	5	16
	3	To Sgt Anderson for Capt George's Company.....	5 1/2	16
	8	To Capt John Dodge for Indians by Col Montgomery	2	6
	19	To Capt George for his own use................	3	9
		Rotten and dried away.........................		14

See Lib: A, fol: 7----

Total - - - - 161 lbs.
[Totals 155 lbs.]

Tobacco issued to sundry persons per order of Capt George, Commandant

			Pounds
		Wm Clark, Secretary....................	3
		Martin Carney........................	2
		Leonard Helm.........................	10
		Edwd Worthington.....................	3 1/2
		John Girault.........................	2
		James Finn...........................	3
		Philip Barbour.......................	4
1781		John Harris, Armourer................	2
April	7	Five men of Capt Georges C^{o}............	2 1/2
	10	Capt Helm..........................	3
Ap^{l}	13	John Donne...........................	3
	"	Martin Carney........................	3
	17	Capt Kellar's C^{o}.....................	2
	24	Six men going to the Falls of Ohio......	6
om^{td}	17	Jacob Pyatte.........................	3
	26	Illinois Regiment....................	21 1/2
	28	One man of Capt George's C^{o}...........	1
May	3	Joshua Archer........................	3
			77 1/2

Account of ammunition delivered by me by Col^{o} Montgomery's Orders -- MC

1780			Powder		Lead	
July	13	To James Finn, Quartermaster, Illinois Reg^{t}....	20		40	
	14	To Ensign Slaughter, going to Oka [?]..........		1/4		1/2
	"	To James Brown, Sg^{t} Major, Illinois Reg^{t}.......	3	1/2	7	
	"	To Lt Gerault, D^{o} D^{o}.........		1/4		1/2
	"	To Sg^{t} Wilson, D^{o} D^{o}.........	5	1/2	11	
Sep^{t}	8	To James King............................		3/4		
	9	To John Dodge, Agent for Indians..............	100		200	
		To Frederick Guion........................		1/2	1	
	10	To Col^{o} Montgomery........................	1			
	"	To James Meriwether, Lt Cavalary............	1		2	
	"	To John Dodge, Agent......................	10		20	
	"	To Capt McCarty's Company....................	4	1/2	9	
	"	To volunteers who came with Col^{o} Montgomery....	1	1/2	3	

(continued)

(continued)

1780			Powder	Lead
	"	To Capt Brashears' Company....................	5	10
	"	To Capt Kellar's Company......................	4	8
	"	To Capt Brashears for the troops at Cahokia....	100	200
	11	To Col^{o} Montgomery for his own use............	1	2
	"	To Doctor Rey D^{o} D^{o}..................	1/2	1
	"	To Lt Gerault.................................	1	2
	"	To Capt Brashears for his own use.............	1	2
	"	To Ensign Williams D^{o} D^{o}.....................	1	2
Sep^{t}	11	To Mr. Monbreun D^{o} D^{o}.....................	1	2
	"	To two men of Capt Brashears' Company..........	1	2
	"	To one man of Capt George's Company...........	1/2	1
	12	To one man of Capt Worthington's Company.......	1/2	1
	13	To Capt Kellar's Company......................	1 1/2	3
	"	To Lt Dalton for two of his men...............	1	2
Oct	24	To Col Montgomery for his journey to New Orleans	10	
	26	To Israel Dodge upon Mr. Bentley's account.....	73	
	28	To Capt Rogers for the use of his men by Lt Clark..................................	20	12
		See Lib: A fol^{o} 2 Total........	370 3/4	[not totaled]

Account of arms received by me in this department, the property of the Commonwealth of Virginia, -- M.C.

1780			Rifles	Muskets
March	1	Rec^{d} of Mr. Donne, Commissary at the Falls of Ohio.............................	2	3
April	8	Rec^{d} of Col Clark at the Falls of Ohio......	3	27
Total		....	5	30
July	13	D^{o} of Lt Wilson at Fort Jefferson................		5
Dec^{r}	12	D^{o} Capt Barbour (with bayonets & belts) with bayonets and belts.........................		120
Ap^{r}	28	Rec^{d} of Capt John Rogers (entered before in another place)...........................	2	
		Purchased from Wm Pope.....................	1	2
		Appraised & taken into service belonging to N. Randolph..........................	1	

The two foregoing also entered in addition
to the 5 rifles & muskets brought from the Falls

Tobacco issued by order of Capt George, Commander

			Pounds
	1781	Amount brought forward from..................	77 1/2
May	10	James Finn..................................	3
	14	Illinois Regiment...........................	27
	17	Capt Worthington............................	3
	18	Martin Carney...............................	3
	21	Mr. Hunter..................................	3
	23	Capt Helm...................................	3
June	2^d	Illinois Regiment...........................	28
			147 1/2
		Wasted and Dried..	1 1/2
	See Lib A, fol. 7	Total Amount...	149

Account of arms delivered by me by order of Capt Robert George, to individuals, -- M:C

1780		Rifles
August 21	To Capt Leonard Helm for his use.....	1
"	To Lt Richard Clark d^o d^o......	1
	See Book A, fol. 1	2

Issued by order of Col. Montgomery July 17, 1781 at the Falls of the Ohio, forty-six pounds of iron to make nails for boat building

Issued to Capt John Rogers August 10, 1781, to shoe public horses = 19 lbs [iron ?]

Account of ammunition delivered by me by order of Capt George -- M.C.

1780			Powder	Lead
Oc^t	4	To Sg^t Pmen [?] of Capt McCarty's Company.......	1/2	1
	5	To the militia at this place..................	5	10
		To eight men of Capt George's Company...........	4	8
	11	To Major Harlan of the militia, for his own use.	1/4	1/2
	"	To John Ash, a soldier in Capt George's Company.	1/4	1/2
	14	To Sg^t Allen of Capt Brashears' Company.........	1 1/2	3
	16	To Frank Little of Capt George's Company........	1/4	1/2
	"	To Sg^t Elms of Capt Brashears' Company..........	1/2	1

(continued)

(continued)

1780			Powder	Lead
Oc^t	18	To two men of Capt Bailey's Company.............	1 1/2	1
	19	To Sg^t Moore of Capt George's Company...........	2 1/2	5
	20	To Bryan, a soldier in Capt Worthington's Company	1/4	1/2
	"	To four men of Capt Bailey's Company...........	1	2
	24	To Lt Dalton for his journey to New Orleans.....	1	10
	27	To Ensign Slaughter, for his own use............	1/2	1
	"	To Capt Abraham Keller for D^o D^o............		2
	28	To Sg^t Vaughan of Capt Bailey's Company.........	1/4	1/2
	"	To Anderson for going express to the Falls of Ohio	1 1/4	3
	31	To Capt John Williams..........................	1	2
	"	To Isreal Dodge, Deputy Agent..................	1/2	1
Nov	2	To Mr. Sherlock for the use of the Kaskaskia Indians............................	80	89
	"	To Capt Helm for his own use...................	2	2
		To three men of Capt Brashears' Company.........	1 1/2	3
	3	To one man of D^o D^o.........................	1/2	1
	5	To Simon Burney, in lieu of 380^{lbs} beef.........	6	
		To Major Harlan for hunting....................	1	2
	6	To two men of Capt George's Company............	1	2
	9	To two men of Capt Bailey's D^o................	1	2
	"	To two men of Capt Brashears' Company...........	1	2
Nov	9	To Two Men of Capt Kellar's Company............	1	2
	19	To four men of d^o d^o d^o...............	1	2
	21	To Major Harlan for hunting....................	2 1/4	4 1/2
	22	To eight men going hunting with Harlan..........	3	6
		Transferred to page 2 Lib: A- -	123 1/4	170

Account of sugar delivered by me by order of Col^o Montgomery at Fort Jefferson -- M.C.

1780			Lbs
Sep^r	8	To two soldiers in Capt Worthington's Company...............	2
	"	To three men of Capt Bailey's Company.........................	3
	"	To one woman and two childern of Capt Worthington's [Company]	2
	"	To Mr. McMeans' family..	3
	"	To two men in Capt George's Company..........................	4
	"	To Matthew Murray and family in Capt Keller's Company........	2
	"	To two soldiers in Capt Worthington's Company................	3
	9	To Nelly Lewis, a soldier's widow..............................	2
	"	To David Allen, a soldier in Worthington's Company...........	1

(continued)

(continued)		Lbs Sugar	
Sepr 9	To Thomas Quirk	1	
"	To Archibald Lockard, Worthington's Company	2	
"	To Col^o Montgomery's order	3	
"	To Graves Morris, a man in Capt Bailey's Company	2	
"	To a man and his sick children	1	
"	To Thomas Quirk	2	
"	To eight sick people of the inhabitants	4	
"	To a sick woman and children of Capt Brashears' Company	2	
"	To James Merriwether, L^t of Cavalry	4	
"	To two men of Capt Bailey's Company	2	
"	To Matthew Jones, a soldier in Capt George's Company	2	
"	To Mr. Donne, Commissary	4	
"	To Mayfield and children	2	
"	To two men of Capt Bailey's Company	1	
"	To Col Montgomery's order	1	
"	To John Bryan, of Capt George's Company	3	
"	To Anthony Lunsford and family	2	
"	To Josuah Archer	3	
"	To George Lunsford, of Capt Bailey's Company		1/2
Sepr 9	To Mary Demore, a soldier's wife	2	
"	To Henry Steward, a militia man	1	
"	To five men of Capt John Bailey's Company	2	1/2
"	To Mrs. Witzel, a widow of militia	3	
"	To Nathan Allen of the militia	2	
"	To Capt Keller for his own use	4	
"	To Mr. Oiler's sick family	4	
"	To Jacob Dittering	1	
Sepr 9	To Charles Evans, a soldier in Capt Worthington's Company	1	
"	To the Widow Meredith	2	
"	To two wounded militia men	2	
"	To George Owens, Capt of Militia	2	
"	To Jacob Shilling, a militia man	2	
"	To Ezekial Johnston, d^o d^o	4	
"	To Joseph Hunter, d^o d^o	3	
"	To Francis Gamlin, d^o d^o	2	1/2
"	To the Widow Hughs, of the militia	3	
"	To Capt Brashears and Doctor Ray	3	
11	To Lt Gerault, for his own use	1	
12	To two men of Capt Abraham Keller's Company	1	
"	To John Smithers in Capt George's Company	1	
"	To a man of Capt Bailey's Company		1/2
13	To Capt Helm for his use	4	

(continued)

(continued)

		Lbs Sugar
Sepr 13	To Capt Dodge, Agent, D^{o}	4
"	To Lt Dalton for his own use	20
"	To Col^{o} Montgomery, D^{o} D^{o}	3
"	To Reubin Kemp, a Sg^{t} in Worthington's Company	1
"	To a man in Capt McCarty Company	1 1/2
"	To Col^{o} Montgomery order	2
"	To Frank Little of Capt George's Company	2
"	To Robert Ford a militia man for 57^{lbs} beef for public use	7
"	To James Young D^{o} D^{o}	3
"	To ten officers in Col^{o} Montgomery's mess	60
"	To Capt Dodge's order by Frank Little	5 1/2
"	To my own use	4
"	To Mr. Graffen for a handmill for public use	6
"	To the Widow Witzel for a flat bottomed boat for public use	7
"	To James King and company for a D^{o} D^{o} D^{o}	7
14	~~To the Widow Hughes of militia by Capt. George's order~~	~~3~~
"	~~To Sgt. Anderson of Capt. George's Company~~	~~2~~
	To Mr. Phelps ~~of militia~~	~~1~~
		247 1/2
		[Totals 248]

Account of sugar delivered by me by order of Capt George at Fort Jefferson, 1780 -- M.C.

		Lbs
Sepr 13	~~To the Widow Hughes of militia~~	3
"	To Sg^{t} Anderson of Capt George's Company	2
"	To Phelps of militia	6
14	To James Thomson, a soldier in Capt Keller's Company	1
"	To two sick soldiers in D^{o} D^{o} D^{o}	2
"	To two sick soldiers in Capt Brashears' Company	2
"	To Joseph Hunter of militia	3
15	To John Hazard of Capt George's Company	1
"	To W^{m} McCauly of militia	1
"	To John Johnston of militia	1
"	To Jacob Ditteren of artillery	1
"	To John Reed of militia	1

(continued)

(continued)

		Lbs Sugar
15	To Zachariah Williams, a soldier in Worthington's Company....	1
"	To John Grimshaw and Mr. Mullens of George's Company.........	2
"	To Edward Murray, a soldier in Capt Bailey's Company.........	2
16	To Andrew Clark, artificer at public work....................	2
"	To Joseph Panther, a soldier in Capt Keller's Company........	1
"	To Potter Helebrand, a militiaman............................	2
"	To four men of Capt John Bailey's Company....................	2
18	To Andrew Johnston of Worthington's Company..................	1
"	To five men of Capt Brashears' Company.......................	5
19	To Mr. Donne, Commissary, for his family.....................	4
"	To James Thomson, a soldier in Capt Keller's Company.........	1
"	To Matthew Jones in Capt George's Company....................	1
Sept 19	To John Dougherty in Capt George's Company..................	2
"	To Breden in Worthington's Company...........................	2
"	To Helms, a soldier..	2
"	To Edward Johnston, a soldier in Worthington's Company.......	1
"	To Wm Crump, a soldier in D^o D^o...........	2
23	To Francis Little, in Capt George's Company..................	1
27	To two men of Capt John Bailey's Company.....................	1
28	To one man of Capt Worthington's Company.....................	1/2
Oct. 1	To Capt Keller for his own use..............................	2
"	To Edward Murray, a soldier in Capt Bailey's Company........	1/2
6	To Wm Carr, in Capt Bailey's Company.........................	1/2
	Transferred to Lib: A folio 4	64 1/2

Account of sugar delivered by me by order of Capt George -- M.C.

		Lbs
Oct. 6	To Wagoner, a soldier in Capt George's Company...............	1/2
"	~~To Capt. Leonard Helm, for his own use......................~~	~~2~~
Nov. 14	To three men for carrying the sugar..........................	3
15	To Nelly Lewis, a soldier's widow............................	1
"	To five sick men of Capt Bailey's Company....................	5
"	To eleven D^o of Capt George's Company......................	11
"	To a sick woman of Capt Bailey's Company.....................	1
16	To a sick man of Capt Worthington's Company..................	1
"	To Joseph Thornton, artificer................................	2
17	To Andrew Johnston and family of Capt Worthington's..........	1 1/2
"	To a soldier of Capt Bailey's Company........................	1

(continued)

(continued)

		Lbs
	" To two men of Capt Brashears' Company	2
	" To a sick woman and child of Do	2
	18 To George Owens, Capt of Militia	3
	" To Capt Keller, for his own use	2
	19 To John Burks, a sick militia man	1
	20 To three men of Capt George's Company	3
	" To two Do Do Do Do	2
	" To a sick woman and a sick child of Capt Worthington's	1
	" To Colo Clark's Negro, sick	1
	21 To Mr. Phelps, for his sick family	2
	" To Mrs. Hughs, a widow of militia	2
	" To myself, for my use	6
	" To John Wilson, Capt Worthington's servant	1
	23 To Capt George's Mess	[No entry]
	" To a soldier of Capt Worthingtons	1
	25 To a sick woman of Capt George's Company	1
Nov.	25 To Joshua Archer of the militia	1
	26 To Mr. Donne, Commissary	6
	27 To Mr. Lunsford and sick family	5
	" To the Widow Meridith, Do Do	3
	28 To Capt Bailey and Mr. Slaughter	12
	29 To Mr. Isreal Dodge, Deputy Agent	4
Nov.	29 To Joseph Hunter's family	2
	" To Capt Brashears' for his use	6
	29 To Major Williams for his own use	6
	30 To a woman and two children of Worthington's Company	2
	" To Capt Abraham Keller for his use	2
Dec.	1 To Lt Richard Clark for his Do	6
	" To Capt Leonard Helm for his Do	6
	" To Ensign Williams and Major Harlan	12
	" To Mr. Harris, armourer at this place	2
	Entd in Lib: A fol: 4 - - - - - - - - - -	137

Account of ammunition delivered by me by order of Capt Robert George at Fort Jefferson, 1780, -- M.C.

1780		Powder	Lead
Nov	26 To Jesse Piner, for two dressed deer skins for the use of the soldiers at this post	1 1/4	2
	" To Mr. William Clark for his use	1	
	" To Mr. Archer, a militia man	1	

(continued)

1780		(continued)	Powder	Lead
	29	To Mr. Donne, Commissary D^{o}	1	3
	"	To Richard Clark, L^{t} in the Illinois Reg^{t}	1/2	1
	"	~~To Mr. Archer, a militia man~~	~~1~~	
	"	To two men of Capt Bailey's Company	1/2	1
	"	To eleven men going on command to the Illinios..	2 3/4	5 1/2
Dec	4	To Major Harlan's hunting party	4	8
	"	To the soldiers going with Major Harlan	2	4
	5	To the D^{o} D^{o} D^{o} D^{o}	2	4
	7	To one man of Capt John Bailey's Company	1/4	1/2
		To two men D^{o} D^{o}	1/2	2
	18	To Capt Bailey	1/2	1
	19	To Abraham Taylor, a militia man	1/4	1/2
	23	To four militia men	2	4
	25	To Capt Bailey's Company	6	12
	26	To Capt Owen and Lt Williams	2	4
	"	To eight men going on a hunting party	4	8
	"	To Capt Brashears' Company	2	4
	"	To the blockhouse for the swivels	11	
	"	To Capt Keller's Company	3 1/4	6 1/2
	28	To Ensign Slaughter	1/2	1
	"	To Lt Clark's blockhouse on the hill	10	
	30	To two men of Capt Brashears' Company	1	2
	"	To Capt Roberts of ~~Col. Slaughters Company~~	~~100~~	~~200~~
	"	To Capt Brashears	1	4
Dec	30	To two men of Capt Roger's Company	1/2	1
	"	To Capt Harrison	4	8
	31	To Capt Keller's blockhouse	8	5
			72 3/4	92

Account of ammunition and flints delivered by me by order of Capt Robert George at Fort Jefferson, -- M.C.

1781			Pwd^{r}	Lead	Flints
Jan^{y}	4	To Mr. Hunter, a militia man	1/4	1	
	8	To three men of Capt Bailey's Company	1	2	
		To friendly Indians going to war	12 1/2	25	50
		To Capt Bailey and Owens, going express to the Falls	1 1/2	4	
		To Capt Roger's Company	3	6	
	10	To Capt George's Company going on command to the Illinois	4	8	

(continued)

		(continued)	Pwd^r	Lead	Flints
1781	12	To Lt Richard Clark...........................	1/2	1	2
		To Major Williams, six cartridges for the swivel..................................	4	6	
		To Capt Bailey's Company....................	6		
1780					
Dec	24	To Capt Benjamin Roberts....................			24
	28	To Ensign Williams and his hunting party.....			22
Dec	28	To Capt George's Company, 28 men, 2 flints each................................			56
	27	To Capt George's Company....................	10	20	
	29	To Capt Brashears' Company..................			20
Dec	29	To Capt Worthington's Company...............			32
		To Capt Bailey's Company....................			36
Jan	19	To three men of Capt Worthington's Company...	1 1/2	3	
Jan	24	To two men of Capt George's Company..........	1/4	1	
	27	To D^o D^o D^o D^o D^o............	1/2	1	
Feb	1	To two men of Capt Keller's Company..........	1/2	1	
	3	To Lt Clark for his use....................	1/2		
		To D^o Calvit for D^o.........................	1/2	1	
	4	To two men of Capt Worthington's Company.....	1	2	
	5	To Abraham Taylor, a militia man at this post	1/4	1/2	
	6	To two men of Capt George's Company..........	1	2	
	7	To three men of D^o D^o D^o...............	3/4	1 1/2	
	"	To the Kickapoo Indians.......................	7	4	
Feb	7	To two militia men going to the Falls........	2	1	
	8	To Capt Bailey's hunting party..............	12	24	
	11	~~To Major Linctot Indians~~....................	~~100~~	~~100~~	
	12	To Zephaniah Blackford........................	1/4	1/2	
	14	To B. Scarcy, express.........................	2 1/2	5	
	15	To Capt Robert's Company going on command....	2 1/4		
			69 1/2	119 1/2	* [Not totaled]

Account of ammunition expended by the artillery at sundry times by order of Cap[t] Robert George, Commandant, at Fort Jefferson, 1780

		Powder lbs.	Lead	Flan[l] yds.
Dec.	20 At Cap[t] Harrison and Cap[t] Roberts'..... arrival from the Falls of Ohio per verbal order........................	6	2	1
	25 For five swivels and one four pounder, both in town and garrison per verbal order.................................	60	7	6
Jan.	11 Expended at other different times.......	17		3 1/2
	Issued Cap[t] Bailey for the use of ~~his~~ artillery at O'Post....................			3
Feb.	16 Expended at the arrival and setting off of some French bateaux................	5		1/2
		88	9	[Not totaled]
	Brought forward - - - -	72 3/4	92	
	Brought forward - - - -	69 1/2	119 1/2	
	Transferred to Lib: A page 2	230 1/4	220 1/2	

Account of ammunition deliverd by order of Cap[t] George

1781		Pwd[r]	Lead	Flints
Feb.	15 Ensign Slaughter...........................	1/2	1	----
	16 To Cap[t] Bailey for the defense of O'Post..	150	100	100
	Major Linctot for the Indian Department...	400	212	300
	L[t] Calvit................................	1/2	----	----
	L[t] Clark Company..........................	3 3/4	7 1/2	--
	19 To L[t] Williams' hunting party............	1	2	
	22 To Peoria Indians..........................	30	30	80
	22 To two men going with Major Harlan to the Falls of Ohio....................	1 1/2	3	
March	6 To three men of Cap[t] Bailey's Company.....	-----	----	6
	8 To Ensign Williams' hunting party.........	1	2	
	9 To L[t] Calvit's command to the Illinois....	3 3/4	7 1/2	
	To Cap[t] M[c]Carty for his use...............	1		
	To Patrick Kennedy for the inhabitants of the Illinois........................	100		

(continued)

1781		(continued)	Pwd^{r}	Lead	Flints
	9	To D^{o} for his use..........................	1/2	1	
		John Burks, militia man....................	1/4		
	10	To Capt Kellar for hunting.............	1/4	1/2	
		To the Kaskaskia Indians..................	20	40	50
	19	To D^{o}..	1 1/2	3	---
Feb	19	To Capt Rogers going to the Falls of the			
		Ohio..	25	20	
		To the regiment................................	10 3/4	21 1/2	
	22	To Mr. Dodge....................................	1/2	1	
Mar	22	To Mr. Wm Clark............................	1/2	2 1/2	
	23	To Mr. Archer..................................	1/2		
		Ensign Williams' hunting party............	1 1/2	3	
	27	Sg^{t} Walker....................................	1/2	1	
	28	Lt R^{d} Clark..................................	1/2	1	
		Militia at Clarksville........................	2 1/2	5	
		To Mr. Donne...................................	1/2		
		To Lt Girault..................................	1/2	1	
	24	To one man of Capt George's Company.......	1/4	1/2	
	28	To Lt Calvitt and Bowman..................	1		
Apr^{l}	13	To Capt Owens of militia...................	1		
		To Mr. Finn, Commissary....................	1/2	1	
	17	To Capt Robert George's Company...........	1	2	
	21	To express from the Falls of the Ohio.....	2	4	
		To Capt Worthington's Company............	1/2	1	
	23	To Mr. Pyatte going on command to			
		the Falls of the Ohio.........................			12
May	2	To Capt Kellar's hunting party...........	2	4	
		To six men on command......................	1 1/2	3	
	6	To one man of Capt George's...............	1/2	1	
		To two men of D^{o} D^{o}.........................	1	1/2	8
	10	To one man of Capt George's Company.......	1/4	1/2	
	11	To Lt Dalton...................................		1	
		To one man of Capt Worthington's..........	1/2	1	
	14	Capt Owens of militia.......................	1/2		
		To Capt Kellar................................	1/2	1	
		To Lt Calvit....................................	1/2		

(continued)

1781	(continued)	Pwd^r	Lead	Flints
15	Ensign Williams...........................	1/2	1	
	Capt Brashears..........................	1/2		1/2
	Col^o Montgomery.........................	1/2	1	
	Lt Clark's blockhouse....................	5 1/2	11	
	To the regiment...........................	113	23	
	Transferred to Lib: A. fol. 2	34 1/2	65	
		[Column adds to 135.75]	[Column adds to 64.5]	[Column adds to 556]

Stores issued by order of Capt Robert George

Date 1780		A.	B.	C.	D.	E.	F.	G.	H*.
Dec. 7	To Capt Kellar..................................					1			
9	To Capt Brashears' Company..........................						2		
28	To three men of Capt Worthington's	1	2						
29	To two D^o Capt Bailey's Company.......		2						
30	To Capt Bailey's Company................................							1	
31	To Capt Harrison..								1
	To Capt Brashear..								1
1781									
Jan 2	To three men Capt George's Company....		3						
~~3~~	~~To B. Pittman (Boat Master)..........................~~					~~1~~			
10	Patrick Kennedy........................		1	1					
11	To a soldier of Capt Bailey's Company..		1	1					
	To Major William........................		[No entry]						
	~~Ditto~~..................................		~~1~~						
12	To Capt Bailey's Company.....................				23				
	To Capt Worthington's D^o.....................				17				
	To Mr. Hunter, of the militia.................				1				
	To James Sherlock...........................				1				
	To Capt George's Company................................							1	
16	To D^o D^o D^o				32				
18	To Capt George's Company...............		1					1	
19	To Mr. Donne, Commissary...............		2	2	1				
				no belts					
Feb. 3	To Lt Calvitt..................................				3	2			
4	To a soldier of Capt Bailey's..........		1	1					
13	To a soldier of D^o Brashears'..........		1	1					
	To Capt Bailey..............................					1			
	To Peoria Indians..............................				7				
	To Buckner Pitman, Boatmaster.........................							1	
	To Capt Worthington's Company.........		2						
	To Capt Worthington for his use..............				26			1	
		1	16	6	85*	4	2	5	2

1781			A.	B.	C.	D.	E.	F.	G.	H.*
		Brought forward	3	15	6	85	4	2	5	2
Jan	25	Capt Brashears' Company				10				
March	10	Lt Calvit's Command								4
	13	Kaskaskia Indians				2				
	16	To Mr. Kennedy								1
	19	Mr. Miles, Quartermaster Sg^{t}		1						
		Capt Rogers going to the Falls		2						5
		Kaskaskia Indians				2				
March	2	Capt Brashears' Company		3						
		Capt Robert George's Company		1						
		D^{o} D^{o} D^{o} no voucher (not del^{d} to me)							1	
Jan.	27	Lt Calvit							1	
Apr.	24	Buckner Pittman, boatmaster								2
Om^{t}	1780									
Dec.	22	Benjamin Roberts, Capt								2
May	27th	To Wm Carn Soldier Cond^{r} Lt Clark		1	1					
June	6th	To Ens^{n} Williams							1	
	D^{o}	To Col Montgomery							1	
	21	Capt Brashears' Comp^{y}		3						
		Capt George's Comp^{y}		1						
		Capt Worthington's D^{o}		1						
		D^{o} D^{o} D^{o}		1	1					
July	25	To Capt George's Comp^{y}		1						
Aug^{t}	6	To Capt Brashears' D^{o}		1						
	10	To Capt Rogers' Troop		1						
Sep^{t}	8	To Capt George's Comp^{y}		1						
	14	To Capt Roberts' D^{o}		8	8					
	24	To John Godfrey, Interpreter		1						

1780 om^{d}		A.	B.	C.	D.	E.	F.	G.	H*.
Decr 7	To Capt George..............................					1			
D^{o} Aug. 14	To Indians...................................						3		
D^{o} Nov. 29	To Lt Clark.................................						3		
D^{o} Decr 1	To Capt Brashears' C^{o}.........................						2		
D^{o}...... 2	To Capt Helm..................................						1		
D^{o}...... 4	To Capt McCarty's C^{o}........................						1		
Octr 4	To Capt Todd...........................				1				
6	To Col^{o} Slaughter's....................				1				
12	To Capt Rogers' Comp^{y}..................				11				
13	To D^{o} John Rogers' D^{o}.................				11				
	To Capt Craig's Comp^{y}......................					10			
	To Capt Taylor............................					1			
	To previous am^{t} - - - - -	1	23	6		99	4	2	10
		3	42	16	25	109*	5	12	10

[*Not correct total]

The above 99 swords issued, are settled on Capt Barbour's Cargo with Capt George the 23^{d} April 1781, at which time remained 51 on hand, out of which the above ment^{d} 10 have been issued. The above issues transferred to their respective acco^{ts} in Lib. A.

*Where A=Rifles; B=Muskets; C=Bayonets with Belts; D=Swords; E=Axes; F=Tomahawks; G=Kettles; and H=Tent or Oil Cloth.

Account of ammunition delivered by me by order of Capt Robt George and Col Montgomery

			Powd^{r}	Lbs Lead	Flints
June	1st	To Major Williams	1	----	----
	Ditto	To Lt Girault	1	2	----
June	5th	To Capt Keller for the use of hunting for the troops going to the Falls........	1	2	----
	Ditto	To Mr. Archer................................	1	1	----
	Ditto	To Lt Clark................................	1/2	1	----
	Ditto	To three men of Capt Worthington's Company..	3/4	1 1/2	---
	Ditto	To three men of Lt Clark's..................	1 1/2	3	----
June	6th	To Col Montgomery..........................	1	2	2
	Ditto	To Capt Owen's Militia......................	4	8	----
	Ditto	To Mr. Finn..................................	1/2	---	----
June	7th	To six men going to the Falls by land........	3	6	----
			15 1/4	26 1/2	2

(continued)

(continued)

			Powd^r	Lbs Lead	Flints
June	7th	To Pat^k Callahan	1	2	----
	D^o	To Dapiae Whitegar..........................	1	2	----
June	5th	To Mr. Kennedy for his voyage to the Falls..	1	2	6
Om^{td}	13	To twenty-three men at Elk Camp............	5 3/4	11 1/2	
July	7	To a hunter by order of Col^o Montgomery.....	2	4	
		To a hunter by order of Capt George.........	1/4	1/2	
Om^{td}	4	To Col^o Slaughter for rejoining Dray........	25	----	
	8	Capt Owen and Pat^k Callahan for hunting.....	1	2	
	18	To two hunters on Beargrass (Creek).........	1	2	
	20	To Capt Kellar for his hunting party........	----	6	
	21	Capt Worthington's Company..................	3	6	----
	23	To Lt Calvit................................	1	----	----
	25	To Capt Worthington's Com^d to Harrodsburg...	4	8	----
July	30	To Capt Kellar by Col^o Montgomery's order for a Publick fish seine		----	80
August	8	To Capt Roger's Company.....................	----	12	
	9	To twenty men of Col^o Slaughter's Corps.....	----	----	20
		Carried forward - - -	61 1/4	158 1/2	34 *

[Incorrect total]

Ammunition Issued/Falls of the Ohio - 1781

			Powd^r	Lead	Flints
August	19	To Mr. Donne for his use................	----	4	----
	20	To artillery at Genl Clark's arrival.....	11	----	----
		To Command going to Harrodsburg..........	----	8	16
Sep^r	3	To Lt Montgomery........................	----	1	----
	8	To a man of Capt Brashears' Company......	----	1/2	---
	13	To eight men of Capt George's D^o.........	----	4	----
	14	To Capt Roberts' Company.................	----	10	----
	14	To Capt Thomas' Company..................	----	12	----
	20	To one man of Col^o Slaughter's Corps.....	----	2	----
	22	To our friendly Indians..................	----	81	200
		Lt Perrault for his use..................		2	
	25	Commissary Finn for his use..............	----	2	
	28	Capt Thomas for his D^o...................	----	2	
	30	To two men of Capt Thomas' Company.......	----	2	
	"	To friendly Indians......................	----	----	50
Oct^r	1	To Capt Brashears' Company...............	----	3	
	2	To Major Williams........................	----	1	
		To Lt Meriwether........................	----	2	----

(continued)

(continued)

		Powd^{r}	Lbs Lead	Flints
Oct^{r}	2 To Capt Fields........................	----	1	
	3 To Col^{o} Montgomery......................	----	2	
	5 To Col^{o} Slaughter.......................	----	2	
	6 Capt Thomas' Company....................	----	3	
	Maj^{r} Williams for his use.............	----	1	
	Amo^{t} brought forward......................	61 1/4	158 1/2	34
	See Lib A: folio 2 - - - - - for the flints See fol. 8.---	72 1/4	304	300

Account of tobacco issued to the troops [at the] Falls [of the Ohio]--1781

August the 6th
Mr. Donne, Commissary, to two carrots tobacco
Six men of Capt George's company, two carrots toabacco
Four men of Capt Worthington's Comp^{y}, 1/3 carrot

August the 8th
Nine men of Capt George's Comp^{y} -- to 9^{lbs} tob^{o}

August the 26th
One man of Capt George's Company -- to 1 carrot tob^{o}
One man of Capt Roger's Company -- to 1^{lb} tob^{o}

Septr the 6th
Capt Roberts to 1 carrot tob^{o}

Septr the 8th
Capt Worthington's Company -- to 3 carrots tob^{o}
Capt Rogers' troop -- to 2 carrots tob^{o}
Maj^{r} Crittenden -- to 1 carrot tob^{o}

Septr the 13th
Capt Taylor's Company -- to 4 ^{lbs} tob^{o}
Mr. Finn, Commissary, -- to 1 carrot tob^{o}

Septr the 19th
Capt Helm -- to 1 carrot tob^{o}

(continued)

(continued)

Septr the 20th
Capt Roger's troop -- 1 carrot tob^{o}
Mr. Pat^{k} Kennedy -- to 1 carrot tob^{o}
Doctor Connard -- to 1 carrot tob^{o}

Septr the 21st
Capt Todd -- to 1 carrot tob^{o}

Septr the 22^{d}
To friendly Indians -- 12 carrots tobacco
Capt Young and Col^{o} Crockett's Reg^{t} -- to 1 carrot tob^{o}

Septr the 23^{d}
Martin Carney --to 1 carrot tob^{o}
Capt Taylor -- to 1 carrot tob^{o}
To one man of Capt Taylor's Company -- 1 ^{lb} tob^{o}
Lt Perrault -- to 1 carrot tob^{o}
To friendly Indians -- to 2 carrots tobacco
Lt Dalton -- to 2 carrots tobacco
Lt Perrault's Company -- to 3 carrots D^{o}

Septr the 25th
Capt Brashears' Company -- to 1 carrot tob^{o}
Capt Rogers' troops -- to 1 carrot tob^{o}
Capt Brashears' D^{o} -- to 4 carrots tobacco

Septr the 30th
To friendly Indians -- to six carrots tobacco

October the 1st
Ensign Williams -- to 1 carrot tobacco
Capt Rogers' troops -- to 4 ^{lbs} tobacco

October the 2nd
Mr. Berrwick -- to one carrot tobacco

October the 3rd
Maj^{r} Crittenden -- to two carrots tobacco
Col^{o} Crockett's Reg^{t} -- to two ^{lbs} tobacco

(continued)

(continued)

October the 6th
Capt Ben Roberts -- to 1 carrot tobacco
Mr. Patk Kennedy -- to 1 carrot tobacco

October the 7th
Capt Taylor's Company -- to 2/3 carrot tobacco

October the 11th
Capt Worthington -- to one carrot tobo
October the 12th
Capt Rogers' troops -- to 2 carrots tobo

October the 14th
Colo Montgomery -- to 2 carrots tobo

October the 16th
Mr. James Moore -- to 1 carrot tobacco
Illinois Regiment -- to 2 2/3 carrots tobacco

Account of brass kettles delivered by me by order of Capt George at Fort Jefferson 1780-----------

		Kettles
Novr	15 To Capt Robert George and Company........................	3
	" To Capt Leonard Helm for his use...........................	1
	" To Capt Abraham Keller and Company........................	2
	" To Majr John Williams for his use..........................	1
	" To Lt Richard Clark for Capt Worthington's Compy..........	2
	" To Ensign Lawrence Slaughter for Capt Baileys Compy.......	2
	" To Capt Richard Brashears.................................	1
	" To John Harry, Armourer at this place.....................	1
	" To my own use...	1
	Transferred to Lib: A folio 10...Total	14

Account of soap delivered by me, by order of Col^{o} Montgomery and Capt George at Fort Jefferson 1780-----------

			Lbs
Sep^{r}	9	To Fredrick Guion..............................	2
	11	To Zephaniah Blackford..........................	1
	"	To Ensign Slaughter.............................	2
	13	To Captain Bailey's Company.....................	12
	"	To Capt Robert George's Company.................	16
	"	To Capt Edward Worthington's Company............	9 1/2
	"	To Capt Brashears' Company.....................	8 1/2
	"	To Mr. Donne Commissary.........................	3
	"	To Capt McCarty's Company......................	15
	"	To Lt Williams for his use...................	1
		Capt Brashears To ~~Lieut. Girault~~ and Doctor Ray................	1
	16	To Mr. Wil^{m} Clark............................	1
	"	To Capt Abraham Keller's Company...............	6
	"	To ~~Mr.~~ Lt Richard Clark.........................	2
	25	To Sergeant Moore of Capt George's Company......	7 1/2
Oct^{r}	6	To Lt Dalton for his use.......................	5 1/2
	"	To Capt Leonard Helm for D^{o} D^{o}..................	2
	9	To Capt George for his own use..................	12
	"	To Capt Bailey for D^{o} D^{o} D^{o}....................	8
	"	To Mr. Donne, Commissary, for his D^{o}............	4
	"	To myself for my use............................	8
	11	To Lt Richard Clark D^{o} D^{o}......................	6
	22	To Frank Little, a soldier in Capt George's Comp^{y}	1
	"	To John Ash a soldier in D^{o} D^{o} D^{o}..	1
	13	To Capt Leonard Helm for his use................	6
	"	To Ensign Jarret Williams.......................	4
	25	To Capt Abraham Keller..........................	2
No^{v}	8	To John Mr. Garr a soldier in Capt George's Com^{y}.	1
	"	To Joseph Thornton, Artificer for public works...	2
	18	To Mr. Blackford Commissary.....................	3
		Transferr'd to Lib: A. page 6 - -	153 1/2

Account of soap delivered by me by order of Capt George at Fort Jefferson 1780-------

			Lbs
Nov^r	18	To eight men of Capt Worthington's Company.........	8
	"	To Sg^t Morgan for Capt George's Company............	15
	19	To Capt Brashears' Company..........................	4 1/2
	"	To Capt Bailey's Company............................	12
	"	To Capt McCarty's Company..........................	1 1/2
	22	To Capt Abraham Kellar's Company....................	6
	23	To Major Harlan for his own use......................	3
	"	To James Sherlock, Interpreter, for his use..........	6
	27	To Mr. Donne, Commissary.............................	6
	"	To Mr. Isreal Dodge..................................	6
	29	To Capt Brashear for his own use....................	6
	"	To Major Williams for his D^o D^o....................	6
Dec^r	3	To John Hazzard of Capt George's Company............	1
	4	To Capt Helm for his use............................	6
	5	To a man of Capt McCarty's Company.................	1/2
	"	To D^o of Capt George's Company.....................	1
	6	To Mr. Harris, Armourer at this place................	2
	7	To Ensign Slaughter for his use......................	6
	10	To Capt George for his use..........................	15
	"	To Negro Ceasar, Artificer...........................	1 1/2
		To Mr. William Clark.................................	6
		To Ensign Williams...................................	6
		To Mr. Carney, Quartermaster.........................	6
		Dried and wasted away................................	13
		Transferr'd to Lib: A. folio 6 - - -	144

Carney's Book

N° - 1 F

1780-1781

Date	Col^{o} John Montgomery D^{d}	Rum G:Q:P	Sugar Lbs.	Tobacco Carrots	Soap Lbs.
May 10	Per orders from day book	.....	12		
17	Per ditto..............	.....	10		
30	Per ditto..............	.....	5		
June 5	Per ditto..............	.....	6		
	Per ditto..............	.....	20		
7	Per ditto..............	.....	.....	1	
July 19	Per ditto..............	.....	6		
Om^{td}	May 18th Per ditto.....	2			
		2	59	1	
Octr 14	Per ditto to ditto.....			2	
		2	59	3	

Date 1781	Capt Robt George D^{d}	Rum G:Q:P	Sugar Lbs.	Tobacco Carrots	Soap Lbs.
May 25	Per orders from day book	5:2:1			
30	Per ditto...............	......	24		
June 6	Per ditto...............	......	150		
Om^{td}	April 23^{d} Per order	......	.....	3	
June 7	Per ditto...............	......	12		
		5:2:1	186	3	

Date 1781	Maj[r] John Williams D[d]	Rum G:Q:P	Sugar Lbs.	Tobacco Carrots	Soap Lbs.
May 3[d]	Per orders from day book	1:1:1	10		
June 6	Per ditto.............	......	.....	6	
"	Per ditto.............	......	2		
Om[td]	May 31st Per ditto.....	......	.....	1	
		1:1:1	12	7	

Date 1781	Cap[t] Rich[d] Brashears	Rum G:Q:P	Sugar Lbs.	Tobacco Carrots	Soap Lbs.
May 3[d]	Per orders from day book	4:1:1			
	Per order..............	......	5		
26	Per ditto..............	......	10		
June 5	Per ditto..............	......	20		
7	Per ditto..............	......	.....	1	
July 21	Per ditto..............	......	25		
Sep[r] 25	Per ditto..............	......	.....	4	
		4:1:1	60	5	

Date 1781	Capt Ed^{d} Worthington	Rum G:Q:P	Sugar Lbs.	Tobacco Carrots	Soap Lbs.
May 14	Per orders from day book	4:1:1			
"	Per ditto..............	......	10		
19	Per ditto..............	......	2		
	Per ditto..............	......	10		
June 7	Per ditto..............	......	10		
24	Per ditto..............	......	10		
July 9	Per ditto..............	......	10		
23^{d}	Per ditto..............	......	24		
Octr 11	Per ditto..............	......	.....	1	
		4:1:1	76	1	

Date 1781	Col^{o} George Slaughter Delivered	Rum G:Q:P	Sugar Lbs.	Tobacco Carrots	Soap Lbs.
July 7	Per order..............	......	100		
22	Per ditto..............	......	.....	6	
			100	6	

Date 1781	Capt Robt Todd D^{d}	Rum G:Q:P	Sugar Lbs.	Tobacco Carrots	Soap Lbs.
Sepr 21	Per order..............	......	.....	1	
				1	

Date 1781	Lt John Girault Dd	Rum G:Q:P	Sugar Lbs.	Tobacco Carrots	Soap Lbs.
May 3	Per orders from day book	1:1:1			
5	Per ditto..............	......	2		
June 2	Per ditto..............	......	10		
5	Per ditto..............	......	5		
7	Per ditto..............	......	.....	2	
"	Per ditto..............	......	3		
		1:1:1	20	2	

Date 1781	Lieut Joseph Calvit Dd	Rum G:Q:P	Sugar Lbs.	Tobacco Carrots	Soap Lbs.
May 3	Per orders from day book	2:1:0			
"	Per ditto..............	......	8		
23	Per ditto..............	......	8		
June 5	Per ditto..............	......	20		
7	Per ditto..............	......	.....	2	
July 9	Per ditto..............	......	10		
17	Per ditto..............	......	20		
		2:1:0	66	2	

Date 1781	Lieu^{t} Richd Clark D^{d}	Rum G:Q:P	Sugar Lbs.	Tobacco Carrots	Soap Lbs.
May 3^{d}	Per order from day book	3:1:0			
5	Per ditto..............	......	8		
25	Per ditto..............	......	.....	1	
"	Per ditto..............	......	6		
July 8	Per ditto..............	......	6		
21	Per ditto..............	......	20		
		3:1:0	40	1	

Date 1781	Lieu^{t} Thos Dalton D^{d}	Rum G:Q:P	Sugar Lbs.	Tobacco Carrots	Soap Lbs.
May 4	Per order from day book	1:0:0			
14	Per ditto..............	......	10		
26	Per ditto..............	......	6		
June 5	Per ditto..............	......	25		
July 20	Per ditto..............	......	10		
Sept 23	Per ditto..............	......	.....	2	
		1:0:0	51	2	

Date 1781	Capt Issac Taylor D^{d}	Rum G:Q:P	Sugar Lbs.	Tobacco Carrots	Soap Lbs.
July 24	Per order from day book	......	20		
Sepr 23	Per order ditto........	......	.....	1	
			20	1	

Date 1781	Mr Meredith Price Dd	Rum G:Q:P	Sugar Lbs.	Tobacco Carrots	Soap Lbs.
July 6	Per order from day book	.....	10		
			10		

Date 1781	Capt Leonard Helm Dd	Rum G:Q:P	Sugar Lbs.	Tobacco Carrots	Soap Lbs.
May 3d	Per order from day book	3:1:1			
5	Per ditto.............	......	8		
25	Per ditto.............	......	8	1	
June 7	Per ditto.............	......	12		
July 9	Per ditto.............	......	10		
Sepr 19	Per ditto.............	......	.....	1	
		3:1:1	38	2	

Date 1781	Capt Ben Roberts Dd	Rum G:Q:P	Sugar Lbs.	Tobacco Carrots	Soap Lbs.
July 23d	Per order from day book	......	25		
Sepr 5	Per ditto.............	......	25	1	
Octr 6	Per ditto.............	......	.....	1	
			50	2	

Date 1781	Capt Mark Thomas Dd	Rum G:Q:P	Sugar Lbs.	Tobacco Carrots	Soap Lbs.
July 8	Per order from day book	......	10		
22	Per ditto.............	......	15		
			25		

Date 1781	Ensign Wil^m Roberts D^d	Rum G:Q:P	Sugar Lbs.	Tobacco Carrots	Soap Lbs.
July 9	Per order from day book	......	10		
			10		

Date 1781	Mr Donne, D^y Conductor Delivered	Rum G:Q:P	Sugar Lbs.	Tobacco Carrots	Soap Lbs.
May 3	Per order from day book	3:0:0			
June 7	Per ditto.............	......	12	1	
July 9	Per ditto.............	......	10	1	
22	Per ditto.............	......	20		
Aug 6	Per ditto.............	......	.....	2	
		3:0:0	42	4	

Date 1781	Mr Pat Kennedy, D^y Conductor D^d	Rum G:Q:P	Sugar Lbs.	Tobacco Carrots	Soap Lbs.
Jume 5	Per order from day book	......	12		
7	Per ditto.............	......	20	2	
July 23	Per ditto.............	......	10	1	
Aug 8	Per ditto.............	......	.....	1	
20	Per ditto.............	......	.....	4	
Octr 6	Per ditto.............	......	.....	1	
			42	9	

Date 1781	Mr Israel Dodge Deputy Agent Dd	Rum G:Q:P	Sugar Lbs.	Tobacco Carrots	Soap Lbs.
May 3	Per order from day book	3:1:0			
"	Per ditto.............	......	8		
19	Per ditto.............	......	6		
29	Per ditto.............	......	10		
June 4	Per ditto.............	......	10		
July 7	Per ditto.............	......	10		
20	Per ditto.............	......	12		
		3:1:0	56		

Date 1781	Mr Finn, Issuing Commisary Dd	Rum G:Q:P	Sugar Lbs.	Tobacco Carrots	Soap Lbs.
May 3	Per order from day book	2:3:1			
8	Per ditto for purchasing for the use of the troops at Fort Jefferson.............	17:1:0			
10	Per ditto for his use..	......	8	1	
19	Per ditto.............	......	1		
June 7	Per ditto.............	......	.....	1	
Omtd	June 1st Per ditto.....	......	10		
July 9	Per order.............	......	6		
21	Per ditto.............	......	.....	1	
24	Per ditto.............	......	25		
Sept 13	Per ditto.............	......	.....	1	
		20:0:1	50	4	

Date 1781	Martin Carney Quartermaster D[d]	Rum G:Q:P	Sugar Lbs.	Tobacco Carrots	Soap Lbs.
May 3	Per order from day book	3:3:0			
5	Per ditto............	......	2		
10	Per ditto............	......	6		
18	Per ditto............	......	.....	1	
June 7	Per ditto............	......	12		
July 9	Per ditto............	......	10		
21	Per ditto............	......	26	1	
Sep[r] 23	Per ditto............	......	.....	1	
				3	

Date 1781	Cap[t] Abr[m] Kellar D[d]	Rum G:Q:P	Sugar Lbs.	Tobacco Carrots	Soap Lbs.
May 3	Per order from day book	3:2:1			
"	Per ditto............	......	3		
21	Per ditto............	......	4		
June 5	Per ditto............	......	24		
July 6	Per ditto............	......	10		
19	Per ditto............	......	1		
		3:2:1	51		

Date 1781	Cornet Thruston D[d]	Rum G:Q:P	Sugar Lbs.	Tobacco Carrots	Soap Lbs.
July 12	Per order from day book	......	20		
			20		

Date 1781	Cap[t] John Rogers D[d]	Rum G:Q:P	Sugar Lbs.	Tobacco Carrots	Soap Lbs.
July 6	Per order from day book	......	15		
			15		

Date 1781	Lieu[t] Merriwether D[d]	Rum G:Q:P	Sugar Lbs.	Tobacco Carrots	Soap Lbs.
July 24	Per order from day book	......	20		
			20		

Date 1781	M[r] Pittman, Boat Master Delivered	Rum G:Q:P	Sugar Lbs.	Tobacco Carrots	Soap Lbs.
June 24	Per order from day book	......	6		
July 12	Per ditto..............	......	6		
23	Per ditto..............	......	6		
			18		

Date 1781	M[r] John Walker Sg[t] Maj[r] D[d]	Rum G:Q:P	Sugar Lbs.	Tobacco Carrots	Soap Lbs.
May 3	Per order from day book	0:2:1			
14	Per ditto..............	......	3		
June 1	Per ditto..............	......	6		
7	Per ditto..............	......	6		
July 23	Per ditto..............	......	6		
23	Per ditto..............	......	4		
			25		

Date 1781	M[r] Miles, Quartermaster Sg[t] D[d]	Rum G:Q:P	Sugar Lbs.	Tobacco Carrots	Soap Lbs.
June 5	Per order from day book	......	4		
7	Per ditto..............	......	12		
24	Per ditto..............	......	5		
July 12	Per ditto..............	......	6		
21	Per ditto..............	......	6		
			33		

Date 1781	Hospital or Sick Accounts Delivered	Rum G:Q:P	Sugar Lbs.	Tob^{o} Car^{ts}	Soap Lbs.
June 1	Per order to 2 men of Worthington's Company...	.....	4		
7	Per order to 1 woman of Capt Brashears'......	.....	4		
"	Per ditto to 1 man & 2 children of Capt George's Company........	.....	6		
	Per ditto to 1 man & woman Capt George's C^{o}........	.....	3		
	Per D^{o}, man in George's C^{o}	.....	2		
24	Per D^{o} D^{o} Worthington's C^{o}	.....	2		
July 7	Per D^{o} D^{o} George's C^{o}.....	.....	2		
8	Per D^{o} D^{o} Lt Clark's C^{o}...	.....	2		
12	Per D^{o} D^{o} Brashears' C^{o}...	.....	2		
	Per D^{o} D^{o} Roger's C^{o}......	.....	4		
18	Per D^{o} Col^{o} Slaughter.....	.....	2		
19	Per ditto to D^{o} of D^{o}.....	.....	3		
	Per ditto to soldier's wife Capt George's C^{o}...	.....	2		
	Per order to man of Lieu^{t} Calvit's Company.......	.....	4		
	Per ditto 1 woman of the regiment.............	.....	2		
	Per ditto 2 men Capt George's Company........	.....	4		
			48		

Date 1781	Militia of Clarksville Delivered	Rum G:Q:P	Sugar Lbs.	Tobacco Carrots	Soap Lbs.
May 3	To M[r] Archer per orders	......	3	1	
5	To Cap[t] Owens per order	......	6		
14	To M[rs] Helebrand D[o]....	......	4		
June 5	To Joseph Hunter D[o]....	......	12		
"	To M[rs] Helebrand D[o]....	......	3		
	To Cap[t] Owens per ditto	......	.....	1	
	To Miles Hart per ditto	......	12		
	To John Burks per ditto	......	6		
	To Cap[t] Owens per ditto	......	6		
	To M[r] Archer per ditto	......	12		
	To Cap[t] Owens per ditto	......	12		
			76	2	

Date 1781	Illinois Regiment Rations and Fatigue	Rum G:Q:P	Sugar Lbs.	Tob^{o} Car^{ts}	Soap Lbs.
May 11	Per order..for rations	2:1:1/4			
	Per D^{o} for fatigue....	0:3:1/4			
12	Per D^{o} for D^{o}.........	0:3:1/4			
	Per D^{o} for D^{o}.........	0:1:1/4			
17	Per D^{o} for D^{o}.........	0:1:1/4			
25	Per D^{o} for rations....	2:0:0			
Om^{td}	May 3^{d} D^{o}, regiment...	....	171		
D^{o}	Per order to 4 men Capt George's C^{o}....	....	8		
D^{o} 5	Per D^{o} to 1 man Capt Worthington's C^{o}....	....	2		
7	Per D^{o}................	....	.....	9	
19	Per D^{o} to a man of Capt Brashears' C^{o}..	....	2		
21	Per D^{o} to regiment....	....	156		
June 1	Per D^{o} to James McMullin, Gunner....	....	3		
	Per D^{o} to one man of Capt George's C^{o}....	....		3	
5	Per D^{o} to 3 D^{o} D^{o}.....	....	8		
7	Per D^{o} 1 man Capt Worthington's C^{o}....	....	4		
	Per order to a man of Capt George's C^{o}....	....	3		
	Per D^{o} to regiment....	....	.....	9 1/2	
24	Per D^{o} to D^{o}..........	....	.....	18	
	Per D^{o} to D^{o}..........	....	95		

(Continued)

Date 1781	Illinois Regiment (continued)	Rum G:Q:P	Sugar Lbs.	Tobacco Carrots	Soap Lbs.
July 1	Per D^{o} to one man Capt George's C^{o}.....	.....	4		
	Per D^{o} Sg^{t} Matthew, prisoner............	.....	2		
18	Per D^{o} to one man Lieu^{t} Clark's C^{o}.....	.....	3		
20	Per D^{o} Capt Brashears' Company.............	.....	2		
	Per D^{o} to D^{o} D^{o} D^{o}....	.....	1		
21	Per D^{o} to regiment.....	.....	182		
	Per D^{o} to D^{o}...........	.....	.....	8	
Aug 4	Per D^{o} to one man Capt George's C^{o}.....	.....	.....	1	
11	Per D^{o} to one man Capt Brashears' C^{o}...	.....	.....	1	
	Per D^{o} to 2 men Capt Taylor's C^{o}.....	.....	.....	1	
		6:2:1	649	47 1/2	

Date 1781		Individuals Delivered	Rum G:Q:P	Sugar Lbs.	Tobacco Carrots	Soap Lbs.
July	12	George Wilson per order	......	20		
	16	Gen[l] Clark's Negro per order............	......	2		
	17	M[r] Ballard per order...	......	20		
Sep[r]	1	M[r] Asher per order.....	......	15		
		M[r] James Moore on Beargrass per order..	......	20		
	8	To Maj[r] Crittendon.....	......	.....	1	
	20	To Doctor Conner.......	......	.....	1	
	22	To Cap[t] Young..........	......	.....	1	
		To Indians.............	......	.....	12	
	23	To Lieu[t] Perault.......	......	.....	1	
		To Indians.............	......	.....	2	
	25	To Indians.............	......	.....	6	
Oct[r]	16	~~Mr. James Shane~~........	......	~~77~~	~~24~~	
	2	To M[r] James Berwick per order............	......	.....	1	
		To Maj[r] Crittendon Per ditto...........	......	.....	2	
		To Col[o] Crockett's Regiment Per ditto...	......	.....	2/3	
	1	To M[r] James Moore......	......	.....	1	
				77	28 2/3	

Date 1781		Cap[t] Rogers' Troops D[d]	Rum G:Q:P	Sugar Lbs.	Tobacco Carrots	Soap Lbs.
July	16	Per order to Sg[t] Key...	......	4		
		Per ditto to a private	......	3		
		Per ditto to ditto.....	......	4		
		Per ditto to ditto.....	......	2		
		Per ditto to 2 men Cap[t] Rogers' Company......	......	4		
Aug[t]	26	Per ditto to 1 D[o]......	......	.....	1	
Sep[t]	8	Per ditto to the troops	......	.....	2	
	20	Per ditto to the D[o]....	......	.....	1	
	25	Per ditto to the ditto	......	.....	1	
Oc[t]	1	Per ditto to ditto	......	.....	1 1/3	
	12	Per ditto to ditto	......	.....	2	
				17	8 1/3	

Date 1781	State of Virginia Dd	Rum G:Q:P	Sugar Lbs.	Tobacco Carrots	Soap Lbs.
May 23	Per order to Mrs Burks for making shirts for Capt George's Company	......	5		
June 5	Per order to a soldier for burning 4 bushels of charcoal..........	......	4		
	To a man for sawing 4 days public work.....	......	4		
	Per order a militia man for rowing 16 days up the Ohio..........	......	16		
	Per order ~~to~~ exchanged for fatigue liquor with Mr Pyatte.......	......	50		
			79		

Date 1781		Regiment Delivered	Rum G:Q:P	Sugar Lbs.	Tobacco Carrots
		Am^{t} bro^{t} from Page 68	6:2:1	649	47 1/2
Aug	11	Per order to a man Capt Brashears' Company...	......	.....	1
Om^{td}	6	Per order to a man Capt Worthington's.......	......	.....	1
		Per ditto to 6 D^{o} Capt George's Company.....	......	.....	2
	8	Per ditto 4 men Capt Worthington's.........	......	.....	1 1/3
	26	Per ditto 9 D^{o} Capt George's Company.....	......	.....	3
		Per ditto 1 D^{o} D^{o}..D^{o}..	......	.....	1
Sep^{t}	8	Per D^{o} to Capt Worthington's C^{o}.....	......	.....	3
	13	Per D^{o} to Taylor's C^{o}..	......	.....	1 1/3
	23	Per ditto to D^{o} D^{o} D^{o}..	......	.....	1
	25	Per D^{o} to to Lt Perault	......	.....	3
		Per D^{o} to Brashears' C^{o}	......	.....	1
Oct^{r}	7	Per D^{o} Taylor's C^{o}.....	......	.....	1
	11	Per D^{o} Worthington's C^{o}	......	.....	1
	14	~~Per ditto Col. Montgomery for his use~~	......	.....	
	16	Per D^{o} Illinois Regiment.............	......	.....	2 2/3
			6:2:1	649	70 2/3 [Not correct total]

John Dodge's Quartermaster Book

1780-1781

JOHN DODGE'S TABLE OF CONTENTS

TABLE OF CONTENTS (continued)

Col. George Rogers Clark
June 10, 1780

Issued to his slaves by verbal orders upon setting off on an expedition: one check linen handkerchief; seven yards osnaburg for two shirts for Negro man; five yards damaged linen for Wench; seven yards osnaburg for Wench and boy; two and 1/2 yards dark green calico for Wench; three yards spotted flannel for Wench; one India handkerchief for Wench; one check linen handkerchief for Wench; four skeins thread; one scalping knife for Negro man; and five and 1/2 yards osnaburg for two pair trousers.

Issued to himself when going to the Falls of the Ohio to make an expedition against the Indian towns: three ruffled shirts (three 1/4 each); one and 3/4 yards blue bath coating; one and 1/2 yards scarlet cloth; 12 yards ribbon; two skeins silk; one clasp knife; one pair scissors; one pair ravelled gartering; and one lb vermilion.

Paid to Mr. Eyler for a mortar, four lbs white sugar and one lb coffee.

Paid Lafont for 18 plates and two saltcellars, 18 check handkerchiefs.

Paid Lafont for two saltcellars, one snaffle bridle.

Sent six gallons tafia to Fort Jefferson with Capt Brashears.

Paid Gratiot for one dozen china plates, 60 L peltry.

Lt Col^{o} John Montgomery — Fort Jefferson, July 12th 1780

Sundry articles issued: six yards brown broadcloth, seven 1/4 wide; five dozen and five metal buttons; and two 1/4 yards fine cambric for stocks.

Issued for six vest and six pair breeches: four yards white casernone; two and 1/2 yards thickset; two and 3/4 quarter cotton spotted velvet; five yards corded dimity; three yards sycee; three yards calendar; and two and 1/2 yards chintz.

Issued to make up sundry garments: two stick silk parit; seven skeins silk; two pair knee garters (one pair overdrawn); and five yards shalloon (2 and 1/2 overdrawn).

Issued twenty one yards white linen for six shirts; five yards coarse linen damaged for lining; eleven skeins thread; three pair thread hose; two silk handkerchiefs; two Indian handkerchiefs; four linen handkerchiefs (two overdrawn); one ivory and one horn comb (overdrawn); and one brass ink stand (overdrawn).

Received from Capt John Dodge the within sundry goods in part of the clothing allowed by law.

Test: J. Donne

John Montgomery,
Lt Col^{o}

Sundry articles overdrawn by Col. Montgomery, beyond his quota of clothing: one pair silk knee garters; two and 1/2 yards shalloon; two linen handkerchiefs; one ivory and one horn comb; one brass ink stand; one English blanket; one snaffle bridle; five and 3/4 yards muslin; one stick ball; and three and 3/4 yards best ribbon.

Septr 12 Issued per order and receipt, 10 lbs coffee; one yard osnaburg, for saddlers; and thirty-two yards linen per order fav^{r} Capt Brashears.

Octr. 6 Issued per order and receipt, two blankets per order fav^{r} Capt Brashears; 40^{w} soap, 40^{w} sugar, three w coffee, four gall^{n} rum tafia, and seven gall^{n} rum.

Major John Williams

Issued two yards fine holland for six stocks and 3/4 yard fine cambric for ruffling six shirts.

Issued for nine vests and breeches: four yards cottonade; two and 1/2 yards sycee; two and one quarter yards calendar; two and 1/2 yards corded dimity; two and 1/2 yards thickset; and two and 1/2 yards spotted cotton velvet.

Issued three pair thread hose; six yards cotton seyree for three vests and breeches; two dozen and nine metal buttons; 21 yards white linen for six shirts; two sticks silk twist; six skeins silk; one pair knee garters; ten skeins white thread; two silk handkerchiefs; two Indian handkerchiefs; two linen handkerchiefs; two and 1/2 yards shalloon; one fine hat; four yards coarse linen for lining; and three yards broadcloth 7/4 wide.

Rec[d] from Cap[t] John Dodge Agent, the within mentioned goods, in part the clothing allowed by law.

Test: J. Donne John Williams, Mj[r] Ill. Batt[n]

Sundry Articles overdrawn by Major Williams above the clothing allowed him by law: one, two and 1/2 point blanket; one snaffle bridle; five and 1/2[w] soap; and two w coffee.

Sept. 29. Issued per order and receipt: eight w coffee; six w soap; and five w sugar.

Oct. 2. Issued five and 1/2 quarts tafia.

3. Issued three 3/4 gallons rum.

Major Richard McCarty

Sundry articles issued: one and 1/2 yards brown broadcloth, seven 1/4 wide; and one and 1/2 yards brown broadcloth, seven 1/4 wide.

Issued for two pair breeches, two and 1/2 yards thickset, and two and 1/2 yards corded dimity.

Issued for four pair breeches and six vests: two and 1/2 yards shalloon; two and 1/4 yards calendar; four yards camlet; six yards calimanco; four yards toile gris; and three yards chintz.

Issued: two dozen metal buttons; 21 yards white linen for six shirts, 3/4 yard fine holland for ruffling; two yards muslin for six stocks; two pair thread hose; one silk handkerchief; one Indian handkerchief; four linen handkerchiefs; two skeins silk; twelve skeins white thread; three yards coarse linen for lining; and three yards broadcloth, 7/4 wide.

Received from Cap[t] John Dodge Ag[t] the within sundry goods in part of the clothing allowed by law.

Test: J. Donne On behalf of Major Richard M[c]Carty

John Williams, Major

1780 Overdrawn by Major McCarty

Sept[r] 13. Issued per order and receipt of L[t] Col. Montgomery, one blanket.

Cap[t] John Rogers

Sundries issued: one and 3/4 yards broadcloth, 7/2 wide; and one and 1/2 yards blue bath coating.

Issued for five vests and breeches: two and 1/2 yards corded dimity; one and 1/4 yards sycee; one and 1/4 yards calendar; and four yards toile gris.

Issued fourteen yards white linen for four shirts; two yards fine holland for six stocks; 1/2 yard cambric for ruffling; two linen handkerchiefs; two silk handkerchiefs; one and 1/4 yards blue persian; twelve skeins silk; one stick silk twist; two and 1/4 yards thickset, for one pair breeches; two pair thread hose; two and one-half yards shalloon; three yards spotted flannel, for two vests and breeches; three yards gray cloth for three vests and breeches, seven yards white linen for two shirts, one-quarter yard fine holland for ruffling; two and one-half yards coarse linen for lining; two linen handkerchiefs; and two and three-quarters yards broadcloth 7/4 wide.

Jn[o]- Rogers

Received from Cap[t] John Dodge, Agent the within mentioned sundry goods, in part the clothing allowed by Law.

Test: J. Donne

John Rogers, Cap[t]
V. L. D.

Sundry articles overdrawn: one English blanket; three and 3/4 ells ribbon; four skeins silk; one comb; and six lbs coffee.

Oct. 25. Issued per order and receipt seven lbs sugar.

Cap[t] Kellar

Sundries issued: one and one-half yards brown broadcloth, 7/4 wide; one and one-half yards scarlet broadcloth; two and one-half yards shalloon, one stick silk twist, one and 1/4 yards sycee for one vest and breeches, six skeins silk, two and 1/2 yards calendar for one vest and breeches; two yards toile gris for two vests or breeches; two and one-half yards thickset for one pair breeches; two and one-half yards corded dimity for one pair breeches; three and one-half yards chintz for three vests; fourteen yards white linen for four shirts; two yards muslin for six stocks; one-half yard fine holland for ruffling; seven skeins white thread; one silk handkerchief; one Indian handkerchief; four linen handkerchiefs; two pair thread hose; one fine hat (returned);

three and one-half yards coarse linen for lining; one pair knee garters; three yards broadcloth, 7/4 wide; and five and one-half yards white linen for two shirts.

Received from Capt John Dodge Agent, the within sundry goods in part of the clothing allowed by law.

Test: J. Donne

Abr^{m} Kellar, Capt
Ill^{n} Batt^{n}

Overdrawn by Capt Ab^{m} Kellar

Sept. 11. Issued per order and receipt, one blanket.

13. Issued per order and receipt four w coffee; four w sugar; three w sugar; 1/2^{w} coffee; and two quarts tafia.
Sundries issued to Capt John Bailey: one and one-half yards brown broadcloth, 7/4 wide; one and one-half yards scarlet, 7/4 wide; one stick silk twist; eight skeins silk; two and one-quarter yards thickset for one vest or breeches; two yards toile gris for one vest or breeches; two and one-half yards shalloon; two yards toile gris for one vest or breeches; four and one-half yards check linen for two vests or breeches; three and one-eighth calendar for three vests and breeches; five-eighths yard sycee for one vest and breeches; and two yards chintz for two vests and breeches.

Capt John Bailey

Sundries issued: 19 and 1/2 yards white linen for six shirts; two yards muslin for six stocks; three-quarters yard fine holland for ruffling; nine skeins white thread; one silk handkerchief; one India handkerchief; four linen handkerchiefs; two pair thread hose; one fine hat (returned); three and one-half yards coarse linen for lining; three yards broadcloth, 7/4 wide; two and three-quarter yards calamanco for one vest or breeches; and three-quarters yard spotted flannel for one vest or breeches.

Received from Capt John Dodge Agent the within sundry goods in part of the clothing allowed by law.

Test: J. Donne

(in behalf of Capt John Bailey)
Lawrence Slaughter, Ensign
Ill^{s} Battalion

Overdrawn by Capt John Bailey four yards osnaburg and 5/8 yard stroud for leggings.

Sep. 10th Issued per rec^{t} of E. Slaughter and order of Lt Col. John Montgomery: one blanket, five yards white flannel and 40 Continental dollars to enlist a recruit.

Capt Richard Brashears

Issued to: one and one-half yards scarlet cloth, 7/4 wide; one and one-half yards broadcloth, 7/4 yards; two and one-half yards shalloon; two yards calendar for two small garments; four yards toile gris for two small garments; eight yards toile gris for four small garments; three yards gray cloth, 7/8 wide for two small garments; nineteen and one-half yards white linen for six shirts; three-quarters yard fine Holland for ruffling; two yards muslin for six stocks, two skeins thread; two and one-half yards check linen for one small garment; two and one-half yards coarse linen for lining; one pair thread hose; one silk handkerchief; one Indian handkerchief; four linen handkerchiefs; four skeins silk, one hat, two and three-quarters yards calamanco for one small garment; and three yards blue cloth, 7/4 wide.

Received from Capt John Dodge, Agent the within mentioned goods in part of the clothing allowed by law.

Test: J. Donne

Jarret Williams, Ensign
Ill^{s} Reg^{t}

Overdrawn by Capt Richard Brashears

Septr 9 Issued per rec^{t} and order of Lt Col. Montgomery, one English blanket.

28 Issued to Capt Brashears: one ivory and one horn comb; three and one-half gallons rum; eight w sugar; four w coffee; and six w soap.

Lt John Girault

Issued to: one and one-half yards brown broadcloth, 7/4 wide; two yards broadcloth, 7/4 wide (damaged); three yards gray cloth, 7/8 wide; two and one-half yards shalloon; four skeins silk; and one stick silk twist.

Issued to make 11 vest and breeches: two, two yards calendar; two, four yards camlet; two and one-half yards dimity; two, two yards chintz; two, four yards toile gris; and two, six yards calamanco, 1/2 yard wide.

Issued to Lt. Girault: one and one-half yards shalloon (error); three and one-half yards coarse linen for lining; one silk handkerchief; one India handkerchief; four check linen handkerchiefs; two yards muslin for six stocks; nineteen and one-half yards white linen for six shirts; three-quarter yards fine holland for ruffling; twelve skeins white thread; two pair thread hose; one pair knee garters, one and one-half yards blue cloth; and one hat.

Issued for one vest or breeches two and one-quarter calamanco, 1/2 yard wide.

Received from Capt John Dodge, Agent the within mentioned quantity of goods, in part of the clothing allowed by law.

Test: J. Donne Girault, L^{t}

Overdrawn by Lt. Girault.

1780 Issued ~~four yards Check~~ error.

Septr 9th Issued per order Lt Col. Montgomery, one English blanket.

Lt Michael Perrault

Issued: three yards brown broadcloth, 7/4 wide; two and one-half yards shalloon; one stick silk twist; three skeins silk; nineteen and one-half yards white linen for six shirts; three-quarters yard white holland for ruffling; and two yards muslin for six stocks.

Issued for 12 vests and breeches: two yards casimir; two and one-half yards chintz; two and one-half yards spotted flannel; three yards camlet; two yards shalloon; four yards toile gris; and two and one-quarter yards check linen.

Issued one silk handkerchief; one India handkerchief; four linen handkerchiefs; eight skeins thread; two pair thread hose; one hat; four yards damaged linen for lining; and three yards broadcloth, 7/4 wide.

Received from Capt John Dodge, Agent the within quantity of goods, in part of the clothing allowed by law.

Test: J. Donne (in behalf of Lieut. Michael Perrault)

A. Rey Surgeon

Overdrawn by Lt. Perrault

Sept 9th Issued per rec^{t} and order of Lt Col. John Montgomery, one English blanket.

Sept 11 Issued two and one-half yards toile gris.

Lt Richard Clark [Note: entire entry x'd out.]

Issued: one and one-half yards scarlet cloth 7/4 wide; one and one-half yards brown cloth; two and one-half yards shalloon; two yards calendar; four yards toile gris; three yards spotted flannel; three yards gray cloth, 7/8 wide; 19 and 1/2 yards white linen; three-quarters yard fine holland; two yards muslin; one pair thread hose; six yards check linen; four skeins silk; one silk handkerchief; one Indian handkerchief; four linen handkerchiefs; twelve skeins thread; and two and one-half dozen buttons.

Jno Rogers

Received from Capt John Dodge, Agent, the within quantity of goods in part of the clothing allowed by law.

Test: J. Donne (on behalf of Lt Richd Clark)
Jno- Rogers Cap^{n}
V. L. D.

Lt Merriwether

Issued: one and one-half yards scarlet cloth, 7/4 wide; one and five-eighth yards brown broadcloth; and two and one-half yards shalloon.

Issued to make four vests and four breeches: two yards calendar; four yards toile gris; three yards spotted flannel; and three yards gray cloth, 7/8 wide.

Issued to Lt. Merriwether: nineteen and one-half yards white linen for six shirts; three-quarters yard fine holland for ruffling; two yards muslin for six stocks; six yards check linen for two vests and two breeches; four skeins silk; twelve skeins thread; one silk handkerchief; one India handkerchief; four linen handkerchiefs, and three yards white cloth, 7/4 wide.

Received from Capt John Dodge, Agent, the above quantity of goods in part of the clothing allowed by law in behalf of Lt James Merriwether.

Test: J. Donne Jno- Rogers, Capt, V.L. Dragoons

Overdrawn by Lt Merriwether, one English blanket and 1/8 brown cloth.

Ensign Jarret Williams

Issued: one and one-half yards scarlet cloth, 7/4 wide; one and one-half yards broadcloth; and two and one-half yards shalloon.

Issued to make five vests and five pair breeches: two yards calendar; four yards toile gris; eight yards toile gris; and three yards gray cloth, 7/8 wide.

Issued to Ensign Jarret Williams: 19 and 1/2 yards white linen for six shirts; two yards muslin for six stocks; three quarters yard fine holland for ruffling; ten skeins thread; two and one-half yards check linen for one pair breeches; two and one-half yards coarse linen for lining; one silk handkerchief; one India handkerchief; four linen handkerchiefs; one hat, two and three-quarters yards black calamanco for breeches; and three yards blue cloth, 7/4 wide.

Received from Capt John Dodge, Agent, the within mentioned quantity of goods in part of the clothing allowed by law.

Test: J. Donne

Jarret Williams, Ensign
Ill^{s} Batt^{n}

Ensign Slaughter

Issued: one and one-half yards broadcloth, 7/4 wide; one and one-half yards scarlet broadcloth; one stick silk twist; two and one-half yards shalloon; and four skeins silk.

Issued to make one vest and one pair breeches, two yards and one quarter thickset and two yards toile gris.

Issued to make three vests or breeches, two yards toile gris and four and one-half yards check linen.

Issued to make three vests or breeches, three and one-eighth yards calendar.

Issued to make two vests or breeches, five-eighths yard sycee and two yards chintz.

Issued to Ensign Slaughter: nineteen and one-half yards linen for six shirts; two yards muslin for six stocks; three-quarters yard fine holland for ruffling; nine skeins thread; one silk handkerchief; one India handkerchief; four linen handkerchiefs; two pair thread hose; one hat; three yards and one half coarse linen for lining; three yards blue cloth, 7/4 wide; two and three-quarters calamanco for one vest; and three-quarters of a yard spotted flannel for one vest.

Received from Capt John Dodge, Agent, the within mentioned quantity of goods in part of the clothing allowed by law.

Test: J. Donne — Lawrence Slaughter, Ensign Ill^s Reg^t

Overdrawn by Ensign Slaughter:

Septr 10. Issued per rec^t and order of Lt Col. Montgomery: one blanket, 1 1/4 yards thickset, and five skeins silk.

Octr 19. Issued by order of Col. Montgomery: one ink holder; one comb; one knife; 10^w sugar; three w coffee; 6lbs soap; one deer skin; 10^w sugar (error); 10^w soap (error); and one bottle rum.

Cornet Thruston

Issued: one and one-half yards scarlet cloth, 7/4 wide; one and five-eighths yards brown cloth; and two and one-half yards shalloon.

Issued for four vests and four breeches: two yards calendar; four yards toile gris; three yards spotted flannel; and three yards gray cloth, 7/8 wide.

Issued to Cornet Thruston: nineteen and one-half yards white linen, for six shirts; three-quarters yard fine holland, for ruffling; two yards muslin for six stocks; six yards check linen for two vests and two breeches; four skeins silk; one silk handkerchief; one India handkerchief; four linen handkerchiefs; twelve skeins thread; three yards white cloth; and one hat (returned).

Received from Capt John Dodge, Agent, the above mentioned quantity of goods, in part of the clothing allowed by law in behalf of Cornet Thruston.

Test: J. Donne — Jno- Rogers, Capt, V.L. Dragoons

Overdrawn by Cornet Thruston: one English blanket, ordered per Capt Rogers; and 1/8 yard brown cloth.

Doctor Rey

Issued: one and one-half yards scarlet cloth, 7/4 wide; one and one-half yards brown cloth; two and one-half yards shalloon; one stick silk twist; three skeins silk; nineteen and one-half yards white linen for six shirts; three-quarters yard fine holland for ruffling; and two yards muslin for six stocks.

Issued to make six vests and six pair breeches: two yards casimir; two and one-half yards chintz; two and one-half spotted flannel; three yards camlet; three yards shalloon; four yards toile gris; and two and one-quarter yards check linen.

Issued to Doctor Rey: one silk handkerchief; one India handkerchief; eight skeins thread; one skein thread; two pair thread hose; one hat; four yards damaged linen for lining; and three yards broadcloth, 7/4 wide.

Received from Capt John Dodge, Agent, the within mentioned quantity of goods in part of the clothing allowed by law.
Test: J. Donne A. Rey Surgeon

Overdrawn by Doctor Rey:

Septr 11 Issued per rec^t and order of Lt Col. Montgomery, one blanket.

Lt MonBreun

Issued: three yards broadcloth 7/4 wide; two yards and a half shalloon; three and 1/2 yards coarse linen for lining; one silk handkerchief; one India handkerchief; four linen handkerchiefs; two yards muslin for six stocks; 19 and 1/2 yards white linen for lining; three-quarters yard fine holland for ruffling; twelve skeins white thread; two pairs thread hose; one pair knee garters; five and one-half yards spotted flannel for three vests; three yards blue cloth, 7/4 wide; and one hat.

Issued to make six breeches and three vests: two yards calendar; four yards camlet; two yards corded dimity, one-half yard camlet; two yards chintz; and four yards toile gris.

Rec^d from Capt John Dodge, Agent, the above mentioned goods in part of the clothing allowed by law.
Test: J. Donne Timothy MonBreun, L^t

Overdrawn by Lt MonBreun

Septr 10 Issued per rec^t and order of Lt Col. Montgomery, one blanket.

25 Issued per order of Lt Col. Montgomery: six yards ferret; one dressed deer skin; four w sugar; two w coffee; 10^W sugar and 10^W soap.

Mr. James Finn, Quartermaster

Issued: nine and three-quarters yards white linen for three shirts; six yards toile gris for three breeches; one yard fine holland for three stocks; three yards damaged linen for lining; ten skeins thread; one silk handkerchief; one linen handkerchief; one ink holder; four and one-half yards camlet for a coat; and one hat.

Issued to Mr. James Finn, Quartermaster for trimmings to his coat: two and one-half yards toile gris, one skein silk; and two skeins thread.

Issued for three trousers, four yards check linen and two and a quarter yards toile gris.

Received from Capt John Dodge, Agent, the above mentioned goods by order of Lt Col. Jno Montgomery.

Test: J. Donne James Finn, Quartermaster

Mr. John Donne, Deputy Conductor

Issued: one and 3/4 yards blue bath coating, 7/4 wide; three yards gray cloth, 7/8 wide (in lieu of 1 1/2 yards of 7/4 wide); three yards coarse linen for lining; five 1/4 yards coarse linen for lining (in lieu of two 1/2 yards shalloon); 21 yards linen for six shirts; two yards cambric for six stocks; and 3/4 yard cambric for ruffling six shirts.

Issued to make six pair breeches: five yards spotted velvet; two and 1/2 yards thickset; two and 1/2 yards check linen; and five yards white linen.

Issued to make six vests, one and 1/2 yards blue persian and three and 3/4 yards ~~Gingham~~ sycee.

Issued to Mr. John Donne, Deputy Conductor: five yards linen handkerchief; one silk handkerchief; one romal handkerchief; four linen check handkerchiefs; 26 skeins thread; four skeins silk; two sticks silk twist; two pair knee garters; six and 1/2 yards ferret; one hat; and two and 3/4 yards white cloth.

Received from Capt John Dodge, Agent, the within mentioned quantity of goods in part of an order drawn on him in my favor by order of Col. George Rogers Clark of the 12th Inst.

Test: Leo^{d} Helm — J. Donne, Deputy Conductor, Western Department

Overdrawn by Deputy Conductor Donne:

Sepr 11 Issued per receipt and order of Lt Col. Montogomery, one blanket.

Capt Leon^{d} Helm, Superintend^{t} of Ind^{n} Affairs

Issued: two yards brown cloth, 7/4 wide; two and 1/2 yards shalloon; and one and 3/4 yards blue bath coating, 7/4 wide.

Issued to make six vests, two and 1/4 yards chintz, two and 1/2 yards cottonade, and one yard chintz.

Issued to make six pair breeches eight and 1/4 yards toile gris, two and 3/4 yards thickset; and ~~two yards toile gris~~ 1 yard chintz.

Issued to Capt Helm: three and 1/2 yards damaged linen for lining; 20 and 3/4 yards linen for six shirts; 3/4 yard fine holland for ruffling; two yards cambric for six stocks; one silk handkerchief; one India handkerchief; and four linen handkerchiefs; two pair thread hose; 16 skeins thread; ~~three ley~~ one stick silk twist; four skeins silk; one hat; and one pair knee garters.

Received from Capt John Dodge, Agent, the within quantity of goods in part of an order drawn on him in my favor by order of Col^{o} George Rogers Clark dated this day.

Test: J. Donne — Leo^{d} Helm, Superintend In^{d} Af.

Overdrawn by Capt Helm Superintendent

Sepr. 13 Issued per order and receipt five w coffee, one English blanket, and one and 1/2 yards ribbon.

Lt Richard Clark

Issued: one and 1/2 yards scarlet cloth, 7/4 wide; one and 1/2 yards brown cloth, 7/4 wide; and two and 3/4 yards shalloon for lining.

Issued to make six vests: two yards calendar; one and 3/4 yards spotted flannel; three yards gray cloth, 7/8 wide; and one and 3/4 yards white casimir; issued to make six breeches, four and 1/2 yards fustian, and six yards check linen.

Issued to Lt Richard Clark: 21 yards fine linen for six shirts; 3/4 yard fine holland for ruffling shirts; two yards muslin for six stocks; four yards coarse linen for lining (damaged); two pair thread hose; one silk handkerchief; one India handkerchief; four check linen handkerchiefs; 17 skeins thread; four skeins silk; one stick silk twist; one hat; two dozen large metal buttons; 1/2 dozen small metal buttons; and three yards blue cloth, 7/4 wide.

Received of Capt John Dodge, Agent, the above quantity of merchandise in part of an order drawn on him in my favor by order of Col. George Rogers Clark, dated the 11th Inst.

Test: J. Donne R^d^ Clark, L^t^
Illinois Reg^t^

Sundry merchandise overdrawn by Lt Clark per receipt of 4th August 1780 say Sept 11. 1780: one English blanket; two handkerchiefs of check linen; two yards silk ferret; one leather ink pot; one fine comb; one coarse comb; seven skeins thread; five yards blue ferret; and four skeins silk.

Major John Williams for his Company

Issued: two ruffled shirts; six plain shirts; fourteen yards blue cloth; twelve yards white flannel; skeins thread, and a dozen buttons.

Issued to Colonel Montgomery for part of the clothing for four men of Capt Quirk's Company: fourteen yards blue cloth; twelve yards white cloth say flannel; four shirts; and thirteen yards linen for four shirts.

Septr 10 Issued per order for Th. Kirk, Gasper Butcher, and S. Stephenson, three shirts.

Issued to Lt John Girault for four men of Maj^r^ Rich^d^ McCarty's Company: fourteen yards blue cloth; twelve yards white flannel; four shirts; and thirteen yards linen for four shirts.

Major McCarty for his Company Septr 10

Per receipt and order of: Lt Col. Montgomery, 63 yards blue cloth and 55 yards flannel.

13 Issued per receipt and order of Lt Col. Montgomery, 14 shirts.

Capt John Bailey for his Company

Issued per Ensign Slaughter: forty-three plain shirts and one ruffled shirt.

Augt 13 Issued to a soldier per C. Bailey, one ruffled and one plain shirt.

Sept. 18 Issued per rect of L. Slaughter and order of Lt Col. Montgomery, 11 blankets.

Capt Abraham Kellar

Issued for his Company per his rect: eighty and one-half yards cloth; sixty-nine yards white flannel; thread and buttons; three ruffled shirts; twenty-four plain ditto; and eleven shirts.

June 30 Issued per order Capt George and rect of James Thompson, eight plain shirts.

Sep. 13 Issued per rect and order of Lt Col. Montgomery, two blankets.

30 Issued per rect and order of Wm Pritchet, one blanket.

Issued to Ensign Slaughter for Captain Bailey's Company by order of Col. Montgomery, two shirts.

Capt Richard Brashears' Co

Issued per receipt of Ensign Jarret Williams for 25 men of Capt Richd Brashears' Company: one ruffled shirt; forty-nine plain shirts; fifty-three plain shirts; twenty-one yards flannel; twenty-four and one quarter yards blue cloth; thread and buttons; and one ink pot to Sergt Brown by Col. Montgomery's orders.

Sep. 13 Issued per rect and order of Lt Col. Montgomery, four blankets.

30 Issued per order Capt. Brashears and rect of John Gils, 10 lb soap.

Capt Worthington's Co **Fort Jefferson Aug. 2, 1780.--**

Issued by order of Capt George and issued to Lt Clark: 14 plain shirts.

12th Issued to Dd Allen per Lt Clark's rect and C. George's order, two shirts.

20 June Issued per order C. George and Rect of Reuben Kemp, three ruffled and three plain shirts.

23 Issued per order and rec^{t} of Reuben Kemp, 15 plain and one ruffled shirt.

Sep. 9 Issued by order of Lt Col. Montgomery for Richd Underwood, and per rec^{t} of Lt Richd Clark: three and one-half yards blue cloth, three yards white flannel, two plain shirts, buttons and thread for cloth.

13 Issued per rec^{t} of R. Clark and order of Lt Col. Montgomery: eight blankets; 18 3/4 yards blue cloth; 15 and 1/2 yards white flannel; and thread and buttons.

Capt John Rogers for his Com^{y}:

July 14 Issued: 78 and 1/2 yards blue cloth; 2 lbs thread; 11 coarse combs; 11 fine combs; three ink pots; two sticks blackball; two pair horse phlegms; 1/2 lb coarse thread ~~24 S~~; and 24 skeins fine thread.

13 Issued: 18 yards osnaburg for saddle pads; one lb thread; and one and 1/2 dozen needles.

10 Issued, 17 ruffled and 45 plain shirts.

Issued for 62 stocks, 11 yards black persian and 15 and 1/2 yards fine linen (damaged).

July 10 Issued per order of Col. Clark, two yards blue persian and one p^{s} silk ferret.

Decr 3 Issued to Serg^{t} Merriwether per order, one check handkerchief.

Issued to Lt Thomas Wilson by order Col. Montgomery, six and 1/2 yards white linen and four and 1/2 yards toile gris.

Issued to 24 men discharged (to take them home) by order of Col. Montgomery per rec^{t} John Wilson Serg^{t}, 24 plain shirts.

Issued in the Indian Department:

July 13 Delivered to Capt Williams by order of Col. Montgomery's orders: seven and 1/2 yards blue stroud; six plain shirts; two and 1/2 yards half-thicks; five yards ribbon (5 ells); and two, 2 1/2 point blankets.

14 Paid Major John Williams for liquor furnished for the Savages in lieu of 120 lb peltry per receipt: three yards blue persian @ 4

D[s] (12); 1/2 yard fine cambric 12 ------- 6; seven and 1/2 yards ribbon one ---- seven and 1/2; thread; one ivory and two horn combs; and seven and 1/2 yards calimanco, two and 1/2 -- 18 3/4 -- 47 1/4.

om[d] June 20th 1780 Issued to a party of friendly Kaskaskia Indians sent to hunt and scout for the garrison while it was weak, and delivered by orders Col. Montgomery: 13 3/4 yards blue stroud for blankets and breech cloths; six 1/4 yards white half-thicks for leggings; 12 yards white linen for shirts; two yards dark green calico for shirts; three scalping knives; two horn combs; eight skeins thread; one bolt ravelled gartering; three linen handkerchiefs; five and 1/2 yards ribbon; one p[s] ribbon; one pair blue stroud leggings; one plain shirt; and two scalping knives.

July 30. Issued: 31 linen handkerchiefs to wear as tokens; 23 yards blue cloth damaged; 13 3/4 yards white half-thicks; 45 yards blue stroud; 15 and 1/2 yards blue stroud; 29 plain shirts; two pairs ravelled gartering; one lb vermilion; one and 1/2[w] thread; 32 scalping knives; one 3/4 yards blue cloth; three ruffled shirts; 15 plain shirts; one small shirt, one 3/4 yards; 1 2 p[s] ribbon; nine, 2 1/2 point blankets; six yards ribbon; one silk handkerchief; one ruffled shirt; one plain shirt; one pair half-thicks; three yards ribbon; one linen check handkerchief; one pair blue stroud half-thicks; one coarse hat bought for 20 dollars paper cur[y]; four yards white flannel; two linen check handkerchiefs; two pairs garters; four scalping knives; two yards ribbon; and eight yards white flannel for hunting shirts.

Aug[t]	28	paid Duplasse his account for bread and tobacco.....	24..0..0
		paid Joneast his account of bread, pork, etc........	145 -----
	29	paid Nich[s] Canada for his account of smithwork per rec[t]..	40 -----
Sept[r]	9	paid Th[s] Bentley for his account....................	93 -----
		paid Tourangean for tafia for the Indians...........	100 -----
	11	paid Fleure d'Epec for repairs on Indian arms.......	40 -----
om[d]	Aug 23.	paid Tourangean for tafia for the Indians.........	100 -----
		paid Tourangean for tafia for the Indians...........	30 -----
			572

four yards flannel for a hunting shirt made
two lbs vermilion
one ruffled shirt

Sept. 4. Issued to Indian department: two ruffled shirts; four plain shirts; nine yards blue cloth (damaged); three and 3/4 yards blue stroud; three yards blue cloth; one English blanket; one, two and 1/2 point blanket, one and 1/2 yards blue cloth for a stroud; 5/8 yard blue cloth for leggings; two yards flannel; one ruffled shirt; six plain shirts; four pcs. containing 200 yards linen; 145 yards white flannel; 50 scalping knives; one, 2 1/2 point blankets; one stroud, one and 3/4 yards; one and 1/4 yards stroud; two linen shirts; four calico shirts; two pieces ribbon; eight gallons tafia; 5/8 yard stroud for leggings; 1/2 yard stroud for breech cloth; 15^{W} flour; one, 2 1/2 point blanket; three gallons tafia; 17 scalping knives; 5/8 yard stroud for leggings; two yards ribbon; four gallons tafia; six check handkerchiefs; one and 1/4 yards blue stroud for two pair leggings; three calico shirts; three and 1/4 yards blue stroud; six yards white linen for two shirts; two white blankets, 2 1/2 points; 16^{W} tobacco; one English blanket; 15 bushels corn; one c^{W} flour; six yards ribbon; six linen shirts; three calico shirts; twenty-four bushels corn; and one c^{W} flour.

Paid to Misere for ferriage, 6^{W} sugar.

Paid to Pierre Gamlin for tafia, five ells.

Issued to the Indian Department: six gallons tafia; four bushels corn; 10^{W} brown sugar; 50^{W} flour; 20^{W} tobacco; 15 combs; 16 scalping knives; two pair ravelled gartering six w coffee; five w brown sugar; one hat; three gallons tafia; two shirts -- plain; 10 bushels corn; 60^{W} flour; three bags - six ells each; 10^{W} tobacco; five bushels corn; 15^{W} flour; 33^{W} bread; five gallons tafia; 12^{W} soap; six w brown sugar; three bushels corn; six check handkerchiefs; two pieces ribbon; two dozen fine combs; one d^{o} coarse comb; 100^{W} flour; four gallons tafia; 17^{W} lead; 20^{W} lead; one bushel salt; 1/2 bushel salt; 10^{W} lead; 1/2 bushel salt; 15^{W} tobacco; 1/2 bushel salt; four d^{o} corn; four looking glasses; four yards gilt lace; two quarts tafia; and two w vermilion.

Paid Isaac Levy 35 livres and 10 dollars for tafia and tobacco.

Paid I. Camp 16 livres for medicine, etc., for the interpreter.

Paid I. Camp 12 livres peltry and cash for a keg for the Savages.

Paid Isaac Levy 193L peltry per receipt for 20 and 1/2 gallons tafia.

Paid Cap[t] Joneast 10 dollars cash per receipt for sundries for Indians at different times 675.

Paid Lafortaine 10 dollars cash per receipt for interpreting 10 days.

Paid Canada 120 livres for repairing Indian arms and 200 flour.

Paid Gratiot 45 livres peltry, for tafia.

Paid Gratiot L7.10[S] peltry for two and 1/2[W] tobacco.

Paid Gratiot 100 livres peltry for five w vermilion.

Paid Gratiot 45 livres peltry, for three ells ticking given for tobacco for Indians.

Paid Major Bosseron four ells cotton de 16 sachaque, for assisting me in the Indian Department at O'Post.

Paid Chapeau three check handkerchiefs, for carrying a speech to the Savages.

Issued to a friendly Indian Chief, eight yards red calimanco, and 1/2 yard casimir, three yards linen for a coat and jacket.

Sept[r] 20 Issued to Major Williams, Commandant at Cahokia, per his order for the Potawatomi Chiefs for four shirts, 13 yards linen.

Issued to the friendly Savages, three clasp knives and six pair scissors.

Paid Tourangean 35 livres peltry, for pork and tafia.

Paid sheriff 554 Cont[l] dollars, for corn and two corn fields, and for the use of the friendly Savages who came to our assistance in time of danger.

Issued to the Indian Department: 11 yards blue cloth; nine yards white flannel; three and 1/2 yards linen; one yard toile gris; thirty skeins thread; four carrots tobacco; one and 3/4 yards cloth; one check handkerchief.

Paid the sheriff for corn and two corn fields &ea &ea for the use of the friendly savages who came to our assistance in time of danger, 554 Doll[s] Cont[l].

Issued to the Indian Department: 11 yards cloth say blue cloth; 9 yards white flannel; three and 1/2 yards linen; one yard toile gris; 30 skeins thread; four carrots tobacco; one and 3/4 yards cloth; and one check handkerchief.

Lt Dalton — Fort Jefferson the 11th Septr 1780

Issued in part of the clothing allowed by law: five yards cotton sesheque; four yards spotted flannel; two and 1/2 yards corded dimity; eight yards camlet; thirteen skeins thread; two and 3/4 yards cambric; and 21 yards white linen.

Overdrawn by Lt Valentine T. Dalton

Septr 10. Issued per order and Lt Col. John Montgomery, four w coffee and one English blanket.

My [Dodge's] own use — Fort Jefferson 18th June 1780

Issued: six yards brown broadcloth, 7/4 wide; two and 1/2 yards shalloon; 5/12 dozen metal buttons; two sticks silk twist; six skeins silk; and one pair knee garters.

Issued for six vests and six breeches: six yards white casimir; two and 1/2 yards corduroy; four yards chintz; two and 1/2 yards corduroy; two and 1/2 yards thickset; one and 1/4 yards spotted persian; and four and 1/2 yards cottonade.

Issued 21 yards linen for six shirts; and 3/4 yard fine holland for ruffling.

Issued for six stocks, one yard fine holland and one yard cambric.

Issued for my [Dodge's] own use: three pair thread hose; two silk handkerchiefs; one red cotton handkerchief; one India handkerchief; two linen check handkerchiefs; one hat; two pairs shoes; and two pairs silk hose.

July 17	Issued eight and 1/2 yards coarse linen for sheets at..................................	6^{drs}	5	6
20	Issued to washerwoman from house expense account, four and 1/2 yards white linen........			
	Issued from house expense account, one paper pin. [No entry]			

(continued)

(continued)

Septr 9	Paid Moses Henry, four ells black calimanco			
	six yards ferret....................................	3		
	three skeins silk....................................	1		
	one ivory comb....................................	1		
	one and 1/2^{w} sugar....................................	1	6	
	one snaffle bridle....................................	2	4	--
	ten skeins silk....................................	2	--	
	three ells ticking bought from Gratiot, 45 L Peltry....................................	9	--	
	twelve ells linen....................................	12	--	
	ten w soap (house expense)....................................			
		29	5	2

Israel Dodge, Deputy Agent **Fort Jefferson 23^{d} June 1780**

Issued: two yards brown cloth, 7/4 wide; three and 1/2 yards blue bath coating, 7/4 wide; two and 1/2 yards shalloon; four and 1/4 dozen metal buttons; two sticks silk twist; six skeins; and one pair knee garters.

Issued to Israel Dodge to make six vests and six pair breeches: five yards cottonade; three yards chintz; two yards toile gris; two and 1/2 yards thickset; four and 1/4 yards casimir; and two and 1/2 yards chintz.

Issued to Israel Dodge: four yards damaged linen for lining; 21 yards linen for six shirts; 3/4 yard fine holland for ruffling; two yards brittannias for six stocks; one silk handkerchief; one India handkerchief; three linen check handkerchiefs; three pair thread hose; and one hat.

James Sherlock, Indian and French Interpreter **July 16**

Issued by order of Capt Robert George, Commandant, for one coat: one and 1/2 yards brown broadcloth, 7/4 wide; one and 1/2 yards shalloon; 1/8 yard scarlet cloth; two and 1/2 dozen buttons; three skeins silk, one stick silk twist, skeins thread, and two yards coarse linen (damaged).

Issued to James Sherlock, for one capote: three and 1/2 yards gray cloth, 7/8 wide; six yards silk ferret for binding; four skeins silk, and four skeins thread.

Issued to James Sherlock, for one summer coat: two and 1/2 yards chintz; two and 1/2 yards linen for lining; and four skeins thread.

Issued James Sherlock, for three vests and two pair breeches: four and 3/4 yards corded dimity; three and 1/2 yards linen for lining; two and 1/2 yards gray cloth, 7/8 wide; one and 1/4 yards cotton 16 de sacheque; skeins silk, and ten skeins thread.

Issued to James Sherlock for two pair trousers, five yards cottonade.

Issued to James Sherlock: four skeins silk thread, four ruffled shirts; four cambric stocks; one silk handkerchief; one romal handkerchief; two check linen handkerchiefs; two pairs thread hose, and one stock hat.

Patrick Kennedy, Assistant Conductor of Stores

Issued: nine and 3/4 yards linen for three shirts; one and 5/8 yards fine holland for three stocks and ruffling for shirts; three and 3/4 yards calendar for three vests; and four and 5/8 yards check linen for three pair trousers.

Issued to Patrick Kennedy for three pair breeches, three and 1/4 yards toile gris and two and 1/2 yards corded dimity.

Issued to Patrick Kennedy: four and 1/4 yards linen for lining; one ink pot; one ivory and one horn comb; and one pair garters.

Issued to Patrick Kennedy per order of Capt Robert George, 15 skeins thread.

Issued to Patrick Kennedy per order of Capt Rogers, six check handerkerchiefs.

Mr. Blackford, Deputy Commissary of Issues

Issued: three and 3/4 yards sycee for three vests and nine and 3/4 yards white linen for three shirts.

Issued to Mr. Blackford to make three pair trousers: five and 1/4 yards cottonade and two and 1/2 yards toile gris.

Issued to Mr. Blackford one and 1/2 yards muslin for three stocks and ruffling; two linen handkerchiefs; nine skeins white thread; one brass ink pot; and three and 3/4 yards linen for lining for jackets.

The above issues to Mr. Blackford were ordered by Capt Robert George.

Capt. Lt. Richard Harrison **June 10, 1780**

Issued: six yards superfine broadcloth; two and 1/2 yards shalloon; three pairs thread hose; five and 1/4 dozen metal buttons; two sticks silk twist; six skeins silk; 12 skeins thread; and one fine hat.

Issued to Capt. Lt. Richard Harrison, for six vests and six pair breeches: eight yards casimir; ten yards thickset; seven and 1/2 yards corduroy; one yard spotted persian; and two and 1/2 yards linen.

Issued to Capt. Lt. Richard Harrison: 19 and 1/2 yards linen; two and 3/4 yards cambric; one silk handkerchief, one romal handkerchief; two cotton handkerchiefs; and two linen handkerchiefs.

The above is a true inventory of the articles issued to Capt Lt Richard Harrison, agreeable to his rec^t taken in Receipt Book A. Certified by me

J. Donne

William Clark, Secretary to Col. Clark **12 June 1780**

Issued for three vests and three pair breeches: five and 1/4 yards fustian; five yards spotted velvet; and two and 1/2 yards sycee.

Issued to William Clark: nine and 3/4 yards linen for three shirts; 3/8 yard cambric for ruffling shirts; one yard muslin for three stocks; two pair thread hose; one silk handkerchief, one check linen handkerchief; thirteen skeins thread; four skeins silk; one stick silk twist; two and 1/2 yards linen for lining vests and breeches; and five yards toile gris for two pair trousers.

The above is a true inventory of the articles issued to Secretary Clark as taken from Receipt Book A., agreeable to his receipt therein by me.

J. Donne

June 17th Issued one hat.

Samuel Smyth, Surgeon, Illinois Department 12 June 1780

Issued for three vests and three breeches: seven and 1/2 yards spotted cotton velvet; one yard spotted persian; two and 1/2 yards ginghams or check; and seven and 1/2 yards linen for lining.

Issued to Samuel Smyth: one and 3/4 yards blue bath coating; seven and 1/2 yards linen for three pairs trousers; nine and 3/4 yards for three shirts; one silk handkerchief; one romal handkerchief; one check linen handkerchief; one and 3/8 yards cambric for three stocks and ruffling three shirts; two sticks silk twist; 15 skeins thread; four skeins silk; one pair knee garters; and six yards ferret.

The above is a true inventory of the articles issued to Samuel Smyth, Surgeon, agreeable to his receipt taken in Receipt Book A. Certified by me. J. Donne

June 14th Issued one clasp knife; one ivory and one horn comb; 1/4 yard white halfthicks for leggings; 1/2 yard bath coating for a breech cloth; four yards gartering for binding; one brass ink stand; one pair blankets, two and 1/2 point, and one bridle.

The above also issued to Surgeon Smyth by order of Capt. Robt George Commdt agreeable to Col. Clark's orders Inventory and rect taken from Receipt Book A by me. J. Donne

Martin Carney, Deputy Quartermaster 14th June 1780

Issued: three yards brown cloth, 7/4 wide, and three yards shalloon; five yards spotted cotton velvet; two and 1/4 yards linen for lining the vest and breeches; 19 and 1/2 yards linen for six shirts; two yards muslin for six stocks, 3/4 yards fine holland for ruffling six yards; one silk handkerchief; one India handkerchief; one red cotton handkerchief; one blue handkerchief; two check linen handkerchiefs; two sticks silk twist; two skeins silk; 12 skeins thread; one pair knee garters; five dozen metal buttons; and one fine hat.

Issued to Martin Carney, for six vests and six pairs breeches: six yards casimir; two and 1/2 yards thickset; four and 1/2 yards cottonade; and five yards sycee.

The above is a true inventory of the articles issued to Martin Carney, Deputy Quartermaster, agreeable to his receipt taken from receipt Book A by me. J. Donne

Capt William Shannon, Conductor General June 12

Issued by orders of Capt Robt George Comd^{t} per Capt Shannon's receipts: five yards check linen for two pair trousers; two and 3/4 yards thickset for one pair breeches; 1 1/2 yards linen for lining; 1/2 yard blue bath coating for breech cloth; one, two 1/2 point blanket; one snaffle bridle; one clasp knife; one ink holder; one stick silk twist; and one ivory and one horn comb.

13th Issued to Capt William Shannon: 1/2 yard white linen; 1/4 yard check linen; one Indian handkerchief; one silk handkerchief; one linen handkerchief; one pair scissors; and six skeins thread.

14th Issued to Capt William Shannon, three yards fine ribbon.

Captain Robert George D^{d} June 15

For sundry articles taken out of the public store for which no return or receipt has been passed.

Two 1/8 yards super fine gray cloth 7/4 wide.

Issued, four yards brown cloth, 7/4 wide, 1/4 overdrawn.

July 5 Issued 1/8 yard scarlet cloth, 7/4 wide and four yards fine white casimir.

Issued for six breeches and six vests, three and 3/4 yards sycee and eight and 3/4 yards chintz.

Issued: 21 yards fine white linen for six shirts; 3/4 yard fine holland for ruffling shirts; two yards fine holland for six stocks; three silk handkerchiefs; three red silk and cotton handkerchiefs; two and 1/2 yards white linen for lining; two and 1/2 yards shalloon for lining; five and 7/12 dozen metal buttons (2/12 dozen overdrawn); five skeins silk; and two skeins silk twist.

Overdrawn by one skein each, 12 skeins fine white thread, and 12 skeins coarse thread.

Issued: 1/4 yard super fine broadcloth, 7/4 wide; one and 1/8 yards chintz; two and 1/2 yards shalloon; one and 3/4 yards linen; one pair scissors; six skeins fine white thread; six skeins coarse white thread; one snaffle bridle; one ruffled shirt; three and 1/2 yards osnaburg; one skein thread; and two metal buttons.

23^{d} Issued four ruffled shirts per order for soldiers going for provisions.

30 Issued five yards cottonade for self.

10 Issued per order issued to Capt Harrison: 26 yards blue stroud; 32 ruffled shirts; 20 plain shirts; 26 butcher knives; one ink holder; one bridle, and 26 skeins thread.

12 Delivered to Capt Harrison, per order and receipt: three clasp knives; two horn and one ivory combs; one and 1/2 yards white half thicks; 1/2 yard blue bath coating; four yards gartering; two, two and 1/2 point blankets; and one leather ink pot.

Delivered to Sg^{t} Walker per order and receipt: two pair thread hose; five and 1/2 yards cottonade; and 12 yards ferret.

12 Issued to Capt Harrison per his receipt: three, 2 1/2 point blankets; 26 horn combs; 13 ivory combs; two and 1/2 yards blue bath coating; and six skeins thread.

Per order and rec^{t} of Martin Carney, 24 yards osnaburg, 15 skeins thread.

13 Per order and rec^{t} of Wm Moore, four, 2 1/2 point blankets.

Per order and rec^{t} of Mark Eyler, 4 yards black calimanco.

14 Per order and rec^{t} John Walker: one ruffled shirt, one plain shirt; one hat; and one, two and 1/2 point blanket.

19 Delivered to Capt George, per order and no rec^{t}, 23 plain and 23 ruffled shirts.

Per order and receipt of Martin Carney: one brass ink pot; one large clasp knife; one ivory and one horn comb; and six yards ferret.

20 Per order and receipt of John Donne: one ink pot; one ivory and one horn comb.

22 Per order and receipt of Andrew Clark: five yards toile gris; one check linen handkerchief; one ivory comb; one horn comb and two skeins thread.

Per order and rec^{t} of Joseph Anderson, one brass ink stand.

28 Per order and rec^{t} of John Johnson, eight plain shirts.

July 3 Per order and rec^{t} of John Donne, one pair garters.

Per order and receipt of Joseph Anderson, two and 1/2 yards half-thicks.

July 13 Issued per order and receipt of Fred Guyon: three and 1/2 yards blue cloth; three yards white flannel; two ruffled shirts; and thread and buttons for clothes.

Issued per order and receipt of Capt Abraham Kellar: one horn comb; one scalping knife; and one ink stand.

14 Issued per order and receipt Fred Guyon, one ivory comb and one horn comb.

Issued per order and receipt Richard Sinett, four plain shirts.

21 Issued per order and receipt Joshua Archer: two and 1/2 yards half-thicks; one yard blue stroud; and one linen handkerchief.

29 Issued per order and receipt Peter Wagoner, one hat.

Augt 3 Issued per order and receipt John Donne, six w coffee.

Issued per order and receipt William Clark, 18^{W} coffee.

8 Issued per order and receipt Martin Carney: one English blanket, one snaffle bridle; and one stick black ball.

10 Issued per order and receipt Richards Hopkins, one scalping knife.

12 Issued per order and receipt Capt George, four plain shirts.

14 Issued per order and receipt D. Bolton, two and 1/2 yards toile gris.

15 Issued per order and receipt Richard Hopkins, one English blanket.

19 Issued per order and receipt John Ash: one ivory comb; one horn comb; and one scalping knife.

Issued per order and receipt Robert George: 21 yards blue cloth; 18 yards white flannel; and thread and buttons.

Issued per order and receipt Richard Clark, 14[w] coffee.

Issued per order and receipt F. Guyon, one ink pot (omitted July 11).

Aug 24 Issued per order and receipt R. Camp, one scalping knife.

25 Issued per order and receipt Thomas Leney, eight plain shirts.

Sep 13 Issued per order and receipt, one, two and 1/2 point blanket.

Issued per order of L[t] Col. Montgomery and receipt of L[t] Dalton for use of his Company, 12, two and 1/2 point blankets.

Issued per order to Company, 10 shirts.

Issued to Martin Carney, per receipt, for making cartridges, 10 yards white flannel and 15 skeins thread.

Issued to dress a wounded man, 1/2 yard white linen, and one piece ravelled gartering.

Issued per order 10 plain shirts, and 11, two and 1/2 point blankets.

19 Issued per order, 1/4 yard white cloth.

22 Issued per order, seven yards linen, and two skeins thread.

24 Issued per order, 5/8 yards blue cloth.

25 Issued per order, five skeins thread.

26 Issued per order, ~~19 and 1/2 yards linen~~ (error)

om[d] 15 Issued per order, eight yards white flannel.

30 Issued per order, four yards white flannel.

Oct 11 Issued per order, six shirts.

13 Issued per order, one yard flannel.

14 Issued per order, 12 yards flannel and six skeins thread.

15 Issued per order: seven yards blue cloth; six yards flannel, and 12 skeins thread.

om^{d} Aug: 27th Issued to John Ash, per order, one and 1/4 yards blue stroud and three pair moccasins.

Acco^{t} of House Expenses:

Issued from the account of house expenses: two and 1/2 yards ribbon; two red handkerchiefs; one clasp knife; one ink pot; eight skeins thread; one ivory comb; one horn comb; one lb coffee; one scalping knife; two yards white flannel; two yards coarse linen; one yard osnaburg; one d^{o} coarse linen to pay for a bag lost by Mr. Lindsay; two scalping knives; one w coffee; one yard ribbon; one India handkerchief; one check linen handkerchief; two dozen fine combs; one dozen fine combs; one silk handkerchief; one snaffle bridle; eight yards camlet; one coarse linen handkerchief; three and 1/4 yards black persian; one and 1/2 yards gauze; one ink holder; two yards ribbon; one yard ribbon; one check handkerchief, paid for two brooms for the store; two yards check; 10^{W} coffee; 20^{W} sugar; eight gallons rum; 10 gallons tafia; and three ells osnaburg for finding a horse.

Paid Gratiot for 70^{W} sugar, 105 livres peltry out of house expense account.

Paid Charles Charleville for flour and pork, 18 ells osnaburg out of the house expense account.

Paid a woman for sundry kitchen services, six yards camlet out of the house expense account.

Paid Mr. John Dodge for sundry articles taken with him to bear his expenses while on public business: 12 yards calimanco; 74 livres, George Slaughter; three and 3/4 yards camlet; eleven check handkerchiefs; three check handkerchiefs; ten paper pins; three paper pins; four razors; three horse phlegms; seven snaffle bridles; and four w coarse thread.

Delivered to Capt Roberts for John Dodge: two and 1/2 yards calimanco; four and 1/2 yards cotton 16 schachque; and two bolts gartering.

Delivered to George Slaughter for John Dodge: five paper ink holders; 10/12 dozen coarse combs; eight fine combs; and one and 1/2^w fine white thread.

State of Virginia to Store: D^d

1780

June 8 Issued to Major Harlan per order Col. Clark for expresses, two 1/4 yards blue cloth, and three scalping knives.

Issued to Martin Carney, Quartermaster, per receipt and order of Col. Clark, four quire writing paper.

Issued to Martin Carney per order of Col. Clark for going to the Falls of the Ohio, six quire writing paper.

9 Issued to Commissary Department per order Col. Clark, two quire writing paper.

Issued for the use of the Commanding Officer per order of Col. Clark, two quire writing paper.

13 Issued to Dr. Walker and his party, per order of Col. Clark: 12 and 1/2 yards cottonade for five pair overalls; two and 1/2 yards toile gris, for one pair drawers; 22 3/4 yards linen for seven shirts; 3/8 yards muslin for ruffling three shirts; one yard blue cloth for one pair leggings; 1/2 yard blue coating for breechcloth; one scalping knife; four and 1/2 yards worsted binding; one pair garters; one ivory comb; and three and one-fourth yards osnaburg for one shirt.

10 Issued for the use of express to the Falls of the Ohio per order of Col. Clark: one and 3/4 yards blue bath coating; one and 1/2 yards scarlet cloth; one yard blue cloth; 12 yards ribbon; two skeins silk; one clasp knife; one pair scissors; one pair ravelled gartering; one w vermilion; and three ruffled shirts, three and three quarter yards each.

16 Issued to Daniel Bolton per order of Capt George, Commandant for making cartridges for the cannon: two and 1/2 yards white flannel; two and 1/2 yards osnaburg; one pair scissors; eight skeins twine; and two needles.

20 Issued to Mary Smith per order Capt George and rec^t for making

one suit of soldiers clothes, four yards flannel.

21 Issued to John Bryan per order Capt George and receipt for making soldiers clothing: one pair chintz N° 23; six and 3/4 yards white linen; one paper pins; two silk handkerchiefs; and one and 1/2 yards ribbon.

July 3 Issued to Joseph Duncan, Samuel Watkins and Jno Cox per order of Capt George for bringing provisions, 16 1/4 yards white linen and three 1/4 yards check linen.

13 Issued to Shadrach Bond per order of Col. Montgomery for public services: six and 1/2 yards linen; two 3/4 yards osnaburg; and four skeins thread.

14 Issued per order of Col. Clark in favor of John White for public services, paid to John Williams per his receipt:

eight yards white linen @ two and 1/2 D^{s}.........	20
one embroidered apron............................	20
two paper pins..................................	2
one English blanket.............................	16
nine and 1/2 yards white linen 2 1/2.............	23 3/4
two and 1/2 yards calimanco 2 1/2.............	6 1/4
	86 3/4
thread..	4/3
	88 1/3

[Not correct total]

15 Issued per order Col. Montgomery for Anne Elms, nurse in the hospital per her rec^{t}, seven yards calico.

17 Issued for the use of the wounded men: five and 1/2 yards linen (damaged); one yard ribbon; and one p^{s} gartering.

Issued to A. Lockart per his receipt, for honing and setting public razors which were damaged, one check linen handkerchief.

20 Issued per order of Col. Montgomery to D. Bolton per his receipt, in lieu of 15 days public work, three yards white linen.

Augt 9 Issued per order Capt George to Lawrence Keinan per his receipt, for making cannon cartridges, three yards white flannel.

om^{d} June 16th

Paid to William Clark per order of Col. John Todd in lieu of 20 Spanish milled dollars for his services in bringing to this place a quality of cloth saved from Col. Rogers' defeat:

	Doll^{s}
one pair, two and 1/2 point blankets....................	15 1/2
one check linen handkerchief...........................	1
one brass ink pot	1
one large clasp knife..................................	1/2
four yards ribbon	2
	20

20 Issued to Zeph. Blackford by order of Capt. George, to purchase provisions and disposed of agreeable to the return made me for 187 hard dollars: one pair damask, five 1/8 yards; one pair flowered lawn, 13 yards; five ells ribbon; one dozen check linen handkerchiefs; one p^{s} chintz N° 12; one p^{s} chintz N° 6; and one p^{s} chintz N° 10.

Paid for writing paper, two India handkerchiefs.

Exchanged for a set of buttons for the interpreters clothes, two and 1/2 yards osnaburg and one yard linen.

Issued six yards osnaburg made into bags for public use.

Paid to Mr. John Girault in lieu of his charge for assisting in translating in public business: one and 1/2 yards shaloon; one ink pot; one ivory and one horn comb; and three yards ribbon.

om^{d} 15 Paid Nancy Hunter per receipt for making six ruffled shirts, one silk and one India handkerchief.

om^{d} 16 Paid Marg^{t} Bolting for making six plain shirts, three yards calico.

Paid N. Dolirhide for making three ruffled shirts, four and 1/2 yards ribbon.

Paid Mary Brien for making six plain shirts, three and 1/4 yards calico.

Paid Mary Damewood for making three ruffled shirts, one and 1/2 yards calico.

Paid M. Brien for making six plain shirts, three yards calico.

Paid Mary Damewood for making three plain shirts, three yards calico.

Paid M. Brien for making seven plain shirts, three and 1/4 yards calico.

16 Paid R. Yates for making three ruffled shirts per receipt, one silk handkerchief.

Paid Mary Lunsford for making five plain shirts, one India and two check linen handkerchiefs.

Paid E. Phelps for making six ruffled and six plain shirts per receipt, five yards calico.

Paid Mary Groots for making six ruffled and six plain shirts per receipt, five yards calico.

Paid B. King for making six ruffled and six plain shirts per receipt, five yards calico.

Paid E. Burk for making six ruffled and six plain shirts per receipt, five yards calico.

Paid M. Shilling for making three ruffled and three plain shirts per receipt: one and 1/2 yards calico, one ivory comb, and 3/8 yard muslin.

Paid Sarah Burk for making six ruffled and one plain shirts, two yards calico and two linen handkerchiefs.

Paid Ann Johnson for making 12 ruffled and 24 plain shirts, 11 and 1/4 yards calico.

Paid C. King for making six ruffled shirts, one and 1/2 yards calico and two linen handkerchiefs.

Paid F. Breeding for making seven plain shirts: one and 1/2 yards chintz; one linen handkerchief; one horn comb; and one pair scissors.

17 Paid M. Young for making nine plain shirts, two and 3/4 yards calico and one linen handkerchief.

Paid E. Johnson for making six ruffled and 12 plain shirts, five yards calico.

Paid E. McCormick for making five ruffled shirts per receipt, one and 1/4 yards calico; one ivory and one horn comb.

Paid E. Wolf for making three ruffled and 15 plain shirts, five yards calico and one paper pin.

Paid Sarah Smith for making nineteen plain shirts, five and 1/4 yards calico.

19 Paid R. Ford for making six plain shirts, two India handkerchiefs.

Paid E. Ford for making six plain shirts: one India handkerchief, one linen handkerchief, and one coarse handkerchief.

Paid C. Owens for making 10 plain shirts, five linen handkerchiefs.

Paid Esther Ford for making six plain shirts per receipt, two linen handkerchiefs and two and 3/4 yards ribbon.

Paid M. Bolton for washing stains out of damaged linen, two yards white linen.

21 Paid S. Burk for making 11 plain shirts, two silk handkerchiefs and one India handkerchief.

Paid Mary Shilling for making six plain shirts, two India handkerchiefs.

Paid S. Winn for making three ruffled shirts, one silk handkerchief.

Paid S. Winn for making six shirts and five trousers, two and 3/4 yards calico and one and 1/4 yards ribbon.

Paid J. Witzel for making ten plain shirts, two India and two linen handkerchiefs.

Paid M. Means for making 12 plain shirts, one and 1/2 yards calico, two India handkerchiefs, and one linen handkerchief.

23 Paid C. Kimly for making three ruffled and three plain shirts, one and 1/4 yards calico and one India handkerchief.

Paid S. Winn for making three plain shirts, one India handkerchief.

Paid R. Kennedy for making four plain shirts, one silk handkerchief.

24 Paid E. Piggot for making three ruffled and four plain shirts: one India handkerchief, two linen handkerchiefs, one paper pins, and one ivory comb.

Paid Jane Archer for making six ruffled shirts: one blue cotton handkerchief; one linen handkerchief; three yards ribbon; one paper pins; and one pair scissors.

26 Paid Andrew McMeans for making two ruffled and nine plain shirts per receipt: 1/2 paper pins; one pair scissors; three and 1/2 yards narrow ribbon; four linen handkerchiefs; and one paper pins.

27 Paid Mary Grootz for making three plain shirts: one ivory comb; one pair scissors; and one paper pins.

Paid M. Lockart for making three plain shirts, one India handkerchief.

28 Paid L. Meredith for making four plain shirts, one India handkerchief and one ivory comb.

Paid E. Phelps for making ten shirts: four linen handkerchiefs; one pair scissors; and one ivory comb.

Paid Ann Helms for making one plain shirt, one paper pins.

29 Paid Charlotte King for making four plain shirts, one India handkerchief, and one yard ribbon.

July 5 Paid Judy King for making six plain shirts, three yards white flannel.

Paid Sidy Smith for making six ruffled shirts, two and 1/4 yards calico, and two and 1/2 yards ribbon.

Paid M. Brien for making eight plain shirts, two India and two coarse check handkerchiefs.

Paid F. McMeans for making six plain shirts, one fine linen and four coarse handkerchiefs.

6 Paid R. Kennedy for making five plain shirts, one India handkerchief, and one linen handkerchief.

Paid E. McCormick for making 14 plain shirts, six yards white flannel, and one razor.

Paid F. Breeding for making ten plain shirts and one pair leggings, five linen handkerchiefs, and one yard ribbon.

6 Paid L. Meredith for making one plain shirt, one coarse linen handkerchief.

14 Paid John Williams for making 40 plain shirts: 20 yards osnaburg; 12 linen handkerchiefs; three and 3/4 yards ribbon; and one paper pins.

Paid E. Phelps for making three plain shirts, one pair scissors and two paper pins.

15 Paid M. Murray for making three plain shirts, one pair scissors and one linen handkerchief.

Paid N. Hunter for making ten plain and three ruffled shirts, seven yards calico.

17 Paid M. McMeans for making three ruffled and three plain shirts: one linen handkerchief; three yards ribbon; one pair scissors; one ivory comb; and one horn comb.

24 Paid J. Piggott for making seven plain shirts, seven yards damaged linen.

Aug. 16 Paid E. Spairinger for plowing and harrowing a turnip patch, for public use, 1/2 yard blue stroud.

Paid C. Kimley for making two hunting shirts, one linen handkerchief.

18 Paid John Bryan for making a suit of clothes for the interpreter: 3/4 yard black persian; 1/2 yard thickset; six yards binding; and two linen handkerchiefs.

Paid L. Meredith for making four hunting shirts, two linen handkerchiefs.

Paid F. Little for opening and drying public clothes, one pair blue stroud leggings.

Paid F. Breeding for making two hunting shirts, one linen handkerchief.

Aug. 22^{d} Paid Anne Elms for making one hunting and three plain shirts, two linen handkerchiefs and one coarse comb.

Paid L. Meredith for making one plain shirt, one paper pins.

26 Paid E. Wolf for making five plain shirts, three yards white flannel.

" Paid E. Wolf for doubling and twisting six lb twine, for making a net for public use, one yard flannel and two yards ribbon.

27 Issued per order, delivered for use of the artillery, per rec^{t} M. Carney, [No entry] yards flannel and thread.

Septr 2 Issued per order paid to J. Archer per rec^{t} for going express to Kaskaskia in time of an attack, five and 1/2 yards linen.

Issued per order of R. George, paid transporting provisions from Illinois, per rec^{t} of Mr. Carney: ten yards white linen and two linen handkerchiefs.

11 Issued per order Col. Montgomery and rec^{t} of Richd Clark, for 14 days services as engineer at Kaskaskia, seven yards linen.

Issued to John Ash for going express per order of Lt Col. Montgomery, one, 2 1/2 point blanket, and one shirt.

19 Issued per Z. Blackford's receipt, paid to Madam Valley for 52 bushels corn, 1417^{W} flour and six empty barrels, paid by order of Lt Col. Montgomery, 29 ells blue cloth and 85 ells white flannel.

20 Issued to Z. Blackford in lieu of 100 dollars worth of goods, per receipt and voucher, to purchase provisions for Fort Jefferson.

23 Issued per order of Col. Montgomery, to buy powder, 19 and 1/2 yards linen.

Sep. 3 Delivered to Patrick Kennedy, Esquire, Deputy Conductor per his receipt and Lt Col. Montgomery's orders to purchase provisions for the relief of Fort Jefferson: 10 ells blue stroud; 10 ells blue cloth; 20 yards osnaburg; 8, two 1/2 point blankets; four 3/8 ells fine linen; 24 ells fine linen; eight ells flowered muslin; six yards spotted flannel; 12 yards calico; nine and 7/8 yards linen; and seven check handkerchiefs.

27 Paid to Windsor Pipes per receipt, for 50 bushels Indian corn: 12 yards white linen; two gallons tafia; two check handkerchiefs; and 27 yards osnaburg.

30 Paid John Alison for 25 bushels corn, 30 yards osnaburg.

Paid John Alison for carting, two check handkerchiefs.

Octr 3 Paid John Holloway for 110 bushels corn: 30 ells osnaburg; 16 ells black calimanco; 10 ells white linen; and five check linen handkerchiefs.

Octr 3 Paid John Holloway for 110 bushels of corn, four papers of pins, and two ells camlet.

Paid Henry Crutcher for 37 bushels corn per receipt: three India handkerchiefs; 1 and 1/2 ells camlet; five fine combs; six ells white linen; 1 Romall handkerchief; and two check linen handkerchiefs.

om^{d} Augt 28

		Livres	Sol	Den
Augt 23	Paid Baptist Charleville his account for Sundries	76	--------	
	Paid Charles Deleale for one quart vinegar......	5	--------	
	Paid Jean Baptist Barbeau for four sides tanned leather for use of the Light Dragoons by order Col. Montgomery.............	100	--------	
	Paid Doctor Rey for medicines per account.......	104	--------	
28	Paid Madame Viree Roban for her account of rent.	100	--------	
Sep. 2	Paid Bienvenue Perce, for oats, hay, and carting	71	5	----
	Paid Picard his account.........................	384	--------	
om^{d} Augt 23	Paid T. Brady for carting, per rec^{t}.............	15	--------	
		855	5	----

Novr 3 Paid Frogget for thrashing per rec^{t}, two gallons tafia and four lbs sugar.

Issued 32 lbs twine used for making a fish net for use of the garrison at Fort Jefferson.

Sep. 12 Paid for one cannon, 20 yard white flannel.

Paid for John Ash going express, four yards flannel.

Paid to Madam Valley for 26 dressed deer skins for the troops, 36 ells linen.

Paid Frank Coleman for 10 flour casks by order Col. John Montgomery, two and 1/2 ells spotted flannel.

25 Paid for transporting goods: six ells check; six lbs brown sugar; and six peltry.

Paid the Interpreter per receipt: two yards blue cloth; five yards linen; and four and 1/4 yards camlet.

25 Paid for making a fishing net for public use: six and 1/2 yards toile gris; one yard blue stroud; one yard white flannel; one scalping knife; two pair garters; two ivory combs; and four linen handkerchiefs.

Paid F. Bredin for making six shirts, two and 1/2 yards linen and four yards flannel.

Paid per receipt of Mary Hunter for doubling, four yards flannel.

Paid for twisting twine for a net for the garrison, one pair garters.

Paid for threshing corn to M. Guire, one and 1/2^{W} soap.

Paid R^{d} Brashears for making six shirts, three yards white linen.

Paid for hay, 16 check handkerchiefs.

Paid Joseph Thornton for two pair moccasins per his rec^{t}, one linen handkerchief.

Paid Andrew Johnson for two dressed skins for moccasins issued for an express in time of danger, two yards cottonade.

Issued for an express in a time of danger, four moccasins.

Paid Martha Hughes for making a shirt, one paper pins.

Issued for dressing a wounded man, 1/2 yard linen, and one linen handkerchief.

Issued to make bags, 21 yards osnaburg.

Paid A. Johnson for a dressed deer skin for use of an express during time of attack, one linen handkerchief.

Paid for sinking a well during time of attack at Fort Jefferson, 20 yards linen.

These are included in another sections where the cattle are charged:

Paid Danl Graffen for a milk cow, one rifle gun and wipers, and seven yards linen.

Capt Robert George to Store D^{d}

For sundry articles taken out of the public store for which no return or receipt has been passed.

June 15	2 1/8 yds supfine gray cloth 7/4 wide	
	4 D^{o} brown D^{o} 7/4 wide	1/4 yd overdrawn
July 5	1/8 D^{o} scarlet cloth 7/4 wide	
	4 D^{o} white casimir fine	
	3 3/4 D^{o} seysays	for 6 breeches and 6 vests
	8 3/4 D^{o} chintz	
	21 yds fine white linen	for 6 shirts
	3/4 yds fine holland	for ruffling D^{o}
	2 D^{o} D^{o}	for 6 stocks
	3 silk handkerchiefs	
	3 red silk & cotton D^{o}	
	2 1/2 yds white linen for lining	
	2 1/2 yds shalloon for D^{o}	
	5 7/12 dozen metal buttons - 2/12 doz. overdrawn	
	5 skeins silk	
	2 skeins silk twist	
	12 skeins fine white thread	6 skeins of each overdrawn
	12 D^{o} coarse D^{o}	
June 15	1/4 yd supfine broad cloth 7/4 wide	
	1 1/8 yds chintz	
	2 1/2 yds shalloon	
	1 3/4 yds linen	
	1 pr scissors	
	6 skeins fine white thread	
	6 skeins coarse white thread	
	1 snaffle bridle	
	1 ruffled shirt	
	3 1/2 yds osnaburg	
	1 skein thread	

2 metal buttons

23 4 ruffled shirts per order for soldiers going for provisions

30 5 yds cottonade for self

10 26 yds blue stroud
32 ruffled shirts
20 plain D^{o}
26 butcher knives per order: D^{d} to Capt Harrison, no rec^{t}
1 ink holder
1 bridle
26 skeins thread

12 3 clasp knives
2 horn combs
1 ivory comb per order: D^{d} to Capt Harrison, per rec^{t}
1 1/2 yds white half-thicks
1/2 yd blue bath coating
4 yds gartering
2 2 1/2 pt blankets
1 leather ink pot

12 2 pr thread hose
5 1/4 yds cottonade per order: D^{d} to Sg^{t} Walker, per rec^{t}
12 D^{o} ferriting

12 3 2 1/2 pts blankets
26 horn combs
13 ivory D^{o} per order: D^{d} to Capt Harrison, per his rec^{t}
2 1/2 yds blue bath coating
6 skeins thread

12 24 yds osnaburg
15 skeins thread per order & rec^{t} Martin Carney

13 4 2 1/2 point blankets per order & rec^{t} Wm Moore

13 4 yds black calimanco per order & rec^{t} Mark Eyler

14 1 ruffled shirt
1 plain shirt per order & rec^{t} John Walker
1 hat

19 23 ruffled shirts
23 plain shirts per order & D^{d} Capt George - no rec^{t}

	19	1 brass ink pot 1 large clasp knife 1 ivory comb 1 horn comb 6 yds ferriting	per order & rec^{t} John Donne
	20	5 yd toile gris 1 check linen handkerchief 1 ivory comb 1 horn comb 2 skeins thread	per order & rec^{t} And^{w} Clark
	22	1 brass ink stand	per order & rec^{t} Joseph Anderson
	28	8 plain shirts	per order & rec^{t} John Johnson
July	3	1 pair garters	per order & rec^{t} John Donne
	3	2 1/2 yds half-thicks	per order & rec^{t} Joseph Anderson
	13	3 1/2 yds blue cloth 3 yds white flannel 2 ruffled shirts thread & buttons for clothes	per order & rec^{t} Fred^{k} Guyon
	13	1 horn comb 1 scalping knife 1 ink stand	per order & rec^{t} Capt Ab^{m} Keller
	14	1 ivory comb 1 horn comb	per order & rec^{t} Fred^{k} Guyon
	14	4 plain shirts	per order & rec^{t} Richd Senet
	21	2 1/2 yds half-thicks 1 yd blue stroud 1 linen handkerchief	per order & rec^{t} Joshua Archer
	29	1 hat	per order & rec^{t} Peter Wagoner
Augt	3	6^{W} coffee	per order & rec^{t} John Donne
	3	18^{W} coffee	per order & rec^{t} Willm Clark
	8	1 English blanket 1 snaffled bridle 1 stick black ball	per order & rec^{t} Martin Carney

	10	1 scalping knife	per order & rec^{t} R^{d} Hopkins
	12	4 plain shirts	per order & rec^{t} Capt George
	14	2 1/2 yds toile gris	per order & rec^{t} Daniel Bolton
	15	1 English blanket	per order & rec^{t} R. Hopkins
	19	1 ivory comb 1 horn comb 1 scalping knife	per order & rec^{t} John Ash
	19	21 yds blue cloth 18 yds white flannel thread & buttons	per order & rec^{t} R. George
	19	14^{W} coffee	per order & rec^{t} Richd Clark
	19	1 ink pot (om^{d} 11th July)	per order & rec^{t} F. Guyon
Aug	24	1 scalping knife	per order & rec^{t} R. Kemp
	25	8 plain shirts	per order & rec^{t} Thos Lavey
Sep	13	1 2 1/2 pts blanket	per order & rec^{t}
	13	12 D^{o} & rec^{t} of Lieut. Dalton for use of your Company	per order Lt Col^{o} Montgomery
Sep	13	10 shirts plain for your Company per order	
	13	10 yds white flannel for making cartridges 15 skeins thread per D^{o} of D^{o}	per rec^{t} Martin Carney
	13	1/2 yd white linen to dress a wounded man 1 piece ravelled gartering D^{o}	
	13	10 shirts (plain) per order 11 2 1/2 pt blankets D^{o}	
	19	1/4 yd white cloth per D^{o}	
	22	7 yds linen per D^{o}	
		2 skeins thread per D^{o}	
	24	5/8 yds blue cloth per D^{o}	

25 5 skeins thread per D^o

26 ~~19 1/2 yds linen per Ditto~~ (error)

om^d 15 8 yds white flannel per D^o

30 4 yds D^o D^o per D^o

Oct 11 6 shirts per D^o

13 1 yd flannel per D^o

14 12 D^o D^o per D^o
6 skeins thread per D^o

15 7 yds blue cloth
6 D^o flannel
12 skeins thread
per order

om^d 27 1 1/4 blue stroud
3 pr moccasins
to John Ash per order

Account of House Expenses:

2 1/2 yds ribbon
2 red handkerchiefs
1 clasp knife
1 ink pot
8 skeins thread
1 ivory comb
1 horn D^o
1 lb coffee
1 scalping knife
2 yds white flannel
2 yds coarse linen
1 D^o osnaburg
1 yd coarse linen to pay for a bag lost by J. Lindsay
1 1/2 yds gauze
2 yds linen
1 check handkerchief paid for two brooms for the store
2 yds check
10 D^o tafia
pd gratiot for 70^W sugar, 105 Livers peltry
18 ells osnaburg p^d Charles Charleville for flour, pork, &ea
3 ells osnaburg for finding a horse
6 yds camblet p^d a woman for sundry kitchen services

2 scalping knives
1^W coffee
1 yd ribbon
1 India handkerchief
1 check linen D^o
2 doz fine combs
1 doz coarse combs
1 silk handkerchief
1 snaffle bridle
8 yds camblet
1 coarse handkerchief
3 1/4 black Persian
1 ink holder
1 yd ribbon
10^W coffee
20^W sugar
8 $gall^s$ rum

State of Virginia:

Issued John Ash, express, per order of Lt Col. John Montgomery, one blanket and one shirt.

Paid Joseph Hunter for a sheep per certificate of John Donne, Deputy Conductor, one pair blue stroud leggings and one blue breech cloth.

Paid Gasper Butcher per order Col. Montgomery, three and 1/2 yards white flannel and five yards white linen.

Four P^{cs} stroud...................... 400 dollars

Paid DeLeyba in part of an order drawn in his favor by Col^{o} Clark for sundries furnished to the troops in this department: 65 and 1/2 yards white linen @ three D^{s} 393 each, 65 and 1/2 yards white linen , seven ells bath coating @ 10 per (70), 31 and 3/4 yards check linen at three (201), and 35 and 1/4 check linen.

one pair chintz No. 24............	20
one pair chintz 6............	20
one pair chintz 35............	22
one pair chintz 12............	22
six cotton handkerchiefs..........	12
one dozen linen handkerchiefs.....	12

Rec^{t} dated 11th July 80 amount, 1172 Dollars

Paid Lafont for three quire paper for public use, three check handkerchiefs.

Paid for two account books for public use to Mon^{r} Lafont, six check handkerchiefs, four ells spotted flannel, two pieces ribbon, and 14 fine combs.

Paid Duplasy for a lock for the store, one clasp knife.

Paid Le Chaunce for three lbs oakum to repair boats, six scalping knives.

Paid Diveny for a hog for the troops per order Col. Montgomery, 15 ells linen.

Paid E. Johnson for a funnel, five w sugar.

For use of the troops, per order Lt. Col. Montgomery, 25 gallons or 1/2 barrack rum, and two bags.

Issued to M. Serpy, for debarking goods by order of Lt. Col. Montgomery, 20 lbs. lead and three bags.

Issued to John Goyles to transport flour to Fort Jefferson per order Capt Rogers, two bags.

Carried to Fort Jefferson by John Goyles per order of Capt Rogers, 16 bags, five files, and 15^{W} steel.

Issued for use of the troops at Fort Jefferson, per rec^{t} of Lt Clark, five bags, 15 brass kettles (68^{W}), seven large dressed deer skins, one cask sugar, and one case soap.

Delivered to the Commissary Department for the use of transporting provisions and lost by the troops per rec^{t} J. Donne, 11 bags, two and 1/4 quarts.

Paid Saml Allen for five days work, per order of Col. Montgomery, two yards linen.

Paid Ch^{s} Honfloy for five days work, per order of Col. Montgomery, two yards linen.

Paid Isaac Allen, for 12 days work per order Lt Col. Montgomery, one blanket.

Paid Isaac Allen, for 12 days work per order Lt Col. Montgomery, 10^{lbs} peltry.

Paid Lacroix, for tobacco, per order Lt Col. John Montgomery, 110 Livres in peltry or 14 ells check linen.

Paid Fred. S. Guion for tafia for the troops per order Lt Col. Montgomerty, 275 dollars.

Paid Charles Gratiot for a pirogue, by order Lt Col. Montgomery, 15 ells linen.

Paid Frank Coleman for barrels, 20 dollars.

Paid William Taylor for making soldiers clothes, two 1/4 yards linen.

Paid William Taylor for making soldiers clothes, two yards linen, and three skeins thread.

Paid Godin for 62^{W} pork for the troops, seven and 1/4 ells osnaburg.

Paid order Lt Col. Montgomery, two and 1/2 ells osnaburg.

Paid Lacroix for a pirogue per order Lt Col. Montgomery, 15 yards linen.

Paid for repairing a public boat per order Capt Brashears, 100 nails.

Paid Ezekiel Johnson for iron per order Col. Montgomery, 9 and 1/2^{W} sugar.

Paid Madam Tonish for hire of three horses to transport artillery to Cahokia, 50 Livres peltry.

Issued by John Dodge on the orders of sundry commanding officiers and sent per receipt for the relief of Fort Jefferson, 2,820^{W} flour, and 327 12/40 bushels corn.

Paid for a fat hog and 45^{W} pork for the troops by order Lt Col. Montgomery, ~~2-----yards ck~~ 15 ells linen.

Paid John Gest for 600^{W} bacon by order Lt Col. John Montgomery, 6^{ds} per order.

Paid Duplassi part of Col. Montgomery's order for a cow and calf, eighty pounds peltry.

Paid Duplassi for 171^{W} pork, 171 livres hard money.

Paid Duplassi for 85^{W} pork, 85 livres peltry.

Issued to Capt Rogers' C^{o} of Dragoons agreeagble to sundry vouchers, eight bushels and 24 quarts corn.

Issued to Capt Rogers' agreeable to sundry vouchers, seven bushels and 18 quarts salt.

Paid to Isaac Levy for pitch, 80^{W} peltry.

Paid Capt Joneast for 200^{W} flour for the troops, 100 livres in money.

Paid Gratiot for 3,876^{W} lead at 12 is 2325.18, peltry.

Paid Gratiot for 89 1/4^{W} gunpowder, 1785 L. peltry.

Paid Madam Roban (260) five peltry in full of her account per rec^{t}.

1780
Oct. 6 Sent to Fort Jefferson by order of Col. Montgomery per Sg^{t} Keesees, 121 bushels corn @ 40 quarts, 265^{W} flour, and three bags - six ells osnaburg.

19 Sent to Fort Jefferson per rec^{t} John Donne, Deputy Conductor, 37 bushels corn.

18 2 bags to transport flour to Fort Jefferson on per order Lt Col. Montgomery.

om^{d} 9 1 snaffle bridle P^{d} Barbeau per order Col. Montgomery on behalf of Col. Todd.

P^{d} Capt Plassy for pitch and oakum, 84 Livres peltry.

P^{d} LeClaires for ferriages, 65 Livres hard money.

P^{d} Edwd Murray for services by order of Lt Col. Montgomery, 10^{W} peltry.

P^{d} Ch^{s} Hansler for three days work, 9 Livres hard cash.

P^{d} Godin for three gallons wine for the sick, 18^{W} peltry.

55 and 1/2^{W} sugar issued for use of the sick at sundry times per order Captain John Rogers.

1 knife issued for use of the ~~Dy.~~ Asst. Conductor per order John Rogers.

Issued for use of the Dragoon Company, 3 brass kettles.

Issued for garrison of Fort Clark, 85^{W} lead.

Issued to Commissisary Crutchfield per rec^{t} and order of Capt Rogers, two shirts, and three linen handkerchiefs.

P^{d} Le'Clere for ferriages at sundry times, 35 Livres peltry.

P^{d} Datcherut for sundries furnished by him for public use by order of Col. Montgomery, 265 Livres. (Charge J. Bailey)

P^{d} Jacque Lasource for his account per order Col. John Montgomery, balance 315 Livres in cash.

Paid Doctor Rey for the use of the sick, 2^{W} coffee 2^{W} sugar.

P^{d} for 50 pair moccasins for the use of the Light Dragoons per order Capt Rogers Comd^{t}, 39 hard dollars.

P^{d} for 4 horses delivered to Capt Rogers per rec^{t}, 1000 L peltry.

Issued to one sick man of Capt Brashears' Company, 1/2^{W} sugar.

Issued to one sick man of Capt Worthington's Company, 1^{W} sugar and 1/2 a pound coffee to one sick man of Capt Worthington's.

Issued for Capt Kellar's Company per rect. and order of Col. Montgomery, one dressed deer skin and 5^{W} soap.

Issued for one man of Capt Bailey's Company per order and rec^{t} of Col. Montgomery one lb. soap and one pair moccasins.

Issued to Capt Kellar's Company per order and rec^{t}. of Col. Montgomery, two dressed deer skins.

Delivered to two sick men of Capt Brashears' Company per order and rec^{t} of Col. Montgomery, 2^{W} sugar and 1/2 coffee.

Issued to David Glen, express, per order of Col. Montgomery, 2^{W} soap.

Issued to three men of Capt George's Company per order Col. Montgomery, 3^{W} soap.

Issued to David Wallis per order of Col. Montgomery, 3^{W} sugar.

Issued to one man of Capt Brashears' Company, 2^{W} soap.

Issued to four sick men of Capt Brashears' Company, 4^{W} D^{o} sugar.

Issued to James Wiley for liquor for the fatigue per order Col. Montgomery, 5^{W} soap.

Issued to ~~Mr~~. Capt. Kellar's Company per order Col. Montgomery, one w soap.

Issued to Capt. George's Company per order Col. Montgomery, two dressed deer skins.

Issued for Capt. Brashears' Company per order Col. Montgomery, five dressed deer.

Issued for two sick men of Capt. Kellar's Company, 2^{W} coffe and 4^{W} sugar, per order Col. Montgomery.

Issued for a sick man of Capt. Bailey's Company 1 pint tafia, 1^{W} sugar and $1/2^{W}$ coffee per order Col. Montgomery.

Issued for three sick men of Capt Brashears' Company per order Col. Montgomery, 3^{W} sugar and one and 1 $1/2^{W}$ coffee.

Issued for three sick men of Capt Brashears' Company per order Col. Montgomery, 3^{W} sugar and $3/4^{W}$ coffee.

Issued for Capt Worthington's Company per order Col. Montgomery, two dressed deer skins, 20^{W} sugar, and 10^{W} coffee.

Issued for Brashears' Company per order of Col. Montgomery, one pair moccasins, and one w soap.

Issued to Patrick McClosky, for the use of the hospital per order of Col. Montgomery, 20^{W} sugar and 9^{W} lead.

P^{d} Dr. Ichabod Camp for medicines for the Light horse men per account per order of Capt. John Rogers, Comd., 332 Livres in peltry.

P^{d} Dr. Ichabod Camp, for a pickle cask, two check handkerchiefs.

P^{d} Dan. Murray for writing paper, two check handkerchiefs, one horn comb and four skeins thread.

P^{d} I. Camp for making: an Indian coat, 30 bags, and 20 shirts; 11 yards linen and three yards chintz.

P^{d} Nicholas Smith for carting public goods, seven and 1/2 bushels corn.

P^{d} Sg^{t} Merriwether 1 qt tafia for assisting to load a boat per order Col. Montgomery.

Issued to two men in Capt. George's Company per order Col. Montgomery, one quart tafia.

Issued for the use of Capt. Rogers' Company per order Col. Montgomery, five gallons tafia.

Issued to Capt. Brashears' Company per his order and per order Col. Montgomery, one and 1/2^{W} coffee and one ^{W} sugar.

Issued to the hospital per order Dr. Rey 3^{W} sugar and 1 1/2 coffee.

Issued to Brashears' Company per order Col. Montgomery, one bottle tafia and one lb. sugar.

Issued to Capt. A. Kellar's Company per order Col. Montgomery, one bottle tafia.

Issued one quart tafia for twelve men per order Col. Montgomery.

Issued two quarts rum for Capt. Roger's Company per order Col. Montgomery.

Issued to John Williams four gallons tafia, 12^{W} sugar, and 20^{W} soap per order Col. Montgomery.

Replaced to Thomas Hutchins per order of Col. Montgomery, two and 1/2 gallons and one and 1/2 pints tafia.

Issued to men on fatigue by order of Col. Montgomery, one quart tafia.

Issued to the Dragoons at Kaskaskia by order of Capt John Rogers, Comd., 200 1/2 bushels corn, 487^{W} flour and two bags.

P^{d} for ferriage of 4 horses to Charles Gratiot, 40 Livres peltry.

P^{d} Mr. Datcherut for salt and flour per order Col. Montgomery, 153 Livres peltry.

P^{d} Willian Datcherut for salt and flour per order Col. Montgomery, 2360 Livres merchandise.

P^{d} Datcherut for provisions &ea per order Col. Montgomery, 963.15 Livres peltry.

Issued to troops at Fort Clark per order Col. Montgomery, 200 lbs. flour.

Paid Col. Montgomery per account and his order in part, 21 dollars.

P^{d} Major Bosseron for sundries for sundries use of the Savages and troops per his account and rec^{t}, 1018 Livres peltry.

Issued to the Commissary per order Major Williams, Comd., 10 bags - 20 ells osnaburg.

Issued for public use per order Major Williams, two bags and four ells osnaburg.

Sent by Giles to Fort Jefferson by order of Capt Rogers, Comd., 224^{W} flour, two bags, and four ells osnaburg.

Issued to Israel Dodge in lieu of sundry articles lost by him in the Ohio the 27th of March, 1780, when accompanying Joseph Lindsay, Esqr on public business: two and 1/2 yards toile gris, one and 1/4 yds calendry, one yd coarse white linen, one skein thread, one English blanket, and one scalping knife.

Issued 125^{W} pork per rec^{t} Major Williams, 125 Livres peltry.

~~Delivered to Martin Carney, Quartermaster, for the use of the troops per his receipt, 149 weight tobacco.~~

Paid Ezekiel Johnson for sundry articles delivered to Quartermaster Carney for the use of Fort Jefferson per rec^{t} L 13.11 hard money, and 3,040 Continental dollars.

Paid sundry inhabitants at Kaskaskia for 5438^{W} flour and 535 bushels corn, not yet delivered, and whose obligations I have delivered to Mr. Donne D^{y} Cond^{r} per his receipt.

Delivered Patrick Kennedy, Ass^{t} Conductor: 519^{W} lead, 17 and 1/2 bushels salt, one pickle cask, 30 Cont^{t} doll^{s}.

Paid J. Donne for assisting in public business with the accounts &ea while hurried: one skein fine thread, three yards toile gris, five yards osnaburg, and one stick twist.

Delivered to J. Donne, D^{y} Cond^{r}, per his rec^{t}, four bags, and eight ells osnaburg.

P^{d} John Donne for assisting in adjusting accounts: 25 yards white flannel, one ^{w} twine, 12 skeins thread, two paper pins, four skeins thread, one yard linen, and one yard blue cloth.

Paid the sheriff for a cow sold at Vendue, 800 Cont^{l} doll^{s}, per rec^{t}.

D^{d} to John Dodge for sundry articles taken with him to bear his expense while on public business:

12 yds calimanco ----	74 L Geo. Slaughter
3 and 3/4 yards camblet	
11 check handkerchiefs-	3 check handkerchiefs D^{o}
10 papers pins ----	3 paper D^{o}
~~three pair brown~~	
2 and 1/2 yards calimanco ----	D^{d} Capt Roberts
4 razors	
3 horse phlegms	
7 snaffle bridles	
5 paper ink holders ----	3 D^{d} Geo. Slaughter
1 10/12 coarse horn combs ----	1 D^{d} Geo. Slaughter
8 fine combs	1 D^{d} Geo. Slaughter
4 1/2 yds cotton 16 a de Sachque	D^{d} Capt Roberts
2 bolts gartering	
1 1/2^{w} fine white thread ----	3 oz D^{d} Geo. Slaughter
4^{w} thread coarse	

Indian Department:

P^{d} the sheriff for corn and 2 corn fields &ea &ea for the use of the friendly Savages who came to our assistance in time of danger, 554 Dollr^{s} Continental.

11 yds cloth say blue cloth	4 carrots tobacco
9 yds white flannel	1 3/4 yds cloth
3 1/2 yds linen	1 check handkerchief
1 yd toile gris	
30 skeins thread	

D[d] State of Virginia:

For sundry articles delivered to Israel Dodge, deputy Agent, for the troops.

1 piece blue cloth
3 remn[ts] D[o] 64 yds Good
2 D[o] white D[o] 2 3/4 D[o]

8 remn[ts] blue cloth 95 1/2 yds
1 D[o] gray D[o] 4 1/2 D[o] Damaged

5 pieces flannel
3 remn[ts] ----------- 5 yds flannel
9 p[s] linen Damaged
8 remn[ts] D[o] cont[g] 50 yds
1 D[o] fine D[o] 82 D[o]

9 remn[ts] D[o] 158 1/2 D[o] D[o]

20 3/4 toile gris
2 yds brown holland ----- Damaged
8 1/2 yds osnaburg
8 paper pins
30[w] thread
35[w] twine
2 boxes brass buttons
131 doz Capt. buttons
30 looking glasses
30 yds tinsel lace
208 gunworms
23 yds camblet
1 1/2 yds calimanco
3/4 yds camblet
4 check handkerchiefs
2 combs
2 clasp knives
6 plain shirts
3 1/3 doz mohair buttons
2 pair knee garters
1 brass cork [Note: not legible]
3 pr. drawers, 6 yds toile gris
1 lg. chest
12 ells linen
P[d] Francois Charleville for 1 hog, 12 ells linen
6 yds black calimanco P[d] for a table for public use

1 large chest issued to Col. Clark to contain public papers, 401 Cont^{l} doll^{s}

40 Cont^{l} Doll^{s} advanced C. Bailey for the recruiting service.

P^{d} Ezekiel Johnston for one horse, 2,000 Cont^{l} dollars, drowned in the Ohio by the soldiers

6 quire writing paper used in the agent's office.

1 p^{r} steelyards bought of Mark Ker, and delivered to John Donne for use of the Commissary Department, 8 D^{s}.

Issued to Capt Rogers going on command to the Falls: 225^{W} flour at 50 Livres p^{ct}; one cask, 24 Livres; and 96^{W} salt pork, 2 Livres p^{lb}.

Issued for use of our friendly Indian chiefs, 13 and 1/2 yards osnaburg made into hunting shirts.

P^{d} Thomas Bentley on account, 530 Livres cash.

Issued at sundry times for public use, 20^{W} thread.

Issued to shirt makers, 400 needles, Doll 3.0.0

Issued to the officers and soldiers for their clothing, 240 sk^{S} silk dollars 5.--.--.

2 boxes wafers used for public use 1 Dollars

Issued to officers for their clothing, 41 doz metal buttons, at 9 reals per dozen.

35 and 1/2 ells holland used for stocks for the troops.

57 3/4 48 ells muslin Brittanias cambric, and lawn for ruffling.

Issued to Capt Worthington on his own account per rec^{t}: 6 check handkerchiefs, 2 yds check linen, and 18 Livres peltry.

Wrecked in transporting goods to Kaskaskia, 1 trunk.

3 3/4 fine white thread issued for making shirts for the troops.

C[r] State of Virginia:

By my obligation in favor Charles Gratiot 452 Livres.---

	Doll[s]
Rec[d] of Col. Montgomery 21 1/2 gallons tafia @ 3.......	64 1/2
also D[d] to Cap[t] Rogers.................	39
1 pirogue........................	25 1/2

By my certificate on the State in favor Major Bosseron [illeg.]
By ~~my~~/ Col. Montg[y] bill favor Cap[t] Rogers for 2,000 Cont[l] dollars.
By 40 Liv. peltry overcharged on account rendered by B. Charleville
By a crosscut saw - per rec[t] M. Carney, D[y] Q[tr] M[str].
~~By amount~~ Rec[d] per rec[t] J. Donne, Deputy Conductor 5.013[W] beef
[illeg.] Venison
[illeg.] Bear Meat

By one piece ribbon - chargeable to J Dodge [illeg.]
By an error in 482 1/2 ells linen [illeg.]

New Orleans invoice including advance.........	18.144.5.6
Montgomery's invoice........D[o]................	8.339.----
Clark's invoice...............................	4.736.----
Total	31,219.5.6

Amount of disbursements exclusive of 7,140 Doll[s] Continenal............................	39,839.1.0
Deduct amounts of invoices....................	31,219.5.6
ball[n] issued in favor of the state	8.619.3.6

Attest

I certify that the foregoing charges have been entered by me agreeable to a number of vouchers produced by Captain John Dodge, & that the said charges are a true abstract of the aforesaid vouchers.---

Fort Jefferson, March 20, 1781.---

J. Donne

Major George Slaughter D^d

74 yards black calimanco
3 check handkerchiefs
3 paper pins
8 small looking glasses
3 ozs fine white thread
1 ivory comb
1 horn - ditto
3 ink stands

Captain Benjamin Roberts D^d

4 1/2 yds sachque
2 1/2 yds scarlet calimanco

Extract of a letter from the Hon^e Jno Page, L^t G^{ov}

Williamsburg 6 Augt 1789 [sic]

Sir, the bearer, Mr. Jno Dodge, from his suffering in the cause of his country is entitled to a bron [illeg.] pence & reward for his services. He wishes to be employed on an expedition against Detroit or as Indian agent in that quarter where his knowledge of the inhabitants & their languages may enable him to be of singular service. The board choose to recommend him to you for an appointment rather than give him one as it might possibly interfere with one of your own. If therefore you have not yet appointed a commerc^l agent according to the Act of Assembly for Establishing the County of Illinois we would recommend Mr. Dodge to you as a proper person to fill that office. I have the honor to be y^r Ob^t Hu^l Servant

Jno Page Lt Govr

A true copy of the original

Jno Dodge

To
Jno Todd, Esqr County
L^t and Commen^t of the
County Illinois---
By Capt Dodge

The commerial agency being already filled it is recommended to Capt Dodge to act as Indian Agent for the State of Virginia in the department for Detroit.

G. R. Clark

Falls of Ohio Nov. 19th C. Cin C. W^d Dep^t
1779

A true Copy Jno Dodge

Instructions from Col. Jno Todd

Louisville

25th Jany 1780--- To Capt Jno Dodge---

You'll proceed as speedily as possible to St Vincennes where you'll hear if the State goods have arrived at Illinois. If arrived, proceed straight way to Kaskaskia and take them into your custody as Assistant Agent to William Lindsey in the trade department. The necessity of keeping the goods untouched until Mr. Lindsey's arrival, who has the invoices and who alone knows the contract below, is all most indispensible. If urgent necessity immediately demands some articles of which at the cautious judge you must deal out very sparingly. Mr. Lindsey's arrival or future orders from me will shortly relieve you from this injunction. Capt Winston will give you any necessary assistance. Reasons the Illinois Act passed in October 1778, which originates your office will point out your duty. If the goods did not arrive in December, you will remain at St Vincennes until, or nearly until, the time they will arrive in which time opportunities may offer whereby you may benefit the State under your appointment in the Indian Department, which will be by no means incompatible with your other office. In your Indian council and speeches, I recommend to you to adhere to the tenor and spirit of those heartfelt delivered by Col. Clark, whom I hope will continue his care and attention to that branch of political office. Your knowledge of the Indian customs and manners and languages will make Perbut [illeg.]. Sir, instructions unnecessary continue your zeal for America liberty and may Heaven reward you with success. I am Sir

Your Humble Servant

A ture copy

Jno Todd J^r

Jno Dodge

Instructions from Col. Todd

Capt Jno Dodge

Sir) Accompanying this is your commission as Trade Agent for the Illinois Department. I am desired by the Board of Trade to reserve the goods from orders for the use of the troops for the Western Department, except what will be necessary for the Indians. You will, therefore as soon as you shall have received of Mr. Lindsey, divide them into two parts: the necessary clothing for the troops and the surplus in mere finery will compose your first division; your second will be made of the necessary Indian goods which may amount 1/4 perhaps 1/3 of the whole. Your store for the troops I think are to be kept for the present at Kaskaskia as the goods are now there although I could wish them at St Vincents [Vincennes]. You will have orders for its removal from Kaskaskia before the fall, probably to the Mouth of Ohio and perhaps have it considerably augmented by that time. The goods requested for the troops are pointed out to you by an Act passed last May with the quantity for each officer and soldier and the prices of certain necessary goods. Besides the allowance to that Act, I refer you for your more special guidance [to] the price [which] must be what they cost the State or an estimated price of what they cost in Europe with 120 P advance whichever will be cheaper. You are to be responsible at present to myself or the Virginia Board of Trade for the just application of the goods and the manner of distributing them. Col. Clark will appoint some one person whose receipt upon a return signed by the commanding officer of the post shall alone authorize you to give out the good. The return must specify for what uses delivered with the names of the persons, and with this addition, is a soldier that they have one year at least to serve. As to the superfluity of necessary articles, let them rest in your care undisturbed until further orders. The Indian goods must be a separate charge which will be entrusted by you to some persons on whom you can depend. The design is to keep up our interest with the Savages which is better done by selling them goods reasonably than by [giving] gifts. The interest of the Wabash Indians is mostly to be consulted. The returns desired will suit better in horses or lead than peltry or any other commodity. Besides the general view of my sentiment, I entrust the matter with you, give such instructions to your satisfaction and enter into such engagements as you shall think most conducive to the trust and honor of our State & your disbursements shall be repaid & your contract approved. Transmit to me an invoice of the goods by Mr. Lindsey with amounts of your proceeding every opportunity. I am your Humble Servant

Louisville 9th Jany 1780 Jno Todd Jr.-

A True Copy Jno Dodge

Extract of a letter from Col. Clark

Louisville February 12th 1780

Sir,
You will receive this by the hands of Mr. Lindsay. I must again select you to purchase at any rate the table furniture I mentioned to you as not any comes for me from New Orleans. I can not do without it as you know my situation. Pray get what you can, some in one some in another; some cows or bulls. Also I daily expect your express from St Vincents. Mr. Lindsay will augment you with all the news. You may easily account for this small letter and consequently will provide me with some paper.

I am Sir Yours,
G. R. Clark

To Capt Jno Dodge

Extract of a letter from Col. Clark

Dr Sir,
By your late supply of paper you have enabled me to write to you as well as others.I thank you for your information. You have given me in your letter respecting the conduct of several persons which you need not doubt of their being called to an account at a proper time. You are in the line of your duty in that as well as satisfying the Savages or any other service you can do. I refer you to Majr Bosseron's letters for the scheme I have taken for supplying the garrison. For a short time, let nothing be wanting in you, as much will be in your power as an Agent. Mr. Lindsay has gone by water to the Illinois expecting you are there to deliver you the goods. If they have arrived, I hope in a short time we shall be able to defy all the enemies we have in the western country and think of them only affording us desertion. Your brother is gone with Mr. Lindsay. I am glad to hear that Mr. Ruland is about things. Pray pay him for it. I will settle it with you. He will deliver them to Capt Bailey, who will lend them to me. Mr.

Conneuye has an account against me. Pray take down the sum in peltry (and) discharge it if you can conveniently, and I will see that you are no loafer by it. Capt Bailey will give you all the news. I am dear Capt, Your very Humble Servant

G. R. Clark

Louisville
February 28, 1780
To Jno Dodge Esqr
Com^l Agent, Illinois

Statement from Lt Col. Montgomery:

I do hereby certify that upon hearing that the troops at Fort Jefferson had no provisions last June and July that at my own and the Agent's request, a party of the Kaskaskia Savages turned out voluntarily went and hunted [and] scouted about the garrison when the troops were not able [to do so] themselves, and must have suffered if they had not gone. And when the garrison was besieged, [the Kaskaskia Indians] behaved with the greatest courage and bravery, one of which ran through the enemy and brought me intelligence. Most of the men under my command [were] at Cahokia [or were] sick so that they could not give immediate relief. I called upon the Savages [Kaskaskia and Peories] who upon the first moments intelligence turned out to a man, [and] went with me to the relief of the garrison to fight as we may say their brother Savages, which is a convincing proof that they are true allies to our cause & worthy [of] every good persons notice. I do likewise certify that it was with my appropriation that the Agent gave them what he has & that it was [as] little as he could possibly satisfy them with. Given under my hand at Kaskaskia, 10 Octo^r, 1780.

Jno Montgomery Lt Col. Command^t

To all whom it may concern

copy
Jno- Dodge

Statement from Capt John Dodge

After Col. Montgomery purchased a quantity of merchandise [he] put [it] into my possession -- it was with great propriety that I issued [it] on his orders.

Statement from John Donne

Received of Capt John Dodge Agent for the State of Virginia, three quarts tafia for use of the Commissary Department, also two quarts spirits for use of a fatigue party on command going for provisions which he has purchased from Mr. Thomas Bentley at my desire. Fort Jefferson, January 1st 1781

J. Donne D^{y} Con^{d}, Western Department

Inventory of Sundry Articles lost by Israel Dodge on his passage from the Falls of Ohio to Post St Vincents on public business:

one broadcloth coat superfine; one waistcoat superfine; two pair fine cloth breeches; one nankeen waistcoat; two shirts; five stocks (one of cambric - four of linen); one black persian stock; one pair silk stockings; one pair worsted stockings; two p^{r} thread stockings; one p^{r} yarn stocking; one, four point blanket, one blanket coat; one butcher knife, and one tomahawk.

Borough of Clarksville:

Personally appeared before me the subscriber John Donne, Clerk of the Borough. Aforesaid Israel Dodge, being duly sworn, did make oath that about the twenty-fifth day of last February through unavoidable accident on his passage from the Falls of Ohio to St Vincennes in company with Mr. Lindsay, and while in public service, he lost the above mentioned articles which he has not yet found, nor has he reason to expect them.

Sworn before me the 7th August 1780

Clarksville J. Donne, Clerk B.C.